Fundamentals of Data Science with MATLAB

Introduction to Scientific Computing, Data Analysis, and Data Visualization

Arash Karimpour

ISBN-10: 1-7352410-1-6
ISBN-13: 978-1-7352410-1-2

" ... Say, "Are those who know equal to those who do not know?" ..." [39:9]

To my parents, my wife, and my family

Preface

This book helps readers to better understand the process involved in scientific data analysis and data visualization with the MATLAB programming language. Although there are many educational resources available for learning general programming with the MATLAB language, there are not as many options available when it comes to practical data analysis with MATLAB. This book intends to fill this gap and provides a practical guide on working with real data for the purpose of scientific computing and data visualization using the MATLAB language.

Scientific studies commonly involve working with some sort of data and mostly require some degrees of data analysis. To achieve that, programming languages are commonly used to analyze and process data. The outcomes of these analyses help to assess and evaluate properties of data which can provide a comprehensive perspective of the studied subject. The MATLAB language is one of the most popular programming languages used for data analysis. Its popularity is due to its simple and yet powerful syntax, its highly capable toolboxes, and its extensive third-party packages.

In this book, readers are walked through steps that are required to analyze and process data with the MATLAB language. This book covers practical guides and approaches to develop codes for data analysis with MATLAB in simple language. This text contains general syntaxes along with many examples to explain how to implement these syntaxes for the purpose of the data analysis. This book is prepared with a practical application in mind. Throughout this book, it is explained how to achieve an intended goal for each section, and through examples, it is shown how to develop a code to analyze data and compute desired values described in that section.

The first two chapters of this book provide an introduction to programming with the MATLAB language. The next three chapters describe how to work with MATLAB arrays and statistical functions. Chapters six, seven, and eight explain how to work with labeled data and time-series. Chapters nine and ten talk about methods to visualize data. The next chapter shows how to interpolate data, fit curve, find roots, and integrate data with MATLAB. Chapters twelve and thirteen provide an introduction to signal processing and digital filtering. The last chapter describes how to read and write data files. In each of these chapters, general syntaxes along with many practical examples are provided to help readers implement each concept for their needs.

Content

Chapter 1
Set Up MATLAB

This book is written to help readers develop and advance their scientific computing skills. This book does not intend to teach programming with MATLAB, rather it explains how to use your programming skills along with MATLAB language strength to solve scientific questions through data analysis. Readers with no prior programming experience might find this book not suitable. Still, in the first two chapters of this book, the basics of programming with MATLAB are explained. Then, in following chapters data analysis and scientific computation with MATLAB are explained more in detail. At the end, it is described how to use MATLAB to visualize and plot scientific data.

In this chapter, it is described how to set up MATLAB programming language on a computer. First, it is explained how to install MATLAB on your system. Then, a MATLAB desktop environment is explained. Next, MATLAB toolboxes and packages are described. Then, it is presented how to run a MATLAB script.

1.1 Introduction to MATLAB Language

MATLAB (MATLAB is a registered trademark of The MathWorks, Inc.; www.mathworks.com) is a proprietary programming language developed by the MathWorks, Inc. MATLAB is one of the most popular scientific and numerical computing programming languages. MATLAB is a simple, easy to learn, and yet powerful computing language with a wide range of applications in science and engineering. Contributions from a MATLAB community, such as the MathWorks File Exchange, provide a large number of third-party packages for developers and users. In all, being powerful, using a simple syntax, having a large number of toolboxes and packages are among the main contributors to MATLAB fame which makes it one of the top choices for commercial companies, businesses, and academic communities. Because of that, users with scientific and engineering backgrounds may find themselves in a need to learn MATLAB language for many different reasons.

1.2 Install MATLAB

MathWorks provides installer files for Windows, Mac, and Linux operating systems. MATLAB is a proprietary software and we need to obtain a proper license to activate MATLAB before using it.

MATLAB has desktop and online versions. To install a desktop version of MATLAB, we need to download a proper installer. To install MATLAB on Windows and Mac systems, run the installer and follow steps on an installation dialog box. To install MATLAB on Linux systems, first, we need to unzip an archive file and then execute an installer command (./install). For more details, refer to a guide for a MATLAB installation with an internet connection (www.mathworks.com/help/install/ug/install-mathworks-software.html).

Figure 1.1
MATALB installer on Windows systems

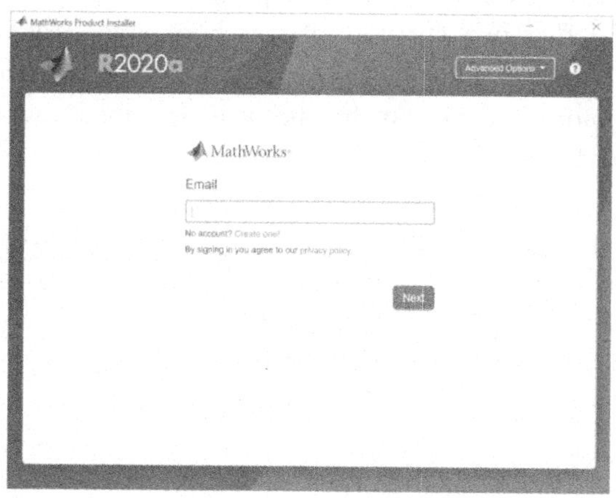

1.3 MATLAB Desktop

The most convenient way to work with MATLAB is to use a MATLAB desktop. Although we do not need anything more than a simple text editor to write and edit your code, it is more convenient to use a software designed for that purpose. A MATLAB desktop provides a graphical user interface (GUI) that serves as a development environment. In addition to a source code editor, a MATLAB desktop contains advanced features such as a debugger, code completion, syntax highlighting, automatic code formatting, command history log, current folder (file explorer), command window, and workspace (variable explorer). Also, a MATLAB desktop lets us run and debug a code within its environment.

It is worth mentioning, there are multi-purpose text editors which are developed to be used with a wide range of programming languages. Some developers may prefer to use these code editors to write and edit their code. Visual Studio Code (Microsoft; code.visualstudio.com), Atom (atom.io), and Sublime Text (Sublime HQ Pty Ltd; www.sublimetext.com) are among the most popular multi-purpose text editors. These editors support a large number of programming language syntaxes.

1.4 MATLAB Toolboxes and Packages

One of the MATLAB valuable assets is its toolboxes. MATLAB offers a series of toolboxes that each aims at a specific task. For example, a MATLAB Curve Fitting Toolbox gives users access to functions that are required to fit a curve or surface to data. Remember that these toolboxes might require separate licenses to be used. Additionally, there a large number of third-party packages developed by MATLAB community contributors. One good source to find third-party packages is the MathWorks File Exchange (The MathWorks, Inc.; www.mathworks.com/matlabcentral/fileexchange). The File Exchange contains a large library of files and packages that may be used for a wide range of applications. MATLAB toolboxes along with these large numbers of packages provide users with a great opportunity to develop sophisticated codes for lots of purposes.

To use the third-party package, we need to download a package and store it on your system. If a packaged is zipped, it should be unzipped first. Now, to use this package, we need to tell MATLAB where to look for this new package. To do that, we should add a folder that contains this package to the MATLAB search path. A folder can be added to the MATLAB search path by using the `addpath` command.

1.5 Run MATLAB Script

To run (execute) a MATLAB script, two methods can be used. In the first method, a MATLAB script is run inside a command window of the MATLAB desktop. In the second method, at first, a MATLAB script is saved in a file, and then, this file is executed.

To run a script inside a MATLAB desktop command window, first, open a MATLAB desktop. After a MATLAB desktop is opened, it may show some information on the top of the command window. After that, we can see >> sign which indicates that we are in a command window. Now, to run any command or script in this window, at first, write it after >> sign, and then pressing an enter key to run that code.

Now, let's run a simple example in a MATLAB command window. In this example, we assign a number 2 to variable a (a=2) and a number 3 to variable b (b=3). Then, we display a value of a+b in command window. This example is written in a MATLAB command window as:

```
>> a=2

a =

     2

>> b=3

b =

     3

>> disp(a+b)
     5

>>
```

The second method to run a MATLAB script is to write and save a MATLAB script in a file and then run that file. An editor in a MATLAB desktop can be used for this purpose. To create a new MATLAB file or to open an existing MATLAB file, go to a Current Folder window of the MATLAB desktop, and choose a destination folder. Then, click on New Script or Open in a ribbon bar. This opens a MATLAB Editor. In this editor, we can write, edit, and save a MATLAB code as a MATLAB file. Note that, a MATLAB file should be saved with .m extension. To run a MATLAB file, first, open a saved file in an editor. Then, go to the EDITOR tab, RUN section, and click on Run. Now, MATLAB starts executing a code saved inside a file and shows the results in a command window. If it is needed, we can change a code while a file is opened inside an editor. However, we need to save a file before we can run it.

As an example, we create a new file and write the MATLAB codes used in a previous example in this new file. Then, we save it as first_program.m. Here is how this program looks like in an editor:

```
a=2
b=3
disp(a+b)
```

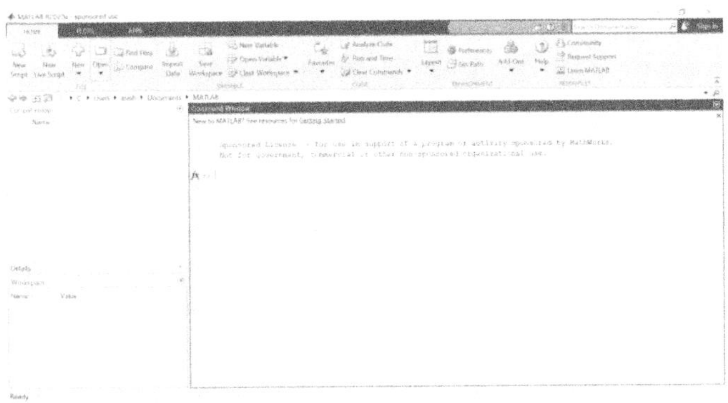

Figure 1.2
MATLAB desktop

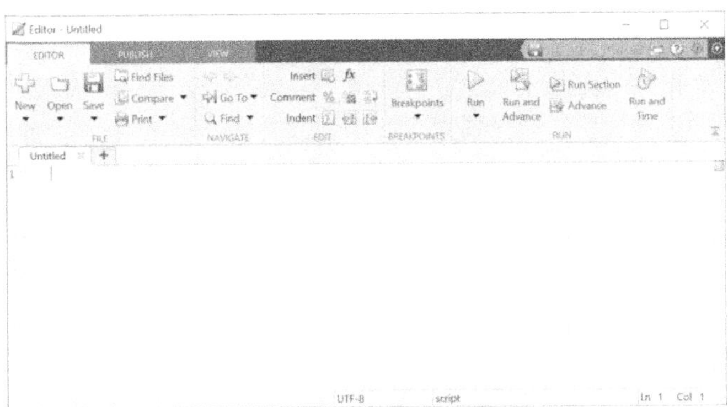

Figure 1.3
MATLAB Editor

Chapter 2
Introduction to MATLAB Programming

In this chapter, the basics of programming with the MATLAB language are described. First, MATLAB syntax style is explained. Then, MATLAB built-in functions, add-on toolboxes, and third-party packages are described. After that, mathematical, comparison, and logical operators are presented. Next, integer, floating point, and complex numbers are described. Then, it is explained how to work with strings. It follows by descriptions of the vector creation. After that, the `if`, `for` and `while` statements are explained. Next, it is described how to define a function. Then, it is demonstrated how to use a tilde. At the end, it is explained how to work with files and directories.

2.1 MATLAB Syntax Style

MATLAB syntax follows sets of standard styles and layouts. Probably, the most distinctive principle of the MATLAB code layout is its use of the **end** keyword to define a block of code. In MATLAB, the **end** keyword is used to mark and define each block of code from other blocks in rest of the code. Every new block of code should finish with the **end** keyword.

Another principle of the MATLAB code layout is that it ignores an indentation. In simple words, indentation is a blank space at the start of each line in a code, which means to start a new line of code further in the left compared with a previous line. In MATLAB, an indentation may be used to structure a code to visually separate each block of code from other blocks in rest of the code. Every time a new block of code is about to start, it can be indented to the left (its lines start further in left) compared with lines in a previous block. In MATLAB, an indentation may be used to structure a code to make it more readable, however, MATLAB does not require it and treats both indented and non-indented code the same way.

MATLAB may not suggest limiting each line of code to a specific number of characters, however, it is a good practice to split a long line of code into two or more lines. In MATLAB, an ellipsis, **...**, is used for a line continuation (a line break). In general, any line of MATLAB code (regardless of its length) can be split into two or more lines by using an ellipsis at the end of each line. Here is an example of how to use an ellipsis for a line continuation. In this example, integers from 1 to 10 are added together.

```
a=1+2+3+4+5 ...
    +6+7+8+9+10;
```

Here is another example for a line continuation. In this example, a text is split into three lines.

```
a=['This is a sample to show a line continuation. ' ...
    'Now let's start the 2nd line, ' ...
    'This is the 3rd line.'];
```

Typically, code developers are expected to include some explanations throughout a source code. These explanations even become more necessary when we are dealing with long codes and complex projects. These extra explanations and descriptions help to add more clarification to a code and provide references for the future. It also can help other developers to understand the logic behind a code. These additional explanations are called comments. In MATLAB, a comment is marked by using a percent sign, **%**, at the start of the comment. This tells MATLAB to ignore anything comes after **%**. A comment can be a separate line, or it can be entered at the end of the line after MATLAB commands. Here is an example of how to use comments in MATLAB:

```
%In the next line, 2+3 is assigned to a
a=2+3;

%In the next line, 2 is raised to the power 3
b=2^3; %A value of b is equal to 8
```

To create multiple lines of comment, one method is to use **%** sign at the start of each line. The easier method to do that, is to use **%{** before the first line of a comment block and use **%}** after the last line of a comment block. In other words, anything comes between **%{** and **%}** is considered as a comment. Here is a general syntax shows how to create a block of comments:

Syntax

```
%{
comment
comment
comment
%}
```

In MATLAB, it is possible to split a code into a series of sections. To do that, double percent signs, **%%**, are used at the start of the line where a new section of code is started. Using sections in a code helps to divide a code into a series of groups as each group serves a specific goal.

Another common syntax style is to use a semicolon at the end of a code line. Every time a MATLAB syntax is run, MATLAB shows outputs at a command window. To stop MATLAB showing results from a line of a code in a command window, a semicolon, **;** , should be used at the end of that line. This is particularly helpful when a MATLAB script file is executed.

MATLAB has specific naming rules for variable names. Here are rules that variable names should follow:

- Variable names can consist of letters (both uppercase, `A-Z`, and lowercase, `a-z`), digits (`0-9`), and an underscore character (_).
- A variable name length should be limited to a number that the **namelengthmax** command returns.
- Variable names should start with a letter. Variable names cannot start with a digit or underscore, _.

- The rest of a variable name, i.e. a part that comes after the first character, can consist of letters, digits, and underscores.
- Variable names cannot be the same as MATLAB keywords. To check if a name is a MATLAB keyword, the `iskeyword('...')` command may be used. The `iskeyword` command returns all MATLAB keywords.
- Variable names are case sensitive. For example, `age=60` and `Age=60` are considered as two separate variables. Although it is allowed to use both age and Age as a variable name, it is highly recommended to avoid using both of them in the same code.
- Space is not allowed in variable names. Therefore, space cannot be used between parts of a compound name. To split a variable name into two or more parts, use an underscore character, _, between parts (This practice is known as snake case). For example, `best age=25` is not correct. Some acceptable alternatives are: `best_age=25`, or `bestage=25`, or `BestAge=25`, or any other combination without a space.
- It is suggested to avoid using the same name for variables and functions, particularly in the same script.

2.2 MATLAB Built-in Functions, Add-on Toolboxes, and Third-Party Packages

MATLAB comes with a large number of built-in functions. All built-in functions are loaded at the moment MATLAB starts and become available to use. Here are some of the MATLAB built-in functions: `abs`, `clear`, `length`, `max`, `min`, and `disp`.

In addition to built-in functions, MATLAB has a list of add-on toolboxes that may be acquired separately. To use any of the toolboxes, its license should be obtained first. Any of these toolboxes includes a series of functions which developed to conduct specific tasks. After a toolbox is obtained, all associated functions in that toolbox become available to use. Some of the MATLAB toolboxes are: Curve Fitting Toolbox, Data Acquisition Toolbox, Image Processing Toolbox, Mapping Toolbox, Optimization Toolbox, Parallel Computing Toolbox, and Signal Processing Toolbox.

Similar to built-in functions, MATLAB comes with pre-defined constants. The most commonly used MATLAB built-in constants are `eps`, `pi`, and `NaN`. Also, MATLAB has a series of keywords such as `if`, `for`, and `while`.

Furthermore, there are tons of popular third-party packages for MATLAB. Unlike the built-in functions that come pre-installed with MATLAB, the third-party packages need to be added manually after MATLAB is installed. To use the third-party package, it should be downloaded and stored on a system. If a packaged is zipped, it should be unzipped first. Now, to use this package,

MATLAB needs to know where to look for this new package. For that purpose, a folder that contains this package should be added to the MATLAB search path. A folder can be added to the MATLAB search path by using the `addpath` command. Each package might have its own installation instruction that users should follow.

2.3 Mathematical Operators

MATLAB has a series of arithmetic operators. When MATLAB starts, these mathematical operators are available to use right away. However, there are other operators or functions that are only available through add-on toolboxes. For example, a plus operator, `+`, is always available to use, while the `periodogram` function which estimates a power spectral density, is only available through the Signal Processing Toolbox (Although it might be obtained from the third-party packages as well). Therefore, to use the periodogram function, the Signal Processing Toolbox should be obtained first.

MATLAB mathematical operators

Operation	Description
`x + y`	Add x and y
`x - y`	Subtract y from x
`x * y`	Multiply x by y (matrix multiplication)
`x .* y`	Multiply x by y (element-wise multiplication)
`x / y`	Divide x by y (matrix right division)
`x ./ y`	Divide x by y (element-wise division)
`A \ B`	Matrix left division: solve systems of linear equations as Ax = B
`mod(x, y)`	Modulo: a reminder of x divided by y
`-x`	Negative x
`abs(x)`	An absolute value of x (magnitude of x, if x is a complex number)
`x^y`	Raise x to the power of y (matrix power)
`x.^y`	Raise x to the power of y (element-wise power)
`x.'`	Transpose of x

There are two types of arithmetic operations in MATLAB., an array operation and a matrix operation. An array operation is used for numerical operation while a matrix operation uses a linear algebra for matrix manipulations.

The first type of arithmetic operations is array operations, which is used for numerical operations. For example, `2*3` is a simple numerical manipulation. As another example for an array operation, consider matrixes `A` and a scaler 2. Now, the `A*2` expression multiplies all elements of matrix `A` by 2. Similarly, `A/2` divides all elements of matrix `A` by 2, the `A+2` adds 2 to all elements of matrix `A`, and the A-2 subtracts 2 from all elements of matrix A. However, 2/A causes an error, as we cannot divide a number by a matrix.

Another situation that an array operation might be used is in computations that element by element (element-wise) operations are required. For example, consider the same-size matrixes B and C. Now, assume a case that we need to multiply all elements in a matrix B by their corresponding elements in a matrix C. To do that we can use B.*C expression. Similarly, B./C divides all elements of a matrix B by their corresponding elements in a matrix C. Here, the period character, ., instructs MATLAB to use array operations rather than matrix operations. As array and matrix operations for + and - are the same, there is no need to use a period before them.

Remember that a 2/A expression causes an error, however, the 2./A divides 2 by all elements of matrix A. Similarly, the A^2 causes an error, however, the A.^2 raises all elements of matrix A to the power of 2. Note that, A.*2 is the same as A*2 and A./2 is the same as A/2.

The second type of arithmetic operations is matrix operations, which is used for matrix manipulations. For example, consider matrixes D and F with compatible sizes. The D*F expression multiplies a matrix D by a matrix F, the D/F divides a matrix D by a matrix F, the D+F adds a matrix D and a matrix F, the D-F subtract a matrix D from a matrix F. Remember, in each of these matrix operations, matrixes should have compatible sizes, otherwise, it causes an error.

Here are examples of the typical arithmetic operators in MATLAB:

```
%Assume x=3, y=2, and z=[1,2,3]

%Add x and y
a=3+2;

%Subtract y from x
a=3-2;

%Multiply x by y
a=3*2;

%Multiply z by y (element-wise)
%Output: [2,4,6]
a=[1,2,3].*2;

%Divide x by y
a=3/2;
```

```
%Divide z by y (element-wise)
%Output: [0.5,1,1.5]
a=[1,2,3]./2;

%Return a remainder of x divided by y
%Output: 1
a=mod(3,2);

%Return x raised to the power of y
%Output: 9
a=3^2;

%Return z raised to the power of y (element-wise)
%Output: [1,4,9]
a=[1,2,3].^2;

%Return a transpose of z
%Output: [1;2;3]
a=[1,2,3].';
```

2.4 Comparison Operators

MATLAB offers a series of comparison operators. These operators compare expressions with each other. These operators typically return `logical 1` (`true`) if a statement is correct and return `logical 0` (`false`) if a statement is not correct. These operators are typically used substantially during numerical computations.

MATLAB comparison operators

Operation	Description
`x < y`	Evaluate if x is less than y
`x <= y`	Evaluate if x is less than or equal to y
`x > y`	Evaluate if x is greater than y
`x >= y`	Evaluate if x is greater than or equal to y
`x == y`	Evaluate if x is equal to y
`x ~= y`	Evaluate if x is not equal to y

Here are examples of comparison operators in MATLAB:

```
%Statement in the next line returns 1 (true)
3>2
```

```
%Statement in the next line returns 0 (false)
3==2

%Statement in the next line returns 0 (false)
3<2
```

2.5 Logical Operators

There are 5 logical operators in MATLAB: `|`, `&`, `||`, `&&`, `~`,. These operators evaluate given expressions and return `logical 1` (`true`) or `logical 0` (`false`). Statement `(x | y)` returns `1` if one of the `x` or `y` is `true`, otherwise, it returns `0`. Statement `(x & y)` returns `1` if both `x` and `y` are `true`, otherwise, it returns `0`. Statement `(~x)` returns `1` if x is `false`, otherwise, it returns `0`. The && represents short-circuiting logical AND. Similarly, the || represents short-circuiting logical OR.

MATLAB logical operators

Operation	Description
`x	y`	Logical OR, return logical 1 if x or y is true
`x || y`	Logical OR (short-circuiting)
`x & y`	Logical AND, return logical 1 if both x and y are true
`x && y`	Logical AND (short-circuiting)
`~x`	Logical NOT, return logical 1 if x is false

Here are examples of logical operators in MATLAB:

```
%Statement in the next line returns 1 (true)
(3>2) | (2<1)

%Statement in the next line returns 0 (false)
(3>2) & (2==1)

%Statement in the next line returns 0 (false)
~(3>2)
```

2.6 Integer and Floating Point

In MATLAB, there are 3 numerical types that are used the most. They are integer, floating point, and complex numbers. Integers are zero, positive, or negative numbers without any decimal point and decimal part such as `a=3`. Floating points are numbers that have a decimal point and a decimal part (a fraction part) such as `a=3.2`. By default, MATLAB considers numerical values as a double-precision floating point.

The `int8(x)` function converts x to 8-bit signed integer. The `double(x)` converts x to a double-precision floating point. The `ceil(x)` round x toward a positive infinity and returns the smallest integer that is greater than or equal to x. The `floor(x)` rounds x toward a negative infinity and returns the largest integer that is less than or equal to x.

If a variable becomes `NaN`, it means that a variable is Not-a-Number. If a variable becomes `Inf`, it means that a variable is an infinity. A value of `eps` in MATLAB is equal 2.2204e-16.

MATLAB number types

Operation	Description
`int8(x)`	Convert x to 8-bit signed integer
`double(x)`	Convert x to a double-precision floating point
`round(x,n)`	Return x rounded to n precision after (for n>0) or before (for n<0) a decimal point (default n=0)
`ceil(x)`	Return the smallest integer greater than or equal to x
`floor(x)`	Return the largest integer less than or equal to x
`fix(x)`	Return x rounded toward 0 (truncate a fractional part)

Here are examples of integers and floating point numbers:

```
%Numbers
a=int8(3.2);
b=double(3);
c=round(3.456);
d=ceil(3.2);
f=floor(3.2);
g=fix(3.2);
h=NaN;
```

To truncate a floating point number `x` to `n` precision after a decimal point without rounding it, we can use a mathematical expression `(fix(x*10^n))/(10^n)`. Here is an example of how to keep only 2 digits after a decimal point:

```
%Following statement returns 2 digits after a decimal point
%Convert 3.45678 to 3.4500
%Output: 3.4500
a=(fix(3.45678*10^2))/(10^2);
```

A scientific notation (a scientific number) is typically presented by a mathematical expression as $m \times 10^n$. In MATLAB, a scientific notation is presented by using a letter `e` or `E`. In this form, a letter `e` or `E` presents "times ten raised to the power of". For example, a mathematical expression of 1.23×10^4 is written as `1.23e4` in MATLAB. Here are examples of scientific notations in MATLAB:

```
%Scientific notations (scientific numbers)
a=1.23e4;
b=4.5e-6;
c=-8E12;
```

2.7 Complex Numbers

A Complex number in MATLAB is defined as $real\ +\ imag \times i$, where $i = \sqrt{-1}$ is an imaginary unit. Typically, an imaginary unit is presented by `i` in mathematical texts, however, MATLAB uses both `i` and `j` for that purpose. Note that, to yield an imaginary number, an imaginary unit `i` or `j` should be always appended to a numeric literal such as `1i`. There should not be any space between a number and `i` or `j`. If `i` or `j` is not attached to a number, then MATLAB may consider them as a variable, not as an imaginary unit.

A complex number in MATLAB can be defined by one of the following methods:

- The first method is to define a complex number by using the `complex` function as `z=complex(real,imag)`, where `z` is a complex number, `real` is a real part of the complex number, and `imag` is an imaginary part of the complex number. Note that, `complex(x)` is considered as `complex(x,0)`.
- The second method is to define a complex number as `z=a+bi` or `z=a+bj`, such as `z=3+2i` or `z=x+y*1j`.

For any given complex number such as `z`, its magnitude can be obtained by `abs(z)`, its real part can be obtained by `real(z)`, its imaginary part can be obtained by `imag(z)`, and its phase can be obtained by `angle(z)`.

MATLAB complex number

Operation	Description
`complex(real,imag)`	A complex number as $(real + imag \times 1i)$, where $i = \sqrt{-1}$
`abs(z)`	Return an absolute value of z (magnitude of z, if z is a complex number)
`real(z)`	Return a real part of a complex number z
`imag(z)`	Return an imaginary part of a complex number z
`angle(z)`	Return a phase of a complex number z

Here are examples of complex numbers in MATLAB:

```
%Return a complex number as z=x+y*1i using the complex function
z=complex(3,2);

%Return a complex number as z=x+y*1i
z=3+2i;

%Return a complex number as z=x+y*1i
x=3;
y=2;
z=x+y*1i;

%Return a real part of the complex number
%Output: 3
real(z)

%Return an imaginary part of the complex number
%Output: 2
imag(z)

%Return a magnitude of the complex number
%Output: 3.6055
abs(z)

%Return a phase of the complex number
%Output: 0.5880
angle(z)
```

2.8 Strings

MATLAB has a series of features and commands for text processing and string manipulation. In MATLAB, a text can be presented by a character array or by a string array. To create a character array from a sequence of characters in MATLAB, one of the following methods can be used:

- Insert a sequence of characters inside single quotes (`'...'`) to create a character array
- Use the `char` function to create a character array

To create a string array from a sequence of characters, one of the following methods can be used:

- Insert a sequence of characters inside double quotes (`"..."`) to create a string array
- Use the string function to create a string array

Also, a series of strings may be used to form a string array or a cell array. There are more details on a cell array in the following chapters. Here are examples of defining strings in MATLAB:

```
%Create a character array
name='MATLAB';
c=char('word');

%Create a string array
txt="This is a text";
s=string("program");
arr=["MATLAB","program"];

%Create a cell array
cll={"MATLAB","program"};

%Create a string from a variable
%Output: 123
a=123;
st=string(a);
disp(st)
```

To add two strings together, which also is known as strings concatenation, two methods can be used. The first one is to use a character array as `['...' , '...' , '...']` to concatenate strings. Note that single quotes are used to define each string. If double quotes are used to define a string, then it generates a string array instead of concatenating strings. The second one is to use the `strcat` function. Here are examples of attaching two strings together. In these examples, we create a 'butterfly' string from 'butter' and 'fly' strings.

```
%Add two strings by ['...','...']
%Output: butterfly
first_part='butter';
second_part='fly';
word=[first_part,second_part];
disp(word)

%Add two strings by strcat
%Output: butterfly
first_part='butter';
second_part='fly';
word=strcat(first_part,second_part);
disp(word)
```

Here is an example of how to insert a numerical variable in a string. In this example, we insert a variable that shows a length of a pool into a string. To do that, at first, we use the **num2str** command to convert a number into a string, and then we use a character array as `['...' , '...' , '...']` to add all strings together. Note that single quotes are used to define each string.

```
%Insert a numerical variable in a string
%Output: Length of this pool is 3m.
a=3;
txt=['Length of this pool is ',num2str(a),'m.'];
disp(txt)
```

Similarly, a string variable can be inserted in a text. Here is an example of how to insert a string variable in a text by using a character array as `['...' , '...' , '...']` to add all strings together. In this example, we insert a string 'pool' into a text.

```
%Insert a string variable in a text
%name is replaced by 'pool'
%Output: Length of this pool is 3m.
name='pool';
txt=['Length of this ',name,' is 3m.'];
disp(txt)
```

Indexes (indices) can be used to call characters stored in a string or elements stored in an array. To access an element (character) in a string (character array), an element is called by using a string name followed by an index of that element inside parentheses, `(...)`. For example, consider a string that is stored in a variable named `txt`. Then, the first element in txt is obtained by `txt(1)` and the second element is obtained by `txt(2)`. MATLAB uses one-based indexing (numbering). It means that, in MATLAB, the first element has an index 1, the second element has an index 2, and so on. Note that, some programming languages, such as Python (Python Software Foundation; www.python.org), use zero-based indexing, where the first element has an index 0.

In MATLAB we can use `end` as an index. In this case, `end` is interpreted as the last elements in a corresponding dimension. For example, to access the last element in txt, we can use `txt(end)`. There are more details on indexing and slicing in the following chapters. Here is how a word 'butterfly', which is stored as a string, is indexed in MATLAB:

Variable:	b	u	t	t	e	r	f	l	y
Index:	(1)	(2)	(3)	(4)	(5)	(6)	(7)	(8)	(9)

Here are examples of calling elements in a string (character array). In this example, the first element is 'b', the second element is 'u', the third element is 't', and so on.

```
%Use indexes to call characters stored in a character array (string)
c='butterfly';
fisrt_character=c(1);
second_character=c(2);
last_character=c(end);
```

Remember, if we are working with a character array, indexes refer to characters in that array. However, if we are working with a string array, indexes refer to elements in that array. Here are examples of calling elements in a string array. In this example, the first element is "butterfly" and the second element is "wings".

```
%Use indexes to call elements stored in a string array
s=["butterfly","wings"];
fisrt_element=s(1);
second_element=s(2);
```

MATLAB has a series of formatting operators to format a string or text. Commonly, the `fprintf` and `sprintf` functions along with formatting operators are used to format a string. The `fprintf` function writes (prints) a text to a file or displays it in a command window. The `sprintf` function creates a string variable.

A simple method to format a string or text in MATLAB is to use special characters. These special characters are generally called escape sequences. For example, an escape sequence `\t` inserts a tab space and an escape sequence `\n` starts a new line in a printed text. Here are some examples of using escape sequences to format a text:

```
%MATLAB interprets escape sequence \n as a new-line
txt='This is the 1st line \n this is the 2nd line';
fprintf(txt)

%MATLAB interprets escape sequence \t as a tab-space
txt='Length of this pool is \t 3m';
fprintf(txt)
```

In some texts, a user may intend to use an escape sequence itself, rather than its interpretation. In other words, a user may want to prevent an interpretation of an escape sequence. In such cases, MATLAB should be instructed to ignore a special interpretation of that escape sequence. To do that, a backslash \ is added in front of the escape sequence. Additionally, for some texts such as the ones in a plot, all string configurations can be disregarded by setting a text interpreter to `'none'`. Here is an example of using a backslash. In this example, we use a backslash to tell MATLAB to ignore `\n` in a string, otherwise, MATLAB interprets `\n` as an escape sequence to start a new line.

```
%Backslash before \n tells MATLAB to ignore this escape sequences
%Therefore, MATLAB ignores \n
txt='C:\\name'
fprintf(txt)
```

The more sophisticated way to format a string in MATLAB is to use a format specifier. To use this method, at first, a section of the string that needs to be formatted is marked by a percent sign followed by a format specifier. Each format specifier presents a placeholder that will be replaced by a given string.

The full format specifier has six fields. These fields from left to right are: identifier, flags, field width, precision, subtype, and conversion character. Except for a conversion character, other fields in a format specifier are optional. To mark a format specifier in MATLAB, a leading percent sign, `%`, should be used right before a format specifier.

In general, to use this method, at first, a format specifier, which serves as a placeholder, is placed inside a text. Then, a string that is intended to replace a format specifier (placeholder) is given afterward. For example, the `sprintf` function is used as `sprintf( '...%format specifier...' , replacement strings )`. A format specifier may have position identifier as `n$`, which refers to position number `n`. If format specifier positions are not defined, then each format specifier is replaced by given strings in an order that format specifiers appear in a text. It means that, the first format specifier is replaced by the first string, the second format specifier is replaced by the second string, and so on. However, if a format specifier has a position identifier, then it is replaced by a string that matches its position. For example, `%1$s` is a string format specifier with a position identifier of `1$`, and is replaced by a string that has the first position in replacement strings. If a text format is not defined, then an imported text from replacement strings follows a default text format.

MATLAB Conversion Specifier

Conversion Specifier	Description	Example
`c`	Single character	`%c`
`d`	Decimal	`%d`
`e`	Exponential (Scientific)	`%e`
`f`	Fixed-point	`%f`
`s`	String	`%s`
`- (minus sign)`	Left-justify	`%-s`
`n$`	Position identifier	`%1$s`

Here are steps to insert a simple format specifier as a placeholder in a text and use the `sprintf` function to replace that format specifier:

- Write the desired text as a string. It can be a standalone string, or it can be assigned to a variable. For example, consider the desired text as `'A butterfly has 4 wings.'`
- Use a format specifier to substitute a part of the text that needs to be repeatedly replaced or formatted. For example, assume in the text `'A butterfly has 4 wings.'`, a number "4" needs to replaced. Therefore, the text is rewritten as `'A butterfly has %d wings.'`. A format specifier `%d` presents a placeholder for a decimal number.
- Use the `sprintf` function to replace a format specifier. Any value that is used as the second input argument of the `sprintf` function replaces a format specifier. In this example, a number 4 should replace `%d` identifier. Therefore, a number 4 is used as the second input argument of the `sprintf` function as `sprintf('A butterfly has %d wings.',4)`. This instructs MATLAB to insert 4 in place of `%d`.

Here are examples of using a format specifier as a placeholder. In these examples, at first, we show how to use and replace a format specifier to insert 4 in a string 'A butterfly has %d wings.'. Then, we present different examples of how to use a format specifier as a placeholder.

```
%Specifier %d defines a decimal placeholder that is replaced by 4
```

```
%Output: A butterfly has 4 wings.
txt=sprintf('A butterfly has %d wings.',4);
disp(txt)

%Specifier %s defines a string placeholder that is replaced by 'four'
%Output: A butterfly has four wings.
txt=sprintf('A butterfly has %s wings.','four');
disp(txt)

%Specifier %d defines a decimal placeholder that is replaced by 4
s='A butterfly has %d wings.';
txt=sprintf(s,4);
disp(txt)

%Specifiers %d and %d define two decimal placeholders
%that are replaced by 4 and 6
%Output: A butterfly has 4 wings and 6 legs.
s='A butterfly has %d wings and %d legs.';
txt=sprintf(s,4,6);
disp(txt)
```

As mentioned, a format specifier may have position identifier as `n$`, which refers to position number `n`. A format specifier with a position identifier is replaced by a string that matches its position in replacement strings. Here are examples of using format specifiers as placeholders that have position identifiers.

```
%Specifiers %1$s, %2$s, and %3$s are three string placeholders
%identified by position identifiers
%Specifier n$ is a position identifier
%Example: 1$ is the first position
%Specifier %1$s reads as: the first position string
%Specifier %1$s refers to a position 1 and is replaced by 'four'
%Specifier %2$s refers to a position 2 and is replaced by 'six'
%Specifier %3$s refers to a position 3 and is replaced by 'two'
%Output: A butterfly has four wings, six legs, and two antennae.
s='A butterfly has %1$s wings, %2$s legs, and %3$s antennae.';
txt=sprintf(s,'four','six','two');
disp(txt)

%Specifiers %1$s, %2$s, and %3$s are three string placeholders
%identified by position identifiers
%Specifier n$ is a position identifier
```

```
%Example: 1$ is the first position
%Specifier %1$s reads as: the first position string
%Specifier %1$s refers to a position 1 and is replaced by t[0]
%Specifier %2$s refers to a position 2 and is replaced by t[1]
%Specifier %3$s refers to a position 3 and is replaced by t[2]
%t is a string array
t=["four","six","two"];
s='A butterfly has %1$s wings, %2$s legs, and %3$s antennae.';
txt=sprintf(s,t(1),t(2),t(3));
disp(txt)
```

Here are examples of using variables to replace format specifiers:

```
%Specifiers %s, %s, and %s are three string placeholders
%First specifier %s refers to a position 1 and
%is replaced by wng='four'
%Second specifier %s refers to a position 2 and
%is replaced by leg='six'
%Third specifier %s refers to a position 3 and
%is replaced by ant='two'
wng='four';
leg='six';
ant='two';
s='A butterfly has %s wings, %s legs, and %s antennae.';
txt=sprintf(s,wng,leg,ant);
disp(txt)

%Specifiers %1$s, %2$s, and %3$s are three string placeholders
%identified by position identifiers
%Specifier n$ is a position identifier
%Example: 1$ is the first position
%Specifier %1$s reads as: the first position string
%Specifier %1$s refers to a position 1 and is replaced by wng='four'
%Specifier %2$s refers to a position 2 and is replaced by leg='six'
%Specifier %3$s refers to a position 3 and is replaced by ant='two'
wng='four';
leg='six';
ant='two';
s='A butterfly has %1$s wings, %2$s legs, and %3$s antennae.';
txt=sprintf(s,wng,leg,ant);
disp(txt)
```

As it is demonstrated, a format specifier is used to mark, format and replace a text in a string. To do that, at first, a format specifier, which serves as a placeholder, is placed inside a text. Then, a string that is intended to replace a format specifier is given afterward. For example, the `sprintf` function is used as `sprintf( '...%format specifier...' , replacement strings )`. If a format specifier has a position identifier as `n$`, which refers to position number `n`, then it is replaced by a string that matches nth position in replacement strings. Otherwise, if a format specifier does not have a position identifier, then each format specifier is replaced by given replacement strings in an order that format specifiers appear in a text.

A format specifier is defined by conversion specifiers. For example, a letter `f` defines a fixed-point (float) number if it is used as a text format conversion. To better describe that, consider `%1$.2f` as a format specifier. It interprets as a format specifier that refers to a position 1 and has a text format of `.2f`. The text format of `.2f` means to use a fixed-point notation with two digits after a decimal point. Here are examples of how to use a format specifier to format a replacement text:

```
%Specifier %1$f defines a fixed-point placeholder
%identified by a position identifier
%Identifier n$ is a position identifier
%Example: 1$ is the first position
%Specifier %1$f reads as: the first position fixed-point float
%Specifier 1$ refers to a position 1 and is replaced by 71
%f converts a number to a float
%Output: About 71.000000 percent of the Earth surface is covered by
water.
s='About %1$f percent of the Earth surface is covered by water.';
txt=sprintf(s,71);
disp(txt)

%Specifier %1$.2f defines a fixed-point placeholder
%identified by a position identifier
%Identifier n$ is a position identifier
%Example: 1$ is the first position
%Specifier %1$.2f reads as: the first position 2 digits decimal float
%Specifier 1$ refers to a position 1 and is replaced by 71
%.2f converts a number to a float with 2 digits after decimal point
%Output: About 71.00 percent of the Earth surface is covered by water.
s='About %1$.2f percent of the Earth surface is covered by water.';
txt=sprintf(s,71);
disp(txt)

%Specifiers %7d, %7d, and %7d are three decimal placeholders
```

```
%Specifier %7d reads as: 7 characters width decimal number
%First specifier %7d refers to a position 1 and is replaced by by 135
%Second specifier %7d refers to a position 2 and is replaced by by 206
%Third specifier %7d refers to a position 3 and is replaced by by 235
%Output: RGB values for sky blue color are:    135,    206,    235.
red=135;
green=206;
blue=235;
s='RGB values for sky blue color are:%7d,%7d,%7d.';
txt=sprintf(s,red,green,blue);
disp(txt)

%Specifiers %-7d, %-7d, and %-7d are three decimal placeholders
%Specifier %-7d reads as: left-justified 7 characters width decimal number
%First specifier %7d refers to a position 1 and is replaced by by 135
%Second specifier %7d refers to a position 2 and is replaced by by 206
%Third specifier %7d refers to a position 3 and is replaced by by 235
%Output: RGB values for sky blue color are:135    ,206    ,235    .
red=135;
green=206;
blue=235;
s='RGB values for sky blue color are:%-7d,%-7d,%-7d.';
txt=sprintf(s,red,green,blue);
disp(txt)

%Specifier %.2e is an exponential placeholder replaced by a=123000
%Specifier %.2e reads as: 2 digits decimal exponential (scientific number)
%Output: 1.23e+05 123000
a=123000;
s='%.2e';
txt=sprintf(s,a);
b=str2num(txt);
disp(txt)
disp(b)

%Specifier %d\n is a decimal placeholder
%Specifier \n interprets as a new-line
a=[1000,2000,3000,4000];
txt=sprintf('%d\n',a);
disp(txt)
```

2.9 Vector Creation

In MATLAB, all variables are considered as a multidimensional array. However, 1-dimensional and 2-dimensional arrays have specific names. In MATLAB, a 1-dimensional array is called vector and a 2-dimensional array is called matrix. There are two types of vectors, a row vector and a column vector. A row vector is a 1-dimensional array with a single row that has a size of (`1xN`), where `N` is a number of elements in a vector. A simple method to create a row vector is to enter a series of numbers separated by a space or comma between two square brackets as `[ ... , ... , ... ]`. A column vector is a 1-dimensional array with a single column that has a size of (`Mx1`), where `M` is a number of elements in a vector. A simple method to create a column vector is to enter a series of numbers separated by a semicolon between two square brackets as `[ ... ; ... ; ... ]`. For example, `A=[1,2,5,3]` is a row vector with 4 elements and `B=[1;2;5;3]` is a column vector with 4 elements.

A vector creation can be used to generate a sequence of numbers. A simple way to generate a sequence of number in MATLAB is to use a colon, `:` , for a vector creation. By using a colon, a sequence of numbers can be generated between a `start` number and a `stop` number with an interval of a given `step`. Here is a general syntax for a vector creation using a colon:

Syntax

```
start : step : stop
```

The `start` defines a starting number in a sequence. The `stop` defines the last number in a sequence. Note that, depending on a `step` value, the `stop` itself may or may not be included in a sequence. The `step` defines an interval between every two consecutive numbers in a sequence. The `step` value is optional. Therefore, if only `start` and `stop` values are defined, then by default, `step` is considered as step=1. Note that, a vector created by a colon is a row vector. Here are different forms that a colon can be used to create a vector:

Vector creation with a colon

Syntax	Default
`start : stop`	step=1
`start : step : stop`	

Here are some notes to consider when using a colon to create a vector:

- All `start`, `stop`, and `step` values should be a number.

- Values for `start`, `stop` and `step` can be positive, zero, and negative. However, if step=0, then an empty row vector is created.
- Depending on a value of the `step`, a created vector may or may not contain a `stop` value.
- The `step` is optional and its default value is step=1.
- A vector created by a colon is a row vector.

Here is an example of using a colon to create a row vector with `start` and `stop` values. In this example, we generate integers from 1 to 10.

```
%Use a colon with start and stop values
%Output: a=[1, 2, 3, 4, 5, 6, 7, 8, 9, 10]
a=1:10;
```

Here is an example of using a colon to create a row vector with `start`, `stop`, and `step` values. In this example, we generate integers from 1 to 9 with step 2.

```
%Use a colon with start, stop, and step values
%Output: a=[1, 3, 5, 7, 9]
a=1:2:10;
```

A colon can be used to generate negative numbers as well. Both negative and positive `step` values can be used when negative integers are generated. Here is an example of using a colon to create a row vector with negative `start`, `stop`, and `step` values. In this example, we generate integers from -1 to -9 with step -2.

```
%Use a colon with negative start, stop, and step values
%Output: a=[-1, -3, -5, -7, -9]
a=-1:-2:-10;
```

Similarly, a colon can be used to generate a sequence of numbers contained both negative and positive numbers. Again, both negative and positive `step` values can be used. Here is an example of using a colon to generate negative, zero, and positive values. In this example, we generate integers from -10 to 10 with step 2.

```
%Use a colon to create negative, zero, and positive outcomes
%Output: a=[-10, -8, -6, -4, -2, 0, 2, 4, 6, 8, 10]
a=-10:2:10;
```

The start, stop, and step can be either integer or non-integer values. Here is an example of using a colon with both integer and non-integer inputs. In this example, we generate numbers from 1.5 to 4 with step 0.5.

```
%Use a colon with non-integers inputs
%Output: a=[1.5, 2, 2.5, 3, 3.5, 4]
a=1.5:0.5:4;
```

Note that, `a=1:2:10` is similar to `a=[1:2:10]`, however, it is not a common practice to use the latter one with square brackets.

As mentioned, a vector created by a colon is a row vector. However, if it is required, a column vector may be generated from a row vector. One method to do that is to use a transpose command. In MATLAB a dot-apostrophe operator, `.'` , is used to transpose an array. Another method to create a column vector from a row vector is to assign a row vector to a column vector by indexing. In MATLAB, `(1,:)` index means all elements in a row number one, and `(:,1)` index means all elements in a column number one. This indexing can be used to generate a column vector from a row vector. There are more details on indexing and slicing in the following chapters. Here are examples of how to obtain a column vector from a row vector:

```
%Create a column vector from a row vector by using a transpose
a=1:10; %A row vector
b=a.'; %A column vector

%Create a column vector from a row vector by indexing
a=1:10; %A row vector
b(:,1)=a; %A column vector
```

Note that, similar methods mentioned above may be used to generate a row vector from a column vector as well.

2.10 The `if` Statement

One of the most well-known and widely-used statements in MATLAB is the `if` statement. The `if` statement is used to check given conditions before running (executing) a part of the code that is embedded inside the `if` statement. This embedded code is known as a body of `if` statement. If a given conditional expression returns `logical 1` (`true`), then a code within a body of `if` statement is executed. Otherwise, if a conditional expression returns `logical 0` (`false`), a code within a body of `if` statement is ignored. Here is a general syntax shows how to use the `if` statement:

Syntax

```
if conditional expression
    body of if
end
```

Pay attention to the `end` keyword at the end of the `if` statement. This `end` keyword defines the end of the `if` statement, and if this `end` keyword is missing, it causes an error. MATLAB considers a part of the code that comes between the `if` statement and the `end` keyword as a body of that `if` statement. Note that, it is a common practice to indent a body of `if` statement to make a code more structured and readable. However, this indentation is not required by MATLAB. Here is an example of using the `if` statement in MATLAB. In this example, at first, a variable `a` is set to 0. Then an expression `a<0.5` is evaluated, and if it is `true` (`logical 1`), a string 'a is smaller than 0.5' is displayed.

```
%A simple if statement
a=0;
if a<0.5
    disp('a is smaller than 0.5')
end
```

It is not common to write the `if` statement in one line. However, if it is needed, an in-line `if` statement can be written by using the following structure:

Syntax

```
if conditional expression, body of if, end
```

Pay attention to the `end` keyword after all statements. This `end` keyword defines the end of the `if` statement, and if this `end` keyword is missing, it causes an error. Here is an example of using an in-line form of the `if` statement in MATLAB. In this example, we re-consider a previous example, but this time, we use an in-line `if` statement.

```
%An in-line if statement
a=0;
if a<0.5, disp('a is smaller than 0.5'), end
```

Here is another example of using the `if` statement in MATLAB. In this example, we use the `rand` function to generate a random number in a range (0 , 1). Note that, 0 and 1 are not included in a range. Here, at first, we used the `rand` function to assign a random number between 0 and 1 to a variable a. Then we use the `if` statement to evaluate an expression `a<0.5`.

```
%Use if statement to check a value of a
a=rand(1,1); %Return a random number between 0 and 1
if a<0.5
    disp('a is smaller than 0.5')
    disp(a)
end
```

In the `if` statement, a combination of several conditional expressions can be used together if needed. In cases that a combination of conditional expressions is used, it is recommended to put each conditional expression in a separate set of parentheses. Here is an example of using multiple conditional expressions with the logical operator in the `if` statement:

```
%Use multiple expressions with logical operator to check a value of a
a=rand(1,1); %A random number between 0 and 1
if ((a<0.5) & (a~=0.5))
    disp('a is smaller than 0.5')
    disp(a)
end
```

The `if` statement can be combined with an optional `else` statement. Each `if` statement can only have one `else` statement, which always comes after the `if` statement. In cases that the `if-else` statement is used, at first, the `if` statement is evaluated. In case that the `if` statement is `true`, a body of `if` statement is executed, and the `else` statement is ignored. It means that, if a conditional expression in the `if` statement returns `logical 1` (`true` value), then the `else` statement is ignored. However, in case that the `if` statement is not `true`, a body of `else` statement is executed. Here is a general syntax shows how to use the `if-else` statement:

Syntax

```
if conditional expression1
    body of if
else
    body of else
end
```

Note that, indentations of body of **if** and body of **else** are not required by MATLAB. Here is an example of using the **if-else** statement in MATLAB:

```
%Use if-else to check a value of a
a=rand(1,1); %A random number between 0 and 1
if a<0.5
    disp('a is smaller than 0.5')
    disp(a)

else
    disp('a is equal or larger than 0.5')
    disp(a)

end
```

Similar to the **if-else** statement, the **if** statement can also be combined with optional **elseif** and **else** statements. In general, the **if** statement can be combined with one, both or none of the **elseif** and **else** statements. The **elseif** statement allows to check for more conditional expressions after the **if** statement.

Each **if** statement can have as many **elseif** statements as required. Remember that each **if** statement can only have one **else** statement. The **elseif** statements always come after the **if** statement and before the **else** statement.

In cases that the **if-elseif** statement is used, at first, the **if** statement is evaluated. In case that the **if** statement is **true**, a body of **if** statement is executed, and all **elseif** statements are ignored. It means that, if a conditional expression in the **if** statement returns **logical 1** (**true** value), then all **elseif** statements are ignored. However, in case that the **if** statement is not **true**, then the first **elseif** statement is evaluated. Now, if this **elseif** statement returns a **true** value, then a body of this **elseif** statement is executed and the rest of **elseif** statements are ignored. If this **elseif** statement returns **logical 0** (**false** value), then the next **elseif** statement is evaluated, and it continues until one **elseif** statement returns a **true** value. If none of the **if** and **elseif** statements returns a **true** value, then all of them are ignored. Note that, if a **true** value is returned by any of the **if** or **elseif** statements, the rest of the **elseif** statements are ignored.

Similar steps are used to evaluate the **if-elseif-else** statement. At first, the **if** statement is evaluated, and if it is **false**, then **elseif** statements are evaluated one by one in an order they appear in a code. Finally, if all previous statements are **false**, then the **else** statement is executed. Similar to the **if-elseif** statement, if a **true** value is returned by any of the **if** or **elseif** statements, the rest of the **elseif** statements and the **else** statement are ignored. Here is a general syntax shows how to use the **if-elseif-else** statement:

Syntax

```
if conditional expression1
    body of if
elseif conditional expression2
    body of elseif
elseif conditional expression3
    body of elseif

...

else
    body of else
end
```

Note that, indentations of body of **if**, body of **elseif**, and body of **else** are not required by MATLAB. Here is an example of using the **if-elseif** statement in MATLAB:

```
%Use if-elseif to check a value of a
a=rand(1,1); %A random number between 0 and 1
if a<0.5
    disp('a is smaller than 0.5')
    disp(a)

elseif a>0.5
    disp('a is larger than 0.5')
    disp(a)

elseif a==0.5
    disp('a is equal to 0.5')
    disp(a)

end
```

Here is an example of using the **if-elseif-else** statement in MATLAB:

```
%Use if-elseif-else to check a value of a
```

```
a=rand(1,1); %A random number between 0 and 1
if a<0.5
    disp('a is smaller than 0.5')
    disp(a)

elseif a>0.5
    disp('a is larger than 0.5')
    disp(a)

else
    disp('a is equal to 0.5')
    disp(a)

end
```

The `if` statement can be used in a nested form as well. A nested `if` statement is a series of `if` statements, where each statement is inside another statement. Here is a general syntax of the nested `if` statement containing 3 statements:

Syntax

```
if conditional expression1
    body of if 1

    if conditional expression2
        body of if 2

        if conditional expression3
            body of if 3
        end

    end

end
```

Pay attention to the **end** keyword at the end of each `if` statement. These **end** keywords define the end of each `if` statement. As mentioned before, an indentation of a body of each `if` statement is only for structuring a code and is not required by MATLAB. In a nested `if` statement, each `if` statement can have optional `elseif` and `else` statements as well. Here is an example of the nested `if` statement. In this example, we use the **`input`** function to request an input between 0 and 1 from a user. Then, we use the nested `if` statement to define a range of the input value.

```
%A nested if statement
a=input('Enter a number between 0 and 1: '); %Read a number
                                              %between 0 and 1

if a<0.5
    if a==0
        disp('a is equal to 0')
    else
        disp('a is smaller than 0.5')
    end

elseif a>0.5
    if a==1
        disp('a is equal to 1')
    else
        disp('a is larger than 0.5')
    end

else
    disp('a is equal to 0.5')

end
```

The `if` statement also may be used to compare character arrays (strings). Here is an example of how to compare two strings in MATLAB:

```
%String (character array) comparison
a=input('Enter yes or no: ','s'); %Read a string yes or no
if strcmp(a,'yes')==1
    disp('a is equal to yes')
else
    disp('a is not equal to yes')
end
```

2.11 The `for` Statement

During a process of code developments, there might be situations that a set of commands (a block of code) needs to be re-executed repeatedly for a certain number of times. In such cases, a loop is used to iterate these commands for a given number of times. One favorite method to create a loop, is to build a loop by using the `for` statement.

The `for` statement runs (executes) a part of the code that is embedded inside the `for` statement for a defined number of times. The embedded code inside the `for` statement is known as a body of `for` statement. Here is a general syntax shows how to use the `for` statement (`for loop`):

Syntax

```
for counter = integer sequence
    body of for
end
```

Pay attention to the `end` keyword at the end of the `for` statement. This `end` keyword defines the end of the `for` statement, and if this `end` keyword is missing, it causes an error. MATLAB considers a part of the code that comes between the `for` statement and the `end` keyword as a body of that `for` statement. Note that, it is a common practice to indent a body of `for` statement to make a code more structured and readable. However, this indentation is not required by MATLAB.

The `for` statement iterates over the elements of an `integer sequence`. A total number of the times that the `for` statement is looped is equal to a total number of elements that are inside a sequence used in the `for` statement.

A `counter` in the `for` statement behaves like a variable. In each iteration, the `counter` receives a content of an element in a `sequence`. In other words, a content of the `counter` changes in each iteration of the `for` loop and becomes equal to a content of the corresponding element inside a `sequence`. It means that, in the first iteration, a `counter` becomes equal to the first element in a `sequence`. In the second iteration, a `counter` becomes equal to the second element in a `sequence`. This continues until the last iteration, which a `counter` becomes equal to the last element in a `sequence`.

The `counter` in the `for` statement can have any name, such as a letter or a word. If it is intended to reference or use the `counter` in a loop, the same exact name of the `counter` should be used inside a body of `for`. Remember, we should never change a value of the `counter` within a body of `for` statement. For example, we should not assign a new value to a `counter` while a loop is iterating. The most common names for a `counter` are: `i`, `j`, `k`, `m`, `n`. In cases that there are complex numbers inside a code, it is suggested to use `i` or `j` as a `counter` with caution to avoid a `counter` being mistaken with an imaginary unit in a complex number.

Any integer **sequence** can be used in the **for** statement. In cases that working with arrays are intended, a vector creation is commonly used as a **sequence**. This is particularly helpful if a value of a **counter** becomes equal to a number of times that a loop has been iterated so far. This helps to use a **counter** as an array index to address different elements of an array.

Here is an example of using a vector creation as a **sequence** in the **for** statement. Assume there is an 1-dimensional array a=[10,11,12,13,14]. By using a vector creation **1:5** as a **sequence** and **i** as a **counter**, the **for** statement is used to raise each element of this array to the power of two.

```
%The for statement with a vector 1:5 as a sequence
a=[10,11,12,13,14];
for i=1:5
    b=a(i)^2;
    disp(b)
end
```

Consider a previous example again. This time we use a vector creation **1:2:5** as a **sequence** and **i** as a **counter** to raise the first, third, and fifth elements of this array to the power of two.

```
%The for statement with a vector 1:2:5 as a sequence
a=[10,11,12,13,14];
for i=1:2:5
    b=a(i)^2;
    disp(b)
end
```

Here is an example of using a numeric row vector **number=[1,2,3,4,5]** as a **sequence** and **num** as a **counter** in the **for** statement. In this example, the **for** statement is used to display a value of **num** in each iteration. Note that, a **counter** only iterates over a row vector. In other words, if we need to use a vector as an integer **sequence** in the **for** statement, it should be a 1-dimensional row array. Therefore, if we have a column vector, it should be transposed to a row vector before it can be used as a **sequence** in the **for** statement.

```
%The for statement with a row vector as a sequence
number=[1,2,3,4,5];
for num=number
    disp(num)
end
```

The `for` statement can be used in a nested form as well. A nested `for` loop is a series of `for` statements, where each loop is inside another loop. Here is a general syntax of the nested `for` statement containing 3 loops:

Syntax

```
for counter1 = integer sequence1
    body of for 1

    for counter2 = integer sequence2
        body of for 2

        for counter3 = integer sequence3
            body of for 3

        end

    end

end
```

Pay attention to the `end` keyword at the end of each `for` statement. These `end` keywords define the end of each `for` statement. As mentioned before, an indentation of a body of each `for` statement is only for structuring a code and is not required by MATLAB.

A nested `for` loop can be very helpful if working with multidimensional arrays are intended. This is particularly helpful if sequences are defined in such a way that a value of a `counter` becomes equal to a number of times that a corresponding loop to that `counter` has been iterated so far. This helps to use counters as array indexes to address different elements of an array.

Here is an example of the nested `for` statement. Assume we have two arrays of coordinate data. The first one contains six x coordinates as x=[0,1,2,5,7,10] and the second one contains six y coordinates as y=[3,4,5,6,8,9]. Now, consider we want to find all pairs of (x,y) that their distances from an origin (0,0) are equal or larger than 10. Remember that a distance of a point (x,y) from an origin (Euclidean norm) is calculated as $\sqrt{x^2 + y^2}$. To find all pairs with a distance equal or larger than 10, we use a nested `for` statement. To print the results, the `fprintf` function is used as `fprintf('(%d,%d), d=%.2f\n',x(i),y(j),dist)`. This displays the results in a form of (x,y), distance=XX.XX.

```
%A nested for statement
x=[0,1,2,5,7,10];
y=[3,4,5,6,8,9];
for i=1:6
    for j=1:6
        dist=sqrt(x(i)^2+y(j)^2); %Distance
        if dist>=10
            fprintf('(%d,%d), distance=%.2f\n',x(i),y(j),dist)
        end
    end
end
```

The `break` and `continue` keywords can be used in a body of `for` statement. The `break` keyword stops a loop and breaks out of the `for` loop. The `continue` keyword stops a current iteration of a loop as ignoring a rest of commands in a loop and continues with the next iteration.

2.12 The `while` Statement

The `while` statement is a loop that is used to re-execute a set of commands (a block of code) repeatedly as long as a given conditional expression is `true`. The `while` statement consists of a conditional expression and a body of `while` statement. A part of the code that is embedded inside the `while` statement is known as a body of `while` statement. At each iteration, first, the `while` statement checks a conditional expression. If a conditional expression returns `logical 1` (`true`), then the `while` statement runs (executes) a body of `while` statement. After running a body of the `while` statement, it checks a conditional expression again. If it is `true`, it re-runs the loop one more time. This procedure continues until a conditional expression becomes `logical 0` (`false`). At any iteration, including the first one, if a conditional expression returns `false`, the `while` statement exits. Here is a general syntax shows how to use the `while` statement (`while loop`):

Syntax

```
while conditional expression
    body of while
end
```

Pay attention to the `end` keyword at the end of the `while` statement. This `end` keyword defines the end of the `while` statement, and if this `end` keyword is missing, it causes an error. MATLAB considers a part of the code that comes between the `while` statement and the `end` keyword as a body of that `while` statement. Note that, it is a common practice to indent a body of `while` statement to make a code more structured and readable. However, this indentation is not required by MATLAB.

When we use the **while** statement, we have to make sure that a conditional expression becomes **false** at some point. The reason is that, if a conditional expression is given in a way that it never becomes **false**, then the **while** statement goes into infinite loop iterations and never stops.

Here is an example of using the **while** statement in MATLAB. In this example, the **while** statement is used to raise elements of an array a=[0,1,2,3,4,5] to the power of two. To do that, at first, a variable `n` is used as an element index and set to 1 as `n=1`. Then, a **while** loop is used to check a value of `n`. If a value of `n` is equal or less than a length of an array, then the nth element of an array, `a(n)`, is raised to the power of two and stored in the variable `b`. After that, a value of `b` is displayed and a value of `n` is increased by one. This loop is repeated until a variable `n` is no longer equal or smaller than a length of an array. To find a length of an array the **length** function is used. In this case, a length of the array **a** (a number of elements in a) is equal to 6.

```
%The while statement
a=[0,1,2,3,4,5];
n=1;
while n<=length(a)
    b=a(n)^2; %Raise a(n) to the power of 2
    disp(b)
    n=n+1;
end
```

The **while** statement can be used in a nested form as well. A nested **while** loop is a series of **while** statements, where each loop is inside another loop. Here is a general syntax of the nested **while** statement containing 3 loops:

Syntax

```
while conditional expression1
    body of while 1

    while conditional expression2
        body of while 2

        while conditional expression3
            body of while 3

        end
```

```
    end
end
```

Pay attention to the end keyword at the end of each while statement. These end keywords define the end of each while statement. As mentioned before, an indentation of a body of each while statement is only for structuring a code and is not required by MATLAB.

The break and continue keywords can be used inside the while statement. The break keyword stops a loop and breaks out of the while loop. The continue keyword stops a current iteration of a loop as ignoring a rest of commands in a loop and continues with the next iteration.

2.13 Define a Function

During a process of a code development, there might be situations that a set of commands (a block of code) needs to be repeatedly included and reused in a different part of a code. Furthermore, these commands might be required to be used in different codes. In such cases, it is practical to define these commands as a function. Then, every time that these commands are required in a code, instead of copying all the codes related to these commands, a function that contains these commands is called. A function provides a practical and simple way to call a set of commands over and over again, which helps to make a code clean and structured. Here is a general syntax shows how to define a function:

Syntax

```
function [output1, output2, ...] = function_name(argument1, argument2, ...)
%function help

body of function
end
```

A block of a code that is embedded inside a function is known as a body of function. Pay attention to the end keyword at the end of the function. This end keyword defines the end of the function, and if this end keyword is missing, it may cause an error. MATLAB considers a part of the code that comes between a function definition line and the end keyword as a body of that function. Note that, we may indent a body of function to make a code more structured and readable. However, this indentation is not required by MATLAB.

A function can have zero or as many as required arguments as inputs. Also, if needed, a function can return a value of any variable used inside that function as an output.

In MATLAB, there are two methods to call a function. In the first method, a function is initially saved in a file with a .m extension, and then, it is called in another file or in a command window. Note that, a file that contains a function should have an exact same name as a function name. For example, if the name of a function is `my_function`, then a name of a file that contains this function should be `my_function.m`. Remember, to call a function, either a current folder of MATLAB should be the same as a folder that contains a function file, or a folder that contains a function file should be added to MATLAB search path, otherwise, MATLAB cannot find the function. In the second method, a function is stored at the end of a script file. In this case, a function can be called anywhere within that script file. Here is a general syntax shows how to call a function:

Syntax

```
[output1, output2, ...] = function_name(argument1, argument2, ...)
```

Here is an example of a function that does not have an input argument and does not return any value. This function is named `squared` and saved in a file `squared.m`. Every time this function is called, it raises each of 0, 1, 2, 3, and 4 to the power of two and displays the results.

```
%Define a function to print squared values of 0,1,2,3,4
function squared()
for i=0:4
     a=i^2;
     disp(a)
end
end
```

To call this function, simply use its name, `squared`, in a code or a command window. Here is an example of how to call this function:

```
%Call a function
squared()
```

Here is another example of defining and using a function. This time, a function gets input arguments and also returns output variables. This function is named `circle` and saved in a file `circle.m`. It gets a radius of a circle as an input argument and returns an area and a circumference of that circle. In this function, the first output is an area and the second output is a circumference of a circle.

```
%Define a function to calculate area and circumference of a circle
function [area,circ]=circle(radius)
area=pi*radius^2; %Area of a circle
circ=2*pi*radius; %Circumference of a circle
end
```

Here are examples of how to call this function in a code or a command window:

```
%Call a function for a circle with radius=5
%Output: A=78.5398, C=31.4159
radius=5;
[A,C]=circle(radius)

%Call a function for a circle with radius=5
%Output: A=78.5398, C=31.4159
[A,C]=circle(5)

%Call a function for a circle with radius=5
%Output: A=78.5398, C=31.4159
r=5;
[A,C]=circle(r)
```

When a function is called in a code, the input variables can have any names. It means that, input variables are not required to have the same names as the ones that are used to define a function, although they can be the same. In this example, 3 different methods are used to call a function to calculate an area and a circumference of a circle with a radius of 5. In the first method, at first, a value of 5 is assigned to a variable `radius` and then it is used as `[A,C]=circle(radius)`. In the second method, an integer 5 is used directly in place of an input argument as `[A,C]=circle(5)`. In the third method, at first, a value of 5 is assigned to a variable `r` and then it is used to in place of an input argument as `[A,C]=circle(r)`. This example shows how to use any variable or number to replace an input argument.

Similarly, when a function is called in a code, the outputs of a function can be assigned to any variable names. It means that, output variables are not required to have the same name as the ones that are used inside a function, although they can be the same. In this example, variable names `area` and `circ` are used for an area and a circumference inside the function. However, when a function is called, variable names `A` and `C` are used. MATLAB assigns a value of `area` into `A` and a value of `circ` into `C`.

During a course of defining a function, a user can assign default values to any input arguments of that function. If input arguments of a function have default values, then, none, some, or all of these arguments with default values may be excluded when a function is called. In a case that any of the input arguments with default values is not given when a function is called, then its default value is used by a function. One method to exclude default arguments is to exclude them in a reverse order from the last default argument toward the first default argument. In this case, all remaining arguments should be in an exact order that is defined in a function. Another method is to assign empty value by using `[]` to input arguments that are not at the end of an argument list. In this case, a default value is used for any argument that is set equal to `[]`.

One method to define default values for input arguments of a function is to use the **`switch`**, **`nargin`** and **`isempty`** functions. The **`switch`** function is similar to the **`if-elseif`** function. Based on a given conditional expression, the **`switch`** function executes one case (a set of commands) from all given cases. The **`nargin`** function gives a number of input arguments that a user used when a function is called. For example, if a function has 5 input arguments and a user only uses the first two, then the **`nargin`** return 2. The **`isempty`** function checks if a variable is empty or not. If a variable is empty it returns `logical 1` (`true`), otherwise, it returns `logical 0` (`false`).

To explain how to use default arguments when a function is called, let's consider a function that calculates a surface area and a volume of a rectangular box (cuboid). This function is named `box` and saved in a file `box.m`. It gets a length, width, and height of a box as inputs and returns a surface area and a volume of that box. In this example, default values are assigned to all three input arguments and set as **`length=1`**, **`width=1`**, and **`height=1`**. In a case that none of the input arguments are given, a function returns a surface area and a volume of a unit cube.

```
%Define a function to calculate surface area and
%volume of a rectangular box
function [area,vol]=box(length,width,height)

switch nargin
    case 0 %if nargin==0
        length=1; width=1; height=1;
    case 1 %elseif nargin==1
        width=1; height=1;
    case 2 %elseif nargin==2
        height=1;
end

if isempty(length)==1
    length=1;
```

```
end
if isempty(width)==1
    width=1;
end
if isempty(height)==1
    height=1;
end

area=2*(length*width+length*height+width*height); %Surface area
                                                  %of a box
vol=length*width*height; %Volume of a box

end
```

Here in this function, we chose an order of input arguments as length, width, height. Remember, any other order for these variables may be considered when a function is defined. Now, we show a couple of different ways to call this function when using its default arguments.

```
%Call a function for a box with length=10, width=5, height=3
%Output: A=190, V=150
[A,V]=box(10,5,3);

%Call a function for a box with length=10, width=5, height=default
%Output: A=130, V=50
[A,V]=box(10,5);

%Call a function for a box with
%length=10, width=default, height=default
%Output: A=42, V=10
[A,V]=box(10);

%Call a function for a box with
%length=default, width=default, height=default
%Output: A=6, V=1
[A,V]=box();

%Call a function for a box with length=10, width=default, height=3
%Output: A=86, V=30
[A,V]=box(10,[],3);

%Call a function for a box with length=default, width=default, height=3
%Output: A=14, V=3
```

```
[A,V]=box([],[],3);
```

In this example, we used `[]` to assign an empty value to input arguments. The reason is that as it mentioned, all arguments should be used in an exact order that is defined in a function. Therefore, if we need to use a default value for an argument which is not the last, we have to use `[]` in its place.

Assigning default values to input arguments of a function is optional. Therefore, during a function definition, a user may assign default values to none, some, or all of the input arguments. In case that only some of the input arguments have default values, all arguments without default values should come first in a function definition line, and then all arguments with default values should follow them. In other words, in a function definition line, all default arguments should follow non-default arguments, and therefore, non-default arguments cannot follow default arguments. It means that, if we only need to define a default value for one argument, that argument should be the last argument in a function argument list. Similarly, if we need to define default values only for two arguments, those two arguments should be the last and the one before the last argument, and so on. Remember, an order of all arguments is defined by a user. The only restriction is that all default arguments should follow non-default arguments.

For example, assume we only need a default value for a height in a previous example. Then a function may be defined as `function [area,vol]=box(length,width,height)` or as `function [area,vol]=box(width,length,height)` . Now, if we only need a default value for a length, a function can be defined as `function [area,vol]=box(width,height,length)` or as `function [area,vol]=box(height,width,length)` . As another example, assume we need a default values for both width and height. Then a function can be defined as `function [area,vol]=box(length, width, height)` , or as `function [area,vol]=box(length, height, width)` .

Here is another example of how to use a default argument in a function. Assume we need to define a function to approximate a value of the Pi number, π. Remember that, an exact value for the Pi number can be obtained from the `pi`. One method to approximate the Pi number is to use the Leibniz formula for Pi (also known as a Gregory-Leibniz series). The Leibniz formula approximates the Pi value as $\frac{\pi}{4} = 1 - \frac{1}{3} + \frac{1}{5} - \frac{1}{7} + \frac{1}{9} - \cdots$. This series may be written as $\frac{\pi}{4} = \sum_{n=1}^{\infty} \pm \frac{1}{2n-1}$, where odd terms are positive and even terms are negative. The function to approximate Pi is named `approx_pi` and saved in a file `approx_pi.m`. It gets a total number of terms to be included in the Leibniz formula as an input and returns an approximated Pi value by this formula. Here is how to use this formula to approximate the Pi number:

```
%Define a function to approximate Pi using Leibniz formula
```

```
%n_terms: number of terms in Leibniz formula
function [PI]=approx_pi(n_terms)
switch nargin
    case 0 %if nargin==0
        n_terms=1000000;
end

sigma=0; %Initialize sigma
sign_value=1; %Define a sign value as 1 or -1

for n=1:n_terms
    %sigma=1-(1/3)+(1/5)-(1/7)+(1/9)-...
    sigma=sigma+sign_value/(2*n-1);
    sign_value=-sign_value;
end

PI=4*sigma; %PI/4=sigma

end
```

Here are examples of how to call this function in a code or a command window:

```
%Call a function to approximate Pi with default n_terms=1000000
[PI]=approx_pi()

%Call a function to approximate Pi with n_terms=10000
[PI]=approx_pi(10000)
```

In this example, at first, a function is called to approximate a value of Pi by using a default number of terms as `[PI]=approx_pi()`. By default, this function uses 1000000 terms in the Leibniz formula for Pi approximation. Then, a function is called again, but this time, a number of terms to be included in the Leibniz formula is set to 10000 as `[PI]=approx_pi(10000)`. Remember that a fraction of (355/113) gives a good approximation for the Pi, which is accurate up to 6 digits after a decimal point. Again, an exact value for the Pi number can be obtained from the `pi`.

It is a common practice to include some documentation with a function. It provides descriptions of a function for users. Also, it helps developers for future references. In MATLAB, comments are used for this purpose. A help for a function is placed right after a definition line of a function. To separate help lines from the rest of the function, leave a blank line (without `%`) between the end of help lines and the rest of commands and comments that do not belong to the help. Note that, in addition to functions, a help text can be used at the beginning of any program.

Here is an example of a function with a help text. This function is named `calc_rectangle` and saved in a file `calc_rectangle.m`. It gets a length and width of a rectangle as inputs and calculates its area and perimeter.

```
function [area,perim]=calc_rectangle(length,width)
%calc_rectangle calculates an area and a perimeter of rectangle.
%Inputs: length and width of a rectangle
%Outputs: area and perimeter of a rectangle.

area=length*width; %Area of a rectangle
perim=2*(length+width); %Perimeter of a rectangle
end
```

Here is an example of how to call this function in a code or a command window:

```
%Call a function for a rectangle with length=10,width=5
%Output: area=50, perim=30
[area,perim]=calc_rectangle(10,5)
```

To access a help text for any function, the `help` function is used. To access a help text, the `help` function should be followed by a function name. Here is an example of how to access a help text in the `calc_rectangle` function:

```
%Access a help text using help function
help calc_rectangle
```

2.14 The `varargin`

We can use `varargin` if we need to define a function with an arbitrary number of input arguments. In other words, if we are not sure how many input arguments might be passed to a function, we can use `varargin` in a function definition line. Here is a general syntax shows how to define a function with an arbitrary number of input arguments:

Syntax

```
function [output1, output2, ...] = function_name(args, varargin)
body of function
end
```

In a function definition, we may have none, one, two, or more input arguments before **varargin**.

Let's explain how to use **varargin** in a function to present an arbitrary number of inputs. The **varargin** represents input arguments as a cell array. A cell array is a MATLAB data container. To access elements in a cell array, we can place an element index inside curly brackets, **{}**. There are more details on cell arrays in the following chapters.

Consider we need to define a function that gets an arbitrary number of inputs and returns a sum of all inputs. This function is named **input_sum**. Remember, the **nargin** function returns a number of input arguments in a function.

```
%Define a function to calculate sum of inputs
function [s]=input_sum(varargin)
s=0;
for i=1:nargin
    s=s+varargin{i};
end
end
```

Now, we call this function to calculate, first, a sum of 1, 2, then a sum of 1, 2, 3, and finally a sum of 1, 2, 3, 4. In the last example, first, we assign 1, 2, 3, 4 to a, b, c, and d variables and then we use these variables when we call a function.

```
%Call a function to add 1,2
%Output: s=3
[s]=input_sum(1,2);

%Call a function to add 1,2,3
%Output: s=6
[s]=input_sum(1,2,3);

%Call a function to add 1,2,3,4
%Output: s=10
a=1;
b=2;
c=3;
d=4;
[s]=input_sum(a,b,c,d);
```

2.15 Define Anonymous Function

In a previous section, it is explained how to define a function. However, there are cases that we only need a small one-line function. These types of functions are anonymous and are defined by using the @ symbol. These functions are called anonymous functions. Here is a general syntax shows how to use the anonymous function:

Syntax

```
@ (arguments) expression
```

Here are some notes about an anonymous function:

- It is a one-line function.
- It may have any number of arguments as inputs.
- It is restricted to have only a single expression.
- It executes this expression and returns results of that.

Here is an example of using the @ symbol to define an anonymous function. This function raises its argument to the power of 3.

```
%Anonymous function to raise input to the power of 3
cubed = @(x) x^3;
```

Now, to use this anonymous function, we can simply pass an argument to it. Here is an example of how to call this anonymous function in a code or a command window:

```
%Call an anonymous function
%Outcome: 125
a=cubed(5);
disp(a)
```

Here is another example of an anonymous function. In this example, we define an anonymous function that gets x and y as its input arguments and returns a distance of a point with (x,y) coordinates from an origin (0,0). Remember that a distance of a point (x,y) from an origin (Euclidean norm) is calculated as $\sqrt{x^2 + y^2}$.

```
%Anonymous function to calculate distance of (x,y) from (0,0)
d = @(x,y) sqrt(x^2+y^2);
```

Here is an example of how to call this anonymous function in a code or a command window:

```
%Call an anonymous function
%Outcome: 5
a=d(3,4);
disp(a)
```

An anonymous function may be used inside another anonymous function. In other words, we can define an anonymous function that contains an anonymous function. By doing that, multiple anonymous functions can be defined. Here is an example of how to use an anonymous function inside another anonymous function. Assume we want to define an anonymous function that raises any number to a given power. Here is how to define this anonymous function. It gets a power value `n` as an input and returns an anonymous function that raises its input argument to the power of `n`.

```
%Anonymous function to raise input to the power of n
power_n = @(n) (@(x) x^n);
```

Now, assume we want a function to raise its input to the power of 3. Here is how to call this anonymous function to do that in a code or a command window. The `f` function raises its input to the power 3.

```
%Call an anonymous function
%Outcome: 1000
f=power_n(3); %Raise to the power 3
a=f(10);
disp(a)
```

As another example, assume we want a function to raise its input to the power of 8. Here is how to call this anonymous function to do that in a code or a command window. The `g` function raises its input to the power 8.

```
%Call an anonymous function
%Outcome: 256
g=power_n(8); %Raise to the power 8
a=g(2);
disp(a)
```

2.16 Name-Value Pair Arguments

In most MATLAB functions, we need to pass some input arguments to a function when we call that function. Besides regular input arguments, some of MATLAB functions also receive one or more optional comma-separated Name-Value pair arguments in a form of `'Name', Value`. In a Name-Value pair argument, the `'Name'` defines a name of the optional argument, while the `Value` contains values to be assigned to this optional argument. In general, we can use none, one, or as many Name-Value pair arguments as accepted by a function. These Name-Value pair arguments may be used in any order. Note that, the `'Name'` and `Value` always should be used as a pair. Here is a general syntax shows how to call a function with both regular arguments and Name-Value pair arguments:

Syntax

```
[out1, ...] = fun_name(arg1, ..., argN, 'Name1', Value1, ..., 'NameN', ValueN)
```

For example, MATLAB has the `plot` function that plots 2-d line. By default, the `plot` function draws a line using a color from a MATLAB default color order. Now, if we need to use a custom color to plot a line, we can use a Name-Value pair argument as `'Color',LineColor` to specify a line color.

Here is an example shows how to use a Name-Value pair argument in the `plot` function. Assume we have two arrays X and Y and we want to plot a line from these two arrays with a gray color. For this purpose, we use a Name-Value pair argument as `'Color',[0.5,0.5,0.5]` which `'Color'` defines a name of the optional argument and `[0.5,0.5,0.5]` contains RGB values for gray color.

```
%Plot line with gray color
X=[1,2,3,4,5]; %X data
Y=[1,2,3,4,5]; %Y data
plot(X,Y,'Color',[0.5,0.5,0.5])
```

2.17 Tilde (~)

In MATLAB, a tilde character, ~ , can be used for two applications. One application for a tilde is to use it as a `logical not`. For example, an expression `(~x)` returns `logical 1` (`true`) if `x` is `false`, otherwise, it returns `logical 0` (`false`).

Another application for a tilde is to use it in a code to ignore a variable or a value. To explain how it works, consider a function that calculates a surface area and volume of a sphere. This function is named `calc_sphere` and saved in a file `calc_sphere.m`. It gets a radius of a sphere as an input and returns a surface area and volume of that sphere. In this function, the first output is a surface area and the second output is a volume. Let's consider a case that we are only interested in a value of a volume which is the second value returned by this function. Now, since we do not need a value of a surface area, assume we prefer to ignore it. To ignore a value of a surface area which is the first value returned by this function, we can simply replace it with a tilde. Here is an example that shows how to use a tilde to ignore an output of a function:

```
%A function to calculate surface area and volume of a sphere
function [area,vol]=calc_sphere(radius)
area=4*pi*radius^2; %Surface area of a sphere
vol=4/3*pi*radius^3; %Volume of a sphere
end
```

Now, we use a tilde to ignore an output of a function:

```
%Ignore the first output of a function
%Output: b=523.5987
[~,b]=calc_sphere(5)
```

A tilde also may be used to ignore input arguments of a function as well. This application of a tilde is beyond a scope of this text.

2.18 Working with File and Directory

There are many instances that it is required to work with files and directories in a code. For that purpose, a path of a file or directory should be obtained or passed to MATLAB. However, the format of a file or directory path depends on an operating system that is on a computer. Windows uses a backslash, \, between folder names in a file or directory path. Mac and Linux use a forward-slash, /, between folder names in a file or directory path. Here are basic structures of paths in Windows, Mac and Linux systems:

Syntax

```
File path on Windows systems:
main_directory\1st_folder\2nd_folder\file_name
```

```
File path on Mac and Linux systems:
/main_directory/1st_folder/2nd_folder/file_name
```

In MATLAB, a file or directory path should always be defined by following an operating system convention. Using a wrong slash in a path to separates folder causes an error. Here are examples of how to use a file path in MATLAB:

```
%File path on Windows System, using a backslash
file_path='C:\test_folder'

%File path on Mac and Linux System, using a forward-slash
file_path='/home/test_folder'
```

In MATLAB, to get a current working directory, the `pwd` function can be used. Here is an example of how to get a current working directory:

```
%Return a current working directory
current_folder=pwd
```

To change a current working directory, the `cd` function can be used. Here is an example of how to change a current working directory:

```
%Change a current working directory
cd('C:\test_folder')
```

Also, the `path` function allows to view or change MATLAB search path.

Chapter 3
Introduction to MATLAB Array

In this chapter, MATLAB arrays and the basics of working with them are described. First, MATLAB arrays are described. Then, vector, matrix, and multi-dimensional arrays are explained. Next, data types and dimensions of a MATLAB array are described. Then, it is explained how to use indexes and slicing to access elements of an array. It follows by descriptions of indexing by an index array. Next, it is demonstrated how to work with logical indexing. Then, it is explained how to change the contents of array elements. At the end, cell and structure arrays are described.

3.1 MATLAB Arrays

Nearly in all programming developments, there is an essential need to store, retrieve, and work with a collection of data. For example, assume a programmer wants to develop a code for a school to analyze student progress. To do that, a programmer needs to import, store, and use students' names and their grades in the program. As another example, consider a scientist that wants to analyze collected data during research. To do that, those data should become accessible within a programming language first.

In MATLAB, arrays are used to store and work with a collection of data. In general, arrays behave as multi-dimensional containers which retain data. Some of the prominent arrays (data containers) in MATLAB are numeric, string, cell, structure, and table arrays. These arrays allow programmers to store, retrieve, and manipulate data. Here are general descriptions of these data containers:

- Array is a multi-dimensional data container.
- Array elements are ordered, which means that each element has a designated position (location) in an array.
- Each element in an array can be accessed by its position (index).
- Array is changeable, which means that an array may be changed after it is created.

Here are simple examples of these arrays. The first example is a numeric array that contains integers 1,2,3. The second one is a string array that contains strings 'four','five','six'. The third one is a cell array that contains seasons and an approximate number of days for these seasons. And, the fourth one is a structure array with seasons as its field names and an approximate number of days for these seasons as its field values.

```
%Numeric array
%Output: 1
N=[1,2,3];
disp(N(1)) %First element in an array

%String array
%Output: five
S=["four","five","six"];
disp(S(2)) %Second element in an array

%Cell array
%Output: 93
C={'spring',93;'summer',93;'fall',90;'winter',89};
disp(C{1,2}) %Content of a cell with indexes {1,2}
```

```
%Structure array
%Output: 93
Str.spring=93;
Str.summer=93;
Str.fall=90;
Str.winter=89;
disp(Str.spring) %Value of field name 'spring'
```

Among these arrays, numeric arrays have the most applications in data analysis. Because of that, the focus is on working with a numeric array in the rest of the chapter.

3.2 Vector, Matrix, and Array

In most programming languages, data can be stored in multi-dimensional data containers. These data containers may have one, two, or more dimensions. In a generic form, a data container that is made up of an ordered collection of elements with the same data type is called an array. In MATLAB, an array is the main data container to store and work with data.

Sometimes programmers tend to use a particular term for an array with a specific number of dimensions. A 1-dimensional array is commonly called a vector. A vector may be a horizontal array of one row or a vertical array of one column. Make sure this is not mistaken for a mathematical vector.

A 2-dimensional array is usually called a matrix. A matrix is like a table that is made up of a series of rows and columns. Make sure this is not mistaken for a mathematical matrix.

An Array with 3 or more dimensions is simply called an array. For example, a 3-dimensional array is made up of two or more 2-d arrays that are put together along the third dimension.

In this book, we do not use these specific names for different types of arrays. Instead, we always explicitly mention an array dimension. For example, instead of using the term "vector", we always use the term "1-d array". Similarly, instead of "matrix", we always use "2-d array".

3.3 Vector

As mentioned earlier, arrays are multi-dimensional data containers. The 1-dimensional and 2-dimensional arrays have specific names. In MATLAB, a 1-dimensional array is called vector and a 2-dimensional array is called matrix.

There are two types of vectors, a row vector and a column vector. A row vector is a 1-dimensional array with a single row that has a size of (`1xN`), where `N` is a number of elements in a vector. A column vector is a 1-dimensional array with a single column that has a size of (`Mx1`), where `M` is a number of elements in a vector.

A vector may be created using one of the following methods:

- To create a row vector, items are placed between two square brackets separated by a space or comma as `[ ... , ... , ... ]`
- To create a column vector, items are placed between two square brackets separated by a semicolon as `[ ... ; ... ; ... ]`
- Use a colon, `:` , to create a row vector.

Note that, a pair of square brackets without any item inside them as `[]` creates an empty vector.

Here are examples of how to create a vector. The first example is a row vector containing integers from 1 to 10. The second example is a column vector containing integers from 1 to 5. In the third example, a colon, `:` , is used to create a row vector containing integers from 1 to 10.

```
%Create a row vector
a=[1,2,3,4,5,6,7,8,9,10];

%Create a column vector
b=[1;2;3;4;5];

%Create a row vector using a colon
c=1:10;
```

To access (call) an element in a vector, we use an index of that element. Here are examples of how to access an element in a vector. In the first example, we call the second element in a row vector. In the second example, we call the third element in a column vector.

```
%Access an element in row vector
%Output: 20
```

```
V_row=[10,20,30,40,50];
d=V_row(2); %Or d=V_row(1,2);
disp(d)

%Access an element in column vector
%Output: 30
V_col=[10;20;30;40;50];
f=V_col(3); %Or f=V_col(3,1);
disp(f)
```

For further details on how to access elements in a vector, refer to indexing and slicing sections.

To change a value of an element in a vector, we assign a new value to that element using its index. Here is an example to show how to change a value of an element in a vector. In this example, we change a value of the first element from 5 to 10.

```
%Change a value of element in vector
%Output: 10    20    30    40    50
V=[5,20,30,40,50];
V(1)=10;
disp(V)
```

3.4 Matrix

As mentioned, a 2-dimensional array is called matrix. In other words, the matrix is a specific name that is used for a 2-dimensional array. A matrix with a size of (`MxN`) has `M` rows and `N` columns.

A matrix may be created using one of the following methods:

- Row vectors are placed between two square brackets separated by a semicolon as `[[ ... , ... , ... ]; [ ... , ... , ...]; ... ]`. In other words, a matrix can be created from semicolon-separated row vectors.
- Column vectors are placed between two square brackets separated by a space or comma as `[[ ... ; ... ; ... ], [ ... ; ... ; ...], ... ]`. In other words, a matrix can be created from space-separated or comma-separated column vectors.

Here is an example of a matrix with a size of `4x3`. This matrix contains 4 row vectors, which each of these vectors contains 3 elements.

```
%A numeric matrix with a size of 4x3
M=[[1,2,3];[4,5,6];[7,8,9];[10,11,12]];
```

This matrix also may be written in a simpler way as:

```
%A numeric matrix with a size of 4x3
M=[1 2 3; 4 5 6; 7 8 9; 10 11 12];
```

A matrix in this example can be illustrated as:

```
M = [[1 , 2 , 3 ];
     [4 , 5 , 6 ];
     [7 , 8 , 9 ];
     [10, 11, 12]];
```

To access (call) an element in a matrix, we use indexes of that element. Here are examples of how to access an element in a matrix. In this example, we call an element that is positioned in the third row and the second column of a matrix.

```
%Access an element in position (3,2)
%Output: 8
M=[[1,2,3];[4,5,6];[7,8,9];[10,11,12]];
a=M(3,2);
disp(a)
```

For further details on how to access elements in a matrix, refer to indexing and slicing sections.

To change a value of an element in a matrix, we assign a new value to that element using its indexes. Here is an example to show how to change a value of an element in a matrix. In this example, we change a value of the element that is positioned in the third row and the second column from 8 to 80.

```
%Change a value of element in in position (3,2)
%Output:
%          1     2     3
%          4     5     6
%          7    80     9
%         10    11    12
M=[[1,2,3];[4,5,6];[7,8,9];[10,11,12]];
M(3,2)=80;
disp(M)
```

3.5 Multi-Dimensional Array

As explained earlier, the main data container in MATLAB is a multi-dimensional array. An array is made up of ordered elements that is able to store data. Each element in an array has a designated position and can be accessed (called) by using its position (index). Also, these positions may be used to retrieve or change the content of array elements.

The simplest method to create a multi-dimensional array is to create 2-dimensional matrixes and then extend them to a multi-dimensional array. For example, a 3-dimensional array with a size of (`3x3x2`) consists of 2 2-dimensional matrixes each with a size of (`3x3`).

To access (call) an element in an array, we use indexes of that element. Similarly, to change a value of an element in an array, we assign a new value to that element using its indexes. There are further details on how to access elements in an array, change content of elements, add items to an array, or delete items from an array in following sections and chapters.

3.6 Array Data Type

Every time we create an array, that array gets a data type based on the data we used to create it. It means that, if we use numbers to create an array, it becomes a numeric array. Similarly, if we use a sequence of characters to create an array, it becomes a character array.

For example, if use [1,2,3] to create an array, its data type is set to a double. Similarly, if we use 'matlab' to create an array, its data type is set to char. Here is an example of creating a double array by using floating-point numbers.

```
%Create a double array
arr=[1.0,2.0,3.0];
```

Some of the common data types for arrays and functions to create them are:

Data Type / Function	Description
`double`	Double precision numerical array
`int8`	8-bit signed integer array
`char`	Character array
`string`	String array
`logical`	Logical 1 (true) and logical 0 (false) array
`table`	Table array

cell	Cell array
Struct	Structure array

One method to create an array with a specific data type is to use values with that specific type. Here is an example of how to create a string array by using string values:

```
%Create a string array
arr="matlab";
```

Another method to create an array with a specific data type is to use appropriate function to create an array with the desired data type. Here is an example of how to create a string array by using the string function:

```
%Create a string array
arr=string("matlab");
```

MATLAB provides a series of functions which are aimed to change a data type of an existing array. Therefore, if we need to change a data type of an array after it is created, we can use a function that is designated to convert an array to the desired type. Here are two common functions to convert a numerical array to a string array and vice versa:

Function	Description
str2num	Convert character or string array to numeric array
num2str	Convert numeric array to character array

Here is an example to show how to use the `str2num` function to change an array data type from string to numeric. In this example, first, we create a string array containing integers. Then, we change its type to double.

```
%Create a string array
%Output: 12345
arr=["12345"];
disp(arr)

%Change array type to double using str2num
%Output: 12345
arr=str2num(arr);
disp(arr)
```

3.7 Array Dimension

MATLAB arrays are multi-dimensional data containers that are made up of an ordered collection of elements. These arrays may have one, two, three, ..., or n dimensions. There are two parameters that describe the dimensional properties of an array: array size and array number of elements.

An array size shows array dimensions. In other words, an array size shows how many elements are in each dimension of an array. An array number of elements shows the total number of elements that an array has. For example, consider a 2-d array with m elements along its first dimension and n elements along its second dimension. This array has a size of (m,n) and the total number of elements of m*n.

In MATLAB arrays, each dimension is identified by one number. In an n-dimensional array, the n-th dimension is identified by number n. For example, in a 2-d array, the first dimension, which denotes rows, is identified by number 1, and the second dimension, which denotes columns, is identified by number 2. Similarly, in a 3-d array, the first dimension is identified by number 1, the second dimension by 2, and the third dimension by 3.

A 1-dimensional array is a single row or a single column of elements. A 1-d row array (row vector) has a size of (1,n) which means it has 1 element in its first dimension and n elements in its second dimension. The total number of elements in this 1-d array is equal to n. Similarly, a 1-d column array (column vector) has a size of (m,1) which means it has m elements in its first dimension and 1 element in its second dimension. The total number of elements in this 1-d array is equal to m.

Here is an illustration of a 1-dimensional row array with a size of (1,n). Numbers in this illustration show element numbers (indexes) in this 1-d array.

2nd dim

Elements:	1	2	3	...	n

Here is an illustration of a 1-dimensional column array with a size of (m,1). Similarly, numbers in this illustration show element numbers (indexes) in this 1-d array.

1st dim

1
2
3
...
m

A 2-dimensional array is like a table of data that each cell in a table is one element. A 2-d array (matrix) has a size of (m,n) which means it has m elements (rows) along its first dimension, and n elements (columns) along its second dimension. The total number of elements in a 2-d array is equal to m*n.

Here is an illustration of a 2-dimensional array. Vertical numbers indicate row numbers (indexes) along the first dimension, and horizontal numbers indicate column numbers (indexes) along the second dimension of this 2-d array.

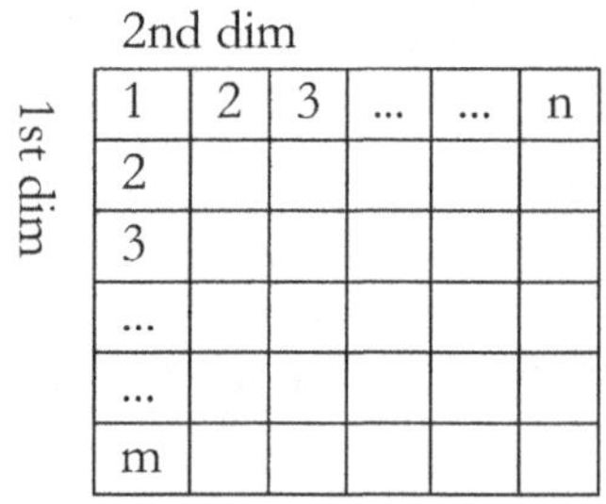

A 3-dimensional array is similar to a cuboid that is made up of elements. One way to visualize a 3-d array is to consider it as an extension of a 2-d array into the third dimension. For that purpose, consider a 2-d array as a sheet. Now, if we place two or more of these sheets together along the third dimension, we have a 3-d array.

A 3-d array has a size of (m,n,p) which means it has m elements (rows) along its first dimension, n elements (columns) along its second dimension, and p elements (sheets) along its third dimension. The total number of elements in a 3-d array is equal to m*n*p.

Here is an illustration of a 3-dimensional array with a size of (3,4,2) and the total number of elements equal to 3*4*2. It has 3 elements (rows) along its first dimension, 4 elements (columns) along its second dimension, and 2 elements (sheets) along its third dimension. Vertical numbers indicate element numbers (rows) along the first dimension and horizontal numbers indicate element numbers (columns) along the second dimension in each sheet. Note that these numbers are the same as element indexes in each dimension.

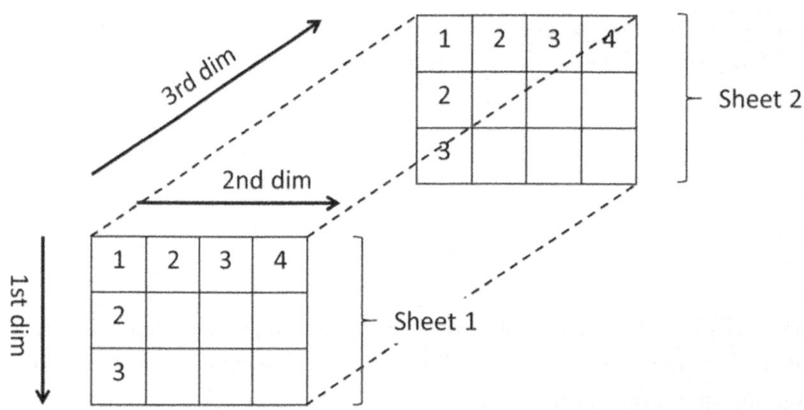

At first, it might seem difficult to visualize an array with more than 3 dimensions. However, after we become comfortable with 2-d arrays, we will find out that working with higher dimensional arrays is not much different from working with 2-d arrays.

3.8 Array Indexing

An index refers to a position (location) of an item in a data container that holds ordered data. Because indexes point to positions of items in a data container, indexes are widely used to access items stored in a data container. These indexes help to retrieve, use, and manipulate data stored in data containers.

A MATLAB array is an ordered data container and its elements can be accessed by using their indexes. MATLAB arrays follow one-based indexing. It means that, in a MATLAB array, the first element in each dimension of an array has a position 1 or an index 1, the second element in that dimension has a position 2 or an index 2, and so on. One helpful index is `end` as it indicates the last position (index) in a corresponding dimension.

To access an element in arrays, an element is called by using an array name followed by an index of that element inside parentheses, `(...)`. For example, consider a 1-d array `A` (vector `A`). Then, the first element in `A` is obtained by `A(1)`, the second element is obtained by `A(2)`, the third element is obtained by `A(3)`, and so on.

Note that, all indexes should be positive integers. If we have a value that is not a positive integer, we cannot use it as an index unless we change its data type to an integer. For example, assume we want to use values in one array as indexes for another array. To use the values of the first array as indexes, either the values in this array should be positive integers or we have to change them to positive integers before using them as indexes. Although MATLAB allows us to use floating-point numbers such as `(1.0)` as an index, it is recommended to use equivalent integer `(1)` instead.

Indexes in a 1-dimensional array (vector) have a form of `( i )`, which `i` refers to an index (position) of an element. Note that, we can also use an indexing format for a 2-d array in a 1-d array indexing by using index 1 for a dimension that has 1 element.

Here is an illustration of indexes for a 1-d row array (row vector) with n elements. Numbers in this illustration show element indexes of this 1-d array.

	2nd dim				
Indexes:	(1)	(2)	(3)	...	(n)

Here is an illustration of indexes for a 1-d column array (column vector) with `m` elements. Numbers in this illustration show element indexes of this 1-d array.

1st dim

(1)
(2)
(3)
...
(m)

Indexes in a 2-dimensional array (matrix) have a form of `( i , j )`, which `i` shows a position of an element along its first dimension, and `j` shows a position of an element along its second dimension. Here is an illustration of indexes for a 2-d array. This 2-d array has a size of (m,n) which means it has `m` elements (rows) along its first dimension, and `n` elements (columns) along its second dimension.

2nd dim

1st dim

(1,1)	(1,2)	(1,3)	...	...	(1,n)
(2,1)	(2,2)	(2,3)	...	...	(2,n)
(3,1)	(3,2)	(3,3)	...	...	(3,n)
...	...	...	...	...	...
...	...	...	...	...	...
(m,1)	(m,2)	(m,3)	...	...	(m,n)

Indexes in a 3-dimensional array have a form of `( i , j , k )`, which `i` shows a position of an element along its first dimension, `j` shows a position of an element along its second dimension, and `k` shows a position of an element along its third dimension. Here is an illustration of indexes for a 3-d array. This 3-d array has a size of (3,4,2) which means it has 3 elements (rows) along its first dimension, 4 elements (columns) along its second dimension, and 2 elements (sheets) along its third dimension.

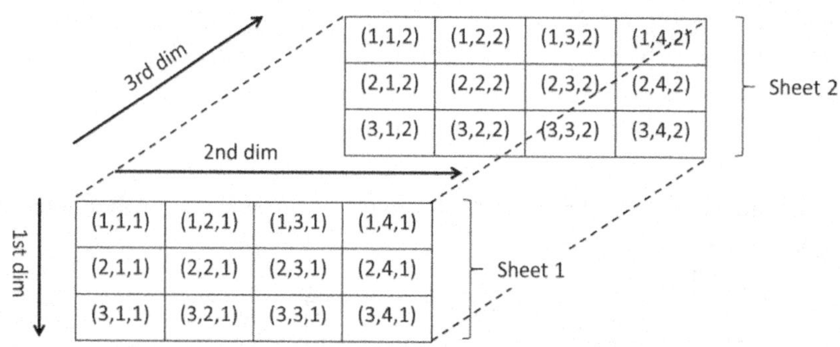

Now, we show how to work with array indexes. Here is an example of calling elements in a 1-d row array [1,2,3,4,5]. In this example, a value in the first element is 1, in the second element is 2, in the third element is 3, and so on.

```
%Create a 1-d row array (row vector) with 5 elements
x=[1,2,3,4,5];

%Use indexes to call elements in a 1-d row array
fisrt_element=x(1);
second_element=x(2);
last_element=x(end); %Equal to x(5)
```

Here is another example of calling elements. This time, we call elements in a 2-d array with a size of (4,3) containing integers from 1 to 12. In this example, the first row is [1,2,3], the second row is [4,5,6], the third row is [7,8,9], and the fourth row is [10,11,12].

```
%Create a 2-d array with a size of (4,3)
%Output:
%        1     2     3
%        4     5     6
%        7     8     9
%       10    11    12
arr=[[1,2,3];[4,5,6];[7,8,9];[10,11,12]];
disp(arr)

%Use indexes to call elements in a 2-d array
element_1_1=arr(1,1);
element_2_2=arr(2,2);
element_4_3=arr(end,end); %Equal to arr(4,3)
```

3.9 Array Slicing

It is explained that an index can be used to access an element in an array. However, using a single index is helpful to access one element at a time and may not be used if we need to call multiple elements at once. There is another method to access elements in an array called slicing. Unlike simple indexing which calls an individual element each time, slicing calls a subset of an array. In other words, slicing is used to call multiple elements in an array at once.

A colon, : , is used to obtain a slice of elements in a MATLAB array. By using a colon, a sequence of indexes can be generated between a start number and a stop number with an interval of a given step. Here is a general syntax of how to define a slice of indexes using a colon in a 1-dimensional array:

Syntax

```
( start : step : stop )
```

The `start` defines a starting index in an index sequence. The `stop` defines the last index in an index sequence. Note that, depending on a `step` value, the `stop` itself may or may not be included in an index sequence. The `step` defines an interval between every two consecutive indexes in an index sequence. The `step` value is optional and by default is step=1. Therefore, if only `start` and `stop` values are defined, then the `step` is considered as step=1.

Here is an illustration of a slice `( i : j )` in a 1-dimensional row array (row vector). Slice indexes are shown in a gray shade. Numbers show element indexes in this 1-d array.

	2nd dim								
Indexes:	(1)	(2)	(3)	...	(i)	...	(j)	(j+1)	...

Here is an illustration of a slice `( i : j )` in a 1-dimensional column array (column vector). Slice indexes are shown in a gray shade. Numbers show element indexes in this 1-d array.

1st dim
(1)
(2)
(3)
...
(i)
...
(j)
(j+1)
...

Here are several formats that a colon can be used to create a slice in a 1-d array:

1-d array slicing with a colon

Syntax	Description
`(i:k:j)`	Elements from i to j with an interval of k
`(i:j)`	Elements from i to j (step=1)
`(i:end)`	Elements from i to the end of an array (step=1)
`(1:j)`	Elements from the beginning of an array to j (step=1)

`(1:k:end)`	Elements from beginning to end with an interval of k
`(end:-1:1)`	All elements from end to beginning (in a reverse order)
`(end:-k:1)`	Elements from end to beginning with an interval of k
`(:)`	All elements in an array (as a single column vector)
`(end)`	The last element
`(end-1:end)`	The last two elements
`(end-(i-1):end)`	The last i elements
`(1:end-1)`	All elements in an array except the last element
`(1:end-2)`	All elements in an array except the last two elements
`(1:end-j)`	All elements in an array except the last j elements

Here are some notes to consider when using a colon for slicing:

- All `start`, `stop`, and `step` values should be an integer.
- A value for `start` should be positive. Values for `stop` and `step` should be chosen in a way that an index sequence only contains positive integers. A value for `step` can be zero. However, if step=0, then an empty row vector is returned.
- Depending on a value of the `step`, a `stop` value may or may not be included in an index sequence created by a colon.
- The `step` is optional and its default value is step=1.

Here are examples of how to use slicing in a 1-d array. In these examples, we show how to use different slicing on a 1-d row array [10,20,30,40,50,60,70,80,90,100].

```
%Create a 1-d row array (row vector) with 10 elements
x=[10,20,30,40,50,60,70,80,90,100];

%Use slicing to assign elements x(3) to x(8) to a
%Output: 30    40    50    60    70    80
a=x(3:8);
disp(a)

%Assign elements x(8) to end of array x to b
%Output: 80    90   100
b=x(8:end);
disp(b)

%Assign elements x(1) to x(4) to c
%Output: 10    20    30    40
c=x(1:4);
```

```
disp(c)

%Assign last 5 elements of array x to d
%Output: 60    70    80    90   100
d=x(end-(5-1):end);
disp(d)

%Assign all elements of array x except last 3 to f
%Output: 10    20    30    40    50    60    70
f=x(1:end-3);
disp(f)
```

Slicing in a 2-d array is similar to a 1-d array. We may use a slice of indexes in one dimension or in both dimensions of a 2-d array. Here is a general syntax of how to define a slice of indexes using a colon in a 2-dimensional array:

Syntax

```
( start1 : step1 : stop1 , start2 : step2 : stop2 )
```

The `start1` defines a starting index in the first dimension and `start2` defines a starting index in the second dimension. The `stop1` defines the last index in the first dimension and the `stop2` defines the last index in the second dimension. Note that, depending on `step1` and `step2` values, the `stop1` and `step2` may or may not be included in index sequences. The `step1` and `step2` define intervals between every two consecutive indexes in the first and second dimensions, respectively. The `step1` and `step2` values are optional. Therefore, if `step1` or `step2` is not given, then by default, the missing `step1` or `step2` is considered to be 1.

Here is an illustration of a slice `( i : j , m : n )` in a 2-dimensional array (matrix). Slice indexes are shown in a gray shade. Numbers show element indexes in this 2-d array.

2nd dim

1st dim

(1,1)	(1,2)	...	(1,m)	...	(1,n)	(1,n+1)	...
(2,1)	...	...	...	...	...	...	...
...	...	...	...	...	...	...	...
(i,1)	...	...	...	...	...	...	...
...	...	...	...	...	...	...	...
(j,1)	...	...	...	...	...	...	...
(j+1,1)	...	...	...	...	...	...	...
...	...	...	...	...	...	...	...

We may use any of the slice formats from a 1-d array and extend it to a 2-d array. Here are some of the practical slice formats that can be used to create a slice in a 2-d array:

2-d array slicing with a colon

Syntax	Description
`(i:j,m:n)`	Elements from i to j in 1st dim and m to n in 2nd dim (step=1)
`(i,:)`	Row i
`(i:j,:)`	Rows i to j
`(i:k:j,:)`	Every k rows from i to j
`(:,m)`	Column m
`(:,m:n)`	Columns m to n
`(:,m:p:n)`	Every p columns from m to n
`(:,:)`	All rows and columns in an array
`(:)`	All elements in an array (as a single column vector)
`(end:-1:1,:)`	All rows and columns with reversed rows
`(:,end:-1:1)`	All rows and columns with reversed columns

Here are examples of how to use slicing in a 2-d array. In these examples, we show how to use different slicing on a 2-d array [[10,20,30];[40,50,60];[70,80,90];[100,110,120]]. This 2-d array has a size of (4,3) and the total elements of 12. In this example, the first row is [10,20,30], the second row is [40,50,60], the third row is [70,80,90], and the fourth row is [100,110,120].

```
%Create a 2-d array with a size of (4,3)
%Output:
%        10    20    30
%        40    50    60
%        70    80    90
%       100   110   120
arr=[[10,20,30];[40,50,60];[70,80,90];[100,110,120]];
disp(arr)

%Use slicing to assign arr(3:4,2:3) to a
%Output:
%        80    90
%       110   120
a=arr(3:4,2:3);
disp(a)

%Assign the first row of array arr to b
%Output: 10    20    30
```

```
b=arr(1,:);
disp(b)

%Assign the first column of array arr to c
%Output:
%        10
%        40
%        70
%       100
c=arr(:,1);
disp(c)
```

Slicing in an n-dimensional array is similar to a 2-d array. We may use a slice of indexes in any dimension of an n-dimensional array.

In array indexing, if given indexes are fewer than available dimensions, then missing indexes are replaced by 1 from the last dimension toward the first dimension. For example, consider `arr` as a 3-d array. Now, `arr(m)` is equivalent to `arr(m,1,1)`. Similarly, `arr(m,n)` is equivalent to `arr(m,n,1)`.

3.10 Indexing by Index Array

Slicing is a powerful method to call multiple elements when their indexes follow a pattern. However, sometimes we may need to call multiple elements that their indexes do not have any pattern. In such cases, we can use an array of indexes to call these elements. This index array contains all indexes for elements we want to call. An index array should only contain positive integers, otherwise it causes an error. Here is a general syntax of how to use this advanced indexing to call multiple elements in an array:

Syntax

```
array([indx1_1, ..., indx1_m], [indx2_1, ..., indx2_n], ...)
```

In this syntax, `[indx1_1, ..., indx1_m]` represent element indexes along the first dimension, `[indx2_1, ..., indx2_n]` represents element indexes along the second dimension, and so on. It means that, it returns all elements that their indexes along the first dimension are `[indx1_1, ..., indx1_m]`, and their indexes along the second dimension are `[indx2_1, ..., indx2_n]`, and so on.

Here are examples of how to use an index array to call multiple elements from a 1-d array. In these examples, we use an index array to call elements from a 1-d row array [10,20,30,40,50,60,70,80,90,100].

```
%Create a 1-d row array (row vector) with 10 elements
x=[10,20,30,40,50,60,70,80,90,100];

%Assign elements x(2), x(4), x(8) to a
%Output: 20    40    80
a=x([2,4,8]);
disp(a)

%Assign elements x(3), x(5), x(8) to b
%Output: 30    50    80
indx=[3,5,8];
b=x(indx);
disp(b)
```

Here are examples of how to use an index array to call multiple elements from a 2-d array. In these examples, we use an index array to call elements from a 2-d array [[10,20,30];[40,50,60];[70,80,90];[100,110,120]].

```
%Create a 2-d array with a size of (4,3)
%Output:
%         10    20    30
%         40    50    60
%         70    80    90
%        100   110   120
arr=[[10,20,30];[40,50,60];[70,80,90];[100,110,120]];
disp(arr)

%Assign elements with row indexes 3,4 and column indexes 1,2 to c
%Output:
%         70    80
%        100   110
c=arr([3,4],[1,2]);
disp(c)

%Assign elements with row indexes 1,3,4 and column indexes 1,2 to d
%Output:
%         10    20
%         70    80
```

```
%        100    110
indx_dim1=[1,3,4];
indx_dim2=[1,2];
d=arr(indx_dim1,indx_dim2);
disp(d)
```

3.11 Logical Indexing

The logical indexing is an advanced indexing method that allows us to select multiple elements that all satisfy a specific condition. For example, assume we have an array that contains students' grades which are between 0 and 100. Now, if we want to find out all elements that have a grade smaller than 60, we can use logical indexing to filter out those elements. Here is a general syntax of how to use logical indexing to call multiple elements in an array:

Syntax

```
array(conditional expression)
```

Here is an example of how to use logical indexing to call multiple elements from a 1-d array. In this example, we use logical indexing to select all elements that are less than 60 in a 1-d row array [10,20,30,40,50,60,70,80,90,100].

```
%Create a 1-d row array (row vector) with 10 elements
x=[10,20,30,40,50,60,70,80,90,100];

%Assign elements less than 60 to a
%Output: 10    20    30    40    50
a=x(x<60);
disp(a)
```

Probably, the most helpful application for logical indexing is to use it to perform the same operation on all elements of an array that satisfy a specific condition. Consider a previous example again. This time, assume we want to add 5 to all elements that their values are less than 60. We can use logical indexing for this purpose.

```
%Add 5 to all elements less than 60
%Output: 15    25    35    45    55    60    70    80    90    100
x=[10,20,30,40,50,60,70,80,90,100];
x(x<60)=x(x<60)+5;
```

```
disp(x)
```

We can use a compound conditional expression in logical indexing as well. Consider a previous example again. This time, we use a compound conditional expression in logical indexing to select all elements that are larger than 30 and less than 60.

```
%Assign elements larger than 30 and less than 60 to b
%Output: 40    50
x=[10,20,30,40,50,60,70,80,90,100];
b=x((x>30) & (x<60));
disp(b)
```

Sometimes we need to select elements in one array based on a condition in another array. For example, assume we have two arrays that one contains students' exam grades and another contains students' homework grades. Grades in both arrays are between 0 and 100. Now, if we want to find out exam grades for students that their homework grades are smaller than 60, we use logical indexing to filter out exam grades based on homework grades.

Here is an example that shows how to select elements in one array based on a condition in another array. Consider an array x as [10,20,30,40,50,60,70,80,90,100] and an array L with the same size as an array x as [0,1,1,0,1,1,0,0,1,0]. Now, assume we need to select elements in x where their corresponding elements in L are equal to 1. We use logical indexing to select all these elements. Note that, both arrays should have the same size, otherwise it causes an error.

```
%Assign elements of x to c where L==1
%Output: 20    30    50    60    90
x=[10,20,30,40,50,60,70,80,90,100];
L=[0,1,1,0,1,1,0,0,1,0];
c=x(L==1);
disp(c)
```

Using logical indexing in a 2-d array is similar to a 1-d array. Here is an example of how to use logical indexing to call multiple elements from a 2-d array. Consider a 2-d array arr as [[10,20,30];[40,50,60];[70,80,90];[100,110,120]]. In this example, we use logical indexing to add 5 to all elements that their values are less than 60.

```
%Create a 2-d array with a size of (4,3)
%Output:
%           10    20    30
%           40    50    60
%           70    80    90
```

```
%        100    110    120
arr=[[10,20,30];[40,50,60];[70,80,90];[100,110,120]];
disp(arr)

%Add 5 to all elements less than 60
%Output:
%          15     25     35
%          45     55     60
%          70     80     90
%        100    110    120
arr(arr<60)=arr(arr<60)+5;
disp(arr)
```

Here is an example that shows how to select elements in a 2-d array based on a condition in another 2-d array. Consider a previous 2-d array arr along with an array M as [[1,0,1];[1,1,0];[0,0,1];[1,1,1]] which has the same size as an array arr. Now, we select all elements in arr where their corresponding elements in M are equal to 0. Note that, both arrays should have the same size, otherwise it causes an error.

```
%Assign elements of arr to d where M==0
%Output:
%         70
%         20
%         80
%         60
arr=[[10,20,30];[40,50,60];[70,80,90];[100,110,120]];
M=[[1,0,1];[1,1,0];[0,0,1];[1,1,1]];
d=arr(M==0);
disp(d)
```

Here is another example to show how to use logical indexing in a 2-d array. Consider a previous 2-d array arr again. Assume we have an array S which contains a sum of each row in an array arr as [60;150;240;330]. Now, we want to select all rows in arr that its sum is larger than 200. We can select those rows by using logical indexing.

```
%Assign rows in arr with sum larger than 200 to f
%Output:
%          70     80     90
%         100    110    120
arr=[[10,20,30];[40,50,60];[70,80,90];[100,110,120]];
S=[60;150;240;330]; %Sum of each row in arr
```

```
f=arr(S>200,:);
disp(f)
```

3.12 Change Element Contents in Array

After a MATLAB array is created, it is very probable that we may need to make some changes in array elements while we are working with it. For this purpose, array elements are accessed by their indexes, and if required, their values can be changed or updated. Here are examples of how to change the values of array elements.

```
%Use an index to change an element value in an array
%Output: 10    20    30    40    50
a=[10,20,30,70,50];
a(4)=40;
disp(a)

%Use an index to change an element value in a string array
%Output: "one"    "two"    "three"    "four"    "five"
b=["one","nine","three","four","five"];
b(2)='two';
disp(b)

%Use slicing to change values of multiple elements in an array
%Output: 1    1    1    2    2    2    3    3    3
c=[1,1,1,5,5,5,3,3,3];
c(4:6)=[2,2,2];
disp(c)

%Use logical indexing to change values of multiple elements in an array
%Output: 1    2    3    4    0    0    0    8    9
d=[1,2,3,4,50,60,70,8,9];
d(d>10)=0;
disp(d)
```

Note that, if we assign data to an array index that is outside the current dimensions of that array, MATLAB automatically expands that array to accommodate data to an index we use. For example, assume we have 2-d array with a size of (2,2). Now, if we assign a value to an element with indexes (4,3), MATLAB automatically grows this array to a new size of (4,3).

3.13 Cell Array

It is very common that we may need to store data with different data types and sizes (heterogeneous data). MATLAB provides three main containers for this purpose, cell array, structure array, and table array. In this section, we explain how to create and work with cell arrays. A cell array is an array that contains data in cells. A distinctive property of these arrays is that they may contain data with different data types and sizes.

A cell array may be created using one of the following methods:

- To create a row cell array, items are placed between two curly brackets separated by a space or comma as `{ [ ... ] , [ ... ] , [ ... ] }`
- To create a column cell array, items are placed between two curly brackets separated by a semicolon as `{ [ ... ] ; [ ... ] ; [ ... ] }`
- To create a 2-d cell array, comma-separated items are placed between two curly brackets separated by a semicolon as `{[ ... ] , [ ... ] , [ ... ] ; [ ... ] , [ ... ] , [ ... ] ; ... }`

Note that, a pair of curly brackets without any item inside them as `{}` creates an empty cell array. Also, we can use the cell function to create an empty cell array.

The items that we use to create a cell array can have different data types and sizes and does not need to be similar to each other.

To explain how to work with a cell array, let's consider an example. In this example, we assume we have a table that contains approximated nutrition facts for milk products from a hypothetical milk producer. In this table, we have four types of milk as whole (3.25%) milk, reduced fat (2%) milk, low fat (1%) milk, and fat free (nonfat) milk. For each of these products, we have amounts of total fat and cholesterol per 100 grams as well as their product ID. Total fat and cholesterol values are in grams. Note that, these numbers are for hypothetical products and do not reflect any real values.

```
Type           Total Fat     Cholesterol     Product ID

whole          3.3           0.010           1
reduced fat    2.0           0.008           2
low fat        1.0           0.005           3
fat free       0.1           0.002           4
```

Now, we show how to create a cell array that contains these data. In this example, we create a cell array with a size of (4,2). The cells {1,1}, {2,1}, {3,1}, and {4,1} contain types of milk as 'whole', 'reduced_fat', 'low_fat', and 'fat_free'. The cells {1,2}, {2,2}, {3,2}, and {4,2} contain data of 'Total Fat', 'Cholesterol', and 'Product ID' for each type of milk. Here, first we define content of each cell and then we create a cell array by using two curly brackets.

```
%Define cells
cell_1_1='whole';
cell_1_2=[3.3, 0.010, 1];
cell_2_1='reduced_fat';
cell_2_2=[2.0, 0.008, 2];
cell_3_1='low_fat';
cell_3_2=[1.0, 0.005, 3];
cell_4_1='fat_free';
cell_4_2=[0.1, 0.002, 4];

%Create cell array
%Output:
%       {'whole'      }    {1×3 double}
%       {'reduced_fat'}    {1×3 double}
%       {'low_fat'    }    {1×3 double}
%       {'fat_free'   }    {1×3 double}
cell_array = {cell_1_1, cell_1_2; cell_2_1, cell_2_2;
              cell_3_1, cell_3_2; cell_4_1, cell_4_2};
disp(cell_array)
```

To access a cell in a cell array, we use indexes of that cell inside two parentheses as `(i, j, ...)`. To access contents of a cell, we use indexes of that cell inside two curly brackets as `{i, j, ...}`. Also, we can access specific elements inside a cell by using indexes as `{i, j, ...}(m, n, ...)`, where `{i, j, ...}` defines cell indexes and `(m, n, ...)` defines indexes of elements inside that cell. Here are examples show how to access data in a cell array.

```
%Access a cell with indexes (1,2)
%Output: [1×3 double]
a=cell_array(1,2);
disp(a)

%Access contents of a cell with indexes {1,2}
%Output: 3.3000    0.0100    1.0000
b=cell_array{1,2};
disp(b)
```

```
%Access an element (1,3) in a cell with indexes {1,2}
%Output: 1
c=cell_array{1,2}(1,3);
disp(c)
```

Similarly, new data can be assigned to a cell in a cell array. Here are examples show how to assign data to a cell array. Note that, here, to preserve the original array, we create a copy of the original array and make changes on that copy. However, all these changes can be made on the original array as well.

```
%Change a cell with indexes (4,2) to {[0, 0, 0]}
%Output:
%        {'whole'      }    {1×3 double}
%        {'reduced_fat'}    {1×3 double}
%        {'low_fat'    }    {1×3 double}
%        {'fat_free'   }    {1×3 double}
d=cell_array;
d(4,2)={[0, 0, 0]};
disp(d)

%Change contents of a cell with indexes {4,2} to 10
%Output: 0     0     0
f=cell_array;
f{4,2}=[0, 0, 0];
disp(f{4,2})

%Change an element (1,3) in a cell with indexes {4,2} to 10
%Output: 0.1000    0.0020   10.0000
g=cell_array;
g{4,2}(1,3)=10;
disp(g{4,2})
```

3.14 Structure Array

MATLAB supports a type of an array called structure array. A structure array is an array that contains data in fields. Similar to cell arrays, these arrays also may contain data with different data types and sizes.

A simple method to create a structure array is to use a dot, `.` , to assign values to a field name of a structure array. In this method, an array name is followed by a dot followed by a field name. Here is a general syntax shows how to create a structure array with a dot:

Syntax

```
structure_array.field_1 = value_1
...
structure_array.field_n = value_n
```

The `field_1`, ..., `field_n` define field names of a structure array. Note that, a field name is a character or string that should begin with a letter. A field name can contain letters, digits, and underscores without any space. The `value_1`, ..., `value_n` define field values for `field_1`, ..., `field_n`, respectively. The `value_1`, ..., `value_n` can have different data types and sizes and does not need to be similar to each other.

Another method to create a structure array is to use the struct function. Here is a MATLAB function to create a structure array:

Function	Description
`struct`	Create structure array

Here is a general syntax shows how to create a structure array using the struct function:

Syntax

```
structure_array = struct('field_1', value_1, ..., 'field_n', value_n)
```

Similarly, the `'field_1'`, ..., `'field_n'` define field names of a structure array, and the `value_1`, ..., `value_n` define field values for `'field_1'`, ..., `'field_n'`, respectively

Here is an example explains how to work with a structure array. Consider a previous table that contains approximated nutrition facts for milk products from a hypothetical milk producer again. In this table, we have four types of milk as whole (3.25%) milk, reduced fat (2%) milk, low fat (1%) milk, and fat free (nonfat) milk. For each of these products, we have amounts of total fat and cholesterol per 100 grams as well as their product ID. Total fat and cholesterol values are in grams. Note that, these numbers are for hypothetical products and do not reflect any real values.

```
Type            Total Fat     Cholesterol     Product ID

whole           3.3           0.010           1
reduced fat     2.0           0.008           2
low fat         1.0           0.005           3
fat free        0.1           0.002           4
```

Now, we show how to create a structure array that contains these data. To do that, we use a dot to define field names for a structure array called milk. The field names in this example define types of milk as whole, reduced_fat, low_fat, and fat_free. We assign field values to each of these field names. Each field value contains data of 'Total Fat', 'Cholesterol', and 'Product ID' for each type of milk.

```
%Create structure array
%Output:
%              whole: [3.3000 0.0100 1]
%        reduced_fat: [2 0.0080 2]
%            low_fat: [1 0.0050 3]
%           fat_free: [0.1000 0.0020 4]
milk.whole=[3.3, 0.010, 1];
milk.reduced_fat=[2.0, 0.008, 2];
milk.low_fat=[1.0, 0.005, 3];
milk.fat_free=[0.1, 0.002, 4];
disp(milk)
```

As mentioned earlier, we can also create a structure array by using the struct function. Consider a previous example again. This time we use the struct function to create a structure array. To do that, first, we define field names. The field names define types of milk as 'whole', 'reduced_fat', 'low_fat', and 'fat_free'. Then, we define values for each of these field names. Each field value contains data of 'Total Fat', 'Cholesterol', and 'Product ID' for each type of milk. Finally, we use these field names and field values to create a structure array by using the struct function.

```
%Define field names
field1='whole';
field2='reduced_fat';
field3='low_fat';
field4='fat_free';

%Define field values
value1=[3.3, 0.010, 1];
value2=[2.0, 0.008, 2];
```

```
value3=[1.0, 0.005, 3];
value4=[0.1, 0.002, 4];

%Create structure array
%Output:
%             whole: [3.3000 0.0100 1]
%       reduced_fat: [2 0.0080 2]
%           low_fat: [1 0.0050 3]
%          fat_free: [0.1000 0.0020 4]
milk = struct(field1, value1, field2, value2, ...
    field3, value3, field4, value4);
disp(milk)
```

To access data in a structure array, we can use a dot and simple indexing. To obtain values for a given field name, we use an array name followed by a dot followed by a field name. To obtain a specific item from field values, we can use its index. Here are examples show how to access data in a structure array.

```
%Access values of a field name 'whole'
%Output: 3.3000    0.0100    1.0000
a=milk.whole;
disp(a)

%Access the 2nd value in a field name 'whole'
%Output: 0.0100
b=milk.whole(2);
disp(b)
```

Similarly, new data can be assigned to a field name in a structure array. Here are examples show how to assign data to a structure array. Note that, here, to preserve the original array, we create a copy of the original array and make changes on that copy. However, all these changes can be made on the original array as well.

```
%Change values of field name 'fat_free' to [0, 0, 0]
%Output:
%             whole: [3.3000 0.0100 1]
%       reduced_fat: [2 0.0080 2]
%           low_fat: [1 0.0050 3]
%          fat_free: [0 0 0]
c=milk;
c.fat_free=[0, 0, 0];
```

```
disp(c)

%Change the third value of field name 'whole' to 10
%Output:
%              whole: [3.3000 0.0100 10]
%        reduced_fat: [2 0.0080 2]
%            low_fat: [1 0.0050 3]
%           fat_free: [0.1000 0.0020 4]
d=milk;
d.whole(3)=10;
disp(d)
```

Chapter 4
Working with MATLAB Array

In this chapter, it is described how to manipulate and work with MATLAB arrays. First, it is described how to copy an array. After that, methods to append, insert, and delete array elements are presented. Next, it is described how to obtain a shape and size of an array. Then, it is explained how to reshape and flip an array. It follows by descriptions of how to concatenate arrays. Next, array initialization and element-wise operation are explained. Then, it is shown how to find indexes of elements that follow a specific condition. After that, `NaN` and `Inf` values are explained. At the end, it is described how to generate a sequence of numbers.

4.1 Copy Array

It is very probable that we need to make a copy of an array in a program. To create a copy of an array, we simply assign that array to a new array. For example, by using `new_array=existing_array` , we copy `existing_array` to `new_array`. In such cases, a new array is independent of an existing array. It means that, if we make any changes in one of these arrays, the changes do not reflect in the other array. A copied array has the same shape and size as an original array. Here is a general syntax shows how to copy an existing array to another array:

Syntax

```
copied_array = existing_array
```

Note that, a single equal sign `=` is used for an assignment while two equal signs `==` are used for comparison.

Here is an example of copying an array. Consider an array `x` as [1,2,3,4,5]. In this example, array a is a copy of the array x.

```
%Create an array with 5 elements
x=[1,2,3,4,5];

%Copy an array
a=x;
```

4.2 Append, Insert, and Delete Array Elements

After an array is created, we may need to make some changes in an array while working with it. We may append (add), insert, or delete array elements after an array is created.

It is very likely that we may need to add an item to an existing array when we are working with arrays. In MATLAB, arrays grow (expand) automatically. It means that, if we assign data to an element index that does not exist, an array grows automatically to allocate data to that index. For example, consider an array `x` with 5 elements as [10,20,30,40,50]. Now, if we want to add an element with a value 60 at the end of this array, we can use x(6)=60 to assign a number 60 to the sixth element of x. Since x(6) is not already existed, MATLAB grows the array to accommodate the 6th element.

Similarly, to add new values at the end of an array, we can simply assign those values to proper indexes. By doing that, given values are added to an array at those indexes.

Here are examples of adding elements to the end of an array.

```
%Add one element to the end of an array
%Output: 10    20    30    40    50    60
d=[10,20,30,40,50];
d(end+1)=60;
disp(d)

%Add two elements to the end of an array
%Output: 10    20    30    40    50    60    70
f=[10,20,30,40,50];
f(end+1:end+2)=[60,70];
disp(f)

%Add one element to the end of an array
%Output: "one"    "two"    "three"    "four"    "five"    "six"
s=["one","two","three","four","five"];
s(end+1)=["six"];
disp(s)
```

Although MATLAB grows (expands) arrays automatically, an incremental array growth can become relatively slow if it is repeated many times. If we know the final size of an array, it is usually faster to initialize a full array first, and then replace the values of an array with desired values. If we do not know the final size of an array, we can speed up a process by reducing the number of times that we grow an array by appending more items at once.

Note that, a common method to add an array to another array is to use the `cat` function. For more details on adding an array to another array, refer to a concatenate arrays section.

To insert new values into an existing 1-d row array, we can use a comma. Here is a general syntax shows how to insert values into a 1-d row array at a given index:

Syntax

```
new_array = [row_arr(1:indx-1), [val1, val2, ...], row_arr(indx:end)]
```

The `row_arr` defines a 1-d row array (row vector) that new values are inserted into that. The `indx` defines an index to insert values in that position. The `val1`, `val2`, ... define values to be inserted into an array.

Similarly, to insert new values into an existing 1-d column array, we can use a semicolon. Here is a general syntax shows how to insert values into a 1-d column array at a given index:

Syntax

```
new_array = [col_arr(1:indx-1,1); [val1; val2; ...]; col_arr(indx:end,1)]
```

The `col_arr` defines a 1-d column array (column vector) that new values are inserted into that. The `indx` defines an index to insert values in that position. The `val1`; `val2`; ... define values to be inserted into an array.

Both of these structures insert items into an array starting at the position defined by an index. In other words, an index of the first inserted value becomes equal to a given index.

Here are examples of inserting elements into an array.

```
%Insert elements [20,30] at index 2
%Output: 10     20     30     40     50
g_row=[10,40,50];
g_row=[g_row(1),[20,30],g_row(2:end)];
disp(g_row)

%Insert elements [20;30] at index 2
%Output:
%       10
%       20
%       30
%       40
%       50
g_col=[10;40;50];
g_col=[g_col(1,1);[20;30];g_col(2:end,1)];
disp(g_col)
```

To remove elements from an array, we can use an empty array as `[]`. Here is a general syntax shows how to delete elements from an array at given indexes:

Syntax

```
arr(indx) = []
```

The `arr` defines an array to remove elements from that. The `indx` defines indexes that elements in those positions are removed. This deletes elements at given indexes from an array. Note that, we can delete an entire variable (remove a variable from a workspace) by using the MATLAB `clear` or `clearvars` functions. To delete (remove) all variables from a workspace we can use `clear all` command.

Here are examples of removing elements from an array and deleting an entire array.

```
%Delete elements with indexes 3 and 4 from an array
%Output: 10    20    50
h=[10,20,30,40,50];
h(3:4)=[];
disp(h)

%Delete an array (an entire variable)
x=[10,20,30,40,50];
clear x

%Delete all variables
clear all
```

4.3 Obtain Array Shape and Size

As mentioned in an earlier chapter, MATLAB arrays are multi-dimensional data containers that may have one, two, three, ..., or n dimensions. Here are functions that describe the dimensional properties of an array:

Function	Description
`ndims`	Number of dimensions in array
`size`	Array dimensions (shape)
`numel`	Total elements in array
`length`	Length of array along largest dimension

Before explaining these functions, let's have a quick reminder about the array dimensions. As mentioned in an earlier chapter, each dimension in a MATLAB array is identified by one number.

For example, assume we have a 3-d array. In this 3-d array, the first dimension is identified by number 1, the second dimension is identified by number 2, and the third dimension is identified by number 3. The first dimension (number 1) denotes rows, the second dimension (number 2) denotes columns, and the third dimension (number 3) denotes sheets in this 3-d array.

To find out how many dimensions an array has, we can use the `ndims` function. For example, for an array with 2 dimensions, `ndims` returns 2. Here is a general syntax shows how to find a total number of dimensions in an array:

Syntax

```
n_dimension = ndims( A )
```

The `A` defines an array that its number of dimensions is returned.

To explain these functions, let's first create a 2-dimensional array with a size of (4,3) containing integers from 1 to 12 as:

```
%Create a 2-d array with a size of (4,3)
arr=[[1,2,3];[4,5,6];[7,8,9];[10,11,12]];
```

This array can be illustrated in a form of a matrix as:

```
arr = [[1 , 2 , 3 ];
       [4 , 5 , 6 ];
       [7 , 8 , 9 ];
       [10, 11, 12]];
```

Now, in this example we show how to use ndims.

```
%Obtain number of dimensions using ndims function
%Here, array is 2-d
%Output: 2
nd=ndims(arr);
disp(nd)
```

We can use the `size` function to get array dimensions (array sizes). This function returns a 1-d row array (row vector) that contains a number of elements in each dimension of an array. For example, a size of a 2-d array with 4 elements in its first dimension and 3 elements in its second dimension is [4,3] which shows a number of elements in each dimension of this array. Here is a general syntax shows how to find a size of an array:

Syntax

```
size_array = size(A, dim)
```

The `A` defines an array that its size is returned. The `dim` defines a dimension that its length is returned. The `dim` is optional. If the `dim` is not defined, the size function returns sizes for all dimensions of an array. However, if the `dim` is defined, then a length along that dimension is returned. The size function returns a 1-d row array (row vector) that contains a size of an array as `[ L1 , L2 , L3 , ... ]`. In this array, `L1` shows the total number of elements in the first dimension, `L2` shows the total number of elements in the second dimension, `L3` shows the total number of elements in the third dimension, and so on. In other words, `L1` is a length of the first dimension, `L2` is a length of the second dimension, `L3` is a length of the third dimension, and so on.

Here we show how to use the size function.

```
%Obtain array size using size function
%Here, array is 4x3
%Output: 4     3
arr=[[1,2,3];[4,5,6];[7,8,9];[10,11,12]];
sz=size(arr); %Or [L1,L2]=size(arr);
disp(sz)
```

By using a dimension identification number in place of a dim, we may use the size function to get a size of an array along one of its dimensions. It is commonly called a length of an array in that dimension. Here we show how to get a length of each dimension using the size function.

```
%Obtain length of array along its first dimension
%Here, array is 4x3
%Output: 4
arr=[[1,2,3];[4,5,6];[7,8,9];[10,11,12]];
L1=size(arr,1);
disp(L1)

%Obtain length of array along its second dimension
%Here, array is 4x3
%Output: 3
```

```
L2=size(arr,2);
disp(L2)
```

The `numel` function shows the total number of elements that an array has. For example, the total number of elements in a 2-d array with 4 elements in its first dimension and 3 elements in its second dimension is 12. Here is a general syntax shows how to find the total number of elements in an array:

Syntax

```
n_elements = numel( A )
```

The `A` defines an array that its total number of elements is returned.

Here we show how to use the numel function.

```
%Obtain number of elements in array using numel function
%Here, array has 12 elements
%Output: 12
arr=[[1,2,3];[4,5,6];[7,8,9];[10,11,12]];
n=numel(arr);
disp(n)
```

To find a length of an array along its largest dimension, we can use the `length` function. For example, consider a 3-d array `x` with 4 elements in its first dimension, 3 elements in its second dimension, and 2 elements in its third dimension. To find a length of the largest dimension in this array, we use `length(x)` which returns 4.

Here is a general syntax shows how to find a length of the largest array dimension:

Syntax

```
dimension_length = length(X)
```

The `X` defines an array that a length of its largest dimension is returned.

Here are examples show how to use the length function to find a length of an array. In the first example, an array has 4 elements, therefore, its length is 4. In the second example, it is shown how to find a length of an array slice. In the third example, the length function is used to find the length of the largest dimension in a 2-d array. An array has a size of (4,3), therefore, its largest length is 4.

```
%Find length of a 1-d row array
%Output: 4
a=[1,4,7,3];
l=length(a);
disp(l)

%Find length of a(1:3)
%Output: 3
a=[1,4,7,3];
l=length(a(1:3));
disp(l)

%Find length of largest array dimension
%Here, array is 4x3
%Output: 4
arr=[[1,2,3];[4,5,6];[7,8,9];[10,11,12]];
l=length(arr);
disp(l)
```

Also, we can use the length function to find a size of an array along one of its dimensions. Consider a previous 3-d array `x` with 4 elements in its first dimension, 3 elements in its second dimension, and 2 elements in its third dimension. Now, to find a length of the first dimension of this array, we can use `length(x(:,1,1))` which returns 4. Similarly, `length(x(1,:,1))` returns a length of the second dimension of an array equal to 3, and `length(x(1,1,:))` returns a length of the third dimension of an array equal to 2.

Consider a 2-d array with a size of (4,3) from a previous example again. Here we show how to get a length of each dimension using the length function.

```
%Obtain length of array along its first dimension
%Here, array is 4x3
%Output: 4
arr=[[1,2,3];[4,5,6];[7,8,9];[10,11,12]];
L1=length(arr(:,1));
disp(L1)

%Obtain length of array along its second dimension
%Here, array is 4x3
```

```
%Output: 3
L2=length(arr(1,:));
disp(L2)
```

The `length` function sometimes is used for indexing. Consider a 1-d array A. An index for the first element of this array is 1, and an index for the last element of this array is length(A). It means that, the first element in this array is A(1), and the last element is A(length(x)). Remember, to access the last element of a 1-d array, it is more common to use A(end) instead of A(length(x)).

4.4 Reshape Array

We can reshape an array with a size `(m, n, p, ...)` to a size `(sz1, sz2, sz3, ...)` as long as a total number of elements stays the same. In other words, a reshaped array should have as many elements as an original array. Both original and reshaped arrays may be multi-dimensional data containers with one, two, three, ..., or n dimensions. Here is a function to reshape an array:

Function	Description
`reshape`	Reshape an array

Here is a general syntax shows how to reshape an array to a new shape:

Syntax

```
reshaped_array = reshape(A, sz1, ..., szN)
```

The `A` defines an array to be reshaped. The `sz1`, ..., `szN` define sizes (dimensions) of a reshaped array. In other words, `sz1`, ..., `szN` are a number of elements in each dimension of a reshaped array. To reshape an array at least two sizes (`sz1` and `sz2`) should be defined.

Here are examples show how to use the `reshape` function to reshape an array. Consider a 2-dimensional array with a shape of (4,3) containing integers from 1 to 12. Now, we reshape this array from a size of (4,3) to an array with a size of (2,6).

```
%Create a 2-d array with a size of (4,3)
%Output:
%       1    2    3
%       4    5    6
%       7    8    9
```

```
%       10     11     12
arr=[[1,2,3];[4,5,6];[7,8,9];[10,11,12]];
disp(arr)

%Reshape an array using reshape function
%Output:
%        1      7      2      8      3      9
%        4     10      5     11      6     12
new_arr=reshape(arr,2,6);
disp(new_arr)
```

When we reshape an array, a reshaped array should have a compatible size with an original array. It means that, both a reshaped array and an original array should have the same total number of elements. One helpful method to make sure both arrays have compatible sizes is to use `[]` as a dimension length when we define a new size. Using `[]` tells MATLAB to calculate a length of a dimension that is marked by `[]`. Note that, we can only replace one dimension in a new size with `[]`.

For example, consider a previous example again. In that example we reshaped an array arr with a size of (4,3) into a new size of (2,6). We repeat this reshaping, but this time, we use `[]` for a length of the second dimension as 2,`[]`. By using `[]`, we tell MATLAB to calculate a required length for the second dimension to make a new size compatible with an original size of an array.

```
%Reshape an array using []
%Output:
%        1      7      2      8      3      9
%        4     10      5     11      6     12
new_arr=reshape(arr,2,[]);
disp(new_arr)
```

Again, remember we only can replace one dimension in a new size with `[]`.

We can convert an array to a 1-d column array (column vector) by using `(:)`. Consider a previous example again. We reshape this array to a 1-d column array (column vector) by using `(:)`.

```
%Reshape an array to 1-d column array using (:)
%Output:
%        1
%        4
%        7
%       10
```

```
%         2
%         5
%         8
%        11
%         3
%         6
%         9
%        12
new_arr=arr(:);
disp(new_arr)
```

4.5 Flip Array

Sometimes we need to reverse elements in an array along a given dimension. Here are functions and indexes to flip an array along one of its dimensions:

Function	Index	Description
`flip`	`end:-1:1`	Reverse elements along given dimension
`flipud`	`(end:-1:1,...)`	Flip an array in up/down direction
`fliplr`	`(:,end:-1:1,...)`	Flip an array in left/right direction

To reverse elements of an array along a given dimension, we can use the **`flip`** function. Here is a general syntax shows how to use the flip function to reverse array elements:

Syntax

```
flipped_array = flip(A, dim)
```

The **`A`** defines an array to be flipped. The **`dim`** defines a dimension that an array is flipped over along that dimension. The **`dim`** is optional. If the **`dim`** is not defined, the **`flip()`** function flips an array based on a size of an array. In 1-d array, elements are reversed along the length of an array. In 2-d array, elements are reversed in each column. In n-d array, elements are reversed along the first dimension that has a size larger than 1.

Here are examples show how to use the **`flip`** function. First, we create a 2-dimensional array with a size of (2,3) containing integers from 1 to 6. Now, we use the **`flip`** function to flip this array along its dimensions.

```
%Create a 2-d array with a size of (2,3)
%Output:
%       1     2     3
%       4     5     6
arr=[[1,2,3];[4,5,6]];
disp(arr)

%Flip an array along its 1st dimension
%Output
%      4     5     6
%      1     2     3
a=flip(arr,1); %Or a=arr(end:-1:1,:);
disp(a)

%Flip an array along its 2nd dimension
%Output
%      3     2     1
%      6     5     4
b=flip(arr,2); %Or b=arr(:,end:-1:1);
disp(b)
```

The **flipud** function flips elements of an array along a up/down dimension. Similarly, the **fliplr** function flips elements of an array along a left/right dimension. Here are general syntaxes show how to use the **flipud** and **fliplr** functions to reverse array elements:

Syntax

```
flipped_array = flipud( A )
flipped_array = fliplr( A )
```

The **A** defines an array to be flipped. As each of these function flips an array along a specific direction, we cannot define a dimension for any of these functions. Note that, **flipud(A)** is equivalent to **flip(A,1)** and **fliplr(A)** is equivalent to **flip(A,2)**.

Consider a previous example again. This time, we show how to use the **flipud** and **fliplr** functions to flip an array.

```
%Create a 2-d array with a size of (2,3)
%Output:
%       1     2     3
```

```
%       4     5     6
arr=[[1,2,3];[4,5,6]];
disp(arr)

%Flip an array along up/down direction
%Output
%       4     5     6
%       1     2     3
c=flipud(arr); %Or c=arr(end:-1:1,:);
disp(c)

%Flip an array along left/right direction
%Output
%       3     2     1
%       6     5     4
d=fliplr(arr); %Or d=arr(:,end:-1:1);
disp(d)
```

4.6 Concatenate Arrays

In MATLAB, two or more arrays can be joined together to create a new array. We can join arrays by using the following functions and square brackets:

Function	Square Brackets	Description
`cat`		Concatenate arrays along an existing dimension
`horzcat`	`[..., ..., ...]`	Concatenate arrays horizontally (column-wise)
`vertcat`	`[...; ...; ...]`	Concatenate arrays vertically (row-wise)

To explain how any of these functions works, let's illustrate how two 2-d arrays may be joined together. Consider two 2-d arrays `A` and `B` with a size of (3,2). First, we show how these two arrays may be joined along their first dimension. The resulted array has a size of (6,2).

1st array

A11	A12
A21	A22
A31	A32

2nd array

B11	B12
B21	B22
B31	B32

Joined arrays along 1st dim.

A11	A12
A21	A22
A31	A32
B11	B12
B21	B22
B31	B32

Now, we show how these two arrays can be joined along their second dimension. The resulted array has a size of (3,4).

1st array

A11	A12
A21	A22
A31	A32

2nd array

B11	B12
B21	B22
B31	B32

Joined arrays along 2nd dim.

A11	A12	B11	B12
A21	A22	B21	B22
A31	A32	B31	B32

The most helpful function to join several arrays is the `cat` function. Here is a general syntax shows how to use the cat function to join arrays along an existing dimension:

Syntax

```
joined_array = cat(dim, A1, A2, ..., An)
```

The `dim` defines an existing dimension that arrays are joined along that dimension. The `dim` is 1 for the first dimension, 2 for the second dimension, and so on. The `A1`, `A2`, ..., `An` define arrays to be joined. Note that, all `A1`, `A2`, ..., `An` arrays should have the same length in all dimensions, except along a dimension that arrays are joined together.

Here is an example shows how to use the cat function. Consider 2-d arrays x and y, both with a size of (3,2). All elements in x are 0 and all elements in y are 1. Now, we use the cat function to join these two 2-d arrays along their first dimension (dim is 1) and create a new array with a size of (6,2).

```
%Create all 0 array with a size of (3,2)
%Output:
%        0      0
%        0      0
```

```
%        0     0
x=[[0,0];[0,0];[0,0]]; %All elements are 0
disp(x)

%Create all 1 array with a size of (3,2)
%Output:
%        1     1
%        1     1
%        1     1
y=[[1,1];[1,1];[1,1]]; %All elements are 1
disp(y)

%Join arrays along 1st dimension using cat
%Output:
%        0     0
%        0     0
%        0     0
%        1     1
%        1     1
%        1     1
a=cat(1,x,y);
disp(a)
```

Now we join these two 2-d arrays with the cat function along their second dimension (dim is 2). The joined array has a size of (3,4).

```
%Join arrays along 2nd dimension using cat
%Output:
%        0     0     1     1
%        0     0     1     1
%        0     0     1     1
b=cat(2,x,y);
disp(b)
```

Functions `horzcat` and `vertcat` are special cases of the cat function. The `horzcat` function joins arrays horizontally (column-wise) and the `vertcat` function joins arrays vertically (row-wise). Here are general syntaxes show how to use these functions:

Syntax

```
horizontally_joined_array = horzcat(A1, A2, ..., An)
vertically_joined_array = vertcat(A1, A2, ..., An)
```

The `A1` , `A2`, ..., `An` are arrays to be joined. As each of these function joins arrays along a specific dimension, we cannot define a concatenation dimension for any of these functions.

Here are examples show how to use these functions to join two arrays.

```
%Create two arrays with a size of (3,2)
x=[[0,0];[0,0];[0,0]]; %All elements are 0
y=[[1,1];[1,1];[1,1]]; %All elements are 1

%Join arrays column-wise using horzcat
%Output:
%       0     0     1     1
%       0     0     1     1
%       0     0     1     1
d=horzcat(x,y); %Or d=cat(1,x,y);
disp(d)

%Join arrays row-wise using vertcat
%Output:
%       0     0
%       0     0
%       0     0
%       1     1
%       1     1
%       1     1
f=vertcat(x,y); %Or f=cat(2,x,y);
size(f)
```

Similarly, we can use square brackets to join arrays. The `[A1, A2, ..., An]` joins arrays horizontally (column-wise) and the `[A1; A2; ...; An]` joins arrays vertically (row-wise). Here are general syntaxes show how to use square brackets to join arrays:

Syntax

```
horizontally_joined_array = [A1, A2, ..., An]
vertically_joined_array = [A1; A2; ...; An]
```

The **A1**, **A2**, ..., **An** are arrays to be joined.

Here are examples show how to use square brackets to join two arrays.

```
%Create two arrays with a size of (3,2)
x=[[0,0];[0,0];[0,0]]; %All elements are 0
y=[[1,1];[1,1];[1,1]]; %All elements are 1

%Join arrays column-wise using horzcat
%Output:
%       0       0       1       1
%       0       0       1       1
%       0       0       1       1
g=[x,y]; %Or g=horzcat(x,y);
disp(g)

%Join arrays row-wise using vertcat
%Output:
%       0       0
%       0       0
%       0       0
%       1       1
%       1       1
%       1       1
h=[x;y]; %Or h=vertcat(x,y);
disp(h)
```

4.7 Array Initialization

In general, a creation of an array before using that array is called an array initialization. Typically, an array is initialized in its final size with all of its elements set to the same value. As mentioned earlier, MATLAB expands an array automatically as it grows. Therefore, it is not necessary to initialize (create) an array before we start working with that array. However, in working with a large array, it often improves the performance of a code if an array is initialized (created) first rather than grown incrementally. These are functions that are typically used to initialize an array:

Function	Description
`zeros`	Create an array filled with 0
`ones`	Create an array filled with 1
`[]`	Create an empty array

Commonly, two approaches are used to initialize an array, initialization by pre-allocation and initialization by an empty array.

Between these two approaches, an array initialization by pre-allocation is a preferable approach for array initialization. It helps to avoid resizing and reshaping arrays and increase a code performance. To initialize an array by pre-allocation, an array is created in its final size while all of its elements are filled with the same value. Typically, a pre-allocated array is composed of all-zero or all-one elements. After an array is initialized, desired values can be assigned to its elements. This pre-allocation helps to avoid resizing and reshaping an array continuously. However, this approach is only helpful when we know the final size of an array from the beginning.

One reason to initialize an array by pre-allocation is to speed up computation when we are working with large arrays. In MATLAB, arrays grow automatically. It means that, after an array is created, if we assign an item to an element index that does not exist, MATLAB grows an array to add a new element. To do that, MATLAB resizes or reshapes an array by copying and re-allocating an entire original array to a new one. This process of incrementally expanding an array as it grows could be very inefficient and slow. Therefore, it is highly recommended to initialize arrays in a way that arrays resizing and reshaping are minimized.

The most common method to initialize an array is to use the `zeros` or `ones` functions. The `zeros` function creates an array that all of its elements are 0. Similarly, the `ones` function creates an array that all of its elements are 1. Here are general syntaxes show how to use the `zeros` or `ones` functions to create an all-zero or all-one array with a size of (sz1, ..., szN):

Syntax

```
array = zeros(sz1, ..., szN)
array = ones(sz1, ..., szN)
```

The `sz1`, ..., `szN` define sizes (dimensions) of an array to be created. In other words, `sz1`, ..., `szN` are a number of elements in each dimension of a returned array. In case that only the `sz1` value is defined, then a 2-d array with a size of `(sz1,sz1)` is returned.

Here are examples explain how to initialize and pre-allocate an array. Here, we create two arrays with a size of (2,3). Elements in the first array are all filled with 0 and in the second array are all filled with 1.

```
%Initialize a 2x3 array with zeros
%Output:
%        0     0     0
%        0     0     0
arr_0=zeros(2,3);
disp(arr_0)

%Initialize a 2x3 array with ones
%Output:
%        1     1     1
%        1     1     1
arr_1=ones(2,3);
disp(arr_1)
```

Another approach to initialize an array is to use an empty array. To use an empty array for array initializing, first, an empty array is created. Then, data are typically added to this empty array by concatenation (using functions such as cat) or by appending (assigning values to new elements). This approach is helpful when we do not know the final size of an array. For example, when we read data from a file, we may not know how many elements are required from the beginning. A disadvantage for this approach is that we may need resizing and reshaping an array continuously, which often decreases the performance of a code.

To initialize an empty array, we use empty square brackets as the `[]`. It creates an array that has no element. Here is a general syntax shows how to use empty square brackets to create an empty array:

Syntax

```
array = []
```

Here is an example of how to create an empty array.

```
%Initialize an empty array with empty square brackets
empty_arr=[];
```

4.8 Element-Wise Operation and Comparison

Typically, we use two types of mathematical operations when we are working with arrays. The first one is an element-wise array operation and the second one is a mathematical matrix operation. For example, consider two arrays `x` and `y`. The `x.*y` expression returns element-wise multiplication of `x` by `y` while the `x*y` or `mtimes(x,y)` returns a matrix multiplication of `x` and `y`. In MATLAB, all standard mathematical operators such as `+`, `-`, `*`, `/`, and `^`, perform mathematical matrix operations on arrays. However, if standard mathematical operators are leading by a dot such as `.*`, `./`, and `.^`, then they perform element-wise operations on arrays. Similarly, if comparison expressions such as `==`, `<`, `<=`, `>`, `>=`, and `~=` are used with arrays, they return results for element-wise comparisons.

Element-wise operations help us to avoid using loops when we need to apply a series of identical operations to all elements of an array. As a result, a code would execute much faster compared to the ones that use loops. Also, it makes code looks clean and easy to follow. This element-wise process is called vectorization.

Here are examples show how to perform element-wise operations on MATLAB arrays. In the first example, we multiply all elements of an array by 5. In the second example, we multiply all elements of one array by their corresponding elements from another array.

```
%Multiply array x by a scaler 5
%Output: 15    30    45    60
x=[3,6,9,12];
a=5*x;
disp(a)

%Multiply elements of two arrays x and y
%Output: 12    48   108   192
x=[3,6,9,12];
y=[4,8,12,16];
b=x.*y;
disp(b)
```

Here is another example of how to perform element-wise operations. In this example, we have two arrays x and y that contain coordinates of points as (x,y). Now, we want to find a distance of each point (x,y) from an origin (0,0). This distance, which is also known as the Euclidean norm, can be obtained from $\sqrt{x^2 + y^2}$. We can use element-wise operations to calculate a distance from this formula.

```
%Distance of (x,y) from (0,0) (Euclidean norm)
%Distance is calculated as d=sqrt(x^2+y^2)
%Output: 5    10    15    20
x=[3,6,9,12];
y=[4,8,12,16];
d=sqrt(x.^2+y.^2);
disp(d)
```

Similarly, we can use element-wise comparisons to check given conditions for all elements in an array. Here are examples of how to perform element-wise comparisons on MATLAB arrays. Note that, outputs from these operations are in the form of logical 1 (true) and logical 0 (false).

```
%Check if x is equal to z
%Output: 1   0   0   1
x=[3,6,9,12];
z=[3,10,30,12];
disp(x==z)

%Check if x+y is larger than z
%Output: 1   1   0   1
x=[3,6,9,12];
y=[4,8,12,16];
z=[3,10,30,12];
disp((x+y)>z)
```

4.9 Find Indexes

It is very probable that we may need to find indexes of array elements that satisfy particular conditions. For example, consider an array that contains students' grades which are between 0 and 100. Now, assume we need to find indexes of elements that have a grade smaller than 60. For that purpose, we can use the `find` function to return elements satisfying this condition. This is a function that finds and returns indexes of array elements that follow a certain condition:

Function	Description
`find`	Find indexes in array

Here is a general syntax shows how to use the **find** function to find indexes of elements that satisfy a specific condition:

Syntax

```
indexes = find( conditional expression )
```

Let's explain how the **find** function finds indexes of elements that satisfy a given condition. First, a conditional expression in the **find** function returns a logical array contains **1** (**true**) and **0** (**false**). Then, it locates indexes of all elements that are not zero. As a result, it returns indexes of elements with true outcomes.

Note that, if we pass an array without any conditional expression to the **find** function, then the **find** function returns indexes of all nonzero elements in that array.

Here is an example shows how to use the **find** function. Consider an array x as [10,20,30,40,50,60,70,80,90,100]. Now, assume we need to know indexes of elements in x that are less than 60. We use the **find** function to find indexes of these elements.

```
%Find elements of x where x<60
%Output: 1     2     3     4     5
x=[10,20,30,40,50,60,70,80,90,100];
indx=find(x<60);
disp(indx)
```

We may also use the **find** function to find elements that satisfy a compound condition. We can use logical operators to create a compound conditional expression. To create a compound condition, although it is not required, it is recommended to put each conditional expression in a separate set of parentheses.

Here is an example shows how to use the **find** function with a compound condition. Consider a previous example again. This time, we use the **find** function to find indexes of elements that are larger than 30 and less than 60.

```
%Find elements of x where x>30 and x<60
%Output: 4     5
x=[10,20,30,40,50,60,70,80,90,100];
indx=find((x>30) & (x<60));
disp(indx)
```

Similar to the logical indexing, we can use the **find** function to find elements in one array based on a condition in another array. For example, consider an array x as [10,20,30,40,50,60,70,80,90,100] and an array L with the same size as [0,1,1,0,1,1,0,0,1,0]. Now, assume we need to select elements in x where their corresponding elements in L are equal to 1. To do that, first, we use the **find** function to find indexes of elements in L that are equal to 1. Then, we use these indexes to select corresponding elements in x.

```
%Find elements of x where L==1
%Output: 20    30    50    60    90
x=[10,20,30,40,50,60,70,80,90,100];
L=[0,1,1,0,1,1,0,0,1,0];
indx=find(L==1);
a=x(indx);
disp(a)
```

Using the **find** function for 2-d arrays is similar to 1-d arrays. Here is an example of how to use the **find** function to find indexes of elements in a 2-d array. Consider a 2-d array arr as [[10,20,30];[40,50,60];[70,80,90];[100,110,120]]. Assume we want to copy all elements in this array that are less than 60 to a new array. To do that, first, we use the **find** function to find indexes of elements that are less than 60. Then, we use these indexes to assign those elements to a new array.

```
%Create a 2-d array with a size of (4,3)
%Output:
%        10    20    30
%        40    50    60
%        70    80    90
%        100   110   120
arr=[[10,20,30];[40,50,60];[70,80,90];[100,110,120]];
disp(arr)

%Find all elements less than 60 to b
%Output:
%        10
%        40
%        20
%        50
%        30
indx=find(arr<60);
b=arr(indx);
disp(b)
```

Note that, in most cases, we can use the logical indexing to find indexes directly. This helps to skip using the `find` function. For example, in a previous example, we can use `b=arr(arr<60)` to skip using the `find` function. For more detail, refer to a logical indexing section.

4.10 NaN and Inf

The values that are not any type of numbers are presented by `NaN` which stands for "Not a Number". One situation that we may have `NaN` is when we are working with a dataset that contains missing data. These missing data, usually are represented by `NaN`.

The `Inf` represents infinity values. A situation that leads to having `Inf` is when there is a calculation error. For example, when a number is divided by zero, the result is represented by `Inf`.

MATLAB supports `NaN` and `Inf`. Here are MATLAB functions for working with `NaN` and `Inf`:

Function	Special Value	Description
`isnan`		Return logical 1 (true) if input is NaN
`isinf`		Return logical 1 (true) if input is Inf
`isfinite`		Return logical 1 (true) if input is not NaN or Inf
`ismissing`		Return logical 1 (true) if input is NaN or Inf
	`NaN`	NaN (Not a Number)
	`Inf`	Inf (Infinity)

Here are examples show situations that can result in having `NaN` or `Inf`.

```
%The NaN output
%Output: NaN
a=0;
disp(a/0)

%The Inf output
%Output: Inf   Inf   Inf
b=[1,2,3];
disp(b/0)
```

We can use the `isnan` and `isinf` functions to check if an array contains `NaN` or `Inf` values. Here is an example shows how to check if there are `NaN` or `Inf` values in an array.

```
%Check for NaN and Inf values
```

```
%Output:
%        NaN   Inf   Inf
%        1     0     0
%        0     1     1
c=[0,1,2];
d=c/0;
nan_chk=isnan(d);
inf_chk=isinf(d);
disp(d)
disp(nan_chk)
disp(inf_chk)
```

MATLAB has special functions to work with arrays that contain `NaN`. For example, the `sum` function returns a sum of elements in an array. Now, if an array contains `NaN`, we cannot use the `sum` function to get a sum of elements in that array, as it returns `NaN` for a sum. Instead, we need to use the `nansum` function to get a sum of elements in that array while excluding `NaN` elements. Some of the other helpful functions to work with arrays that contain `NaN` are `nanmin`, `nanmax`, and `nanmean`. Remember, these functions are generally slower than their counterpart functions that do not work with `NaN`. For example, the `nansum` function is usually slower than the `sum` function, and therefore, we should avoid using `nansum` unless it is necessary.

4.11 Generate Sequence of Numbers

We may need to generate a sequence of numbers between two values with an evenly spaced step. Here are MATLAB functions to create a sequence of numbers:

Function/Operator	Description
`:`	Generate evenly spaced sequence of numbers
`linspace`	Generate evenly spaced sequence of numbers

The `:` (colon) generates an evenly spaced sequence of numbers over an interval of `[start,stop]`. A resulted sequence includes a `start` value, but depending on a `step` value, it may or may not include a `stop` value. Here is a general syntax shows how to use the colon:

Syntax

```
sequence = start : step : stop
```

The `start` defines a starting number in a sequence. The `stop` defines the end value in a sequence. Note that, depending on a `step` value, the `stop` itself may or may not be included in a sequence. The `step` defines an interval between every two consecutive numbers in a sequence. The `step` is optional and by default is 1. If only `start` and `stop` values are defined, then by default, `step` is considered as step=1. Here are different forms that the colon can be used:

: (colon) Syntaxes	Default
`start : stop`	step=1
`start : stop : step`	

Here are some notes to consider when using the colon:

- Values for `start` and `stop` can be positive, zero, and negative. A `step` value can be positive and negative, but not zero. If a `step` value is set equal to zero, MATLAB returns an empty array.
- Depending on a `step` value, a returned sequence from the colon may or may not include a `stop` value.
- The `step` is optional and its default value is step=1.

Here are examples show how to use the colon to generate a sequence of numbers.

```
%The colon with start and stop values
%Output: 1     2     3     4     5     6     7     8     9    10
seq=1:10;
disp(seq)

%The colon with start, step, and stop values
%Output: 1     3     5     7     9
seq=1:2:10;
disp(seq)

%The colon with negative start, step, and stop values
%Output: -1    -3    -5    -7    -9
seq=-1:-2:-10;
disp(seq)

%The colon with negative, zero, and positive outcomes
%Output: -10    -8    -6    -4    -2     0     2     4     6     8    10
seq=-10:2:10;
disp(seq)
```

Another method to generate a sequence of numbers is to use the `linspace` function. The `linspace` function generates an evenly spaced sequence of numbers over an interval of `[start,stop]`. A resulted sequence includes both `start` and `stop` values. Here is a general syntax shows how to use the linspace function:

Syntax

```
sequence = linspace(start, stop, n)
```

The `start` defines a starting number in a sequence. The `stop` defines the end value in a sequence. Note that, a sequence includes both `start` and `stop` values. The `n` defines a number of samples to be generated. The `n` is optional and by default is 100.

Here are examples show how to use the `linspace` function to generate a sequence of numbers.

```
%Generate 10 numbers between 0 and 9
%Output: 0     1     2     3     4     5     6     7     8     9
seq=linspace(0,9,10);
disp(seq)

%Generate 5 numbers between 1 and 9
%Output: 1     3     5     7     9
seq=linspace(1,9,5);
disp(seq)

%Generate 11 numbers between 0 and 5
%Output: 0   0.5   1.0   1.5   2.0   2.5   3.0   3.5   4.0   4.5   5.0
seq=linspace(0,5,11);
disp(seq)

%Generate 5 numbers between -0.1 and -0.9
%Output: -0.1   -0.3   -0.5   -0.7   -0.9
seq=linspace(-0.1,-0.9,5);
disp(seq)

%Generate 4 numbers between -1 and 0.5
%Output: -1.0   -0.5    0    0.5
seq=linspace(-1,0.5,4);
disp(seq)
```

In general, we can generate any sequence of numbers using the `:` (colon) or `linspace` function. However, sometimes we may need to generate a sequence of float numbers from a sequence of integers. In such cases, first, we generate a sequence of integers using the `:` (colon). Then, by using a proper `step` value, we generate a float sequence from this integer sequence.

Here is an example shows how to generate a sequence of float numbers from a sequence of integers. In this example, we use an integer sequence of [0,1,2,3,4,5,6] to generate a sequence of floats between 1.0 and 10.0 with a step of 1.5.

```
%Define start, stop, step
start=1.0;
stop=10.0;
step=1.5;

%Generate float sequence from integer sequence
%Output: 1.0000    2.5000    4.0000    5.5000    7.0000    8.5000   10.0000
N=fix((stop-start)/step);
seq_arr=start+[0:N]*step;
disp(seq_arr)
```

Chapter 5
Basic Statistics

In this chapter, the basic statistics with MATLAB are described. First, MATLAB array dimensions are revisited. Then, a list of common statistical functions in MATLAB is presented. After that, it is explained how to find the sum and mean values of an array. Next, it is described how to find a minimum and maximum values of an array. Then, it is explained how to sort an array. It follows by descriptions of how to generate random values. At the end, it is explained how to calculate a histogram and probability density function of a dataset.

5.1 Array Dimension

Before explaining MATLAB statistical functions, let's have a quick reminder about an array dimension. As mentioned in an earlier chapter, each dimension in a MATLAB array is identified by one number. In an n-dimensional array, the n-th dimension is identified by number n. For example, assume we have a 2-dimensional array. In this 2-d array, the first dimension, which denotes rows, is identified by number 1, and the second dimension, which denotes columns, is identified by number 2. Similarly, in a 3-dimensional array, the first dimension is identified by number 1, the second dimension by number 2, and the third dimension by number 3. In this 3-d array, the first dimension (number 1) denotes rows, the second dimension (number 2) denotes columns, and the third dimension (number 3) denotes sheets.

The reason for this reminder is that, when we calculate the statistical values of an array, we may be interested in finding these values in an entire array or finding them along one dimension. For example, assume we want to obtain a maximum value in a 2-d array. We may need a maximum value in an entire array, or we may need a maximum value in each row or in each column. The proper application of the dimension identification number helps us to get statistical values that fit our needs.

5.2 Statistical Functions

MATLAB provides a series of functions for statistical applications. Here is a list of the most common MATLAB functions for basic statistics:

Function	Description
`abs`	Return absolute values of array
`sum`	Return sum of array
`mean`	Return the mean of array
`min`	Return the minimum value of array
`max`	Return the maximum value of array
`sort`	Return sorted array in ascending order
`std`	Return standard deviation of array
`var`	Return variance of array
`rand`	Return uniformly distributed random values in (0,1)
`randn`	Return normally distributed random values with $\mu = 0$ and $\sigma = 1$
`histogram`	Return histogram of array
`histogram2`	Return bivariate histogram of 2 arrays

The values that are not any type of numbers are considered as `NaN` which stands for "Not a Number". MATLAB has special functions to work with arrays that contain `NaN`. For example, the `sum` function returns a sum of elements in an array. Now, if an array contains `NaN`, we cannot use the `sum` function to get a sum of elements in that array, as it returns `NaN` for a sum. Instead, we need to use the `nansum` function to get a sum of elements in that array while excluding `NaN` elements. Some of the other helpful functions to work with arrays that contain `NaN` are `nanmin`, `nanmax`, and `nanmean`. Remember, these functions are generally slower than their counterpart functions that do not work with `NaN`. For example, the `nansum` function is usually slower than the `sum` function, and therefore, we should avoid using `nansum` unless it is necessary.

5.3 Sum and Mean of Array

We can find the sum and mean values of the MATLAB arrays by using the following functions:

Function	Description
`sum`	Return sum of array
`mean`	Return mean of array
`nansum`	Return sum of array ignoring NaN
`nanmean`	Return mean of array ignoring NaN

In this section, we explain how to work with the `sum` function. Working with the other functions presented above is more or less similar to the `sum` function.

To find a sum of an array, we may use the `sum` function. Here is a general syntax shows how to find a sum of an array:

Syntax

```
array_sum = sum(A, dim)
```

The `A` defines an array that a sum of its elements is returned. The `dim` defines a dimension that the sum values are calculated along that dimension. The `dim` is optional and if it is not defined, the `sum` function returns the sum values of elements along the first dimension of an array that its size is larger than 1. However, if the `dim` is defined, then the sum values along that dimension are given. To get a sum of all elements in an array either use `'all'` in place of the dim or use `(:)` indexing to indicate all elements.

Here is an example of how to use the `sum` function for a 1-d array:

```
%Create a 1-d array with 10 elements
x=[9,5,7,2,1,8,3,6,4,10];

%Sum of array using sum function
%Output: 55
s=sum(x);
disp(s)
```

Here is an example shows how to use the **sum** function for a 2-d array. In this example, first, we create a 2-d array with a size of (4,3) containing integers from 1 to 12. Then, we use the **sum** function to find a sum of all elements in this array. Note that, we use **(:)** indexing as **sum(arr(:))** to get a sum of all elements in an array.

```
%Create a 2-d array with a size of (4,3)
%Output:
%        1     5    12
%        3    10     2
%        7     4     9
%        6    11     8
arr=[[1,5,12];[3,10,2];[7,4,9];[6,11,8]];
disp(arr)

%Sum of array using sum function
%Output: 78
s=sum(arr(:));
disp(s)
```

We may use the **sum** function to get a sum of an array along one of its dimensions. For example, in a 2-d array, we can find a sum of each row by summing along all columns (dim is 2). Similarly, we can find a sum of each column by summing along all rows (dim is 1).

To better understand how defining dimension works in the **sum** function, consider it as this given dimension is removed from an array during the sum process. It means that, when we set the dim equal 1, we tell MATLAB to remove the first dimension (remove rows). By doing that, we have one row with all columns. Similarly, when we set the dim equal 2, we tell MATLAB to remove the second dimension (remove columns). Then, we have one column with all rows.

Here are examples show how to find a sum of an array along its dimensions.

```
%Create a 2-d array with a size of (4,3)
```

```
arr=[[1,5,12];[3,10,2];[7,4,9];[6,11,8]];

%Sum of each row
%Output:
%       18
%       15
%       20
%       25
s_row=sum(arr,2);
disp(s_row)

%Sum of each column
%Output: 17    30    31
s_col=sum(arr,1);
disp(s_col)
```

We can also find a sum value for a slice of elements. Here, we show how to find a sum of the first column in an array.

```
%Sum of an array slice
%Output: 17
s=sum(arr(:,1));
disp(s)
```

Similarly, we can find a sum of elements using the logical indexing. Here, we show how to find a sum of all elements that are less than 6 in an array.

```
%Sum of elements less than 6
%Output: 15
s=sum(arr(arr<6));
disp(s)
```

5.4 Minimum and Maximum of Array

We can find the minimum and maximum values of the MATLAB arrays by using the following functions:

Function	Description
min	Return the minimum value of array
max	Return the maximum value of array

`nanmin`	Return the minimum value of array ignoring NaN
`nanmax`	Return the maximum value of array ignoring NaN

In this section, we explain how to work with the `min` function. Working with the other functions presented above is more or less similar to the `min` function.

To find a minimum value of an array, we can use the `min` function. Here is a general syntax shows how to find a minimum value of an array:

Syntax

```
array_min = min(A, [], dim)
```

The `A` defines an array that its minimum value is returned. The `dim` defines a dimension that minimum values are returned along that dimension. The `dim` is optional and if it is not defined, the `min` function returns minimum values of elements along the first dimension of an array that its size is larger than 1. However, if the `dim` is defined, then minimum values along that dimension are given. To get a minimum value of all elements in an array either use `'all'` in place of the dim or use `(:)` indexing to indicate all elements.

We can use the `min` function to find an index of a minimum value in an array as well. Here is a general syntax shows how to find a minimum value and its index in an array:

Syntax

```
[array_min, indexes] = min(A, [], dim)
```

Here is an example of how to use the `min` functions for a 1-d array:

```
%Create a 1-d array with 10 elements
x=[9,5,7,2,1,8,3,6,4,10];

%Minimum of array using min functions
%Output:
%       1
%       5
[m,indx]=min(x);
disp(m)
disp(indx)
```

Here is an example shows how to use the `min` function for a 2-d array. In this example, first, we create a 2-d array with a size of (4,3) containing integers from 1 to 12. Then, we use the `min` function to find the minimum value of all elements in this array. Note that, we use `(:)` indexing as `min(arr(:))` to get a minimum value of all elements in an array.

```
%Create a 2-d array with a size of (4,3)
%Output:
%        1     5    12
%        3    10     2
%        7     4     9
%        6    11     8
arr=[[1,5,12];[3,10,2];[7,4,9];[6,11,8]];
disp(arr)

%Minimum of array using min function
%Output: 1
m=min(arr(:));
disp(m)
```

We may use the `min` function to find minimum values of an array along one of its dimensions. For example, in a 2-d array, we can find a minimum value of each row by using 2 in place of the dim. Similarly, we can find a minimum value of each column by using 1 in place of the dim.

Here are examples show how to find minimum values of an array along its dimensions.

```
%Create a 2-d array with a size of (4,3)
arr=[[1,5,12];[3,10,2];[7,4,9];[6,11,8]];

%Minimum of each row
%Output:
%        1
%        2
%        4
%        6
m_row=min(arr,[],2);
disp(m_row)

%Minimum of each column
%Output: 1     4     2
m_col=min(arr,[],1);
```

```
disp(m_col)
```

5.5 Sort Array

We can sort elements of a MATLAB array by using the following function:

Function	Description
`sort`	Return sorted array in ascending order

To sort an array, we may use the `sort` function. The `sort` function returns a sorted array in ascending order unless it is specified to sort in descending order. Here are general syntaxes show how to sort an array:

Syntax

```
sorted_array = sort(A, dim, direction)
```

The `A` defines an array to be sorted. The `dim` defines a dimension that an array is sorted along that dimension. The `dim` is optional and if it is not defined, the `sort` function sorts an array along the first dimension of an array that its size is larger than 1. However, if the `dim` is defined, then an array is sorted along that dimension. The `direction` defines a direction that an array to be sorted. The direction is optional and by default is `'ascend'` which sorts an array in ascending order. To sort an array in descending order, use `'descend'` in place of the direction.

We can use the `sort` function to find indexes of sorted elements as well. Here is a general syntax shows how to find indexes of sorted elements:

Syntax

```
[sorted_array, indexes] = sort(A, dim, direction)
```

Here is an example shows how to use the sort for a 1-d array:

```
%Create a 1-d array with 10 elements
x=[9,5,7,2,1,8,3,6,4,10];

%Sort array using sort functions
```

```
%Output:
%        1      2      3      4      5      6      7      8      9     10
%        5      4      7      9      2      8      3      6      1     10
[y, indx]=sort(x);
disp(y)
disp(indx)
```

The **sort** function sorts an array in ascending order, from the smallest to the largest values. To sort an array in descending (reverse) order, we use **'descend'** in place of the **direction**. Consider a previous example again. This time, we sort an array in descending order.

```
%Sort an array in descending order
%Output: 10     9      8      7      6      5      4      3      2      1
x=[9,5,7,2,1,8,3,6,4,10];
y=sort(x,'descend');
disp(y)
```

We may use the **sort** function to sort an array along one of its dimensions. For example, in a 2-d array, we can sort rows by sorting an array along all columns (dim is 2). Similarly, we can sort columns by sorting an array along all rows (dim is 1).

Here are examples show how to use the **sort** function for a 2-d array. In this example, first, we create a 2-d array with a size of (4,3) containing integers from 1 to 12. Then, we show how to sort this array along each of its dimensions by using the **sort** function.

```
%Create a 2-d array with a shape of (4,3)
%Output:
%        1      5     12
%        3     10      2
%        7      4      9
%        6     11      8
arr=[[1,5,12];[3,10,2];[7,4,9];[6,11,8]];
disp(arr)

%Sort rows
%Output:
%        1      5     12
%        2      3     10
%        4      7      9
%        6      8     11
y_row=sort(arr,2);
```

```
disp(y_row)

%Sort columns
%Output:
%        1     4     2
%        3     5     8
%        6    10     9
%        7    11    12
y_col=sort(arr,1);
disp(y_col)
```

Similar to 1-d array, we can sort rows and columns of a 2-d array in descending (reverse) order by using `'descend'` in place of the `direction`. Consider a previous example again. This time, we sort rows and columns in descending order.

```
%Sort rows in descending order
%Output:
%       12     5     1
%       10     3     2
%        9     7     4
%       11     8     6
y_row=sort(arr,2,'descend');
disp(y_row)

%Sort columns in descending order
%Output:
%        7    11    12
%        6    10     9
%        3     5     8
%        1     4     2
y_col=sort(arr,1,'descend');
disp(y_col)
```

5.6 Random Number

MATLAB has several functions to generate various types of random values. Here is a list of most common functions to generate random values:

Function	Description
`rand`	Return uniformly distributed random values in (0,1)

`randi`	Return uniformly distributed random integers in [imin,imax]
`randn`	Return normally distributed random values with $\mu = 0$ and $\sigma = 1$
`normrnd`	Return normally distributed random values with μ and σ
`datasample`	Return random values from given array

The most basic random values are the ones that are uniformly distributed. The **rand** function returns uniformly distributed random values. These random values are generated over an open interval of (0,1) where 0 and 1 are not included in this interval. Here is a general syntax shows how to generate uniformly distributed random values:

Syntax

```
random_array = rand(sz1, ..., szN)
```

The `sz1`, ..., `szN` define dimensions of the returned array. In other words, `sz1`, ..., `szN` are a number of elements in each dimension of a returned array. If the `rand` function is used without any argument, it returns a single random value. In case that only the **sz1** value is defined, then a 2-d array with a size of `(sz1,sz1)` is returned.

Here are examples show how to generate uniformly distributed random values. In these examples, first, we generate a single random value. Next, we generate a 1-d random array with 10 elements. Then, we generate a 2-d random array with a size of (4,3). Note that, since data are generated randomly, we get different results each time we run this code.

```
%Generate one random value
r=rand()

%Generate a 1-d random array with 10 elements
r=rand(1,10)

%Generate a 2-d random array with a size of (4,3)
r=rand(4,3)
```

The `rand` function returns uniformly distributed random values over (0,1) interval. However, we may need uniformly distributed random values between two given numbers. To generate uniformly distributed random values between any two given numbers, first, random values are generated over an open interval of (0,1) using the `rand` function. Then, these random values are scaled to an interval of (low,high). Here is a general syntax shows how to generate random values between two given limits:

Syntax

```
random_array = low + (high-low) .* rand(sz1, ..., szN)
```

The `low` and `high` define an open interval as (low,high) where random values are generated over that interval.

Note that, working with the other random functions is more or less similar to the `rand` function. Here are general syntaxes show how to generate uniformly distributed random integers using the `randi` function and normally distributed random values using the `randn` function:

Syntax

```
random_array = randi([imin, imax], sz1, ..., szN)
random_array = randn(sz1,...,szN)
```

The `sz1`, ..., `szN` define dimensions of the returned array. In other words, `sz1`, ..., `szN` are a number of elements in each dimension of a returned array. If the `randn` function is used without any argument, it returns a single random value. In case that only the `sz1` value is defined, then a 2-d array with a size of `(sz1,sz1)` is returned. The `imin` and `imax` define an interval [imin,imax] where random integers are generated over that interval. The `imin` is optional and by default is 1.

To generate normally distributed random values with a mean equal to zero ($\mu = 0$) and a standard deviation equal to 1 ($\sigma = 1$), we can use the `randn` function. Note that, $\mu = 0$ and $\sigma = 1$ represent a standard normal distribution. Similarly, to generate normally distributed random values with any given mean, μ, and standard deviation, σ, we can use the `normrnd` function. Another method to generate normally distributed random values with any given mean, μ, and standard deviation, σ, is:

Syntax

```
random_array = mu + sigma .* randn(sz1, ..., szN)
```

The `mu` defines a mean value. The `sigma` defines a standard deviation value.

5.7 Generate Reproducible Random Number

Every time we use any of random methods to generate random values, we receive a new set of random values. However, sometimes we may need to generate the same random values over and over again. To do that, we need to tell a random generator to produce a reproducible set of random numbers. Here is a function to generate reproducible random values:

Function	Description
`rng`	Set random generator and initial seed

To generate reproducible random values, we need to define a random seed in the **`rng`** function. Note that, a random seed is a numerical sequence that is used to initialize a random generator. Therefore, by defining a random seed, we can set a random generator to generate reproducible random values.

Here is a general syntax shows how to initiate a random generator:

Syntax

```
Generator = rng(seed, generator)
```

The **`seed`** defines a random seed to initialize a random generator. As mentioned earlier, a random seed is a numerical sequence that is used to initialize a random generator. The **`seed`** is optional and by default is 0. If the **`seed`** is not defined, unpredictable random values are returned. The **`generator`** defines a type of a random generator to be used. The **`generator`** is optional and by default is **`'twister'`**.

Here is an example shows how to generate reproducible random values. In this example, we define a random seed in a random generator to generate reproducible random values. To do that, every time we need to generate random values, first, we initiate a random generator with the seed equal to 0. Then, we use the **`randi`** function to generate 5 reproducible random integers with a size of (1,5) over [0,10] interval.

```
%Generate 5 random integer over [0,10] interval
%Output: 8     9     1    10     6
rng1=rng(0);
r1=randi([0,10], 1, 5);
disp(r1)
```

```
%Reproduce 5 random integer over [0,10] interval
%Output: 8     9     1    10     6
rng2=rng(0);
r2=randi([0,10], 1, 5);
disp(r2)
```

5.8 Histogram and Probability Density Function of Dataset

A histogram shows a distribution of data in a dataset. Assume we have a dataset that we want to find its histogram. To do that, first, a data range in this dataset is split into several bins (intervals), and then, numbers of data points fall into each bin are counted. A histogram is a presentation of data counts in each bin. We can use MATLAB to find a histogram of a dataset. Here is a list of functions to find a histogram of a dataset:

Function	Description
`histogram`	Plot and return histogram of array
`histogram2`	Plot and return bivariate histogram of 2 arrays
`histcounts`	Return histogram of array
`histcounts2`	Return bivariate histogram of 2 arrays
`hist`	Return histogram of array (legacy function)

The **`histogram`** function calculates and plots a histogram of a dataset. Here is a general syntax shows how to find a histogram of a dataset:

Syntax

```
histogram_object = histogram(X, nbins)
```

The **`X`** defines an array that its histogram is calculated. The **`nbins`** defines the total number of bins in a histogram. The **`nbins`** is optional. If the **`nbins`** is not defined, then the total number of bins are defined automatically.

Note that, besides a histogram calculation, the **`histogram`** function also plots a histogram of a dataset. To calculate a histogram without plotting it, we can use the **`histcounts`** function. For more details on how to display data, refer to the advanced data visualization chapter.

Here is an example shows how to calculate and display a histogram of a dataset. In this example, first, we generate 1000 random data points drawn from a standard normal distribution using the `randn` function. Then, we calculate and display a histogram of these data within 20 bins. Note that, since data are generated randomly, we get slightly different results each time we run this code.

```
%Generate Data
x=randn(1000,1); %Generate 1000 random data points
                 %with normal distribution

%Histogram of data
h = histogram(x,20);

%Add labels
title('Histogram')
xlabel('Bins')
ylabel('Counts')
```

Figure 5.1
Histogram of dataset

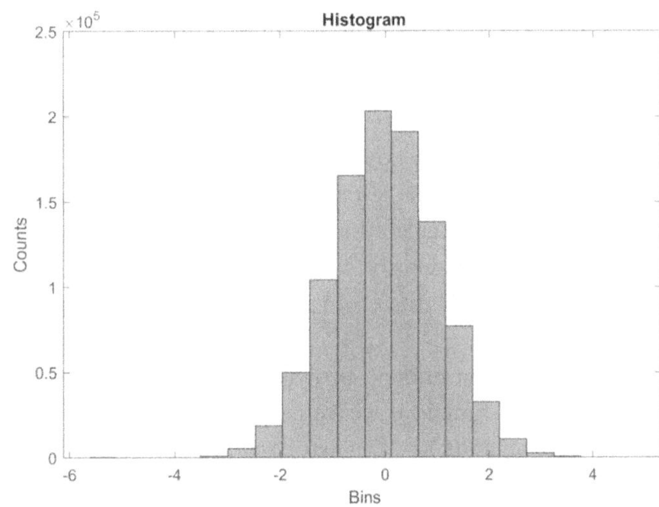

The **`histogram`** function returns a histogram object that contains all information about a calculated histogram. To obtain or specify any property of a histogram, we trail a histogram object with dot notation followed by a histogram property. For example, the **`NumBins`** property is used to obtain or specify the total number of bins in a histogram. To get how many bins are in a histogram we use **`histogram_object.NumBins`**. Similarly, to change the total number of bins in a histogram, we assign a new bins number to **`histogram_object.NumBins`**. Assume we want to change the total number of bins in a histogram to 30 after a histogram is calculated. To do that, we use **`histogram_object.NumBins=30`**. Here is a list of common histogram properties:

Function	Description
histogram_object.NumBins	Return/specify total number of bins in histogram
histogram_object.BinWidth	Return/specify width of bins
histogram_object.BinEdges	Return/specify edges of bins
histogram_object.Values	Return number of data points in each bin
histogram_object.Normalization	Specify normalization method

The `histogram_object.Normalization` defines how a histogram is normalized. By default the `histogram_object.Normalization` is set to `'count'` which returns the total number (counts) of data points that fall in each bin (frequency of observation). To get a probability density function (pdf), we need to use `histogram_object.Normalization='pdf'`.

As mentioned above, to get a probability density of a dataset we can use the `histogram_object.Normalization='pdf'`. However, sometimes we have histogram data and we need to calculate a probability density function (pdf) from these data. In such cases, we can find a probability density function of a dataset by dividing its histogram by the total area under its histogram.

Here is an example shows how to calculate a probability density function of a dataset from its histogram. In this example, first, we generate 1000 random data points and calculate their histogram. Then, we calculate bin widths, bin centers, and area under each bin. After that, we calculate a probability density function of this dataset. Note that, since data are generated randomly, we get slightly different results each time we run this code.

We know that the area under a probability density function should be one. After we calculate a probability density function, we can check to see if its area is equal to one or not by using `sum(pdf.*bin_widths)`.

```
%Generate Data
x=randn(1000,1); %Generate 1000 random data points
                 %with normal distribution

%Histogram of data
h = histogram(x,20);

%Find bin edges
bin_edges=h.BinEdges;

%Find bin widths
bin_widths=h.BinWidth;
```

```
%Or bin_widths=diff(bin_edges);

%Find bin centers
bin_centers=(bin_edges(1:end-1)+bin_edges(2:end))/2;
%Or bin_centers=bin_edges(1:end-1)+bin_widths/2;

%Find area under each bin
bin_areas=h.Values*bin_widths;

%Calculate probability density function
pdf=h.Values./(sum(bin_areas));
%Note: sum(pdf.*bin_widths) should be 1
```

Note that, MATLAB has a legacy `hist` function that returns a histogram of a dataset. Although the `hist` function is sufficient for most general purposes, it has limited capabilities compared with the `histogram` function. Here is a general syntax shows how to find a histogram of a dataset using the `hist` function:

Syntax

```
[counts, centers] = hist(x, nbins)
```

The `x` defines an array that its histogram is calculated. The `nbins` defines the total number of bins in a histogram. The `nbins` is optional and by default is 10. Note that, if the `hist` function is called without any output argument, then it plots a histogram of data.

Chapter 6
Introduction to MATLAB Table

In this chapter, the basics of working with labeled data are described. First, it is described how to create a MATLAB table. Then, properties of tables are presented. Next, it is explained how to use indexes and slicing to access items in tables. At the end, it is explained how to change the contents of items in tables.

6.1 Table

MATLAB provides support for manipulation and analysis of 2-dimensional table-like arrays called table. Table helps to eliminate the complexity of working with structured datasets. MATLAB provides tools to create and manipulate structured datasets in the same way that we used to work with tables in spreadsheets. It results in easier code development and cleaner syntax.

6.2 Create Table

The MATLAB table is a 2-dimensional labeled array. In this section, we explain how to create a table. Here are MATLAB functions to create a table:

Function	Description
`table`	Create table (2-d tabular labeled array)
`array2table`	Convert array to table

MATLAB tables are 2-d labeled arrays. It means that, it is a 2-d array where each row and each column has its own label. We may visualize it as a table in a spreadsheet where we can select each row or each column by its label. Here is a general syntax shows how to create a MATLAB table:

Syntax

```
Table = table(var1, ..., varN, 'VariableNames', varNames, 'RowNames', rowNames)
```

The `var1`, ..., `varN` contains data that a table is created from them. They may have different sizes and data types but they all should have the same number of rows. We can set column and row names (labels) by using an optional Name-Value pair arguments `'VariableNames', varNames` and `'RowNames', rowNames`. The `'VariableNames'` indicates that the following variable contains variable names (labels). The `varNames` is a cell array of character vectors or a string array that contains variable names (labels) and by default is the same as `var1`, ..., `varN`. The `'RowNames'` indicates that the following variable contains row names (labels). The `rowNames` is a cell array of character vectors or a string array that contains row names (labels). The `'VariableNames', varNames` pair and `'RowNames', rowNames` pair are optional.

To explain how to work with a MATLAB table, let's consider an example. Assume we have a table that contains approximated nutrition facts for milk products from a hypothetical milk producer. In this table, we have four types of milk as whole (3.25%) milk, reduced fat (2%) milk, low fat (1%) milk, and fat free (nonfat) milk. For each of these products, we have amounts of total fat, cholesterol, sodium, and potassium per 100 grams. These values are in grams. Note that, these numbers are for hypothetical products and do not reflect any real values. These values can be presented as:

```
                 Total Fat     Cholesterol     Sodium     Potassium

whole            3.3           0.010           0.043      0.132
reduced fat      2.0           0.008           0.047      0.140
low fat          1.0           0.005           0.044      0.150
fat free         0.1           0.002           0.042      0.156
```

Now, we show how to create a MATLAB table that contains these data. To do that, first, we define row labels and column labels. The row labels in this table are 'whole', 'reduced fat', 'low fat', and 'fat free'. The column labels in this table are 'Total Fat', 'Cholesterol', 'Sodium', and 'Potassium'. Then, we create 1-d column arrays (column vectors) that each contains numerical values associated with one column in a table. Finally, we use these data to create a table (labeled 2-d array) by using the `table` function.

```
%Create row labels
row_label={'whole';'reduced fat';'low fat';'fat free'};

%Create column labels
col_label={'Total Fat','Cholesterol','Sodium','Potassium'};

%Create 1-d column arrays containing data
col1=[3.3;2.0;1.0;0.1];
col2=[0.010;0.008;0.005;0.002];
col3=[0.043;0.047;0.044;0.042];
col4=[0.132;0.140;0.150;0.156];

%Create table
%Output:
%                     Total Fat    Cholesterol    Sodium    Potassium
%                     _________    ___________    ______    _________
%
%       whole            3.3            0.01       0.043      0.132
%       reduced fat        2           0.008       0.047       0.14
%       low fat            1           0.005       0.044       0.15
%       fat free         0.1           0.002       0.042      0.156
T=table(col1, col2, col3, col4, ...
     'VariableNames', col_label, 'RowNames', row_label);
```

```
disp(T)
```

We can create a MATLAB table from an array by using the `array2table` function. Here is a general syntax shows how to create a MATLAB table from an array:

Syntax

```
Table = array2table(A, 'VariableNames', varNames, 'RowNames', rowNames)
```

The `A` is an array that a table is created from that. We can set column and row names (labels) by using an optional Name-Value pair arguments `'VariableNames', varNames` and `'RowNames', rowNames`. The `'VariableNames'` indicates that the following variable contains variable names (labels). The `varNames` is a cell array of character vectors or a string array that contains variable names (labels). The `'RowNames'` indicates that the following variable contains row names (labels). The `rowNames` is a cell array of character vectors or a string array that contains row names (labels). The `'VariableNames', varNames` pair and `'RowNames', rowNames` pair are optional.

Here is an example shows how to create a previous table by using an array.

```
%Create row labels
row_label={'whole';'reduced fat';'low fat';'fat free'};

%Create column labels
col_label={'Total Fat','Cholesterol','Sodium','Potassium'};

%Create array containing data
val=[[3.3, 0.010, 0.043, 0.132];
     [2.0, 0.008, 0.047, 0.140];
     [1.0, 0.005, 0.044, 0.150];
     [0.1, 0.002, 0.042, 0.156]];

%Create table
%Output:
%                    Total Fat    Cholesterol    Sodium    Potassium
%                    _________    ___________    ______    _________
%
%    whole              3.3          0.01        0.043       0.132
%    reduced fat          2         0.008        0.047        0.14
%    low fat              1         0.005        0.044        0.15
%    fat free           0.1         0.002        0.042       0.156
```

```
T=array2table(val, 'VariableNames', col_label, 'RowNames', row_label);
disp(T)
```

Note that, we may use other data types such as a string to create a MATLAB table. For example, to create a string table, we can simply use string data by using a cell array of character vectors such as `{' ... ' ; ' ... ' ; ' ... ' }` in the `table` function. Also, we may create a table that contains different data types. For example, we may have a 2-columns table with one column filled with numbers and one filled with strings.

6.3 Table Properties and Functions

MATLAB tables have several properties, each developed for a particular purpose. In general, each of these properties returns or specifies a particular table property. For example, a table has a property `table.Properties.RowNames` which return row names (labels) of a table and has a property `table.Variables` which returns an array containing data in a table.

To use a table property, a table name is followed by a dot and followed by Properties.PropertyName or by PropertyName, depending on which property we use. Here are general syntaxes show how to use a table property:

Syntax

```
results = table.Properties.PropertyName
results = table.PropertyName
```

Here are some of the most common table properties:

Property	Description
`table.Properties.RowNames`	Return/specify row names (labels)
`Table.Row`	Return/specify row names (labels)
`table.Properties.VariableNames`	Return/specify variable (column) names (labels)
`table.Variables`	Return array from a table
`table.Properties.Description`	Return/specify table description

Here, we show how to use table properties. First, we create a table with a size of (3,4), row names (labels) of 'one', 'two', 'three', column names (labels) of 'A', 'B', 'C', 'D', and data of [[1,2,3,4];[5,6,7,8];[9,10,11,12]].

```
%Create row labels
row_label={'one';'two';'three'};

%Create column labels
col_label={'A','B','C','D'};

%Create array containing data
val=[[1,2,3,4];
     [5,6,7,8];
     [9,10,11,12]];

%Create table
%Output:
%                A    B     C     D
%                _    __    __    __
%
%       one      1     2     3     4
%       two      5     6     7     8
%       three    9    10    11    12
T=array2table(val, 'VariableNames', col_label, 'RowNames', row_label);
disp(T)
```

Here are examples show how to use table properties:

```
%Row labels
%Output:
%       'one'
%       'two'
%       'three'
row_lb=T.Properties.RowNames;
disp(row_lb)

%Column labels
%Output: 'A'    'B'    'C'    'D'
col_lb=T.Properties.VariableNames;
disp(col_lb)

%Create array from table
%Output:
%       1     2     3     4
%       5     6     7     8
%       9    10    11    12
```

```
arr=T.Variables;
disp(arr)
```

MATLAB also has several functions, each developed to perform a particular operation on a table. Here are some of the most common functions to work with tables:

Function	Description
`addvars`	Add columns to table
`movevars`	Remove columns from table
`readtable`	Read table from file
`writetable`	Write table to file
`rows2vars`	Reorient table as rows become variables
`sortrows`	Sort row of table
`ismissing`	Find missing data
`fillmissing`	Fill missing data
`innerjoin`	Inner join two tables
`outerjoin`	Outer join two tables

6.4 Table Indexing and Slicing

In most cases, working with MATLAB tables is similar to working with 2-d arrays. Similar to arrays, items in tables can be accessed by indexing and slicing. There are two main methods of indexing for tables. In the first method, items are accessed by their position similar to arrays. In the second method, items are accessed by their row and column names (labels) similar to spreadsheets.

Here are methods to access items in MATLAB tables:

Method	Output	Description
`table( i:j , m:n )`	Table	Return table from items in table using positions
`table({'label_i',...}, {'label_m',...})`	Table	Return table from items in table using labels
`table{ i:j , m:n }`	Array	Return array from items in table using positions
`table{{'label_i',...}, {'label_m',...}}`	Array	Return array from items in table using labels
`table.col_label`	Array	Return array from values of column with label 'col_label'
`table.('col_label')`	Array	Return array from values of column with label 'col_label'

`table.(m)`	Array	Return array from values of column with index m

Note that, if we use parentheses as `( ... , ... )` for indexing, the returned result is a table, however, if we use curly brackets as `{ ... , ... }` for indexing, the returned result is an array. This is correct for both position and label indexing. For example, assume we have a table `T`. The statement `R=T(1,:)` returns the first row of table `T` as a table and assigns it to `R`. Therefore, `R` becomes a table. However, the statement `Arr=T{1,:}` returns the first row of table `T` as an array and assigns it to `Arr`. Therefore, `Arr` becomes an array.

First, we explain how to access items in a table by their position. Items in a table can be accessed by their indexes (positions). Similar to 2-d arrays, each table dimension is identified by a number. In a table, the first dimension is identified by number 1 and the second dimension is identified by number 2. In other words, the first dimension (number 1) denotes rows and the second dimension (number 2) denotes columns in a table. In this method, indexes in a table have a form of `( i:j , m:n )`, which `i:j` shows locations of items along its first dimension (number 1), and `m:n` shows locations of items along its second dimension (number 2).

Here are general syntaxes show how to access items in a table by their position:

Syntax

```
results_table = Table( i : j , m : n )
results_array = Table{ i : j , m : n }
```

Here is an illustration of indexes for a table. This table has a size of (3,4) which means it has 3 rows along its first dimension (number 1), and 4 columns along its second dimension (number 2).

	Col 1	Col 2	Col 3	Col 4
Row 1	(1,1)	(1,2)	(1,3)	(1,4)
Row 2	(2,1)	(2,2)	(2,3)	(2,4)
Row 3	(3,1)	(3,2)	(3,3)	(3,4)

To show how to use indexing and slicing, first, we create a table with a size of (3,4), row labels of 'one', 'two', 'three', column labels of 'A', 'B', 'C', 'D', and data of [[1,2,3,4];[5,6,7,8];[9,10,11,12]].

```
%Create labels
row_label={'one';'two';'three'};
col_label={'A','B','C','D'};
```

```
%Create array containing data
val=[[1,2,3,4];[5,6,7,8];[9,10,11,12]];

%Create table
%Output:
%                A     B     C     D
%                _     __    __    __
%
%       one      1     2     3     4
%       two      5     6     7     8
%       three    9     10    11    12
T=array2table(val, 'VariableNames', col_label, 'RowNames', row_label);
disp(T)
```

Here are examples show how to access items in a table using item positions.

```
%Table first Row
%Output:
%               A    B    C    D
%               _    _    _    _
%
%         one   1    2    3    4
r=T(1,:);
disp(r)

%Table first column
%Output:
%                A
%                _
%
%       one      1
%       two      5
%       three    9
c=T(:,1);
disp(c)

%Table slice
%Output:
%              A    B
%              _    _
%
%       one    1    2
```

```
%        two    5    6
s=T(1:2,1:2);
disp(s)
```

Now, we explain how to access items in a table by their names (labels). To access items in table, we use indexes in a form of `( {'label_i', 'label_j', ...} , {'label_m', 'label_n', ...} )`, which `{'label_i', 'label_j', ...}` shows row names (labels), and `{'label_m', 'label_n', ...}` shows column names (labels).

Here are general syntaxes show how to access items in a table by their labels:

Syntax

```
results_table = Table( {'label_i', 'label_j', ...}, {'label_m', 'label_n', ...} )
results_array = Table{ {'label_i', 'label_j', ...}, {'label_m', 'label_n', ...} }
```

Here are examples show how to access items in a table using row and column names (labels).

```
%Table first Row
%Output:
%               A    B    C    D
%               _    _    _    _
%
%        one    1    2    3    4
r=T('one',:);
disp(r)

%Table first column
%Output:
%                 A
%                 _
%
%        one      1
%        two      5
%        three    9
c=T(:,'A');
disp(c)

%Table slice
%Output:
%                  A    B     C
```

```
%                    _    __    __
%
%         one        1     2     3
%         two        5     6     7
%         three      9    10    11
s=T({'one','two','three'},{'A','B','C'});
disp(s)
```

If we only need to access values from a single column in a table, we can use a table name followed by a dot notation followed by a column label. Note that, in such cases, the returned result is an array, not a table. Here is an example shows how to access the values of one column in a table.

```
%Return values of column 'A' as an array
%Output:
%        1
%        5
%        9
c=T.A; %Or c=T.('A'); Or c=T.(1);
disp(c)
```

We can also use logical indexing in tables. It is in particular helpful to select all rows of a table that all satisfy a condition in a given column. Here is an example shows how to use logical indexing. In this example, we use the logical indexing to select all rows in a table that their values in a column 'A' are larger than 4.

```
%Logical indexing
%Output:
%                    A    B     C     D
%                    _    __    __    __
%
%         two        5     6     7     8
%         three      9    10    11    12
rows=T.A>4; %Or rows=T.('A')>4;
b=T(rows,:);
disp(b)
```

6.5 Change Item Contents in Tables

After a MATLAB table is created, it is very probable that we may need to make some changes in table data while we are working with it. For this purpose, table items are accessed by their indexes or labels, and if required, their values can be changed or updated. Note that, if we use parentheses as `( ... , ... )` for indexing, then assigned values to an existing table should be a table or cell array, however, if we use curly brackets as `{ ... , ... }` for indexing, the assigned values should be an array.

Here are examples show how to change the values of a table. In these examples, we use positions of items for indexing and slicing.

```
%Create table
%Output:
%              A    B    C
%              _    _    _
%
%      one     1    2    3
%      two     4    5    6
row_label={'one';'two'}; %Row labels
col_label={'A','B','C'}; %Column labels
val=[[1,2,3];[4,5,6]];   %Data
T=array2table(val, 'VariableNames', col_label, 'RowNames', row_label);
disp(T)

%Use an index to change values of the 1st column to 0
%Output:
%              A    B    C
%              _    _    _
%
%      one     0    2    3
%      two     0    5    6
T(:,1)={0;0}; %Or T{:,1}=[0;0]; Or T(:,1)=array2table([0;0]);
disp(T)

%Use an index to change values of the 1st row to 0
%Output:
%              A    B    C
%              _    _    _
%
%      one     0    0    0
%      two     4    5    6
T=array2table(val, 'VariableNames', col_label, 'RowNames', row_label);
T(1,:)={0,0,0}; %Or T{1,:}=[0,0,0]; Or T(1,:)=array2table([0,0,0]);
disp(T)
```

```
%Use slicing to change values of the 1st column to 10
%and 2nd column to 100
%Output:
%             A      B     C
%             __     ___   _
%
%      one    10     100   3
%      two    10     100   6
T=array2table(val, 'VariableNames', col_label, 'RowNames', row_label);
T(:,1:2)=array2table([[10,100];[10,100]]);
%Or T{:,1:2}=[[10,100];[10,100]];
disp(T)
```

Here are examples show how to change the values of a table. This time, we use labels of items for indexing and slicing.

```
%Create table
%Output:
%             A    B    C
%             _    _    _
%
%      one    1    2    3
%      two    4    5    6
row_label={'one';'two'}; %Row labels
col_label={'A','B','C'}; %Column labels
val=[[1,2,3];[4,5,6]];   %Data
T=array2table(val, 'VariableNames', col_label, 'RowNames', row_label);
disp(T)

%Use a label to change values of the 1st column to 0
%Output:
%             A    B    C
%             _    _    _
%
%      one    0    2    3
%      two    0    5    6
T(:,'A')={0;0};
%Or T{:,'A'}=[0;0]; Or T.A=[0;0]; Or T(:,'A')=array2table([0;0]);
disp(T)

%Use a label to change values of the 1st row to 0
%Output:
```

```
%               A    B    C
%               _    _    _
%
%       one     0    0    0
%       two     4    5    6
T=array2table(val, 'VariableNames', col_label, 'RowNames', row_label);
T('one',:)={0,0,0};
%Or T{'one',:}=[0,0,0]; Or T('one',:)=array2table([0,0,0]);
disp(T)

%Use slicing to change values of the 1st column to 10
%and 2nd column to 100
%Output:
%               A      B      C
%               __    ___     _
%
%       one     10    100     3
%       two     10    100     6
T=array2table(val, 'VariableNames', col_label, 'RowNames', row_label);
T(:,{'A','B'})=array2table([[10,100];[10,100]]);
%Or T{:,{'A','B'}}=[[10,100];[10,100]];
disp(T)
```

Chapter 7
Working with Table

In this chapter, it is described how to manipulate and work with MATLAB tables. First, MATLAB functions and table properties are explained. Then, methods to append, insert, and delete table items are presented. After that, it is described how to concatenate tables. Next, it is explained how to merge and join tables. It follows by descriptions of how to rearrange columns in a table. Next, arithmetic and element-wise operation are explained. Then, it is shown how to apply a function to data in a table. After that, it is described how to group similar data together. Then, it is shown how to clean and fill missing data. At the end, a rolling window is explained.

7.1 Functions and Properties

MATLAB has a series of functions that allow us to work with tables. Each of these functions is developed for a particular purpose. For example, MATLAB has a function named `readtable` which reads data from a file and returns a table containing these data.

To use a MATLAB function, we usually pass some data along with required or optional arguments to that function, and the function returns the results. Here is a general syntax shows how to use MATLAB functions:

Syntax

```
results = function(argument1, argument2, ...)
```

As mentioned in an earlier chapter, MATLAB tables have several properties, each provides or specifies a particular table property. For example, a table has properties `table.Properties.RowNames` and `table.Properties.VariableNames` which return row names (labels) and column names (labels) of a table, respectively. Similarly, a table property `table.Variables` returns an array containing data in a table. Note that, `table.Variables` syntax is equivalent to `table{:,:}`.

To use a table property, a table name is followed by a dot and followed by Properties.PropertyName or by PropertyName, depending on which property we use. Here are general syntaxes show how to use a table property:

Syntax

```
results = table.Properties.PropertyName
results = table.PropertyName
```

7.2 Append, Insert, and Delete Single Row or Single Column

After a table is created, we may need to make some changes to a table while working with it. We may append (add), insert, or delete items after a table is created. Here are MATLAB functions and methods to append, insert, or delete a single row or single column from a table:

Function/Method	Description
`table.col_label=[...]`	Add a column named 'col_label' to the end of table
`table.('col_label')=[...]`	Add a column named 'col_label' to the end of table
`Table{:,'col_label'}=[...]`	Add a column named 'col_label' to the end of table
`table(:,'col_label')={...}`	Add a column named 'col_label' to the end of table
`Table{'row_label',:}=[...]`	Add a row named 'row_label' to the end of table
`table('row_label',:)={...}`	Add a row named 'row_label' to the end of table
`addvars`	Insert columns at given location into table
`table.('col_label')=[]`	Remove a column named 'col_label' from table
`table.col_label=[]`	Remove a column named 'col_label' from table
`table('row_label',:)=[]`	Remove a row named 'row_label' from table
`removevars`	Remove columns from table

It is very likely that we may need to add a single row or column to an existing table when we are working with tables. The simplest method to add a single column to the end of a table is to assign values to a column with a new name (label). Note that, we may use any acceptable indexing to assign values to a column with a new name (label).

Here is an example shows how to add a new column to a table. In this example, we have a table with a size of (2,2), row names (labels) of 'one', 'two', column names (labels) of 'A', 'B', and numerical values of [[1,2];[4,5]]. Now, we add a column 'C' with values [3;6] to this table.

```
%Create table
%Output:
%               A     B
%               _     _
%
%        one    1     2
%        two    4     5
row_label={'one';'two'}; %Row labels
col_label={'A','B'};     %Column labels
val=[[1,2];[4,5]];       %Data
T=array2table(val, 'VariableNames', col_label, 'RowNames', row_label);
disp(T)

%Add column 'C' as [3;6] to table
%Output:
%               A     B     C
%               _     _     _
%
%        one    1     2     3
```

```
%           two     4     5     6
T.C=[3;6]; %Or T.('C')=[3;6]; Or T{:,'C'}=[3;6]; Or T(:,'C')={3;6};
disp(T)
```

The simplest method to add a single row to the end of a table is to assign values to a row with a new name (label). Note that, we may use any acceptable indexing to assign values to a row with a new name (label).

Here is an example shows how to add a new row to a table. In this example, we have a table with a size of (2,2), row names (labels) of 'one', 'two', column names (labels) of 'A', 'B', and numerical values of [[1,2];[3,4]]. Now, we add a row 'three' with values [5,6] to this table.

```
%Create table
%Output:
%                   A     B
%                   _     _
%
%           one     1     2
%           two     3     4
row_label={'one','two'}; %Row labels
col_label={'A','B'};     %Column labels
val=[[1,2];[3,4]];       %Data
T=array2table(val, 'VariableNames', col_label, 'RowNames', row_label);
disp(T)

%Add row 'three' as [5,6] to table
%Output:
%                     A     B
%                     _     _
%
%           one       1     2
%           two       3     4
%           three     5     6
T{'three',:}=[5,6]; %Or T('three',:)={5,6};
disp(T)
```

Note that, when we add a new column or new row to the end of a table by assigning values to this column or row, we can use numerical indexing as well if we do not need to give a name (label) to this new column or row.

If we need to insert a single column at a specific location into an existing table, we can use the **addvars** function. Here are general syntaxes show how to insert a column into a table at a given index:

Syntax

```
T2 = addvars(T1, var1, 'Before', location, 'NewVariableNames', newNames)
T2 = addvars(T1, var1, 'After', location, 'NewVariableNames', newNames)
```

The **T1** is an existing table that a new column is inserted into that. The **var1** contains values of an inserted column. The **'Before'** and **'After'** define if a new column to be inserted to the left or right of a given position in a table. The **location** defines a position that a new column is inserted into a table. Note that, if an optional **'Before', location** pair or **'After', location** pair are not defined, then a new column is added (appended) to the end of a table. The **'NewVariableNames'** indicates that the following variable contains a variable name (label) of an inserted column. The **newNames** is a cell array of character vectors or a string array that defines a name (label) of an inserted column.

Here is an example of inserting a column at a given location into a table. In this example, we have a table with columns 'A' as [1;4] and 'C' as [4;6]. Now, we insert a column 'B' with data [2;5] as the second column with a position of 2 to this table.

```
%Create table
%Output:
%               A    C
%               _    _
%
%        one    1    3
%        two    4    6
row_label={'one';'two'}; %Row labels
col_label={'A','C'};     %Column labels
val=[[1,3];[4,6]];       %Data
T=array2table(val, 'VariableNames', col_label, 'RowNames', row_label);
disp(T)

%Insert column 'B' as [2;5] to table
%Output:
%               A    B    C
%               _    _    _
%
```

```
%        one    1    2    3
%        two    4    5    6
B_label={'B'}; %Column B label
B_val=[2;5];   %Column B data
T = addvars(T, B_val, 'After', 'A', 'NewVariableNames', B_label)
disp(T)
```

The simplest method to remove a single row or column from a table is to assign an empty array as `[]` to that row or column. Note that, we can delete an entire variable by using the MATLAB `clear table` statement.

Here is an example shows how to remove a column from a table. In this example, we have a table with a size of (2,3), row names (labels) of 'one', 'two', column names (labels) of 'A', 'B', 'C', and numerical values of [[1,2,3];[4,5,6]]. Now, we remove a column 'C' from this table. Then we use the clear statement to delete an entire table.

```
%Create table
%Output:
%               A    B    C
%               _    _    _
%
%        one    1    2    3
%        two    4    5    6
row_label={'one';'two'}; %Row labels
col_label={'A','B','C'}; %Column labels
val=[[1,2,3];[4,5,6]];   %Data
T=array2table(val, 'VariableNames', col_label, 'RowNames', row_label);
disp(T)

%Remove column 'C' from table
%Output:
%               A    B
%               _    _
%
%        one    1    2
%        two    4    5
T.C=[]; %Or T.('C')=[]; Or T.(3)=[];
disp(T)

%Delete a table (an entire variable)
clear T
```

7.3 Append, Insert, and Delete Multiple Rows or Multiple Columns

We may append (add), insert, or delete multiple items after a table is created. Here are MATLAB functions and methods to append, insert, or delete multiple rows or columns from a table:

Function/Method	Description
`Table{:,{'label_m',...}}=[...]`	Add columns named 'label_m', ... to the end of table
`Table{{'label_i',...},:}=[...]`	Add rows named 'label_i', ... to the end of table
`addvars`	Insert columns at given location into table
`table(:,{'label_m',...})=[]`	Remove columns from table
`table({'label_i',...},:)=[]`	Remove rows from table
`removevars`	Remove columns from table

In general, adding multiple columns or rows to the end of a table is similar to adding one column or row to the end of a table. The simplest method to add multiple columns to the end of a table is to assign values to columns with new names (labels).

Here is an example of adding columns to a table. In this example, we have a table with columns 'A' as [1;5] and 'B' as [2;6]. Now, we add columns 'C' as [3;7] and 'D' as [4;8] to this table.

```
%Create table
%Output:
%              A    B
%              _    _
%
%       one    1    2
%       two    5    6
row_label={'one';'two'}; %Row labels
col_label={'A','B'};     %Column labels
val=[[1,2];[5,6]];       %Data
T=array2table(val, 'VariableNames', col_label, 'RowNames', row_label);
disp(T)

%Add columns 'C' as [3;7] and 'D' as [4;8] to table
%Output:
%              A    B    C    D
%              _    _    _    _
%
%       one    1    2    3    4
%       two    5    6    7    8
```

```
T{:,{'C','D'}}=[[3,4];[7,8]];
%Or T(:,{'C','D'})=array2table([[3,4];[7,8]]);
disp(T)
```

Similarly, to add multiple rows to the end of a table, we can assign values to rows with new names (labels). Here is an example of adding rows to the end of a table. In this example, we have a table with rows 'one' as [1,2] and 'two' as [3,4]. Now, we add rows 'three' as [5,6] and 'four' as [7,8] to this table.

```
%Create table
%Output:
%                A    B
%                _    _
%
%       one      1    2
%       two      3    4
row_label={'one';'two'}; %Row labels
col_label={'A','B'};     %Column labels
val=[[1,2];[3,4]];       %Data
T=array2table(val, 'VariableNames', col_label, 'RowNames', row_label);
disp(T)

%Add rows 'three' as [5,6] and 'four' as [7,8] to table
%Output:
%                  A    B
%                  _    _
%
%       one        1    2
%       two        3    4
%       three      5    6
%       four       7    8
T{{'three','four'},:}=[[5,6];[7,8]];
%Or T({'three','four'},:)=array2table([[5,6];[7,8]]);
disp(T)
```

Note that, when we add new columns or new rows to the end of a table by assigning values to these columns or rows, we can use numerical indexing as well if we do not need to give names (labels) to these new columns or rows.

To insert multiple columns at a specific location to an existing table, we can use the `addvars` function. Here are general syntaxes show how to insert columns to a table:

Syntax

```
T2 = addvars(T1, var1, ..., varN, 'Before',location, 'NewVariableNames',newNames)
T2 = addvars(T1, var1, ..., varN, 'After',location, 'NewVariableNames',newNames)
```

The `T1` is an existing table that new columns are inserted into that. The `var1`, ..., `varN` contain values of inserted columns. The `'Before'` and `'After'` define if new columns to be inserted to the left or right of a given position in a table. The `location` defines a position that new columns are inserted into a table. Note that, if an optional `'Before', location` pair or `'After', location` pair are not defined, then new columns are added (appended) to the end of a table. The `'NewVariableNames'` indicates that the following variable contains variable names (labels) of inserted columns. The `newNames` is a cell array of character vectors or a string array that defines names (labels) of inserted columns.

Here is an example of inserting columns at a given location into a table. In this example, we have a table with columns 'A' as [1;5] and 'B' as [2;6]. Now, we add columns 'C' as [3;7] and 'D' as [4;8] to this table.

```
%Create table
%Output:
%               A    B
%               _    _
%
%       one     1    2
%       two     5    6
row_label={'one';'two'}; %Row labels
col_label={'A','B'};     %Column labels
val=[[1,2];[5,6]];       %Data
T=array2table(val, 'VariableNames', col_label, 'RowNames', row_label);
disp(T)

%Add columns 'C' as [3;7] and 'D' as [4;8] to table
%Output:
%               A    B    C    D
%               _    _    _    _
%
%       one     1    2    3    4
%       two     5    6    7    8
C_val=[3;7];           %Column C data
D_val=[4;8];           %Column D data
```

```
new_labels={'C','D'}; %Column C and D labels
T = addvars(T, C_val, D_val, ...
    'After', 'B', 'NewVariableNames', new_labels)
disp(T)
```

Also, we may use the `cat`, `innerjoin`, and `outerjoin` functions to add a table to another table. For more details on adding a table to another table, refer to concatenate, merge, and join sections.

If we need to remove single or multiple rows or columns from a table, we can assign an empty array as `[]` to those rows or columns. Another method to remove single or multiple columns is to use the `removevars` function. Here is a general syntax shows how to remove columns from a table:

Syntax

```
T2 = removevars(T1, vars)
```

The `T1` is an existing table that its columns to be removed. The `vars` is a cell array of character vectors or a string array that defines names (labels) of columns to be removed.

Here is an example of removing rows and columns from a table. In this example, we have a table with a size of (3,4), row names (labels) of 'one', 'two', 'three', column names (labels) of 'A', 'B', 'C', 'D', and data of [[1,2,3,4];[5,6,7,8];[9,10,11,12]]. Now, we remove a row 'three' and columns 'B' and 'C' from this table.

```
%Create table
%Output:
%                 A    B    C    D
%                 _    __   __   __
%
%      one        1     2    3    4
%      two        5     6    7    8
%      three      9    10   11   12
row_label={'one';'two';'three'};          %Row labels
col_label={'A','B','C','D'};              %Column labels
val=[[1,2,3,4];[5,6,7,8];[9,10,11,12]]; %Data
T=array2table(val, 'VariableNames', col_label, 'RowNames', row_label);
disp(T)

%Remove row 'three' and columns 'B' and 'C' from table
```

```
%Output:
%              A    D
%              _    _
%
%       one    1    4
%       two    5    8
T('three',:)=[];
T=removevars(T, {'B','C'});
disp(T)
```

7.4 Concatenate Tables

In MATLAB, two or more tables can be added together to create a new table. We can add tables by using the following function or by using their equivalent square brackets:

Function	Square Brackets	Description
`cat`		Concatenate tables (arrays) along an existing dimension
`horzcat`	`[..., ..., ...]`	Concatenate tables (arrays) horizontally (column-wise)
`vertcat`	`[...; ...; ...]`	Concatenate tables (arrays) vertically (row-wise)

To explain how any of these functions works, let's illustrate how two tables may be concatenated together. Consider two tables with a size of (3,2). First, we show how these two tables may be concatenated along their first dimension. The resulted table has a size of (6,2).

1st table

	A	B
0	A1	B1
1	A2	B2
2	A3	B3

2nd table

	A	B
3	A4	B4
4	A5	B5
5	A6	B6

Concatenated tables along 1st dim.

	A	B
0	A1	B1
1	A2	B2
2	A3	B3
3	A4	B4
4	A5	B5
5	A6	B6

Now, we show how these two tables can be concatenated along their second dimension. The resulted table has a size of (3,4).

1st table

	A	B
0	A1	B1
1	A2	B2
2	A3	B3

2nd table

	C	D
0	C1	D1
1	C2	D2
2	C3	D3

Concatenated tables along 2nd dim.

	A	B	C	D
0	A1	B1	C1	D1
1	A2	B2	C2	D2
2	A3	B3	C3	D3

Here is a general syntax shows how to use the `cat` function to concatenate several tables:

Syntax

```
concatenated_table = cat(dim, A1, A2, ..., An)
```

The `dim` defines an existing dimension that tables (or arrays) are concatenated along that dimension. The `dim` is 1 for the first dimension, 2 for the second dimension, and so on. Note that, if `dim` is 1 then tables are concatenated along the rows, and if `dim` is 2 then tables are concatenated along the columns. The `A1`, `A2`, ..., `An` define tables (or arrays) to be joined. Note that, all `A1`, `A2`, ..., `An` tables (arrays) should have the same length in all dimensions, except along a dimension that tables (arrays) are concatenated together.

Functions `horzcat` and `vertcat` are special cases of the cat function. The `horzcat` function joins tables (arrays) horizontally (column-wise) and the `vertcat` function joins tables (arrays) vertically (row-wise). Here are general syntaxes show how to use these functions:

Syntax

```
horizontally_concatenated_table = horzcat(A1, A2, ..., An)
vertically_concatenated_table = vertcat(A1, A2, ..., An)
```

The **A1**, **A2**, ..., **An** are tables (arrays) to be concatenated.

Similarly, we can use square brackets to concatenate tables. The `[A1, A2, ..., An]` concatenates tables (arrays) horizontally (column-wise) and the `[A1; A2; ...; An]` concatenates tables (arrays) vertically (row-wise). Here are general syntaxes show how to use square brackets to concatenate tables (arrays):

Syntax

```
horizontally_joined_array = [A1, A2, ..., An]
vertically_joined_array = [A1; A2; ...; An]
```

The **A1**, **A2**, ..., **An** are tables (arrays) to be concatenated.

Here is an example shows how to use the cat function. Consider tables T1 and T2, both with a size of (3,2). All data in T1 are 1 and all data in T2 are 2. Now, we use the cat function to concatenate these tables along their first dimension (dim is 1) and create a new table with a size of (6,2).

```
%Create table
%Output:
%                A    B
%                _    _
%
%       one      1    1
%       two      1    1
%       three    1    1
row_label_1={'one';'two';'three'}; %Row labels
col_label_1={'A','B'};             %Column labels
val_1=[[1,1];[1,1];[1,1]];         %Data
T1=array2table(val_1, ...
    'VariableNames', col_label_1, 'RowNames', row_label_1);
disp(T1)
```

```
%Create table
%Output:
%              A    B
%              _    _
%
%       four   2    2
%       five   2    2
%       six    2    2
row_label_2={'four';'five';'six'}; %Row labels
col_label_2={'A','B'};             %Column labels
val_2=[[2,2];[2,2];[2,2]];         %Data
T2=array2table(val_2, ...
    'VariableNames', col_label_2, 'RowNames', row_label_2);
disp(T2)

%Concatenate tables along rows
%Output:
%              A    B
%              _    _
%
%       one    1    1
%       two    1    1
%       three  1    1
%       four   2    2
%       five   2    2
%       six    2    2
T_concat=cat(1,T1,T2);
%Or T_concat=[T1;T2]; Or T_concat=vertcat(T1,T2);
disp(T_concat)
```

Now, we concatenate two tables with the cat function along their second dimension (dim is 2). Consider tables T1 and T3, both with a size of (3,2). All data in T1 are 1 and all data in T3 are 3. We use the cat function to concatenate these tables along their second dimension (dim is 2) and create a new table with a size of (3,4).

```
%Create table
%Output:
%              A    B
%              _    _
%
%       one    1    1
%       two    1    1
```

```
%        three    1    1
row_label_1={'one';'two';'three'}; %Row labels
col_label_1={'A','B'};             %Column labels
val_1=[[1,1];[1,1];[1,1]];         %Data
T1=array2table(val_1, ...
    'VariableNames', col_label_1, 'RowNames', row_label_1);
disp(T1)

%Create table
%Output:
%                 C    D
%                 _    _
%
%        one      3    3
%        two      3    3
%        three    3    3
row_label_3={'one';'two';'three'}; %Row labels
col_label_3={'C','D'};             %Column labels
val_3=[[3,3];[3,3];[3,3]];         %Data
T3=array2table(val_3, ...
    'VariableNames', col_label_3, 'RowNames', row_label_3);
disp(T3)

%Concatenate tables along columns
%Output:
%                 A    B    C    D
%                 _    _    _    _
%
%        one      1    1    3    3
%        two      1    1    3    3
%        three    1    1    3    3
T_concat=cat(2,T1,T3);
%Or T_concat=[T1,T3]; Or T_concat=horzcat(T1,T3);
disp(T_concat)
```

7.5 Merge and Join Tables

In MATLAB, two tables can be merged or joined together to create a new table. We can merge or join tables by using the following functions:

Function	Description
`innerjoin`	Inner join two tables
`outerjoin`	Outer join two tables
`join`	Combine two tables

In general, to merge two tables, we choose one column from each table to be compared. These two columns are called key columns. In the merging process, these two columns are compared with each other and then their comparison results are used as a base for merging.

The `innerjoin` function merges tables based on similar (overlapped) key values in the key columns of both tables. The `outerjoin` function merges tables based on all key values in the key columns of both tables. The `join` function merges tables based on key values in the key column of a left table, providing all key values from a left table also presented in a right table. Here are general syntaxes show how to use join functions to merge two tables:

Syntax

```
merged_table = innerjoin(Tleft, Tright, 'Name1', Value1, ..., 'NameN', ValueN)
merged_table = outerjoin(Tleft, Tright, 'Name1', Value1, ..., 'NameN', ValueN)
merged_table = join(Tleft, Tright, 'Name1', Value1, ..., 'NameN', ValueN)
```

The `Tleft` and `Tright` define a left (1st) and right (2nd) tables to be joined together.

The `'Name1', Value1`, ..., `'NameN', ValueN` define optional comma-separated Name-Value pair arguments. In Name-Value pair arguments, the `'Name'` specifies a name of the optional argument, while the `Value` contains values to be assigned to this optional argument. Here is a list of common Name-Value pair arguments to be used in these functions:

'Name'	Value	Description
`'Keys'`	`'col_label'`	Specify name (label) of a key column
	`col_index`	Specify index of a key column
	`'Row'`	Use row names (labels) as a key column
`'LeftKeys'`	`'col_label'`	Specify name (label) of a key column in left table
	`col_index`	Specify index of a key column in left table
`'RightKeys'`	`'col_label'`	Specify name (label) of a key column in right table
	`col_index`	Specify index of a key column in right table
`'MergeKeys'`	`false`	Outer joined table contains two key columns
	`true`	Outer joined table contains one key column
`'Type'`	`'full'`	Outer join using key value from both tables

`'left'`	Outer join using key value from left table
`'right'`	Outer join using key value from right table

The `'Keys'` defines a key column in both left and right tables that are used as a base to compare and merge two tables. If we use a column name (label) to define a key column, both tables should have a column with that name (label). The `'Row'` defines to merge tables based on the row names of two tables.

The `'LeftKeys'` and `'RightKeys'` define a key column in the left and right tables that are used to compare and merge two tables. This is helpful if we need to use a different column name (label) from each table for comparison.

The `'MergeKeys'` defines if a merged table by the **`outerjoin`** function has one merged key column or has two separate key columns, each represents one table.

The `'Type'` defines how to outer join two tables. The `'full'` defines to include all key values from both tables. The `'left'` defines to include all key values from a left table. The `'right'` defines to include all key values from a right table.

To explain how the **`innerjoin`** and **`outerjoin`** functions work, let's illustrate how two tables may be merged together. Consider two tables with a size of (2,3). Both tables have a column with a similar label 'key'.

T_left

	key	A	B
1	X	A1	B1
2	Y	A2	B2

T_right

	key	C	D
3	Y	C2	D2
4	Z	C3	D3

Now, we show how these two tables may be merged with the **`innerjoin`** function and **`'Keys','key'`**. In this case, first, the **`innerjoin`** function finds columns with similar names (labels) in both tables. Here, both tables have a column with a name (label) 'key'. Then, the **`innerjoin`** function chooses and merges rows in these tables that have the same values in their 'key' columns. Here, both tables have a 'Y' in their 'key' columns, and therefore, rows associated with them are merged.

key

innerjoin, 'Keys','key'

T_left	T_right
X	
Y	Y
	Z

key	A	B	C	D
Y	A2	B2	C2	D2

Now, tables are merged with the `outerjoin` function, `'Keys','key'`, and `'MergeKeys',true`. Again, first, the `outerjoin` function finds columns with similar names (labels) in both tables. Here, both tables have a column with a name (label) 'key'. Then, the `outerjoin` function merges all rows in these tables based on their values in their 'key' columns.

key

outerjoin, 'Keys','key'
'MergeKeys',true

T_left	T_right
X	
Y	Y
	Z

key	A	B	C	D
X	A1	B1	NaN	NaN
Y	A2	B2	C2	D2
Z	NaN	NaN	C3	D3

Here, tables are merged with the `outerjoin` function, `'Keys','key'`, `'Type','left'`, and `'MergeKeys',true`. First, the `outerjoin` function finds columns with similar names (labels) in both tables. Here, both tables have a column with a name (label) 'key'. Then, the `outerjoin` function chooses and merges rows in these tables based on values in the 'key' column of the left table.

key

outerjoin, 'Keys','key'
'Type','left', 'MergeKeys',true

T_left	T_right
X	
Y	Y
	Z

key	A	B	C	D
X	A1	B1	NaN	NaN
Y	A2	B2	C2	D2

Now, tables are merged with the `outerjoin` function, `'Keys','key'`, `'Type','right'`, and `'MergeKeys',true`. First, the `outerjoin` function finds columns with similar names (labels) in both tables. Here, both tables have a column with a name (label) 'key'. Then, the `outerjoin` function chooses and merges rows in these tables based on values in the 'key' column of the right table.

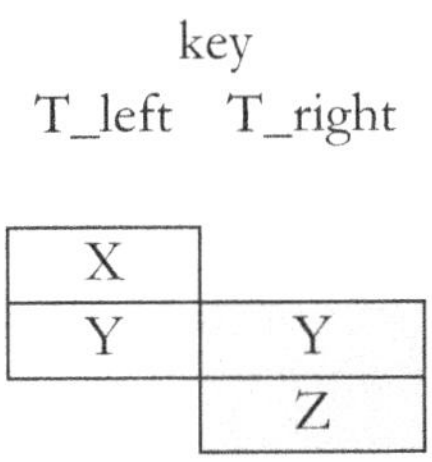

outerjoin, 'Keys','key'
'Type','right', 'MergeKeys',true

key	A	B	C	D
Y	A2	B2	C2	D2
Z	NaN	NaN	C3	D3

Here, tables are merged with the `outerjoin` function and `Keys','Row'`. First, the `outerjoin` function finds columns with similar names (labels) in both tables. Here, both tables have a column with a name (label) 'key'. Then, the `outerjoin` function chooses and merges all rows in these tables based on row names (labels) of the left and right tables.

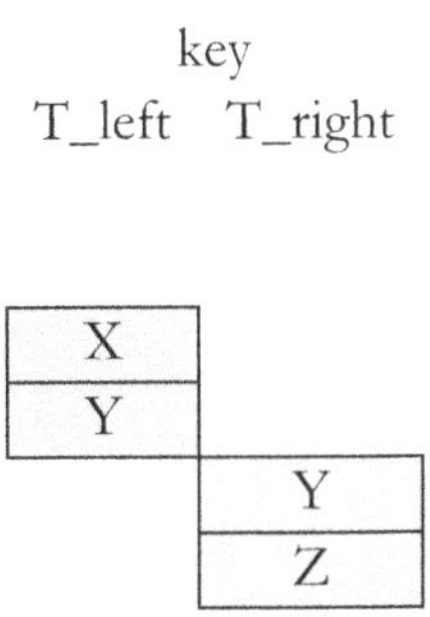

outerjoin, Keys','Row'

	key_left	A	B	key_right	D	D
1	X	A1	B1	NaN	NaN	NaN
2	Y	A2	B2	NaN	NaN	NaN
3	NaN	NaN	NaN	Y	C2	D2
4	NaN	NaN	NaN	Z	C3	D3

Here are examples that show previous demonstrations.

```
%Create left table
%Output:
%             key       A         B
%           _____    ______    ______
%
%       1   {'X'}    {'A1'}    {'B1'}
%       2   {'Y'}    {'A2'}    {'B2'}
row_label_left={'1';'2'};           %Row labels
col_label_left={'key','A','B'}; %Column labels
col1_left={'X';'Y'};                %Data in 1st column
col2_left={'A1';'A2'};              %Data in 2nd column
col3_left={'B1';'B2'};              %Data in 3rd column
T_left=table(col1_left, col2_left, col3_left, ...
    'VariableNames', col_label_left, 'RowNames', row_label_left);
```

```
disp(T_left)

%Create right table
%Output:
%            key        C          D
%           _____     ______     ______
%
%      3    {'Y'}     {'C2'}     {'D2'}
%      4    {'Z'}     {'C3'}     {'D3'}
row_label_right={'3';'4'};         %Row labels
col_label_right={'key','C','D'}; %Column labels
col1_right={'Y';'Z'};             %Data in 1st column
col2_right={'C2';'C3'};           %Data in 2nd column
col3_right={'D2';'D3'};           %Data in 3rd column
T_right=table(col1_right, col2_right, col3_right, ...
    'VariableNames', col_label_right, 'RowNames', row_label_right);
disp(T_right)

%Merge tables with innerjoin, 'Keys','key''
%Output:
%       key       A          B          C          D
%      _____    ______     ______     ______     ______
%
%      {'Y'}    {'A2'}     {'B2'}     {'C2'}     {'D2'}
T_merged=innerjoin(T_left,T_right,'Keys','key');
disp(T_merged)

%Merge tables with outerjoin', 'Keys','key', 'MergeKeys',true
%Output:
%       key          A               B               C               D
%      _____    __________     __________     __________     __________
%
%      {'X'}    {'A1'     }    {'B1'     }    {0×0 char}     {0×0 char}
%      {'Y'}    {'A2'     }    {'B2'     }    {'C2'     }    {'D2'     }
%      {'Z'}    {0×0 char}     {0×0 char}     {'C3'     }    {'D3'     }
T_merged=outerjoin(T_left,T_right,'Keys','key','MergeKeys',true);
disp(T_merged)

%Merge tables with outerjoin, 'Keys','key', 'Type','left', 'MergeKeys',true
%Output:
%       key       A         B           C             D
%      _____    _____     _____     __________     __________
%
```

```
%       {'X'}    {'A1'}    {'B1'}    {0×0 char}    {0×0 char}
%       {'Y'}    {'A2'}    {'B2'}    {'C2'    }    {'D2'    }
T_merged=outerjoin(T_left,T_right, ...
    'Keys','key','Type','left','MergeKeys',true);
disp(T_merged)

%Merge tables with outerjoin, 'Keys','key', 'Type','right', 'MergeKeys',true
%Output:
%        key         A            B           C          D
%       _____    __________   __________   _______   _______
%
%       {'Y'}    {'A2'     }  {'B2'     }  {'C2'}    {'D2'}
%       {'Z'}    {0×0 char}   {0×0 char}   {'C3'}    {'D3'}
T_merged=outerjoin(T_left,T_right, ...
    'Keys','key','Type','right','MergeKeys',true);
disp(T_merged)

%Merge tables with outerjoin, 'Keys','Row'
%Output:
%      key_T_left      A           B         key_T_right      C            D
%      __________   __________  __________   ___________  __________   __________
%
%   1  {'X'      } {'A1'     } {'B1'     }  {0×0 char}   {0×0 char}  {0×0 char}
%   2  {'Y'      } {'A2'     } {'B2'     }  {0×0 char}   {0×0 char}  {0×0 char}
%   3  {0×0 char}  {0×0 char}  {0×0 char}   {'Y'      }  {'C2'     } {'D2'     }
%   4  {0×0 char}  {0×0 char}  {0×0 char}   {'Z'      }  {'C3'     } {'D3'     }
T_merged=outerjoin(T_left,T_right,'Keys','Row');
disp(T_merged)
```

Remember, if we have only one column with similar labels in both tables, then we can skip defining `'Keys','col_label'`. However, if we have more than one column with similar labels in both tables, we can use `'Keys','col_label'` to tell the `innerjoin` or `outerjoin` function which overlapping column is the base of merging. For example, assume we have two tables that both have three columns with similar labels 'key_1', 'key_2', and 'key_3'. Now, if we want these tables merged based on values in columns 'key_1', we use `'Keys','key_1'`. Similarly, if we want to these tables merged based on values in columns 'key_1' and 'key_2', we use `'Keys',{'key_1', 'key_2'}`, and so on.

7.6 Rearrange Columns

We can rearrange columns of a table in MATLAB. This allows us to change an existing table to match new names (labels). Here is a function to rearrange table columns:

Function	Description
`movevars`	Move columns in table

Here are general syntaxes show how to rearrange table columns:

Syntax

```
rearranged_table = movevars(T1, vars, 'Before', location)
rearranged_table = movevars(T1, vars, 'After', location)
```

The `T1` defines a table that its columns to be rearranged. The `vars` defines column names (labels) or indexes to be moved to a new location. The `'Before'` and `'After'` define if columns to be moved to the left or right of a new location. The `location` defines a name or index of a new location that columns are moved to that.

To show how to rearrange table columns, first, we create a table with a size of (3,3), row names (labels) of 'one', 'two', 'three', column names (labels) of 'A', 'B', 'C', and data of [[1,2,3];[4,5,6];[7,8,9]].

```
%Create table
%Output:
%                 A    B    C
%                 _    _    _
%
%       one       1    2    3
%       two       4    5    6
%       three     7    8    9
row_label={'one';'two';'three'}; %Row labels
col_label={'A','B','C'};         %Column labels
val=[[1,2,3];[4,5,6];[7,8,9]];   %Data
T=array2table(val, 'VariableNames', col_label, 'RowNames', row_label);
disp(T)
```

Here is an example of how to rearrange columns in a table. In this example, we rearrange columns by exchanging a place of a column 'A' with a column 'B'.

```
%Rearrange table columns
%Output:
%                 B    A    C
```

```
%                    _    _    _
%
%        one         2    1    3
%        two         5    4    6
%        three       8    7    9
T_rearranged = movevars(T, 'A', 'After', 'B');
%Or T_rearranged = movevars(T, 1, 'After', 2);
disp(T_rearranged)
```

To move multiple columns at the same time, we can identify desired columns by their names (labels) in a cell array or by their indexes. Here is an example of how to rearrange multiple columns in a table. In this example, we rearrange columns by moving columns 'A' and 'B' after a column 'C'.

```
%Rearrange table columns
%Output:
%                    C    A    B
%                    _    _    _
%
%        one         3    1    2
%        two         6    4    5
%        three       9    7    8
T_rearranged = movevars(T, {'A','B'}, 'After', 'C');
%Or T_rearranged = movevars(T, [1,2], 'After', 3);
disp(T_rearranged)
```

7.7 Arithmetic and Element-Wise Operation

Typically, we use two types of mathematical operations when we are working with arrays. The first one is operations between scaler and array and the second one is element-wise array operations. For example, consider two arrays `arr_1` and `arr_2`. The `arr_1*10` expression returns element-wise multiplication of `arr_1` by `10`. Similarly, the `arr_1.*arr_2` expression returns element-wise multiplication of `arr_1` by `arr_2`. However, such operations cannot easily be used for tables. One method to use such operations on tables is to use element replacement. To do that, first, we use curly brackets indexing such as `{ ... , ... }` to extract values in a table as an array. Then we apply mathematical operations on these extracted values the same way as we do for arrays. Finally, we replace existing values in a table with these newly calculated ones.

Here is an example of how to perform element-wise operations on MATLAB tables. In this example, we multiply all elements of a table by 3. To do that, first, we extract all values in a table by using `{:,:}` indexing and multiply them by 3. Then we replace existing values in a table with these new values.

```
%Create table
%Output:
%             A    B    C    D
%             _    _    _    _
%
%      one    1    2    3    4
%      two    1    2    3    4
row_label={'one';'two'};      %Row labels
col_label={'A','B','C','D'}; %Column labels
val=[[1,2,3,4];[1,2,3,4]];    %Data
T=array2table(val, 'VariableNames', col_label, 'RowNames', row_label);
disp(T)

%Multiply table T by a scaler 3
%Output:
%             A    B    C    D
%             _    _    _    __
%
%      one    3    6    9    12
%      two    3    6    9    12
T{:,:}=T{:,:}.*3;
disp(T)
```

Another method to use mathematical operations on a table is to apply a function on a table. For more details on how to apply a function to a table refer to the apply function section.

7.8 Apply Function

After we create a table, we may apply a function to its data. Here are methods to apply a function to data in MATLAB table:

Function	Description
`varfun`	Apply function to columns of table
`rowfun`	Apply function to rows of table

Here are general syntaxes show how to use the `varfun` and `rowfun` functions to apply a function to a table:

Syntax

```
B = varfun(func, A)
B = rowfun(func, A)
```

The `func` defines a function to be applied to data. The `A` defines a table that function is applied to that.

To show how to apply a function to data, first, we create a table with a size of (5,1), row names (labels) from 'one' to 'five', a column name (label) of 'A', and data of [1;2;3;4;5].

```
%Create table
%Output:
%                A
%                _
%
%       one      1
%       two      2
%       three    3
%       four     4
%       five     5
row_label={'one';'two';'three';'four';'five'}; %Row labels
col_label={'A'};                               %Column labels
val=[1;2;3;4;5];                               %Data
T=array2table(val, 'VariableNames', col_label, 'RowNames', row_label);
disp(T)
```

Here are examples show how to use the `varfun` function to apply a function to data in this table. In the first example, we define an anonymous function that adds 5 to its input. Then we use this function to add 5 to values of a table. In the second example, we use the `sqrt` function to return a square root of a column in a table. In the third example, we use the `mean` function to get a mean value of a column in a table. Then we use the `sqrt` function to return a square root of this mean value.

```
%Apply anonymous function to table
%Output:
%       Fun_A
%       _____
%
```

```
%           6
%           7
%           8
%           9
%          10
f = @ (x) x+5; %Function
T_new=varfun(f,T);
disp(T_new)

%Apply sqrt function to table
%Output:
%        sqrt_A
%        ______
%
%             1
%        1.4142
%        1.7321
%             2
%        2.2361
T_new=varfun(@ sqrt, T);
disp(T_new)

%Apply sqrt function to table mean
%Output:
%        Fun_A
%        ______
%
%        1.7321
f = @ (x) sqrt(mean(x)); %Function
T_new=varfun(f, T);
disp(T_new)
```

7.9 Group Data

Sometimes we need to work with a subset of data in a dataset that has a particular property. For example, consider we have a table that contains details about the sales of several products. Now, if we want to look into the sales of each product, we can group them based on their name and evaluate each of them separately. Here, grouping sales data helps to split an original dataset into a series of subsets which members in each subset have the same product name. In general, grouping data based on a particular property is beneficial in many analyses. Here are functions to group data in MATLAB tables:

Function	Description
`findgroups`	Group data in table and return group numbers
`groupsummary`	Return properties of each group
`splitapply`	Group data in table and apply function to each group

The **`findgroups`** function groups data in a table and assigns one number to each group. Then, it returns these group numbers. Here is a general syntax shows how to use the **`findgroups`** function to group data in a table:

Syntax

```
G = findgroups(T)
```

The `T` defines a table that its data to be grouped. The **`G`** contains group numbers for each row in a table. For example, all the rows in **`G`** that contain value **`1`** are corresponding to all the rows in a table that fall in the first group. All the rows in **`G`** that contain value **`2`** are corresponding to all the rows in a table that fall in the second group, and so on.

In most cases, we want to group data in a table based on data in one of its columns. To do that, we use that column in the **`findgroups`** function to group data in that particular column and return group numbers for that column. Then we use these group numbers to group data in a table.

To show how to group data in a table, first, we create a table with a size of (9,3), row names (labels) from '1' to '9', column names (labels) of 'A', 'B', 'C'. The column 'A' contains two groups of string data 'one' and 'two'. Similarly, the column 'B' contains three groups of string data 'X', 'Y' and 'Z'. The column 'C' contains numerical values of 10, 20, and 30.

```
%Create table
%Output:
%              A          B       C
%          _______      _____    __
%
%    1     {'one'}      {'X'}    10
%    2     {'one'}      {'Y'}    20
%    3     {'one'}      {'Y'}    20
%    4     {'one'}      {'X'}    10
%    5     {'two'}      {'Z'}    30
%    6     {'two'}      {'X'}    10
%    7     {'two'}      {'Z'}    30
```

```
%       8     {'two'}     {'Z'}     30
%       9     {'two'}     {'X'}     10
row_label={'1';'2';'3';'4';'5';'6';'7';'8';'9'}; %Row labels
col_label={'A','B','C'};                         %Column labels
col1={'one';'one';'one';'one';
      'two';'two';'two';'two';'two'};            %Data in 1st column
col2={'X';'Y';'Y';'X';'Z';'X';'Z';'Z';'X'};      %Data in 2nd column
col3=[10;20;20;10;30;10;30;30;10];               %Data in 3rd column
T=table(col1, col2, col3, 'VariableNames', col_label, 'RowNames',
row_label);
disp(T)
```

Here are examples show how to use the **findgroups** function to group data in this table. Here, first, we group data based on values in a column 'A', then based on values in column 'B', and finally based on values in columns 'A' and 'B'.

```
%Group data based on column 'A'
%Output:
%   Group: 1
%                 A          B       C
%             _______    _____    __
%
%       1     {'one'}     {'X'}     10
%       2     {'one'}     {'Y'}     20
%       3     {'one'}     {'Y'}     20
%       4     {'one'}     {'X'}     10
%
%   Group: 2
%                 A          B       C
%             _______    _____    __
%
%       5     {'two'}     {'Z'}     30
%       6     {'two'}     {'X'}     10
%       7     {'two'}     {'Z'}     30
%       8     {'two'}     {'Z'}     30
%       9     {'two'}     {'X'}     10
G=findgroups(T.A);
for i=1:max(G)
    T_grouped=T(G==i,:);
    disp(['Group: ', num2str(i)])
    disp(T_grouped)
end
```

```
%Group data based on column 'B'
%Output:
%   Group: 1
%              A          B       C
%           _______     _____    __
%
%      1    {'one'}     {'X'}    10
%      4    {'one'}     {'X'}    10
%      6    {'two'}     {'X'}    10
%      9    {'two'}     {'X'}    10
%
%   Group: 2
%              A          B       C
%           _______     _____    __
%
%      2    {'one'}     {'Y'}    20
%      3    {'one'}     {'Y'}    20
%
%   Group: 3
%              A          B       C
%           _______     _____    __
%
%      5    {'two'}     {'Z'}    30
%      7    {'two'}     {'Z'}    30
%      8    {'two'}     {'Z'}    30
G=findgroups(T.B);
for i=1:max(G)
    T_grouped=T(G==i,:);
    disp(['group: ', num2str(i)])
    disp(T_grouped)
end

%Group data based on columns 'A' and 'B'
%Output:
%   Group: 1
%              A          B       C
%           _______     _____    __
%
%      1    {'one'}     {'X'}    10
%      4    {'one'}     {'X'}    10
%
```

```
%   Group: 2
%                 A           B        C
%              _______     ______     __
%
%         2    {'one'}     {'Y'}      20
%         3    {'one'}     {'Y'}      20
%
%   Group: 3
%                 A           B        C
%              _______     ______     __
%
%         6    {'two'}     {'X'}      10
%         9    {'two'}     {'X'}      10
%
%   Group: 4
%                 A           B        C
%              _______     ______     __
%
%         5    {'two'}     {'Z'}      30
%         7    {'two'}     {'Z'}      30
%         8    {'two'}     {'Z'}      30
G=findgroups(T(:,{'A','B'}));
for i=1:max(G)
    T_grouped=T(G==i,:);
    disp(['Group: ', num2str(i)])
    disp(T_grouped)
end
```

To access each group in a table T, we can use the `T( G==group_number , : )` indexing to return a group that matches a given group number. For example, to call all rows in a table T that fall in the first group, we use `T(G==1,:)`.

Here is an example shows how to use the `( G==group_number , : )` indexing to access a group. In this example, first, we group data based on values in a column 'A', and then, we get the first group.

```
%Group by column 'A' and return the first group
%Output:
%                 A           B        C
%              _______     ______     __
%
%         1    {'one'}     {'X'}      10
```

```
%       2    {'one'}    {'Y'}    20
%       3    {'one'}    {'Y'}    20
%       4    {'one'}    {'X'}    10
G=findgroups(T.A);
grouped_one=T(G==1,:);
disp(grouped_one)
```

To access a column in a group, we can use `T( G==group_number , 'column_name' )` indexing. In other words, the way we access a column in a group is similar to how we access a column in a table.

Here is an example shows how to access a column in a group. In this example, first, we group data based on values in a column 'A', and then, we get a column 'C' in a grouped data.

```
%Group by column 'A' and return column 'C'
%Output:
%   Group: 1
%             C
%             __
%
%       1    10
%       2    20
%       3    20
%       4    10
%
%   Group: 2
%             C
%             __
%
%       5    30
%       6    10
%       7    30
%       8    30
%       9    10
G=findgroups(T.A);
for i=1:max(G)
    grouped_C=T(G==i,'C');
    disp(['Group: ', num2str(i)])
    disp(grouped_C)
end
```

To access a row in a group, first, we use the `T( G==group_number , : )` indexing to extract data in a group and then we can use `( row_index , : )` indexing to retrieve a row in that group.

Here is an example shows how to access a row in a group. In this example, first, we group data based on values in a column 'A', and then, we get the third row in each group.

```
%Group by column 'A' and return column 'C'
%Output:
%   Group: 1
%            C
%            __
%
%       1    10
%       2    20
%       3    20
%       4    10
%
%   Group: 2
%            C
%            __
%
%       5    30
%       6    10
%       7    30
%       8    30
%       9    10
%Group by column 'A' and return the 3rd row in each group
%Output:
%   Group: 1
%                A          B       C
%             _______    _____    __
%
%       3    {'one'}    {'Y'}    20
%
%   Group: 2
%                A          B       C
%             _______    _____    __
%
%       7    {'two'}    {'Z'}    30
G=findgroups(T.A);
for i=1:max(G)
    T_grouped=T(G==i,:);
```

```
        grouped_nth=T_grouped(3,:);
        disp(['Group: ', num2str(i)])
        disp(grouped_nth)
    end
```

After we group data, we can use the **groupsummary** function to get the properties of each group. Here is a general syntax shows how to use the **groupsummary** function to get properties of each group:

Syntax

```
groups_summary = groupsummary(T, groupvars)
```

The `T` defines a table that its data to be grouped. The **groupvars** defines column names (labels) that a table to be grouped based on them.

Here is an example shows how to use the **groupsummary** function to get properties of groups.

```
%Group by column 'A' and return descriptive statistics
%Output:
%          A        GroupCount
%       _______    __________
%
%       {'one'}         4
%       {'two'}         5
groups_summary=groupsummary(T,'A');
disp(groups_summary)
```

We can also apply a function to each group. To do that, we use the **splitapply** function. Here is a general syntax shows how to use the **splitapply** function to apply a function to each group:

Syntax

```
Y = splitapply(func, T, G)
```

The `func` defines a function to be applied to each group. Note that, an output of the `func` should be either one scalar (value) or one row array (row vector). The `T` defines a table that its data to be grouped. The `G` defines group numbers that a table to be grouped based on them.

We can apply several MATLAB functions to grouped data and get the properties of each group. Here is a list of some of the available functions to be used with grouped data:

Function	Description
`min`	Return minimum of groups
`max`	Return maximum of groups
`mean`	Return mean of groups
`sum`	Return sum of groups
`std`	Return standard deviation of groups
`var`	Return variance of groups
`size`	Return size of groups
`numel`	Return number of elements in each group

Here are examples show how to apply a function to grouped data. In the first example, we define an anonymous function that squares its inputs and returns their sum. Then, we group a table based on a column 'A'. Next, we use this function to square and sum data in a column 'C' of each group. In the second example, we use the `min` function to return a minimum value of data in a column 'C' of each group. In the third example, we use the `mean` function to get a mean value of data in a column 'C' of each group.

```
%Group by column 'A'
%and apply anonymous function to column 'C' in each group
%Output:
%       15
%       22
f = @ (x) sum(x.^2); %Function
G=findgroups(T.A);
grouped_squared=splitapply(f,T.C,G);
disp(grouped_squared)

%Group by column 'A' and return min of column 'C' in each group
%Output:
%       10
%       10
G=findgroups(T.A);
grouped_min=splitapply(@ min,T.C,G);
disp(grouped_min)

%Group by column 'A' and return mean of column 'C' in each group
%Output:
%       15
```

```
%        22
G=findgroups(T.A);
grouped_mean=splitapply(@ mean,T.C,G);
disp(grouped_mean)
```

Note that, the `varfun` and `rowfun` functions can be used to apply a function to table columns or rows, respectively. They also may be used to apply a function to columns and rows of grouped data by using `'GroupingVariables','Col_Name'` Name-Value pair arguments in those functions.

7.10 Clean and Fill Missing Data

When we are working with real-world data, it is very probable that a series of data points in a dataset are missing or are not acceptable. For example, we may attain air temperature data from a meteorological station. For any reason, a sensor in that station may stop reading for a while or may report unacceptable temperature values such as -999 degrees. In such cases, we need to clean data and replace all missing values. If we know the correct values for missing data, we can simply replace those values. For example, we may attain missing air temperatures from a nearby weather station. However, in general, we do not have correct values for missing data and we need to use numerical methods to estimate and replace those values from existing values.

Here are functions to fill and replace missing data in MATLAB:

Function	Description
`fillmissing`	Fill missing values
`rmmissing`	Remove missing values
`standardizeMissing`	Replace missing values with standard missing values
`ismissing`	Detect missing values

We can use the **`fillmissing`** function to fill missing data with a constant value. Here is a general syntax shows how to use the **`fillmissing`** function to fill missing values with a constant value:

Syntax

```
F = fillmissing(A, 'constant', v)
```

The `A` defines a table (or array) that its missing values to be filled. The `v` defines a value that is used to replace missing data.

We can also use the **fillmissing** function to fill and replace missing data by their neighboring data points. Here is a general syntax shows how to use the **fillmissing** function to fill missing values by adjacent values:

Syntax

```
F = fillmissing(A, method)
```

The **A** defines a table (or array) that its missing values to be filled. The **method** defines how to fill missing data. Here is a list of the available methods that may be used to fill missing data by their neighboring data points:

Method	Description
'previous'	Use previous data point to fill missing values
'next'	Use next data point to fill missing values
'nearest'	Use nearest data point to fill missing values

If the **method** is **'previous'**, it uses a previous data point to fill missing values. It is called forward filling. If the **method** is **'next'**, it uses the next data point to fill missing values. It is called backward filling.

To show how to fill missing data, first, we create a table with a size of (5,1), row names (labels) from 'one' to 'five', a column name (label) of 'A', and data of [1;NaN;NaN;4;5].

```
%Create table
%Output:
%                  A
%                 ___
%
%        one        1
%        two      NaN
%        three    NaN
%        four       4
%        five       5
row_label={'one';'two';'three';'four';'five'}; %Row labels
col_label={'A'};                               %Column labels
val=[1;NaN;NaN;4;5];                           %Data
T=array2table(val, 'VariableNames', col_label, 'RowNames', row_label);
disp(T)
```

First, we use the **ismissing** function to check a table for any missing values. The **ismissing** function returns `logical 1` (`true`) if it detects missing data, otherwise, it returns `logical 0` (`false`).

```
%Check for missing values
%Output:
%        0
%        1
%        1
%        0
%        0
TF=ismissing(T);
disp(TF)
```

Now, we show how to fill missing data in this table. In this example, first, we fill all missing value by 0, then, we fill them with a previous data point by using a 'previous' method, and finally, we fill them with the next data point by using a 'next' method.

```
%Fill missing values with 0
%Output:
%                  A
%                  _
%
%        one       1
%        two       0
%        three     0
%        four      4
%        five      5
T_filled=fillmissing(T,'constant',0);
disp(T_filled)

%Fill missing values with 'previous' method
%Output:
%                  A
%                  _
%
%        one       1
%        two       1
%        three     1
%        four      4
%        five      5
```

```
T_filled=fillmissing(T,'previous');
disp(T_filled)

%Fill missing values with 'next' method
%Output:
%                A
%                _
%
%       one      1
%       two      4
%       three    4
%       four     4
%       five     5
T_filled=fillmissing(T,'next');
disp(T_filled)
```

Another method to fill missing values is to interpolate missing values from their neighboring data points. To do that, we set the method in the `fillmissing` function to one of the interpolating methods. Here is a list of available methods that may be used to interpolate missing data:

Method	Description
`'linear'`	Interpolate missing values using linear interpolation
`'spline'`	Interpolate missing values using piecewise cubic spline interpolation
`'pchip'`	Interpolate missing values using piecewise cubic spline interpolation
`'makima'`	Interpolate missing values using modified Akima cubic Hermite interpolation

Note that, the `fillmissing` function assumes data points are equally spaced unless `'SamplePoints',Sample_Locations` Name-Value pair arguments are used. Here, `Sample_Locations` contains the location of values. We can consider `Sample_Points` as x values assuming values in a table (array) representing y values. Also, we can use `'DataVariables','Col_Name'` Name-Value pair arguments to specify in which column of table missing values to be filled.

Here are examples show how to interpolate missing data in a table. In this example, first, we create a table with a size of (3,1), row names (labels) of '1', '2', '10', a column names (label) of 'A', and data of [10;NaN;100]. Then, we use the `fillmissing` function to interpolate missing values. When we do not use `'SamplePoints',Sample_Locations` pair arguments, the `fillmissing` function assumes data points are equally spaced. When we use `'SamplePoints',Sample_Locations` pair arguments, the `fillmissing` function uses `Sample_Locations` to define space between data points. In the last example, we use row names (indexes) as locations of data.

```
%Create table
%Output:
%              A
%             ___
%
%       1      10
%       2     NaN
%       10    100
row_label={'1';'2';'10'}; %Row labels
col_label={'A'};          %Column labels
val=[10;NaN;100];         %Data
T=array2table(val, 'VariableNames', col_label, 'RowNames', row_label);
disp(T)

%Interpolate missing values with 'linear' method
%Output:
%              A
%             ___
%
%       1      10
%       2      55
%       10    100
T_interpolated=fillmissing(T,'linear');
disp(T_interpolated)

%Interpolate missing values with 'linear' method
%relative to given locations
%Output:
%              A
%             ___
%
%       1      10
%       2      20
%       10    100
row_labels=T.Row; %Row names (indexes)
row_indexes=cellfun(@ str2num, row_labels); %Convert to numbers
T_interpolated=fillmissing(T,'linear','SamplePoints',row_indexes);
disp(T_interpolated)
```

Note that, functions that are explained in this section may be used the same way to fill missing values in arrays.

7.11 Rolling Window

When we are working with an unprocessed raw dataset, it is often not easy to identify a trend in a dataset and arrive at a fact or draw a conclusion. It is particularly more challenging when we work with a time-series. One tool that may help to process and better understand a raw dataset is a rolling window. A rolling window, also known as a moving or sliding window, refers to a subset of data that is used in each step of a particular operation. For example, consider we have a time-series of daily air temperature for a year and we want to study weekly air temperature variations throughout that year. To do that, we use a rolling average with a window size of 7 to calculate a moving average. By doing that, a rolling window returns average air temperature at each data point by averaging an air temperature from 7 neighboring data points, which includes a data point itself. This can provide us with some understanding about the average weekly air temperature. Here are functions to apply a rolling window to data in MATLAB:

Function	Description
`movmin`	Return minimum of moving window
`movmax`	Return maximum of moving window
`movmean`	Return mean of moving window
`movsum`	Return sum of moving window
`movmedian`	Return median of moving window
`movstd`	Return standard deviation of moving window
`movvar`	Return variance of moving window
`smoothdata`	Smooth data

In this section, we explain how to work with the **`movsum`** function. Applications of the other functions presented above are more or less similar to the **`movsum`** function.

To find a moving sum of an array, we may use the **`movsum`** function. Here is a general syntax shows how to find a moving sum of an array:

Syntax

```
M = movsum(A, k)
```

The `A` defines an array that a rolling window (moving window) rolls over it. The `k` defines a number of data points used in a rolling window. If the `k` is scalar, then a centered window with a length of `k` is used. If the `k` is defined as `[kb kf]`, then a window from `kb` elements before to `kf` elements after a data point is used. In such cases, a window has a length of `kb+1+kf`.

One potential problem with a rolling window is when a rolling window slides at the beginning or at the end of the dataset. In these conditions, there might not be enough neighboring data points for points that are close to the edges. To define how to treat a rolling window when it approaches either end of the dataset, the `'Endpoints','Treating_Method'` Name-Value pair arguments can be used. By default, MATLAB uses `'shrink'` as a `'Treating_Method'`, which shrinks a window size when it approaches the edges of a dataset. To replace non-existing values with `NaN`, we can use `'fill'`. Other options are `'discard'`, or numerical or logical scalar.

In this section, we explain how to use rolling window functions for tables. However, these functions are mainly developed for working with arrays rather than tables. Because of that, to use these functions, first, we extract values in a table as an array, then we use an extracted array as an input for these functions, and finally, we replace existing values in a table with an output of these functions.

To explain how a rolling window works, let's consider an example. Consider a dataset with 10 data points from 1 to 10. Now, we want to calculate a rolling sum of this dataset. A rolling sum returns a sum of each data point and its neighboring data points. If we use a central rolling window with a size of 3, then a rolling sum returns a sum of each point with its two neighbors, except for the first and last points where each has only one neighbor. For example, a rolling sum returns 1+2 at point 1, returns 1+2+3 at point 2, returns 2+3+4 at point 3, and so on. Since we use a central window with a size of 3, one neighbor is on the left and one neighbor is on the right side of each point, which with a point itself they become 3 data points in total. Here is an illustration of a rolling sum on this dataset with 10 data points. Each window contains data points that are used to calculate a sum in that window.

data	1	2	3	4	5	6	7	8	9	10
rolling window 1	1	2								
rolling window 2	1	2	3							
rolling window 3		2	3	4						
rolling window 4			3	4	5					
rolling window 5				4	5	6				
rolling window 6					5	6	7			
rolling window 7						6	7	8		
rolling window 8							7	8	9	
rolling window 9								8	9	10
rolling window 10									9	10
rolling sum	3	6	9	12	15	18	21	24	27	19

To show how to use a rolling window, first, we create a table with a size of (10,1), row names (labels) from 'one' to 'ten', a column name (label) of 'A', and data of [1;2;3;4;5;6;7;8;9;10].

```
%Create table
%Output:
%                   A
%                   __
%
%       one          1
%       two          2
%       three        3
%       four         4
%       five         5
%       six          6
%       seven        7
%       eight        8
%       nine         9
%       ten         10
row_label={'one';'two';'three';'four';'five';
           'six';'seven';'eight';'nine';'ten'}; %Row labels
col_label={'A'};                                %Column labels
val=[1;2;3;4;5;6;7;8;9;10];                     %Data
T=array2table(val, 'VariableNames', col_label, 'RowNames', row_label);
disp(T)
```

Here are examples show how to use a rolling window in this table. In these examples, we show how to use the `movsum` function to calculate a rolling sum over a window size of 3.

```
%Rolling sum with window size of 3
%Output:
%                   A
%                   __
%
%       one          3
%       two          6
%       three        9
%       four        12
%       five        15
%       six         18
%       seven       21
%       eight       24
```

```
%       nine     27
%       ten      19
T_rolled=T; %Make a copy
T_rolled.A = movsum(T_rolled.A,3);
disp(T_rolled)

%Rolling sum with window size of 3 and 'Endpoints','fill'
%Output:
%                 A
%                ___
%
%       one      NaN
%       two        6
%       three      9
%       four      12
%       five      15
%       six       18
%       seven     21
%       eight     24
%       nine      27
%       ten      NaN
T_rolled=T; %Make a copy
T_rolled.A = movsum(T_rolled.A,3,'Endpoints','fill');
disp(T_rolled)

%Rolling sum with window size of [2 0]
%Output:
%                A
%                __
%
%       one       1
%       two       3
%       three     6
%       four      9
%       five     12
%       six      15
%       seven    18
%       eight    21
%       nine     24
%       ten      27
T_rolled=T; %Make a copy
T_rolled.A = movsum(T_rolled.A,[2 0]);
```

```
disp(T_rolled)

%Rolling sum with window size of [2 0] and 'Endpoints','fill'
%Output:
%                  A
%                 ___
%
%       one       NaN
%       two       NaN
%       three       6
%       four        9
%       five       12
%       six        15
%       seven      18
%       eight      21
%       nine       24
%       ten        27
T_rolled=T; %Make a copy
T_rolled.A = movsum(T_rolled.A,[2 0],'Endpoints','fill');
disp(T_rolled)
```

Here is another example shows how to use the **movmean** function to calculate a rolling mean or a moving average with a window size of 3.

```
%Rolling mean with window size of 3
%Output:
%                A
%       one     1.5
%       two     2.0
%       three   3.0
%       four    4.0
%       five    5.0
%       six     6.0
%       seven   7.0
%       eight   8.0
%       nine    9.0
%       ten     9.5
T_rolled=T; %Make a copy
T_rolled.A = movmean(T_rolled.A,3);
disp(T_rolled)
```

Note that, functions that are explained in this section may be used the same way to roll a window in arrays.

Chapter 8
Date, Time, and Time-Series

In this chapter, it is described how to create and work with date, time, and time-series. First, it is explained how to create date and time variables in MATLAB. Then, it is described how to generate a time-series in MATLAB. After that, it is described how to create a time-table. Next, it is explained how to index and slice data in a time-table. It follows by descriptions of how to shift data in a time-table. Next, it is explained how to clean and fill missing data in a time-table. At the end, the resampling methods of data in a time-table are explained.

8.1 Date and Time in MATLAB

When we develop a code, it is very likely that we need to use date and time in our code. In fact, a wide range of applications require to access and use dates and times in some ways. MATLAB provides several functions to work with dates and times. Some of the functions to work with date and time are:

Function	Description
`datetime`	Return date and time
`duration`	Represent time difference (duration)
`years`	Return duration in years
`days`	Return duration in days
`hours`	Return duration in hours
`minutes`	Return duration in minutes
`seconds`	Return duration in seconds

The date and time variables may be created in MATLAB by using the **`datetime`** function. Here is a general syntax shows how to use the **`datetime`** function to create date and time data:

Syntax

```
date_time = datetime(Y, M, D, H, MI, S)
```

The `Y`, `M`, `D`, `H`, `MI`, and `S` define a year, month, day, hour, minute, and second, respectively. The `H`, `MI`, and `S` are optional. If only `Y`, `M`, and `D` are defined, then the result is a date without time. Note that, we may also define millisecond and time zone in the **`datetime`** function.

Here are examples show how to use the **`datetime`** function to create date and time data. In these examples, first, we create date 2050/10/20, then we create date and time 2050/10/20 20:30:10.

```
%Create datetime 2050/10/20
%Output: 20-Oct-2050
t_date=datetime(2050, 10, 20);
disp(t_date)

%Create datetime 2050/10/20 20:30:10
%Output: 20-Oct-2050 20:30:10
t_datetime=datetime(2050, 10, 20, 20, 30, 10);
disp(t_datetime)
```

In MATLAB, a duration of time may be defined by using the `duration` function. Here is a general syntax shows how to use the `duration` function to define a time duration:

Syntax

```
time_duration = duration(H, MI, S)
```

The `H`, `MI`, and `S` define an hour, minute, and second, respectively. Note that, we may also define milliseconds in the `duration` function.

Similarly, we can use one of the `years`, `days`, `hours`, `minutes`, and `seconds` function to define a duration. In this section, we explain how to work with the `hours` function. Applications of the other functions presented above are more or less similar to the `hours` function.

To define a duration in hours, we may use the `hours` function. Here is a general syntax shows how to use the `hours` function to define a time duration:

Syntax

```
duration_hours = hours(X)
```

The `X` defines a duration in hours.

Here are examples show how to define and use a time duration in MATLAB. In these examples, first, we create a duration equal to 20 hours, 30 minutes, and 10 seconds. Then we calculate a time duration between 2050/10/20 and 2050/10/25. After that, we show how to add 5 days to 2050/10/20. Finally, we show how to add 12 hours to 2050/10/20 20:30:10.

```
%Create duration 20:30:10
%Output: 20:30:10
dt=duration(20, 30, 10);
disp(dt)

%Duration from 2050/10/20 to 2050/10/25
%Output: 5 days
t1=datetime(2050,10,20);
t2=datetime(2050,10,25);
a=t2-t1;
```

```
a.Format='d'; %Convert format to days
disp(a)

%Add 5 days to 2050/10/20
%Output: 25-Oct-2050 00:00:00
t=datetime(2050,10,20);
dt=days(5);
b=t+dt;
disp(b)

%Add 12 hours to 2050/10/20 20:30:10
%Output: 21-Oct-2050 08:30:10
t=datetime(2050, 10, 20, 20, 30, 10);
dt=hours(12);
c=t+dt;
disp(c)
```

MATLAB has several functions to manipulate date and time. In this section, we show how to use some of these functions.

One popular date and time format is a numerical date and time format known as date number. The date number is a numerical presentation equivalent to the regular date and time format. Here is a function to work with a date number format:

Function	Description
`datenum`	Return date number from date and time

Here are general syntaxes show how to use the `datenum` function to work with a date number format:

Syntax

```
DateNumber = datenum(t)
date_time  = datetime(DateNumber, 'ConvertFrom', 'datenum')
```

The `t` defines date and time to be converted to date number.

Here are examples show how to use a date number format. In these examples, first, we create a datetime variable for 2050/10/20 20:30:10, and convert it to a date number format. Then, we show how to convert this date number format back to the regular date and time format.

```
%Convert datetime format to date number format
%Output: 7.4904e+05 (7.490418542824074e+05)
t_datetime=datetime(2050, 10, 20, 20, 30, 10);
t_datenumber=datenum(t_datetime);
disp(t_datenumber)

%Convert date number format to datetime format
%Output: 20-Oct-2050 20:30:10
t_datenumber=7.490418542824074e+05;
t_datetime=datetime(t_datenumber, 'ConvertFrom', 'datenum');
disp(t_datetime)
```

Another popular date and time format is date and time presented as a string. It is particularly helpful when we need to read or write date and time to or from a file. Here is a function to work with date and time in a string format:

Function	Description
`datestr`	Return string from date and time

Here are general syntaxes show how to use the **`datestr`** function to work with date and time in a string format:

Syntax

```
DateString = datestr(t, dt_format)
date_time  = datetime(DateString, 'InputFormat', dt_format)
```

The **`t`** defines date and time to be converted to a string format. The **`dt_format`** defines a format of a string date and time.

In general, when we read or write date and time as a string, we need to define a date and time format. To define a date and time format, we use a character vector or string scalar to present a specific date or time. For example, **`yyyy`** represents a four digits year and **`yy`** represents a two digits year.

Note that, the **`datetime`** function uses a different format as a date and time specifier compared with the **`datestr`** and **`datenum`** functions. Here is a list of common date and time formats in MATLAB:

Format datetime	Format datestr datenum	Description	Example
eee	ddd	Abbreviated weekdays name	Sun, ..., Sat
eeee	dddd	Full weekdays name	Sunday, ..., Saturday
e		Numeric weekdays	1, ..., 6
dd	dd	Numeric days	01, ..., 31
MMM	mmm	Abbreviated month name	Jan, ..., Dec
MMMM	mmmm	Full month name	January, ..., December
MM	mm	Numeric month	01, ..., 12
yy	yy	Two digits year	00, ..., 99
yyyy	yyyy	Four digits year	..., 2010, 2011, ...
HH	HH	24-hour	00, ..., 24
hh		12-hour	00, ..., 12
mm	MM	Minute	00, ..., 59
SS	SS	Second	00, ..., 59

For example, consider date and time 2050/10/20 20:30:10. To present this date and time in the `datetime` function we can use date and time format as `'yyyy/MM/dd HH:mm:SS'`. Similarly, we can specify a format in a way that it only presents either date or time. For example, we can present date in the `datetime` function as `'MMM dd, yyyy'`. This format represents 2050/10/20 as a string Oct 20, 2050.

Here are examples show how to work with date and time in a string format. In these examples, first, we define a date and time format as `'yyyy-mmm-dd HH:MM:SS'`. Next, we create a datetime variable for 2050/10/20 20:30:10, and convert it to a string format. Then, we show how to convert this string format back to the regular date and time format using a date and time format as `'yyyy-MMM-dd HH:mm:SS'`. Note that, we use two different date and time formats because the `datestr` and `datetime` functions use different date and time specifiers.

```
%Covert datetime format to string
%Output: 2050-Oct-20 20:30:10
datetime_format='yyyy-mmm-dd HH:MM:SS'; %Date format
t_datetime=datetime(2050, 10, 20, 20, 30, 10);
t_string=datestr(t_datetime,datetime_format);
disp(t_string)

%Convert string to datetime format
%Output: 20-Oct-2050 20:30:00
datetime_format='yyyy-MMM-dd HH:mm:SS'; %Date format
```

```
t_string='2050-Oct-20 20:30:10';
t_datetime=datetime(t_string,'InputFormat',datetime_format);
disp(t_datetime)
```

8.2 Generate Time-Series with MATLAB

One of the common types of data that has a wide range of applications is data that are collected in time. These data are commonly known as time-series data. Data in a time-series are time-stamped and presented as a dependent of time. For example, a daily time-series of meteorological data may contain daily air temperature, air pressure, precipitation, etc.

A simple method to create a series of dates and times in MATLAB is to use the `datetime` function. To explain how to do that, let's consider an example. Assume we need to create a series of 6 days that starts on date 2050-10-20 and ends on date 2050-10-25. To generate a time-series, first, we create datetime values for these dates. Then, we create a time duration equal to 1 day. Next, we generate a time-series of 6 dates from 2050-10-20 to 2050-10-25 by using the colon operator.

Here is an example shows how to create a time-series of 6 days from 2050-10-20 to 2050-10-25 using the datetime function.

```
%Create datetime values for start and end dates
%Output:
%       start_date = 2050-Oct-20 00:00:00
%       end_date   = 2050-Oct-25 00:00:00
start_date=datetime(2050, 10, 20, 0, 0, 0);
end_date=datetime(2050, 10, 25, 0, 0, 0);
disp(['start_date = ',datestr(start_date,'yyyy-mmm-dd HH:MM:SS')])
disp(['end_date   = ',datestr(end_date,'yyyy-mmm-dd HH:MM:SS')])

%Create duration equal to 1 day
%Output: 1 day
dt=days(1); %Or dt=(end_date-start_date)/5; Or dt=duration(24,0,0);
disp(dt)

%Create daily time-series from 2050/10/20 to 2050/10/25
%Output:
%       20-Oct-2050
%       21-Oct-2050
%       22-Oct-2050
%       23-Oct-2050
```

```
%        24-Oct-2050
%        25-Oct-2050
ts=start_date:dt:end_date; %Or ts=linspace(start_date,end_date,6);
disp(ts.')
```

It is also possible to create a series of dates and times by using a date number format. Consider a previous example of creating a series of 6 days from 2050-10-20 to 2050-10-25 again. To generate a time-series, first, we create datetime values for start and end dates. Then, we convert these two dates from a datetime format to a date number format. Next, we generate a series of 6 date numbers from equivalent date numbers for 2050-10-20 to 2050-10-25. Finally, we convert these date numbers back to a datetime format.

Here is an example shows how to create a time-series of 6 days from 2050-10-20 to 2050-10-25 using a date number format.

```
%Create datetime values for start and end dates
%Output:
%        start_date = 2050-Oct-20 00:00:00
%        end_date   = 2050-Oct-25 00:00:00
start_date=datetime(2050, 10, 20, 0, 0, 0);
end_date=datetime(2050, 10, 25, 0, 0, 0);
disp(['start_date = ',datestr(start_date,'yyyy-mmm-dd HH:MM:SS')])
disp(['end_date   = ',datestr(end_date,'yyyy-mmm-dd HH:MM:SS')])

%Convert start_date and end_date to datenum format
%Output:
%        t1 = 749041
%        t2 = 749046
t1=datenum(start_date);
t2=datenum(end_date);
disp(['t1 = ',num2str(t1)])
disp(['t2 = ',num2str(t2)])

%Generate 6 dates between t1 and t2 with datenum format
%Output:
%        749041     749042     749043     749044     749045     749046
t=linspace(t1,t2,6);
disp(t)

%Create daily time-series from 2050/10/20 to 2050/10/25
%Convert time-series from timestamp format to datetime format
```

```
%Output:
%       20-Oct-2050
%       21-Oct-2050
%       22-Oct-2050
%       23-Oct-2050
%       24-Oct-2050
%       25-Oct-2050
ts=datetime(t, 'ConvertFrom', 'datenum');
disp(ts.')
```

Sometimes we may need to convert a time-series to a string, particularly when we want to write data to a file. Here is an example shows how to convert a time-series from a previous example to a string.

```
%Convert time-series to string format
%Output:
%       2050-Oct-20 00:00:00
%       2050-Oct-21 00:00:00
%       2050-Oct-22 00:00:00
%       2050-Oct-23 00:00:00
%       2050-Oct-24 00:00:00
%       2050-Oct-25 00:00:00
datetime_format='yyyy-mmm-dd HH:MM:SS'; %Date format
ts_str=datestr(ts,datetime_format);
disp(ts_str)
```

Note that, we can use the **`timeseries`** function to create a timeseries object. Similarly, we can use the **`dateshift`** function to generate a time-series or to shift dates.

8.3 Generate Time-Table

MATLAB time-table provides convenient ways to create, manipulate, and work with a time-series. We can create a time-table that contains time-series data similar to how we create the regular table.

Here are MATLAB functions to create and work with a time-table:

Function	Description
`timetable`	Create time-table (2-d tabular labeled time array)
`array2timetable`	Convert array to time-table
`table2timetable`	Convert table to time-table

`readtimetable`	Read time-table from file

Now, we explain how to create and work with a time-table that contains time-series data. Here is a general syntax shows how to create a MATLAB time-table:

Syntax

```
Time_Table = timetable(rowTimes, var1, ..., varN, 'VariableNames', varNames)
```

The `rowTimes` contains date and time data. The `var1`, ..., `varN` contains data that a table is created from them. They may have different sizes and data types but they all should have the same number of rows. Except for the `rowTimes` columns, we can set column names (labels) by using optional Name-Value pair arguments `'VariableNames', varNames`. The `'VariableNames'` indicates that the following variable contains variable names (labels). The `varNames` is a cell array of character vectors or a string array that contains variable names (labels) and by default is the same as `var1`, ..., `varN`. The `'VariableNames', varNames` pair are optional.

Here is an example shows how to create a time-table. This time-table has a size of (2,5), row times (labels) of '2050-10-20' to '2050-10-24', column names (labels) of 'A', 'B', and data of [1;2;3;4;5] and [6;7;8;9;10]. In this example, we create row dates and times using the colon operator.

```
%Row date and time from 2050/10/20 to 2050/10/24
start_date=datetime(2050, 10, 20);
end_date=datetime(2050, 10, 24);
dt=days(1);
row_times=[start_date:dt:end_date].';

%Column labels
col_label={'A','B'};

%Data (1-d column arrays)
col1=[1;2;3;4;5];
col2=[6;7;8;9;10];

%Create timetable
%Output:
%         row_times      A     B
%        ___________     _    __
%
%        20-Oct-2050     1     6
```

```
%         21-Oct-2050     2      7
%         22-Oct-2050     3      8
%         23-Oct-2050     4      9
%         24-Oct-2050     5     10
TT=timetable(row_times, col1, col2, 'VariableNames', col_label);
disp(TT)
```

We can create a MATLAB time-table from an array by using the **array2timetable** function. Here is a general syntax shows how to create a MATLAB time-table from an array:

Syntax

```
Time_Table = array2timetable(X, 'RowTimes', rowTimes, 'VariableNames', varNames)
```

The **X** is an array to create a time-table from that. We can set row and column names (labels) by using optional Name-Value pair arguments `'RowTimes', rowTimes` and `'VariableNames', varNames`. The `'RowTimes'` indicates that the following variable contains time and date data. The **rowTimes** is an array that contains date and time associated with each row. The **'VariableNames'** indicates that the following variable contains variable names (labels). The **varNames** is a cell array of character vectors or a string array that contains variable names (labels). The `'VariableNames', varNames` pair are optional.

Here is an example shows how to create a previous time-table by using an array.

```
%Row date and time from 2050/10/20 to 2050/10/24
start_date=datetime(2050, 10, 20);
end_date=datetime(2050, 10, 24);
dt=days(1);
row_times=[start_date:dt:end_date].';

%Column labels
col_label={'A','B'};

%Data
val=[[1,6];[2,7];[3,8];[4,9];[5,10]];

%Create timetable
%Output:
%            Time         A    B
%         ___________     _    __
```

```
%
%         20-Oct-2050    1     6
%         21-Oct-2050    2     7
%         22-Oct-2050    3     8
%         23-Oct-2050    4     9
%         24-Oct-2050    5    10
TT=array2timetable(val, ...
    'RowTimes', row_times, 'VariableNames', col_label);
disp(TT)
```

When we work with tabular time-series data, it is a common occurrence that date and time data are stored in one column of a table. It particularly happens when data are stored in a file. Now, if we read data from this file and convert them to a table, then a table has a column that its data are date and time. However, it is more convenient to have a time-table rather than having a table that one of its columns contains dates and times. For example, it is much easier to access data based on their dates and times when we are working with a time-table. In such cases, we can convert date and time data in a table to a datetime format and then convert a table to a time-table.

We can create a MATLAB time-table from a table by using the `table2timetable` function. Here is a general syntax shows how to create a MATLAB time-table from a table:

Syntax

```
Time_Table = table2timetable(T, 'RowTimes', timeVarName)
```

The `T` is a table to create a time-table from that. We define a column in a table that contains date and time data by using optional Name-Value pair arguments `'RowTimes', timeVarName` pair. The `'RowTimes'` indicates that the following variable contains a name of a column in a table that holds time and date data. The `timeVarName` is a column name (label) that contains date and time data. The `'RowTimes', timeVarName` pair are optional.

Here is an example shows how to convert a table to a time-table. In this example, we have a table with a size of (3,5), row names (labels) of 'one' to 'five', and column names (labels) of 'Date', 'A', 'B'. Here, first, we convert data in a column 'Date' from a string format to a datetime format. Then, we use this datetime data to convert a table to a time-table. Finally, we remove the column 'Row' from a time-table.

```
%Create labels
row_label={'one';'two';'three';'four';'five'};
col_label={'Date','A','B'};
```

```
%Data (1-d column arrays)
col1={'2050-10-20';'2050-10-21';'2050-10-22';
      '2050-10-23';'2050-10-24'};
col2=[1;2;3;4;5];
col3=[6;7;8;9;10];

%Create time-series table
%Output:
%                     Date          A     B
%                ______________     _    __
%
%       one      {'2050-10-20'}     1     6
%       two      {'2050-10-21'}     2     7
%       three    {'2050-10-22'}     3     8
%       four     {'2050-10-23'}     4     9
%       five     {'2050-10-24'}     5    10
T=table(col1, col2, col3, ...
    'VariableNames', col_label, 'RowNames', row_label);
disp(T)

%Convert column 'Date' to datetime
T.Date=datetime(T.Date);

%Convert table to time-table
%Output:
%          Date            Row         A     B
%       ___________    _________      _    __
%
%       20-Oct-2050    {'one'  }      1     6
%       21-Oct-2050    {'two'  }      2     7
%       22-Oct-2050    {'three'}      3     8
%       23-Oct-2050    {'four' }      4     9
%       24-Oct-2050    {'five' }      5    10
TT=table2timetable(T,'RowTimes','Date');
disp(TT)

%Remove column 'Row' from time-table
%Output:
%          Date         A     B
%       ___________     _    __
%
```

```
%         20-Oct-2050    1     6
%         21-Oct-2050    2     7
%         22-Oct-2050    3     8
%         23-Oct-2050    4     9
%         24-Oct-2050    5    10
TT.Row=[];
disp(TT)
```

8.4 Time-Table Indexing and Slicing

Indexing and slicing a time-table are similar to the regular table. Here are methods to access items in MATLAB time-tables:

Method	Output	Description
`table( i:j , m:n )`	Table	Return table from items in table using positions
`table({'label_i',...}, {'label_m',...})`	Table	Return table from items in table using labels
`table{ i:j , m:n }`	Array	Return array from items in table using positions
`table{{'label_i',...}, {'label_m',...}}`	Array	Return array from items in table using labels
`table.col_label`	Array	Return array from values of column with label 'col_label'
`table.('col_label')`	Array	Return array from values of column with label 'col_label'
`table.(m)`	Array	Return array from values of column with index m

Here is a general syntax shows how to access items in a time-table by their position:

Syntax

```
results = TimeTable( i : j , m : n )
```

Here is a general syntax shows how to access items in a time-table by their labels:

Syntax

```
results = TimeTable( {'label_i', 'label_j', ...} , {'label_m', 'label_n', ...} )
```

Note that, if we use parentheses as `( ... , ... )` for indexing, the returned result is a time-table, however, if we use curly brackets as `{ ... , ... }` for indexing, the returned result is an array. This is correct for both position and label indexing. For example, assume we have a time-table `TT`. The statement `R=TT(1,:)` returns the first row of time-table `TT` as a time-table and assigns it to `R`. Therefore, `R` becomes a time-table. However, the statement `Arr=TT{1,:}` returns the first row of time-table `TT` as an array and assigns it to `Arr`. Therefore, `Arr` becomes an array.

Besides regular indexing and slicing methods, MATLAB lets us access data simply by using their time-stamp indexes. For example, we can access all data on a particular date by simply using that date as an index of a time-table.

Also, MATLAB provides functions to call and access data in a time-table. Here are MATLAB functions to access data in a time-table:

Function	Description
`timerange`	Return time range for time-table indexing
`withtol`	Return time tolerance for time-table indexing

To define a range of dates and times we can use the **`timerange`** function. Here is a general syntax shows how to create a time range:

Syntax

```
time_range = timerange(startTime, endTime, intervalType)
```

The `startTime` and `endTime` define start and end times of a time range. The `intervalType` defines if start and end times to be included in a time range or not. The intervalType is optional and by default is `'openright'`. If the intervalType is not defined, a time range is generated over a half-open time interval of `[startTime,endTime)`. In such cases, the `endTime` is not included in a time range. The `intervalType` takes one of `'open'`, `'closed'`, `'openleft'`, `'openright'`, `'closedright'`, and `'closedleft'`. To include both start and end times in a time range, we should use `'closed'` in place of `intervalType`.

To show how to use date and time indexing and slicing in a time-table, first, we create a time-table with a size of (10,1), row names (labels) of random dates from '2050-10-20' to '2051-02-22', a column name (label) of 'A', and data of [1;2;3;4;5;6;7;8;9;10].

```
%Row date and time from 2050/10/20 to 2050/10/24
Date={'2050-10-20';'2050-10-27';
```

```
        '2050-11-17';'2050-11-25';
        '2050-12-13';'2050-12-17';
        '2051-01-19';'2051-01-20';
        '2051-02-14';'2051-02-22'};
row_times=datetime(Date);

%Column labels
col_label={'A'};

%Data
val=[1;2;3;4;5;6;7;8;9;10];

%Create time-table
%Output:
%           Time         A
%       ___________     __
%
%       20-Oct-2050      1
%       27-Oct-2050      2
%       17-Nov-2050      3
%       25-Nov-2050      4
%       13-Dec-2050      5
%       17-Dec-2050      6
%       19-Jan-2051      7
%       20-Jan-2051      8
%       14-Feb-2051      9
%       22-Feb-2051     10
TT=array2timetable(val, ...
    'RowTimes', row_times, 'VariableNames', col_label);
disp(TT)
```

Here are examples show how to access items in a time-table using dates and times.

```
%Select all rows in '2050'
%Output:
%           Time         A
%       ___________     _
%
%       20-Oct-2050     1
%       27-Oct-2050     2
%       17-Nov-2050     3
%       25-Nov-2050     4
```

```
%        13-Dec-2050    5
%        17-Dec-2050    6
TR=timerange('2050-01-01','2050-12-31');
r=TT(TR,:);
disp(r)

%Select all rows in '2051-01'
%Output:
%           Time         A
%        ___________    _
%
%        19-Jan-2051    7
%        20-Jan-2051    8
TR=timerange('2051-01-01','2051-01-31');
r=TT(TR,:);
disp(r)

%Select all rows from '2050-11' to '2051-01'
%Output:
%           Time         A
%        ___________    _
%
%        17-Nov-2050    3
%        25-Nov-2050    4
%        13-Dec-2050    5
%        17-Dec-2050    6
%        19-Jan-2051    7
%        20-Jan-2051    8
TR=timerange('2050-11-01','2051-01-31');
r=TT(TR,:);
disp(r)

%Select all rows from '2050-11-25' to '2051-01-19'
%Output:
%           Time         A
%        ___________    _
%
%        25-Nov-2050    4
%        13-Dec-2050    5
%        17-Dec-2050    6
%        19-Jan-2051    7
TR=timerange('2050-11-25','2051-01-20');
```

```
r=TT(TR,:);
disp(r)

%Select a row with datetime '2050-10-20'
%Output:
%           Time        A
%       ___________     _
%
%       20-Oct-2050     1
r=TT('2050-10-20',:);
disp(r)
```

8.5 Shift Data in Time-Table

We may need to shift data in a time-table back or forward in time. Here is a function to shift data in a time-table:

Method	Description
`lag`	Shift time in time-table

We can use the `lag` function to shift data in a time-table. Here are general syntaxes show how to use the `lag` function to shift data in a time-table:

Syntax

```
TT2 = lag(TT1, n)
TT2 = lag(TT1, dt)
```

The `TT1` defines a time-table to shift its data in time. The `n` defines a number of time steps to shift data. The `n` should be an integer. The positive `n` shifts data forward and negative `n` shifts data backward. The `dt` defines a time interval to shift data.

To show how to shift data in a time-table, first, we create a time-table with a size of (6,1), row times from '2050-10-20' to '2050-10-25', a column name (label) of 'A', and data of [0;1;2;3;4;5].

```
%Create time-table
%Output:
%           Time        A
%       ___________     _
```

```
%
%       20-Oct-2050    0
%       21-Oct-2050    1
%       22-Oct-2050    2
%       23-Oct-2050    3
%       24-Oct-2050    4
%       25-Oct-2050    5
start_date=datetime(2050, 10, 20);
end_date=datetime(2050, 10, 25);
dt=days(1);
row_times=[start_date:dt:end_date].'; %Row times
col_label={'A'};                      %Column labels
val=[0;1;2;3;4;5];                    %Data
TT=array2timetable(val, ...
    'RowTimes', row_times, 'VariableNames', col_label);
disp(TT)
```

Now, we use the **lag** function to shift data in this time-table. Here, first, we shift 1 time step forward, and then we shift 1 time step backward.

```
%Shift data 1 time step forward
%Output:
%          Time         A
%       ___________    ___
%
%       20-Oct-2050    NaN
%       21-Oct-2050      0
%       22-Oct-2050      1
%       23-Oct-2050      2
%       24-Oct-2050      3
%       25-Oct-2050      4
TT_shifted=lag(TT,1);
disp(TT_shifted)

%Shift data 1 time step backward
%Output:
%          Time         A
%       ___________    ___
%
%       20-Oct-2050      1
%       21-Oct-2050      2
%       22-Oct-2050      3
```

```
%        23-Oct-2050      4
%        24-Oct-2050      5
%        25-Oct-2050    NaN
TT_shifted=lag(TT,-1);
disp(TT_shifted)
```

8.6 Clean and Fill Missing Data in Time-Table

When we are working with a time-series, sometimes data in a time-series might be missing. In some cases, there might be several dates in a time-series that data in those dates are missing or unacceptable. In other words, there might be dates in a time-series without any reliable data. In other cases, dates and their values both might be missing. In other words, there are gaps in a time-series. In such cases that we have gaps or unreliable data in a time-series, we need to clean data and replace all missing values. If we know the correct values for missing data, we can simply replace those values. However, if we do not have the correct values for missing data, we can use numerical methods to estimate and replace those values from existing values.

Here are functions to fill and replace missing data in MATLAB:

Function	Description
`fillmissing`	Fill missing values
`rmmissing`	Remove missing values
`standardizeMissing`	Replace missing values with standard missing values
`ismissing`	Detect missing values

We can use the **`fillmissing`** function to fill missing data with a constant value. Here is a general syntax shows how to use the **`fillmissing`** function to fill missing values with a constant value:

Syntax

```
F = fillmissing(A, 'constant', v)
```

The **`A`** defines a time-table (or array) that its missing values to be filled. The **`v`** defines a value that is used to replace missing data.

We can also use the **`fillmissing`** function to fill and replace missing data by their neighboring data points. Here is a general syntax shows how to use the **`fillmissing`** function to fill missing values by adjacent values:

Syntax

```
F = fillmissing(A, method)
```

The **A** defines a time-table (or array) that its missing values to be filled. The **method** defines how to fill missing data. Here is a list of the available methods that may be used to fill missing data by their neighboring data points:

Method	Description
`'previous'`	Use previous data point to fill missing values
`'next'`	Use next data point to fill missing values
`'nearest'`	Use nearest data point to fill missing values

If the **method** is **'previous'** it uses a previous data point to fill missing values. It is called forward filling. If the **method** is **'next'** it uses the next data point to fill missing values. It is called backward filling.

To show how to fill missing data in a time-table, first, we create a time-table with a size of (3,1), row names (labels) of '2050-10-20', '2050-10-24', '2050-10-25', a column name (label) of 'A', and data of [0;4;5].

```
%Create time-table
%Output:
%          Time         A
%       ___________     _
%
%       20-Oct-2050     0
%       24-Oct-2050     4
%       25-Oct-2050     5
Date={'2050-10-20','2050-10-24','2050-10-25'};
row_times=datetime(Date); %Row times
col_label={'A'};          %Column labels
val=[0;4;5];              %Data
TT=array2timetable(val, ...
    'RowTimes', row_times, 'VariableNames', col_label);
disp(TT)
```

Now, assume we need a time-series from '2050-10-20' to '2050-10-25'. In a previous time-table, dates '2050-10-21', '2050-10-22', and '2050-10-23' are missing. Now, we use the colon operator to create dates from '2050-10-20' to '2050-10-25'. Then, we use the retime function to add missing dates to a time-table. For more details on how to use the retime function, refer to the resampling time-table section.

```
%Create dates from 2050-10-20 to 2050-10-25
%Output:
%        20-Oct-2050
%        21-Oct-2050
%        22-Oct-2050
%        23-Oct-2050
%        24-Oct-2050
%        25-Oct-2050
start_date=datetime(2050, 10, 20);
end_date=datetime(2050, 10, 25);
dt=days(1);
date_index=[start_date:dt:end_date]';
disp(date_index)

%Resample time-table
%Output:
%           Time        A
%        ___________   ___
%
%        20-Oct-2050     0
%        21-Oct-2050   NaN
%        22-Oct-2050   NaN
%        23-Oct-2050   NaN
%        24-Oct-2050     4
%        25-Oct-2050     5
TT_resampled=retime(TT,date_index);
disp(TT_resampled)
```

Now, we use the **fillmissing** function to fill missing data in this time-table. In this example, first, we fill missing data with a previous data point by using a 'previous' method, and then, we fill them with the next data point by using a 'next' method.

```
%Fill missing values with 'previous' method
%Output:
%           Time       A
%        ___________   _
%
%        20-Oct-2050   0
```

```
%        21-Oct-2050    0
%        22-Oct-2050    0
%        23-Oct-2050    0
%        24-Oct-2050    4
%        25-Oct-2050    5
TT_filled=fillmissing(TT_resampled,'previous');
%Or TT_filled=retime(TT,date_index,'previous');
disp(TT_filled)

%Fill missing values with 'next' method
%Output:
%           Time        A
%        ___________    _
%
%        20-Oct-2050    0
%        21-Oct-2050    4
%        22-Oct-2050    4
%        23-Oct-2050    4
%        24-Oct-2050    4
%        25-Oct-2050    5
TT_filled=fillmissing(TT_resampled,'next');
%Or TT_filled=retime(TT,date_index,'next');
disp(TT_filled)
```

Another method to fill missing values is to interpolate missing values from their neighboring data points. To do that, we set the method in the `fillmissing` function to one of the interpolating methods. Here is a list of available methods that may be used to interpolate missing data:

Method	Description
`'linear'`	Interpolate missing values using linear interpolation
`'spline'`	Interpolate missing values using piecewise cubic spline interpolation
`'pchip'`	Interpolate missing values using piecewise cubic spline interpolation
`'makima'`	Interpolate missing values using modified Akima cubic Hermite interpolation

Now, we use the `fillmissing` function to interpolate missing data in a previous time-table. In this example, we use a `'linear'` method. The `fillmissing` function uses time indexes to define space between data points.

```
%Interpolate missing values with 'linear' method
%Output:
%           Time        A
```

```
%         ___________    _
%
%         20-Oct-2050    0
%         21-Oct-2050    1
%         22-Oct-2050    2
%         23-Oct-2050    3
%         24-Oct-2050    4
%         25-Oct-2050    5
TT_interpolated=fillmissing(TT_resampled,'linear');
%Or TT_interpolated=retime(TT,date_index,'linear');
disp(TT_interpolated)
```

Note that, we can also fill or interpolate missing data at the same time that we resample a time-table. For more details on how to resample a time-table, refer to the resampling time-table section.

8.7 Resampling Time-Table

When we are working with time-series data it is very probable that we need to resample a time-series into a new interval. For example, we may have a weekly air temperature and we want to resample it into monthly averaged air temperature. Similarly, we may have daily rainfall values and we want to resample it into hourly rainfall values.

If we resample data into a less frequent interval we down-sample data and if we resample data into a more frequent interval we up-sample data. Here is a function to resample a time-table:

Function	Description
`retime`	Return a resampled time-table

We can use the `retime` function to resample a time-table. Here are general syntaxes show how to resample a time-table:

Syntax

```
TT_resampled = retime(TT, 'regular', 'TimeStep', dt)
TT_resampled = retime(TT1, newTimes)
```

The `TT` defines a time-table to be resampled. The `'regular'` indicates that a time-table is resampled on regularly spaced times at a time step dt. We can set a time-table to be sampled at a given time step by using Name-Value pair arguments `'TimeStep', dt`. The `'TimeStep'` indicates that the following variable contains a time step value. The **dt** defines a time step to resample a time-table. The **newTimes** contains new dates and times to resample a time-table on them.

To show how to resample a time-series, first, we create a time-table with a size of (6,3), daily row names (labels) from '2050-10-20' to '2050-10-25', column names (labels) of 'A', 'B', and data of [[1,10];[2,20];[3,30];[4,40];[5,50];[6,60]].

```
%Row times from 2050/10/20 to 2050/10/25
start_date=datetime(2050, 10, 20);
end_date=datetime(2050, 10, 25);
dt=days(1);
row_times=[start_date:dt:end_date].';

%Column labels
col_label={'A','B'};

%Data
val=[[1,10];[2,20];[3,30];[4,40];[5,50];[6,60]];

%Create time-table
%Output:
%          Time         A    B
%       ___________     _    __
%
%       20-Oct-2050     1    10
%       21-Oct-2050     2    20
%       22-Oct-2050     3    30
%       23-Oct-2050     4    40
%       24-Oct-2050     5    50
%       25-Oct-2050     6    60
TT=array2timetable(val, ...
    'RowTimes', row_times, 'VariableNames', col_label);
disp(TT)
```

Here are examples show how to resample this time-table. In these examples, first, we down-sample a time-table into 2-day bins, then we up-sample a time-table into 12-hour bins, and finally, we up-sample a time-table into 12-hour bins and return a slice of data with (1:6,:) indexes.

```
%Down-sample time-table into 2-day bins
%Output:
```

```
%                 Time               A       B
%         ________________________    ___     ___
%
%         20-Oct-2050 00:00:00          1      10
%         22-Oct-2050 00:00:00          3      30
%         24-Oct-2050 00:00:00          5      50
%         26-Oct-2050 00:00:00        NaN     NaN
dt=days(2);
TT_resampled=retime(TT,'regular','TimeStep',dt);
disp(TT_resampled)

%Up-sample time-table into 12-hour bins
%Output:
%                 Time               A       B
%         ________________________    ___     ___
%
%         20-Oct-2050 00:00:00          1      10
%         20-Oct-2050 12:00:00        NaN     NaN
%         21-Oct-2050 00:00:00          2      20
%         21-Oct-2050 12:00:00        NaN     NaN
%         22-Oct-2050 00:00:00          3      30
%         22-Oct-2050 12:00:00        NaN     NaN
%         23-Oct-2050 00:00:00          4      40
%         23-Oct-2050 12:00:00        NaN     NaN
%         24-Oct-2050 00:00:00          5      50
%         24-Oct-2050 12:00:00        NaN     NaN
%         25-Oct-2050 00:00:00          6      60
dt=hours(12);
TT_resampled=retime(TT,'regular','TimeStep',dt);
disp(TT_resampled)

%Up-sample time-table into 12-hour bins and return (1:6,:) indexes
%Output:
%                 Time               A       B
%         ________________________    ___     ___
%
%         20-Oct-2050 00:00:00          1      10
%         20-Oct-2050 12:00:00        NaN     NaN
%         21-Oct-2050 00:00:00          2      20
%         21-Oct-2050 12:00:00        NaN     NaN
%         22-Oct-2050 00:00:00          3      30
%         22-Oct-2050 12:00:00        NaN     NaN
```

```
dt=hours(12);
TT_resampled=retime(TT,'regular','TimeStep',dt);
TT_resampled=TT_resampled(1:6,:);
disp(TT_resampled)
```

In case that we up-sample data, MATLAB fills data for new times with `NaN`. To avoid that, we can fill these `NaN` data with neighboring data points.

Here are general syntaxes show how to fill missing data in a resampled time-table:

Syntax

```
TT_resampled = retime(TT, 'regular', method, 'TimeStep',dt)
TT_resampled = retime(TT, newTimes, method)
```

The `method` defines how the missing data are filled or interpolated by their neighboring data points. Here is a list of available methods that may be used to fill missing data:

Method	Description
`'previous'`	Use previous data point to fill missing values
`'next'`	Use next data point to fill missing values
`'nearest'`	Use nearest data point to fill missing values

Here is a list of available methods that may be used to interpolate missing data:

Method	Description
`'linear'`	Interpolate missing values using linear interpolation
`'spline'`	Interpolate missing values using piecewise cubic spline interpolation
`'pchip'`	Interpolate missing values using piecewise cubic spline interpolation
`'makima'`	Interpolate missing values using modified Akima cubic Hermite interpolation

Here are examples show how to use the `retime` function to resample and fill missing values. In these examples, first, we up-sample a time-table into 12-hour bins, and then we use the `'previous'`, `'next'`, and `'nearest'` methods to fill missing values.

```
%Up-sample into 12-hour bins and fill NaN with previous data
%Output:
%              Time             A    B
%       ____________________    _    __
```

```
%
%       20-Oct-2050 00:00:00    1    10
%       20-Oct-2050 12:00:00    1    10
%       21-Oct-2050 00:00:00    2    20
%       21-Oct-2050 12:00:00    2    20
%       22-Oct-2050 00:00:00    3    30
%       22-Oct-2050 12:00:00    3    30
%       23-Oct-2050 00:00:00    4    40
%       23-Oct-2050 12:00:00    4    40
%       24-Oct-2050 00:00:00    5    50
%       24-Oct-2050 12:00:00    5    50
%       25-Oct-2050 00:00:00    6    60
dt=hours(12);
TT_resampled=retime(TT,'regular','previous','TimeStep',dt);
disp(TT_resampled)

%Up-sample into 12-hour bins and fill NaN with next data
%Output:
%               Time            A    B
%       ____________________    _    __
%
%       20-Oct-2050 00:00:00    1    10
%       20-Oct-2050 12:00:00    2    20
%       21-Oct-2050 00:00:00    2    20
%       21-Oct-2050 12:00:00    3    30
%       22-Oct-2050 00:00:00    3    30
%       22-Oct-2050 12:00:00    4    40
%       23-Oct-2050 00:00:00    4    40
%       23-Oct-2050 12:00:00    5    50
%       24-Oct-2050 00:00:00    5    50
%       24-Oct-2050 12:00:00    6    60
%       25-Oct-2050 00:00:00    6    60
dt=hours(12);
TT_resampled=retime(TT,'regular','next','TimeStep',dt);
disp(TT_resampled)

%Up-sample into 12-hour bins and fill NaN with nearest data
%Output:
%               Time            A    B
%       ____________________    _    __
%
%       20-Oct-2050 00:00:00    1    10
```

```
%        20-Oct-2050 12:00:00    2    20
%        21-Oct-2050 00:00:00    2    20
%        21-Oct-2050 12:00:00    3    30
%        22-Oct-2050 00:00:00    3    30
%        22-Oct-2050 12:00:00    4    40
%        23-Oct-2050 00:00:00    4    40
%        23-Oct-2050 12:00:00    5    50
%        24-Oct-2050 00:00:00    5    50
%        24-Oct-2050 12:00:00    6    60
%        25-Oct-2050 00:00:00    6    60
dt=hours(12);
TT_resampled=retime(TT,'regular','nearest','TimeStep',dt);
disp(TT_resampled)
```

During a resampling process, we can apply several methods to resampled data to return the required values from each bin. For example, consider we have daily readings of air temperature and we want to down-sample them into averaged weekly temperature. To do that, we can use the `'mean'` method. By doing that, the `retime` function first resample data into weekly bins and then calculate and returns a mean value in each bin. Here is a list of common methods to be applied on resampled data:

Method	Description
`'min'`	Return minimum
`'max'`	Return maximum
`'mean'`	Return mean of data points
`'sum'`	Return sum of data points
`'prod'`	Return product of data points
`'count'`	Return total number of data points
`'firstvalue'`	Return first value
`'lastvalue'`	Return last value
`@func`	Apply a function

Here are examples show how to apply these methods to resampled data and return an evaluated value in each bin. In these examples, first, we down-sample a time-table into 2-day bins, and then we apply the `'sum'`, `'mean'`, and `'max'` methods to data of each bin.

```
%Down-sample into 2-day bins and return sum of each bin
%Output:
%               Time              A      B
%        ____________________    ___    ___
%
```

```
%        20-Oct-2050 00:00:00     3     30
%        22-Oct-2050 00:00:00     7     70
%        24-Oct-2050 00:00:00    11    110
dt=days(2);
TT_resampled=retime(TT,'regular','sum','TimeStep',dt);
disp(TT_resampled)

%Down-sample into 2-day bins and return mean of each bin
%Output:
%                Time              A      B
%        ____________________     ___    __
%
%        20-Oct-2050 00:00:00    1.5     15
%        22-Oct-2050 00:00:00    3.5     35
%        24-Oct-2050 00:00:00    5.5     55
dt=days(2);
TT_resampled=retime(TT,'regular','mean','TimeStep',dt);
disp(TT_resampled)

%Down-sample into 2-day bins and return max of each bin
%Output:
%                Time              A    B
%        ____________________     _    __
%
%        20-Oct-2050 00:00:00     2    20
%        22-Oct-2050 00:00:00     4    40
%        24-Oct-2050 00:00:00     6    60
dt=days(2);
TT_resampled=retime(TT,'regular','max','TimeStep',dt);
disp(TT_resampled)
```

We can also apply a function to resampled data. To do that, we use the `@ func` method. Here are general syntaxes show how to apply a function to resampled data:

Syntax

```
TT_resampled = retime(TT, 'regular', @ func, 'TimeStep',dt)
TT_resampled = retime(TT, newTimes, @ func)
```

The `@ func` defines a function to be applied to resampled data. Note that, an output of the `func` should be either one scalar (value) or one row array (row vector).

Here are examples show how to apply a function to resampled data. In the first example, we define an anonymous function that squares its inputs and returns their sum. Then, we use this function to square and sum a time-table that is down-sampled into 2-day bins. In the second example, we use the `@ median` function to return a median of a time-table that is down-sampled into 2-day bins.

```
%Down-sample into 2-day bins and apply anonymous function
%Output:
%               Time                A      B
%       ____________________       __     ____
%
%       20-Oct-2050 00:00:00        5      500
%       22-Oct-2050 00:00:00       25     2500
%       24-Oct-2050 00:00:00       61     6100
f = @ (x) sum(x.^2); %Function
dt=days(2);
TT_resampled=retime(TT,'regular',f,'TimeStep',dt);
disp(TT_resampled)

%Down-sample into 2-day bins and apply median function
%Output:
%               Time                 A      B
%       ____________________       ___     __
%
%       20-Oct-2050 00:00:00       1.5     15
%       22-Oct-2050 00:00:00       3.5     35
%       24-Oct-2050 00:00:00       5.5     55
dt=days(2);
TT_resampled=retime(TT,'regular',@ median,'TimeStep',dt);
disp(TT_resampled)
```

Note that, to fill missing data with a constant value, we can use `'fillwithconstant'` for filling method and then define a constant value by using Name-Value pair arguments `'Constant',Value`. For example, `TT2 = retime(TT1, 'regular', 'fillwithconstant', 'TimeStep', dt, 'Constant', -1)` replaces all missing values with -1.

Chapter 9
Introduction to Data Visualization with MATLAB

In this chapter, the basics of data visualization with MATLAB are described. First, MATLAB plotting functions for data visualization are introduced. Next, it is presented how to create a 2-d line plot. Then, it is explained how to customize a plot by setting its color and line style. It follows by descriptions of how to add markers and labels, set axis properties, and add grid lines and text. Then, it is demonstrated how to display multiple datasets in one figure or how to plot them in multiple figures. After that, it is explained how to further customize a figure with the `get` and `set` functions. Then, it is described how to remove white space around a figure. At the end, it is explained how to customize a MATLAB figure interactively.

9.1 MATLAB Plots

MATLAB may be used for plotting and data visualization. It provides many different plot types and a wide range of features to draw and visualize data. MATLAB is one of the most widely used software for data visualization. It helps to prepare high-quality figures to be used in publications or interactive environments. MATLAB provides two methods of plotting, procedural and object-oriented. Most of the MATLAB plots may be drawn with both of these methods. Here is a list of common MATLAB plotting functions to plot and visualize data:

Function	Description
`plot`	Create line plot
`scatter`	Create scatter plot
`bar`	Create bar plot
`loglog`	Create plot with log scaling
`boxplot`	Create box plot
`errorbar`	Create plot with error bars
`stem`	Create stem plot
`histogram`	Create histogram
`hist`	Create histogram (legacy version)
`binscatter`	Create binned scatter plot
`spectrogram`	Plot spectrogram
`contourf`	Create filled contour plot
`imshow`	Plot image
`pcolor`	Create pseudocolor plot
`quiver`	Plot field of arrows
`streamline`	Plot streamlines
`pie`	Create pie plot
`polarplot`	Create polar plot
`fill`	Plot filled polygons
`figure`	Create new figure

In addition to plotting functions which are used to create a plot and display data, MATLAB provides several functions that let us customize a plot after it is created. Here is a list of common MATLAB functions to customize a plot:

Function	Description
`gca`	Get current axes or chart
`gcf`	Get current figure handle
`axes`	Create Cartesian axes
`axis`	Set axis properties

title	Add title to plot
xlabel	Set label for x-axis
ylabel	Set label for y-axis
xlim	Set x limits for x-axis
ylim	Set y limits for y-axis
xticks	Set tick locations for x-axis
yticks	Set tick locations for y-axis
xticklabels	Set tick labels for x-axis
yticklabels	Set tick labels for y-axis
legend	Add legend to plot
colorbar	Add colorbar to plot
grid	Add or hide grid lines
box	Turn axes outline on or off
text	Add text to data points
annotation	Create annotations
uitable	Create table user interface
refresh	Redraw current figure
reset	Restore default properties of graphics object
clf	Clear current figure
close	Close figure
print	Save figure to specific file format
savefig	Save figure to .fig file
imread	Read image from file
imwrite	Save array with image data into image file
hold	Retain current plot to add new drawings
get	Return graphics object properties
set	Set graphics object properties
alpha	Make plot transparent

In this chapter, first, we explain how to create a 2-d line plot, and then, we show how to customize this plot. In the next chapter, we explain more advanced plotting options to visualize data and manipulate plots.

9.2 Line Plot

The most common plot is a 2-d line plot. In this type of plot, a series of (x,y) pairs are visualized by straight lines connecting them together. In other words, y data are plotted versus x data using lines. In this chapter, first, we explain how to create a 2-d plot, and then, we show how to customize this plot. Here are MATLAB functions to create a 2-d line plot:

Function	Description
`plot`	Create line plot
`axes`	Create Cartesian axes
`print`	Save figure to specific file format
`savefig`	Save figure to .fig file

Here is a general syntax shows how to create a 2-d line plot:

Syntax

```
line_object = plot(X, Y, LineSpec, 'Name1', Value1, ..., 'NameN', ValueN)
```

The `X` and `Y` contain data to be plotted. The `X` and `Y` may be a scalar or array. The `line_object` is a line object which can be used to modify properties of a plotted line.

There are two methods to customize line style, marker type, and line color in a 2-d line plot. The first method uses the `LineSpec` argument and the second method uses comma-separated Name-Value pair arguments. In the first method, the `LineSpec` is defined as a character vector or string which contains symbols that specify line style, marker type, and line color. For example, to plot a line with a dashed line, circle marker, and black color, we can use `'--ok'` in place of the `LineSpec`. Here, `'--'` defines a line to be plotted as a dashed line. The `'o'` set a marker type to circle. The `'k'` set a color of a line to black. Note that, we may use any combination of line style, marker type, and line color symbols. For example, we may only use line color symbol without defining line style or marker type. Here is a list of optional `LineSpec` (line specifications):

LineSpec	Description	Example
Line Style	Set line style	`'--'`
Marker	Set marker type	`'o'`
Color	Set line color	`'k'`

The `'Name1', Value1`, ..., `'NameN', ValueN` define optional comma-separated Name-Value pair arguments. The `plot` function has several optional Name-Value pair arguments that may be used to customize a plot. As explained in an earlier chapter, in Name-Value pair arguments, the `'Name'` specifies a name of the optional argument, while the `Value` contains values to be assigned to this optional argument. Here is a list of common Name-Value pair arguments to customize a 2-d line plot. All arguments in this list are optional.

'Name'	Description	Example
`'Color'`	Set line color	`'Color', [0.5,0.5,0.5]`
`'LineStyle'`	Set line style	`'LineStyle', '--'`
`'LineWidth'`	Set line width	`'LineWidth', 2`
`'Marker'`	Set marker type	`'Marker', 'o'`
`'MarkerEdgeColor'`	Set marker edge color	`'MarkerEdgeColor', [0.5,0.5,0.5]`
`'MarkerFaceColor'`	Set marker face color	`'MarkerFaceColor', [0.5,0.5,0.5]`
`'MarkerSize'`	Set marker size	`'MarkerSize', 10`
`'DatetimeTickFormat'`	Set date and time tick format	`'DatetimeTickFormat', 'yyyy-MM-dd'`

We may use these pair arguments separately or in combination with other proper pair arguments to customize a plot. In the rest of a chapter, we explain how to use some of these pair arguments to customize a plot.

Note that, as mentioned above, we can set line style, marker type, and line color either with `LineSpec` argument or with Name-Value pair arguments.

Also, we can create axes using the **`axes`** function and then add a plot to that axes. For more details on how to create axes and add a plot to that axes refer to axes section.

To explain how to visualize data with MATLAB, let's consider an example. Assume we have six pairs of data points in a form of (x,y) as (1,0), (2,30), (3,20), (4,50), (5,40), and (6,70). Now, we put all x values together in an array x=[1,2,3,4,5,6] and all y values together in an array y=[0,30,20,50,40,70]. When we pass these two arrays to MATLAB, it assigns each value in an array x to its corresponding value in an array y to create all six (x,y) pairs. Because of that, x and y should have the same number of items. Here is an example shows how to plot these data using the **`plot`** function.

```
%x and y data
x=[1,2,3,4,5,6];
y=[0,30,20,50,40,70];

%Plot y versus x
plot(x,y)
```

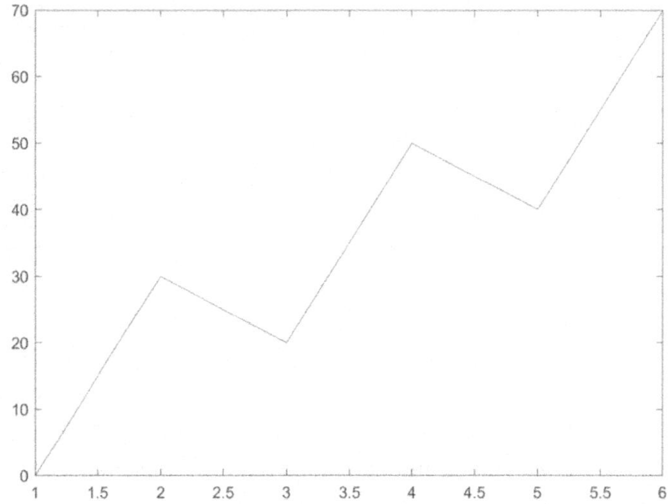

Figure 9.1
Line plot using the `plot` function

After we create a plot, we can save that plot to a file. To do that, we use the `print` function. Here is a general syntax shows how to save a plot:

Syntax

```
print(filename, formattype, resolution)
```

The `filename` defines a path and name of a file to be saved. The `resolution` defines a figure resolution in dots per inch. The `resolution` is optional. The `resolution` is defined by a character vector or string that contains `-r` followed by a resolution value. For example, to save an image with 300 dpi we use `'-r300'`. To save an image with a screen resolution, we can use `'-r0'` for resolution. The `formattype` defines a format of a file to be saved. Here is a list of common file formats to save an image with:

formattype	Saved File Extension
`'-djpeg'`	.jpg
`'-dpng'`	.png
`'-dtiff'`	.tif
`'-dbmp'`	.bmp
`'-dpdf'`	.pdf
`'-deps'`	.eps
`'-dsvg'`	.svg
`'-dpsc'`	.ps

MATLAB may leave some space between plotted lines and a plot boundary. We can use the **axis tight** command to fit a plot boundary to data ranges before saving a figure.

Here is an example shows how to save a figure to a file. In this example, we save a figure from a previous example with a name and extension 'Figure.png' in 'C:\Figure_Example' directory with 300 dpi. Here, we use the '-dpng' image format to save an image with .png extension. We may use other image format to save an image with extensions such as .tif, .jpg, .pdf., .ps, .eps, and .svg extensions.

```
%Save figure as png file
print('C:\Figure_Example\Figure.png', '-dpng', '-r300')
```

9.3 Set Color

When we create a plot, MATLAB uses a color from a default color order to assign a color to its drawings. If we find default colors are suitable for our purpose, we simply let MATLAB uses them. However, if we need to use a particular color, we can use the Name-Value pair arguments `'Color', Color_Value` to assign a user-defined color to a plot. Here are Name-Value pair arguments to set a drawing color in the `plot` function:

'Name'	Description
'Color'	Set plot color

Here is a general syntax shows how to set a color in a 2-d line plot:

Syntax

```
plot(X, Y, 'Color', Color_Value, ...)
```

The `'Color'` indicates that the following variable contains a color value. The `Color_Value` contains a color that data to be drawn with that color. The `Color_Value` may be RGB as [Red, Green, Blue], hexadecimal color code, or classic string values.

Note that, in an RGB format, each of Red, Green, and Blue values should be between 0 and 1 (closed interval of [0,1]). For example, RGB value for a black color is [0,0,0], for a white color is [1,1,1], and for the dark midnight blue is [0, 0.2, 0.4]. It is common to report RGB values in a range of [0,255]. In such cases, we simply divide each RGB value by 255 to convert them to a range of

[0,1]. For example, the dark slate gray has RGB values in a 0-255 scale as [47, 79, 79]. To use this color in MATLAB, we change it to a 0-1 scale as [47/255, 79/255, 79/255].

By default, MATLAB uses a color from a default color order if a color is not defined. It means that, MATLAB uses the first color from a default color order to draw data. If we add a second line to a plot, it uses the second color from a color order. If we add the third line to a plot, it uses the third color from a color order, and so on. This helps to distinguish each line from other lines. Each color in a default color order has a Hexadecimal color code. To get a list of colors in a default color order, we can use the `colororder` function. Here is a list of default Hexadecimal color codes and their RGB values that MATLAB uses:

Hexadecimal Color Code	RGB
'#0072BD'	[0.000, 0.447, 0.741]
'#D95319'	[0.850, 0.325, 0.098]
'#EDB120'	[0.929, 0.694, 0.125]
'#7E2F8E'	[0.494, 0.184, 0.556]
'#77AC30'	[0.466, 0.674, 0.188]
'#4DBEEE'	[0.301, 0.745, 0.933]
'#A2142F'	[0.635, 0.078, 0.184]

Figure 9.2
MATLAB default color order

The simplest way to assign a user-defined color to a drawing is to select a color from the `lines` colormap. To get colors from the lines colormap, we can use the `lines` function. For example, to draw a line with the third color from the lines colormap, first, we obtain first 7 colors from the lines colormap by using `col=lines(7)` , and then we set a line color to the third color by using `'Color', col(3,:)`.

Another method to assign a user-defined color is to use RGB color values. As mentioned above, the RGB color should be passed to MATLAB as a [Red, Green, Blue] row array (row vector) with its values between 0 and 1. For example, a gray color has RGB values equal to [0.5,0.5,0.5]. Therefore, to draw a line with a gray color, we can use `'Color', [0.5,0.5,0.5]`.

Also, we can use classic color strings to set a user-defined color. For example, to draw a line with a classic blue color, we can use `'Color', 'b'`. Here is a list of classic colors to be used in MATLAB:

Classic Color String	Description
'b'	Blue
'g'	Green
'r'	Red
'c'	Cyan
'm'	Magenta
'y'	Yellow
'k'	Black

Here is an example shows how to plot data with a gray color. For this purpose, we use RGB values for a gray color as `'Color', [0.5,0.5,0.5]`.

```
%x and y data
x=[1,2,3,4,5,6];
y=[0,30,20,50,40,70];

%Plot y versus x with gray color
plot(x, y, 'Color', [0.5, 0.5, 0.5])
```

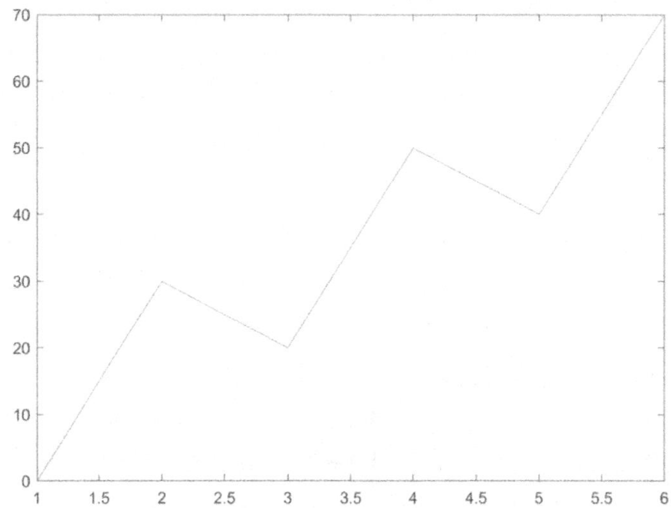

Figure 9.3
Line plot with gray color

9.4 Set Line Style and Line Width

We can define a line style and line width of drawings in MATLAB. We can use the Name-Value pair arguments `'LineStyle', Style_Value` to assign a line style to a drawing. Similarly, we can use the Name-Value pair arguments `'LineWidth', Width_Value` to assign a user-defined line width to a drawing. Here are Name-Value pair arguments to set a line style and line width in the `plot` function:

'Name'	Description
`'LineStyle'`	Set line style
`'LineWidth'`	Set line width

Here is a general syntax shows how to define a line style and line width in a 2-d line plot:

Syntax

```
plot(X, Y, 'LineStyle', Style_Value, 'LineWidth', Width_Value, ...)
```

The `'LineStyle'` indicates that the following variable contains a line style value. The `Style_Value` contains a line style that data to be drawn with that style. By default, MATLAB draws data with a solid line. The `'LineWidth'` indicates that the following variable contains a line width value. The `Width_Value` contains a line width in points. By default, MATLAB draws data in 0.5 points.

We may use several line styles to plot data in MATLAB. Here is a list of common line styles that MATLAB accepts.

Line Style	Description
`'-'`	Solid line
`'--'`	Dashed line
`'-.'`	Dash-dotted line
`':'`	Dotted line
`'none'`	No line

Figure 9.4
MATLAB line styles

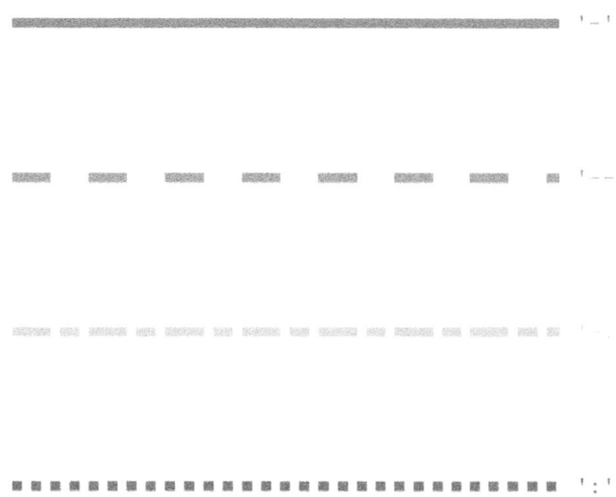

Here is an example shows how to plot data with a dashed line style and a line width equal to 4 points.

```
%x and y data
x=[1,2,3,4,5,6];
y=[0,30,20,50,40,70];

%Plot y versus x with dashed line style and 4 points line width
plot(x, y, 'LineStyle', '--', 'LineWidth', 4)
```

Figure 9.5
Line plot with a dashed line style and 4-points line width

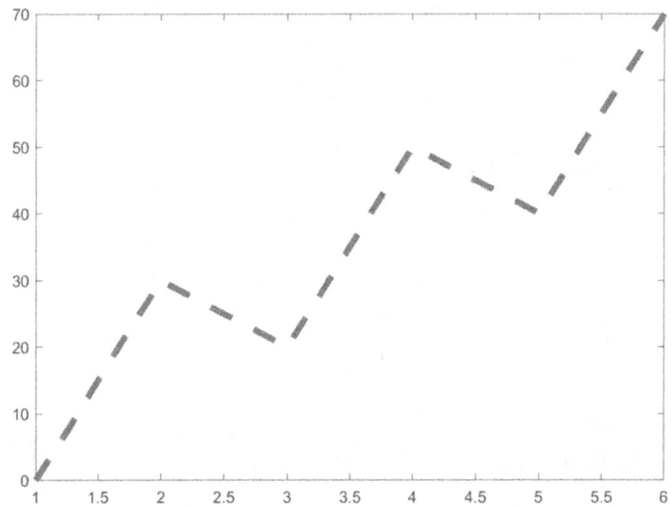

We may combine a line style with a classic color string by using the `LineSpec` argument. To do that, we simply use a string that contains a line style followed by a classic color string after x and y data. For example, to plot y versus x with a dashed line style and a classic blue color we use `plot(x, y, '--b')`. Note that, in this format, we only use the `LineSpec` argument and do not use any Name-Value pair arguments for a line style or color.

9.5 Add Marker

We may add markers to a plot to mark data points in that plot. We can use the Name-Value pair arguments `'Marker', Marker_Value` to add markers to a plot. Here are Name-Value pair arguments to add markers in the `plot` function:

'Name'	Description
`'Marker'`	Set marker type
`'MarkerEdgeColor'`	Set marker edge color
`'MarkerFaceColor'`	Set marker face color
`'MarkerSize'`	Set marker size

Here is a general syntax shows how to add markers to a 2-d line plot:

Syntax

```
plot(X, Y, 'Marker', Marker_Value, ...)
```

The `'Marker'` indicates that the following variable contains a marker type. The `Marker_Value` contains a marker type to be added to a plot. By default, MATLAB does not use markers in a line plot. Here is a list of common markers that MATLAB uses.

Marker	Description
`'.'`	Point marker
`'o'`	Circle marker
`'s'`	Square marker
`'p'`	Pentagon marker
`'h'`	Hexagon marker
`'d'`	Diamond marker
`'x'`	Cross marker
`'+'`	Plus marker
`'*'`	Star (asterisk) marker
`'v'`	Downward pointed triangle marker
`'^'`	Upward pointed triangle marker
`'<'`	Left pointed triangle marker
`'>'`	Right pointed triangle marker
`'none'`	No marker

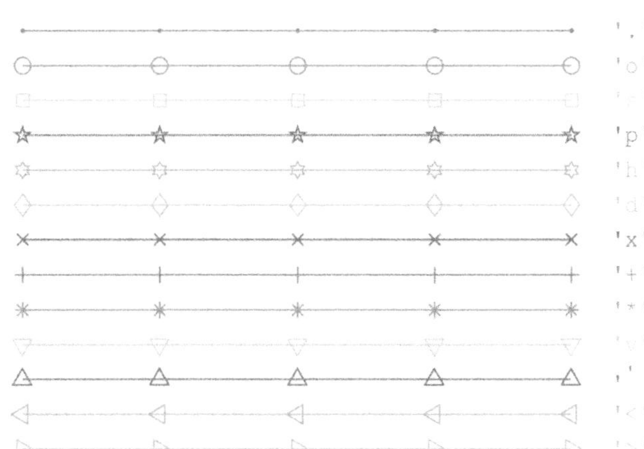

Figure 9.6
MATLAB markers

We may use the Name-Value pair arguments `'MarkerEdgeColor', MarkerEdgeColor_Value` , `'MarkerFaceColor', MarkerFaceColor_Value` , and `'MarkerSize', MarkerSize_Value` to customize the appearance of markers.

Here is an example shows how to plot data with a circle marker. In this example, we set a marker size equal to 10 points.

```
%x and y data
x=[1,2,3,4,5,6];
y=[0,30,20,50,40,70];

%Plot y versus x with circle marker and 10 points marker size
plot(x, y, 'Marker', 'o', 'MarkerSize', 10)
```

Figure 9.7
Line plot with circle markers and 10 points marker size

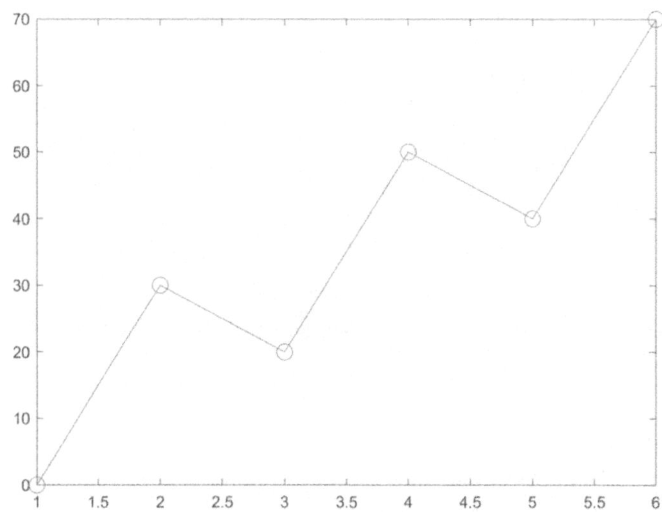

We may combine a line style with a marker sign by using the `LineSpec` argument. To do that, we simply use a string that contains a line style followed by a marker sign after x and y data. For example, to plot y versus x with a dashed line style and a circle marker we use `plot(x, y, '--o')`. Note that, in this format, we only use the `LineSpec` argument and do not use any Name-Value pair arguments for a line style or marker.

Similarly, we may combine a line style, a marker sign, and a classic color string together by using the `LineSpec` argument. To do that, we simply use a string that contains a line style followed by a marker sign followed by a classic color string after x and y data. For example, to plot y versus x with a dashed line style, a circle marker, and a classic blue color we use `plot(x, y, '--ob')`. Note that, in this format, we only use the `LineSpec` argument and do not use any Name-Value pair arguments for a line style, marker, or color.

Also, we may only draw markers and skip drawing lines. For example, to plot y versus x with a circle marker without any line we use `plot(x, y, 'o')`. The result is similar to `plot(x, y, 'LineStyle', 'none', 'Marker', 'o')`.

9.6 Add Labels

We can add labels to a plot and its axes. Here are MATLAB functions to add labels to a plot:

Function	Description
`title`	Add title to plot
`xlabel`	Set label for x-axis
`ylabel`	Set label for y-axis

Here are general syntaxes show how to add labels to a plot:

Syntax

```
title(txt_title)
xlabel(txt_xlabel)
ylabel(txt_ylabel)
```

The `txt_title` defines a plot title. The `txt_xlabel` and `txt_ylabel` define labels of x-axis and y-axis, respectively.

Here is an example shows how to add labels to a plot. In this example, we set a plot title as 'Line Plot', x-axis label as 'X Data', and y-axis label as 'Y Data'.

```
%x and y data
x=[1,2,3,4,5,6];
y=[0,30,20,50,40,70];

%Plot y versus x
plot(x,y)

%Add labels
title('Line Plot')
xlabel('X Data')
ylabel('Y Data')
```

Figure 9.8
Line plot with labels

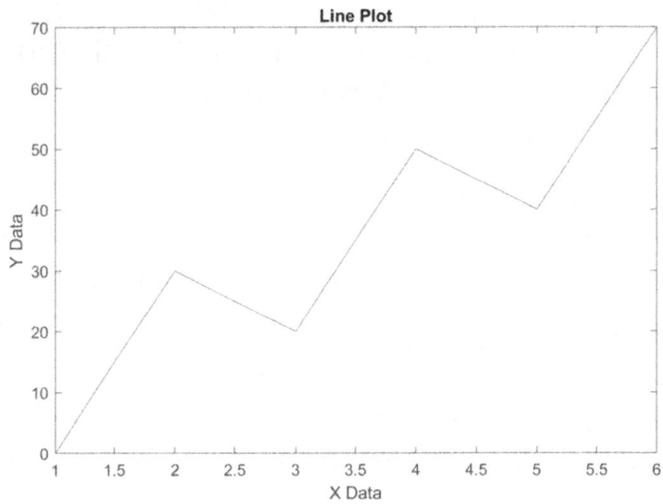

For details on how to use mathematical text in labels, refer to add mathematical text section.

9.7 Set Axis Limits and Ticks

We may customize axis limits and ticks. Here are MATLAB functions to customize axes of a plot:

Function	Description
`xlim`	set x limits for x-axis
`ylim`	set y limits for y-axis
`xticks`	Set tick locations for x-axis
`yticks`	Set tick locations for y-axis
`xticklabels`	Set tick labels for x-axis
`yticklabels`	Set tick labels for y-axis
`axis`	Set axis properties

Here are general syntaxes show how to set axis limits in a plot:

Syntax

```
xlim(limits)
ylim(limits)
```

The `limits` defines limits of an axis. For the x-axis, it defines the left and right sides of an x-axis as `[xmin,xmax]`. For the y-axis, it defines the bottom and top of a y-axis as `[ymin,ymax]`.

Here are general syntaxes show how to set axis ticks in a plot:

Syntax

```
xticks(ticks)
yticks(ticks)
```

The `ticks` is a vector of positions that defines positions of ticks.

Here are general syntaxes show how to set tick labels in a plot:

Syntax

```
xticklabels(labels)
yticklabels(labels)
```

The `labels` is a string array or a cell array of character vectors that defines labels of ticks.

Here is an example shows how to set axis limits and ticks. In this example, we set the x-axis limits from 1 to 6 and y-axis limits from 0 to 70. Also, we set the x-axis to have ticks at positions 1, 3, 5 and y-axis to have ticks at positions 0, 20, 40, 60.

```
%x and y data
x=[1,2,3,4,5,6];
y=[0,30,20,50,40,70];

%Plot y versus x
plot(x,y)

%Set axis limits
xlim([1,6])
ylim([0,70])

%Set axis tick positions
xticks([1,3,5])
yticks([0,20,40,60])
```

Figure 9.9
Line plot with axis limits and tick positions

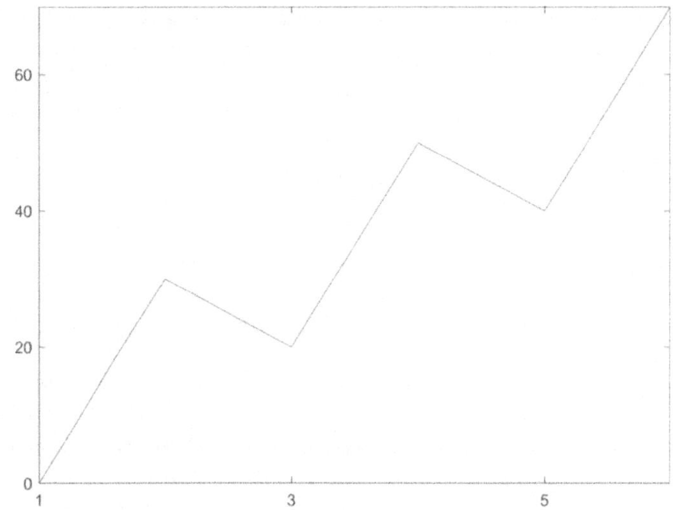

We can also use the `axis` function to customize plot axes. Here is general syntax shows how to set axes properties using the axis function:

Syntax

```
axis value
```

The `value` defines how the axes should be customized. Here is a list of common axis customization values to be used in the axis function.

Value	Description
`on`	Turn on (show) axis lines and labels
`off`	Turn off (do not show) axis lines and labels
`equal`	Set equal length for data units along all axes
`tight`	Set axis limits to fit tightly around the data
`auto`	Automatically set all axis limits
`image`	Similar to combination of equal and tight values
`square`	Set equal length for all axes

For example, to plot data without showing axes, we use the `axis off` command to turn off axes. By doing that, MATLAB does not draw axes.

9.8 Add Grid Lines

We may add grid lines to a plot. Here is a MATLAB function to add grid lines to a plot:

Function	Description
`grid`	Add or hide grid lines

Here is a general syntax shows how to add grid lines to a plot:

Syntax

```
grid value
```

The **`value`** defines how the grids should be drawn. By default, MATLAB does not draw grid lines. To draw grid lines, we need to use the **`grid on`** command. Here is a list of common values to be used in the grid function.

Value	Description
`on`	Turn on (display) major grid lines
`off`	Turn off (remove) all grid lines
`minor`	Turn on or off (display or remove) minor grid lines

Here is an example shows how to add grid lines to a plot. In this example, we add major grid lines to both axes.

```
%x and y data
x=[1,2,3,4,5,6];
y=[0,30,20,50,40,70];

%Plot y versus x
plot(x,y)

%Add grid lines
grid on %Or grid
```

Figure 9.10
Line plot with grid lines

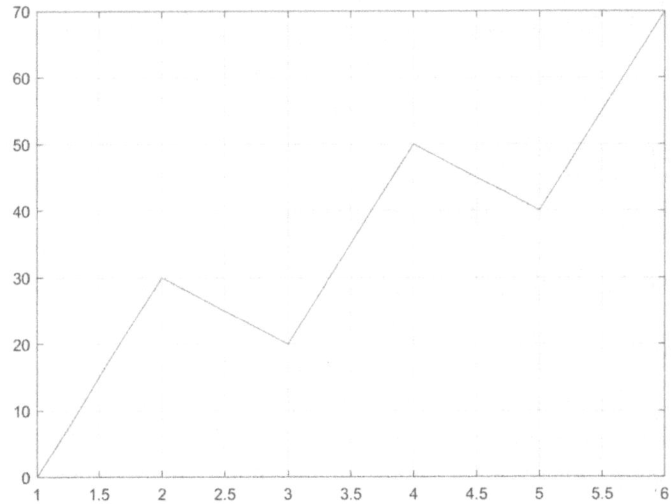

9.9 Add Text and Annotation

After we create a plot, we may need to add a text or annotate a point in that plot. Here are MATLAB functions to add text or annotate a point in a plot:

Function	Description
`text`	Add text to data points
`annotation`	Create annotations

Here is a general syntax shows how to add a text to a plot:

Syntax

```
text(x, y, txt, 'Name1', Value1, ..., 'NameN', ValueN)
```

The `x` and `y` define a position to add a text. The `txt` defines a text (string) to be added to a plot.

The `'Name1', Value1`, ..., `'NameN', ValueN` define optional comma-separated Name-Value pair arguments. We may use several Name-Value pair arguments to customize a text. Here is a list of common Name-Value pair arguments to customize a text. All arguments in this list are optional.

'Name'	Description	Example
`'Color'`	Set color of text	`'Color', [0,0,0]`

'FontName'	Set text font name	'FontName', 'FixedWidth'
'FontSize'	Set text font size	'FontSize', 12
'Interpreter'	Set marker type	'Interpreter', 'latex'

To use a fixed-width font for a text use `'FontName', 'FixedWidth'` pair arguments. The `'Interpreter', Interpreter_Value` pair arguments take one of `'tex'`, `'latex'`, and `'none'` as an `Interpreter_Value`.

Here is an example shows how to add a text to a plot. In this example, we add a text 'This is the first peak' at a position (1,35) with a font size of 12 to a plot.

```
%x and y data
x=[1,2,3,4,5,6];
y=[0,30,20,50,40,70];

%Plot y versus x
plot(x,y)

%Add text at (1,35)
text(1, 35, 'This is the first peak', 'FontSize', 12)
```

Figure 9.11
Line plot with a text

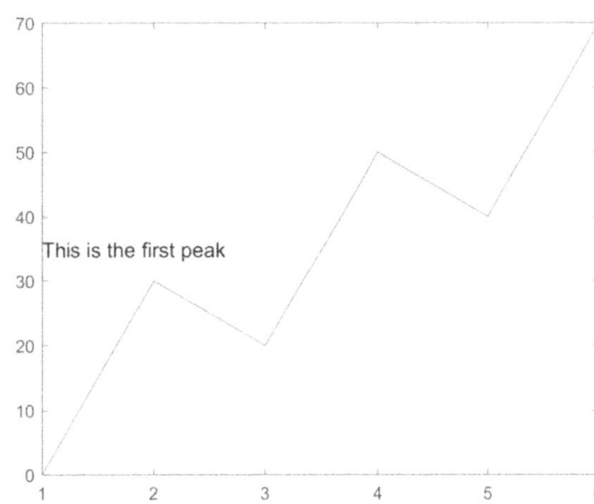

We can also annotate a point in a plot with a text. Here is a general syntax shows how to annotate a point with a text in a plot:

Syntax

```
annotation(lineType, x, y, 'Name1', Value1, ..., 'NameN', ValueN)
```

The `lineType` defines how to draw a line for annotation. The `lineType` takes one of `'line'`, `'arrow'`, `'doublearrow'`, and `'textarrow'`. The `x` and `y` define beginning and end positions of annotation as `[x_begin,x_end]` and `[y_begin,y_end]`. The position values in the `x` and `y` are normalized and should be between 0 and 1. The normalized position for the lower-left corner of the figure is (0,0) and for the upper-right corner is (1,1). We may use Name-Value pair arguments to customize an annotation.

To create a text arrow annotation, we need to set the `lineType` as `'textarrow'`. Here is a general syntax shows how to create a text arrow annotation:

Syntax

```
annotation('textarrow', x, y, 'String', txt, 'Name1', Value1, ...,
'NameN', ValueN)
```

The `'String', txt` pair arguments define a text of an annotation. The `txt` contains a text (string) of an annotation.

Here is an example shows how to annotate a point in a plot. In this example, we annotate a point at (2,30). To do that, we use normalized coordinates (0.26,0.6) for the beginning and normalized coordinates (0.28,0.48) for the end of annotation. Therefore, we use [0.26,0.28] to define the beginning and end of an annotation along the x-axis and use [0.6,0.48] to define the beginning and end of an annotation along the y-axis. We place a text 'This is the first peak' with a font size of 12. To set a font size we use `'FontSize', FontSize_Value` pair arguments. Also, we set a color of annotation by using RGB values [0,0,0]. To set an annotation color we use `'Color', Color_Value` pair arguments.

```
%x and y data
x=[1,2,3,4,5,6];
y=[0,30,20,50,40,70];

%Plot y versus x
plot(x,y)

%Annotate point at (2,30)
```

```
pos_x_norm = [0.26,0.28];
pos_y_norm = [0.6,0.48];
annotation('textarrow', pos_x_norm, pos_y_norm, 'String', ...
    'This is the first peak', 'FontSize', 12, 'Color', [0,0,0])
```

Figure 9.12
Line plot with annotation

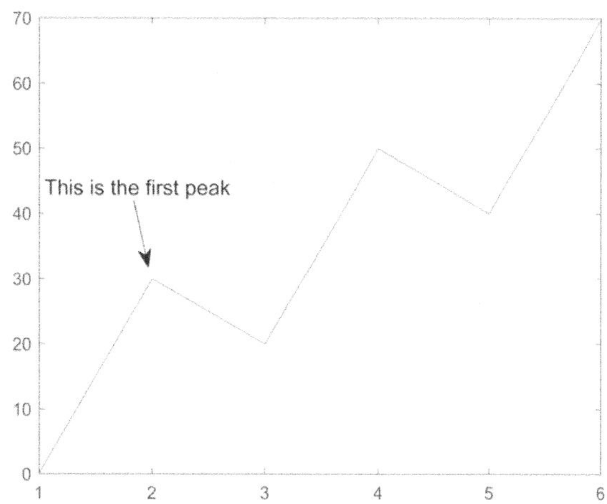

9.10 Add Mathematical Text

It is often required to add formula or mathematical text to a plot. Probably, the best way to add and show mathematical text is to use LaTeX. To add LaTeX, we need to write a text string in a particular format. Here is a general syntax shows how to write a text as a LaTeX:

Syntax

```
'$ TeX String $'
```

Note that, the string should be placed between two **$** signs to be considered as LaTeX, otherwise it will be considered as a TeX markup. Additionally, we need to tell MATLAB to use a LaTeX interpreter to display LaTeX in a proper format. To do that, every time we use a LaTeX in a function, we need to specify a proper interpreter by using `'Interpreter', 'latex'` pair arguments. Also, there are special characters that may be displayed correctly only if represented by unique character sequences. For example, a single quotation mark should be represented by ''. Here is a list of common TeX markups.

TeX	Symbol	TeX	Symbol
\alpha	α	\omega	ω
\beta	β	\Delta	Δ
\gamma	γ	\Sigma	Σ
\delta	δ	\Omega	Ω
\epsilon	ε	\nabla	∇
\eta	η	\infty	∞
\theta	θ	\times	$\times$
\lambda	λ	\pm	$\pm$
\mu	μ	\approx	$\approx$
\nu	ν	\neq	$\neq$
\pi	π	\circ	$\circ$
\rho	ρ	\rightarrow	$\rightarrow$
\sigma	σ	\rm	Normal Font
\tau	τ	\bf	Bold font
\phi	ϕ	\	Control (add) space

We can combine TeX markups to generate a desired mathematical text. Remember, to use any TeX strings as LaTeX, it should be placed between two $ signs as `'$ ... $'`, otherwise it would be considered as TeX. For example, we can use a caret symbol ^ to raise to the power. Now, to show an expression x^y, we need to write it in LaTeX as `'$x^y$'`. Also note that, when we work with mathematical texts, we may need to apply an operator to an expression. In such conditions, we need to put that expression inside curly braces `{...}`. For example, to raise x to the power of y, we can use `'$x^y$'`, however, to raise x to the power of y+z, we need to put y+z inside curly braces as `'$x^{y+z}$'`. Here we present several examples that show how to use TeX strings to produce common mathematical expressions.

TeX String	Result
x \times y	$x \times y$
\pm x	$\pm x$
x^y	x^y
x^{y+z}	x^{y+z}
x_i	x_i
x_{i,j}	$x_{i,j}$
{x_i}^y	${x_i}^y$
x/y	x/y
\frac{x}{y}	$\frac{x}{y}$
\sqrt{x}	$\sqrt{x}$

`\sqrt[3]{x}`	$\sqrt[3]{x}$
`\sqrt[3]{x^2+y^2}`	$\sqrt[3]{x^2+y^2}$
`\sin (2\pi)`	$\sin(2\pi)$
`\int_{a}^{b} x dx`	$\int_{a}^{b} x dx$
`\sum_{n=1}^{\infty} a_n`	$\sum_{n=1}^{\infty} a_n$
`\lim_{x\rightarrow\infty} \frac{1}{x}`	$\lim_{x\rightarrow\infty} \frac{1}{x}$
`10^{\circ} C`	$10^{\circ} C$
`\bar x`	$\bar x$
`\overline{xyz}`	$\overline{xyz}$
`\hat x`	$\hat x$
`\widehat{xyz}`	$\widehat{xyz}$
`abcd`	$abcd$
`{\rm abcd}`	abcd
`{\bf abcd}`	$\mathbf{abcd}$
`ab \ cd`	$ab\ cd$

Here is an example shows how to add a mathematical text to a plot. In this example, first, we generate a sequence of 1000 numbers between 0.001 and 2π. Then, we calculate y values as $y = \sin(2\pi x)/x$. After that, we plot y versus x and label x-axis as x using `'$x$'` and y-axis as $\sin(2\pi x)/x$ using `'$\sin(2 \pi x)/x$'`. Finally, we add a text $y = \frac{\sin(2\pi x)}{x}$ using `'$y=\frac{\sin(2 \pi x)}{x}$'` at a position (1,1.5) to a plot. Note that, we specify a proper interpreter by using `'Interpreter', 'latex'` pair arguments in the xlabel, ylabel, and text functions.

```
%x and y data
x=linspace(0.001,2*pi,1000); %Generate 1000 points
                             %between 0.001 and 2pi
y=sin(2.*pi.*x)./x;          %y=sin(2*pi*x)/x

%Plot y versus x
plot(x,y)

%Add labels
xlabel('$x$', 'Interpreter', 'latex')
ylabel('$\sin(2 \pi x)/x$', 'Interpreter', 'latex')

%Add text at (1,1.5)
text(1, 1.5, '$y=\frac{\sin(2 \pi x)}{x}$', 'Interpreter', 'latex')
```

Figure 9.13
Line plot with mathematical text

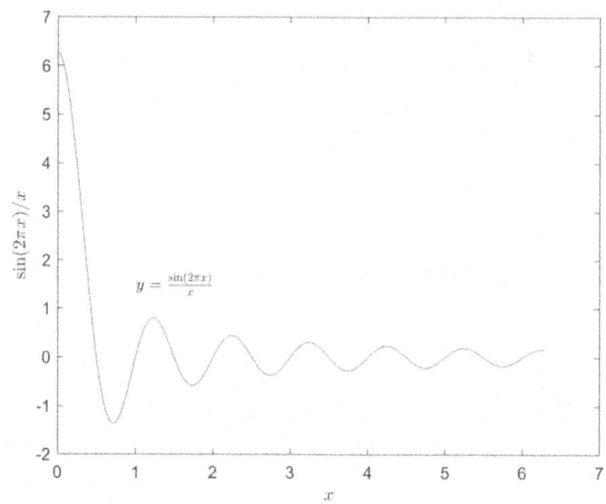

9.11 Plot Multiple Lines and Add Legend

We can draw multiple datasets in one figure. To do that, first, we need to call the `hold` function, and then, we simply use the `plot` function multiple times (once for each dataset) to draw all datasets. Datasets are plotted in an order that the `plot` function is called.

After we draw all datasets, we may need to identify which dataset each drawing presents. In other words, we may need to label drawings to be recognizable from each other. To do that, we can label drawings by adding a legend to a plot. Here are MATLAB functions to draw multiple datasets and add a legend to a plot:

Function	Description
`hold`	Retain current plot to add new drawings
`legend`	Add legend to plot

Here are general syntaxes show how to add new drawings to a plot:

Syntax

```
plot(x1,y1)
hold on
plot(x2,y2)
plot(x3,y3)
...
```

Here are general syntaxes show how to add a legend to a plot:

Syntax

```
legend(label1, ..., labelN, 'Name1', Value1, ..., 'NameN', ValueN)

legend([obj1, ..., objN], {label1, ..., labelN}, 'Name1', Value1, ...,
'NameN', ValueN)
```

The **label1**, ..., **labelN** contain labels for drawings (lines). If **label1**, ..., **labelN** are not given, then MATLAB automatically assigns legends. The **obj1**, ..., **objN** defines graphics objects to be labeled in a legend.

The **'Name1', Value1**, ..., **'NameN', ValueN** define optional comma-separated Name-Value pair arguments. We may use several Name-Value pair arguments to customize a plot legend. Here is a list of common Name-Value pair arguments to customize a plot legend. All arguments in this list are optional.

'Name'	Description	Example
'Location'	Set location of legend	'Location', 'northeast'
'TextColor'	Set color of text	'TextColor', [0,0,0]
'FontSize'	Set text font size	'FontSize', 12
'NumColumns'	Set number of columns	'NumColumns', 3
'Orientation'	Set orientation of legend	'Location', 'horizontal'

We can use the **'Location', Location_Value** pair arguments to set a location of a legend in a figure. Here is a list of common location values we can use to set a location of a legend:

Location Value	Description
'best'	Best location
'north'	Inside top
'south'	Inside bottom
'east'	Inside right
'west'	Inside left
'northeast'	Inside top-right
'northwest'	Inside top-left
'southeast'	Inside bottom-right
'southwest'	Inside bottom-left

There are a couple of methods to add a legend to a plot. In the first method, we add a legend to a plot by using the `legend` function without passing any arguments to it. To do that, first, we draw all datasets using the `plot` function. Then, we call the `legend` function without passing any arguments to it. This function automatically labels drawings as 'data1', 'data2', ... and adds a legend to a plot.

Here is an example shows how to add a legend to a plot without passing any arguments to the `legend` function. In this example, first, we draw three lines of y1, y2, and y3 versus x using the `plot` function. Then, we use the `legend` function without any arguments to add a legend to a plot. MATLAB labels lines as 'data1', 'data2', and 'data3' and adds a legend to a plot.

```
%x, y1, y2, and y3 data
x=[1,2,3,4,5,6];
y1=[0,30,20,50,40,70];
y2=[10,40,30,60,50,80];
y3=[20,50,40,70,60,90];

%Plot y1, y2, and y3 versus x
plot(x,y1)
hold on
plot(x,y2)
plot(x,y3)

%Add legend
legend
```

The second method to add a legend to a plot is to pass legend labels to the `legend` function. To do that, first, we draw all datasets using the `plot` function. Then, we call the `legend` function while passing legend labels to it. This function assigns given labels to drawings and adds a legend to a plot.

Here is an example shows how to add a legend to a plot by passing legend labels to the `legend` function. In this example, first, we draw three lines of y1, y2, and y3 versus x. Then, we pass legend labels as 'y1','y2','y3' to the `legend` function to add a legend to a plot. MATLAB assigns given labels to drawings and adds a legend to a plot.

```
%x, y1, y2, and y3 data
x=[1,2,3,4,5,6];
y1=[0,30,20,50,40,70];
y2=[10,40,30,60,50,80];
```

```
y3=[20,50,40,70,60,90];

%Plot y1, y2, and y3 versus x
plot(x,y1)
hold on
plot(x,y2)
plot(x,y3)

%Add legend
legend('y1','y2','y3')
```

Figure 9.14
Line plot with legend

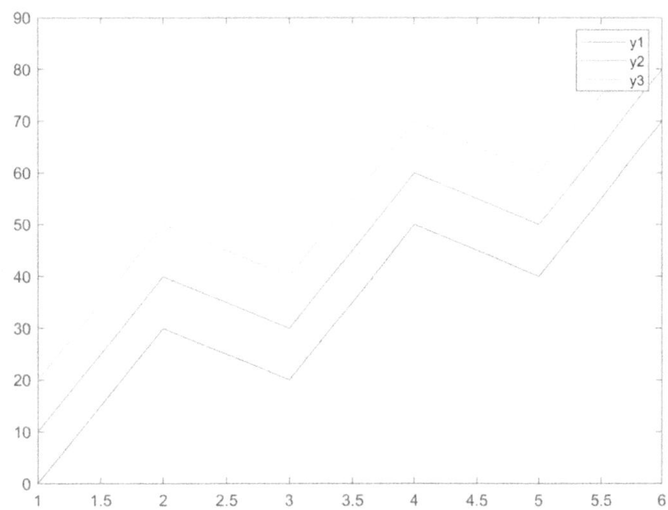

The third method to add a legend to a plot is to pass graphics objects and labels to the `legend` function. To do that, first, we draw all data while assigning each drawing to a graphics object using the `plot` function. Then, we call the `legend` function with passing graphics objects and labels to it. This function assigns each label to a corresponding graphics object and adds a legend to a plot.

Here is an example shows how to add a legend to a plot by passing both graphics objects and labels to the `legend` function. In this example, first, we draw three lines of y1, y2, and y3 versus x. We assign these drawings to graphics objects p1, p2, and p3 while we draw them. Then, we pass graphics objects as [p1,p2,p3] and legend labels as {'y1','y2','y3'} to the `legend` function to add a legend to a plot. MATLAB assigns each label to a corresponding graphics object and adds a legend to a plot.

```
%x, y1, y2, and y3 data
x=[1,2,3,4,5,6];
y1=[0,30,20,50,40,70];
```

```
y2=[10,40,30,60,50,80];
y3=[20,50,40,70,60,90];

%Plot y1, y2, and y3 versus x
p1 = plot(x,y1);
hold on
p2 = plot(x,y2);
p3 = plot(x,y3);

%Add legend
legend([p1,p2,p3],{'y1','y2','y3'})
```

9.12 Create Multiple Figures

When we draw multiple datasets, instead of drawing them all on one figure, we may need to plot them on several separate figures. For example, we may want to plot each dataset on a separate figure, or we may want to plot subsets of data on several figures. To do that, we should create each figure before plotting data on that figure. It means that, for the first figure, we create a figure and we plot all data to be displayed on the first figure on that figure. Then, we create another figure and we plot all data to be displayed on the second figure on that figure. We repeat this process until we create all figures. Here are MATLAB functions to work with a figure:

Function	Description
`figure`	Create new figure
`clf`	Clear current figure
`close`	Close figure

Here is a general syntax shows how to create a figure:

Syntax

```
fig = figure(n, 'Position', Position_Value)
```

The `n` defines a figure number. The `n` is optional. If `n` is not defined, the next incremented figure number is used. The `'Position', Position_Value` pair arguments define figure position and size. The `Position_Value` takes position and size of a figure as `[left, bottom, width, height]`. The `'Position', Position_Value` pair arguments are optional.

Note that, if we need to add drawings to an existing figure, we can use its figure number in the figure function to switch to that figure. By doing that, a specified existing figure becomes a current figure and all new drawings are added to that figure. Also, if we need to clear a current figure, we can use the `clf` function.

Here is an example shows how to plot 3 sets of data in 3 figures. In this example, we plot three lines of (x,y1), (x,y2), and (x,y3) on three figures.

```
%x, y1, y2, and y3 data
x=[1,2,3,4,5,6];
y1=[0,30,20,50,40,70];
y2=[10,40,30,60,50,80];
y3=[20,50,40,70,60,90];

%Plot y1 versus x in figure 1
figure(1)
plot(x,y1)

%Plot y2 versus x in figure 2
figure(2)
plot(x,y2)

%Plot y3 versus x in figure 3
figure(3)
plot(x,y3)
```

9.13 The get and set Functions

After a plot is created, MATLAB allows changing a wide range of plot properties to customize an existing plot. Here are MATLAB functions to customize an existing plot:

Function	Description
`get`	Return graphics object properties
`set`	Set graphics object properties
`gca`	Get current axes or chart
`gcf`	Get current figure handle
`reset`	Restore default properties of graphics object

In MATLAB, we can customize a graphics after it is created. To do that, commonly, a graphics is assigned to a graphics object at the time of its creation. Then, we use that graphics object to get access and customize associated graphics. To get or set properties of a graphics objects, we can use the `get` or `set` functions. Here are general syntaxes show how to get or set properties of a graphics object:

Syntax

```
Property_Value = get(graphics_object, 'Property_Name')
set(graphics_object, 'Property_Name', New_Property_Value)
```

The `graphics_object` defines a graphics object to get or set its properties. The `'Property_Name'` defines a property name to be get or set. The `New_Property_Value` defines a new value to be set for the `'Property_Name'`.

Here is an example shows how to set plot properties after it is created. In this example, first, we create a plot and assign it to a graphics object. Then, we use that graphics object to set line width to 4 points and a line style to dashed-line.

```
%x and y data
x=[1,2,3,4,5,6];
y=[0,30,20,50,40,70];

%Plot y versus x
p = plot(x,y);

%Set line width to 4 pints
set(p, 'LineWidth', 4)

%Set line style to dashed line '--'
set(p, 'LineStyle', '--')
```

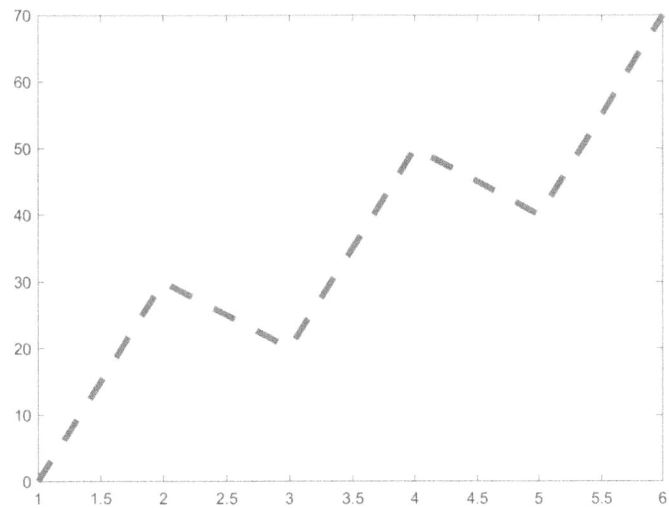

Figure 9.15
Line plot with customized style

We may use the `get` or `set` functions for any graphics objects. For example, assume we add a text to a plot and assign it to an object. We can use the `set` function to change an orientation of this text (object) in a plot.

Here is an example shows how to rotate a text in a plot. In this example, we add a text 'This is the first peak' at a position (2,35) with a font size of 12 to a plot and assign it to a text object. Then, we use the `set` function to change an orientation of this text object to 90 degrees.

```
%x and y data
x=[1,2,3,4,5,6];
y=[0,30,20,50,40,70];

%Plot y versus x
plot(x,y)

%Add text at (2,35)
t = text(2, 35, 'This is the first peak', 'FontSize', 12);

%Rotate text 90 degrees
set(t, 'Rotation', 90)
```

Figure 9.16
Line plot with 90 degrees text

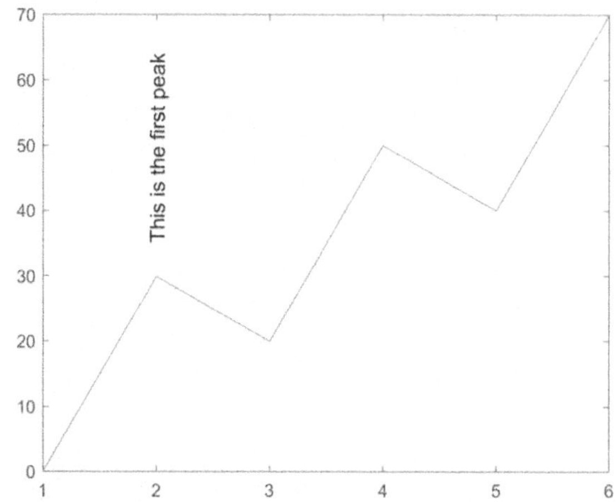

To get or set properties of axes or figure, first, we use the **gca** or **gcf** functions to get current axes or current figure respectively and assign it to an object. Then, we use this object to get access and customize axes or figure properties. Here are general syntaxes show how to get current axes or current figure and assign it to a graphics object:

Syntax

```
axes_object = gca
figure_object = gcf
```

Here is an example shows how to use the **set** function to change axes properties. In this example, first, we create a plot and then we use the **gca** function to assign current axes to an object. Then, we use this object to change axes properties. Here, first, we set axes background color to the light steel blue with RGB values of [0.69, 0.77, 0.87]. Next, we add grid lines and set a grid line color to a white color with RGB values of [1,1,1]. Finally, we set an axes line width to 1.

```
%x and y data
x=[1,2,3,4,5,6];
y=[0,30,20,50,40,70];

%Plot y versus x
plot(x,y)

%Assign current axes to object
ax = gca;
```

```
%Set background color to [0.69, 0.77, 0.87]
set(ax, 'Color', [0.69, 0.77, 0.87])

%Add grid lines and set color to [1,1,1]
grid on
set(ax, 'GridColor', [1,1,1])

%Set axes line width to 1
set(ax, 'LineWidth', 1)
```

Figure 9.17
Line plot with colored background

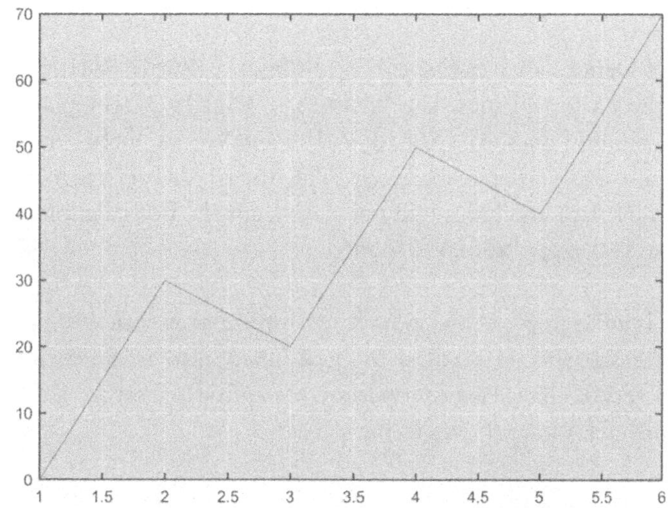

We may set axes scale using the `set` function. Here is a general syntax shows how to set axes scales in a plot:

Syntax

```
set(ax, 'XScale', XScale_Value, 'YScale', YScale_Value)
```

The `ax` defines an axes object to be scaled. The `'XScale', XScale_Value` pair arguments define the x-axis scale. The `'YScale', YScale_Value` pair arguments define the y-axis scale. The `XScale_Value` and `YScale_Value` contain scale values for the x and y axes, respectively. The scale value can be `'linear'` or `'log'` which refer to a linear scale and logarithmic scale, respectively. For example, to set a logarithmic scale for the x-axis, we use `set(ax, 'XScale', 'log')`.

Note that, MATLAB has several functions that create scaled plots without any need to scale axes. For example, the `loglog` function creates a plot with logarithmic axes. Similarly, the `semilogx` and `semilogy` functions create a plot with a logarithmic scale on the x-axis and y-axis, respectively.

Similarly, we can display or hide grid lines for the x and y axes. Here is a general syntax shows how to add or remove axes grid lines:

Syntax

```
set(ax, 'XGrid', XGrid_Value, 'YGrid', YGrid_Value)
```

The `ax` defines an axes object. The `'XGrid', XGrid_Value` pair arguments define to display or hide the x-axis grid lines. The `'YScale', YScale_Value` pair arguments define to display or hide the y-axis grid lines. The `XGrid_Value` and `YGrid_Value` define how the grids should be drawn for the x and y axes, respectively. The `XGrid_Value` and `YGrid_Value` can be `'on'` or `'off'` which displays and hides grid lines, respectively. For example, to display grid lines for the x-axis, we use `set(ax, 'XGrid', 'on')`.

Here is an example shows how to customize axes scales and grid lines. In this example, first, we create a plot and then we use the `gca` function to assign current axes to an object. Then, we use this object to change axes properties. Here, first, we set a scale for the x-axis to a logarithmic scale, and then we add grid lines to the x-axis.

```
%x and y data
x=[1,2,3,4,5,6];
y=[0,30,20,50,40,70];

%Plot y versus x
plot(x,y)

%Assign current axes to object
ax = gca;

%Set x-axis to logarithmic scale and y-axis to normal scale
set(ax, 'XScale', 'log', 'YScale', 'linear')

%Turn on x-grid lines and turn off y-grid lines
set(ax, 'XGrid', 'on', 'YGrid', 'off')
```

Figure 9.18
Line plot with logarithmic x axis

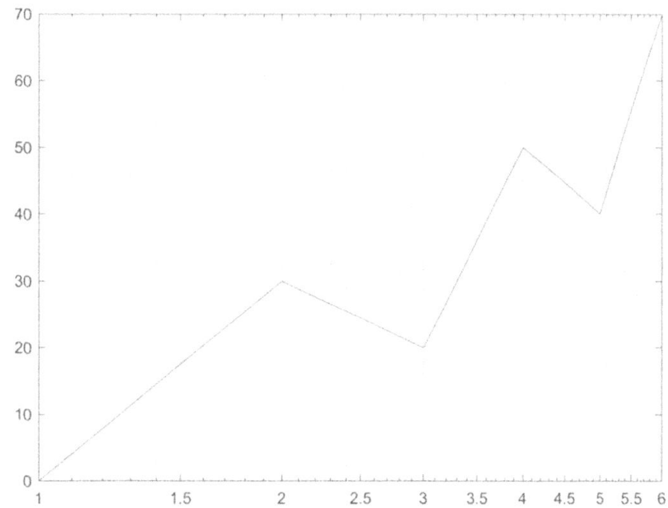

To reset graphics object properties to their default values, we can use the **`reset`** function. Here is a general syntax shows how to reset graphics object properties to their default values:

Syntax

```
reset(graphics_object)
```

9.14 Remove White Space around Axes

When we draw data in MATLAB, it leaves some space between a plot and a figure boundary. We may need to adjust and fit a plot to a figure boundary and remove white space around axes.

Here is an example shows how to remove white space around axes after a plot is drawn.

```
%x and y data
x=[1,2,3,4,5,6];
y=[0,30,20,50,40,70];

%Plot y versus x
plot(x,y)

%Get current axes
ax = gca;
```

```
%Get outer size and location of axes
outerpos = get(ax, 'OuterPosition');

%Get tight margins (size and location) around axes
ti = get(ax, 'TightInset');

%Find tight size and location of axes
left = outerpos(1) + ti(1);
bottom = outerpos(2) + ti(2);
ax_width = outerpos(3) - ti(1) - ti(3);
ax_height = outerpos(4) - ti(2) - ti(4);

%Remove white space around axes by change size and location of axes
set(ax,'Position', [left, bottom, ax_width, ax_height]);
```

9.15 Explore Plot Interactively

Every time we create a plot, a figure window opens to show plotted data. It is possible to visually inspect a plot and interactively customize a plot in this figure window. Exploring and customizing plots interactively can be helpful when we want to assess plot views or when we prepare a limited number of plots. However, to prepare consistent plots regularly, it is often suggested to use customizing syntaxes to prepare plots.

Chapter 10
Advanced Data Visualization with MATLAB

In this chapter, details of data visualization with MATLAB are described. First, MATLAB colormaps and how to work with them are explained. Then, it is described how to create a scatter plot, contour plot, bar plot, and histogram plot. After that, plot axes and how to create subplots are presented. Next, procedural and object-oriented plotting are described. Then, it is explained how to create a time-series plot. It follows by descriptions of how to display data in 3-dimensional space. At the end, it is shown how to create a map to display geospatial data.

10.1 Colormaps

Colormap is one of the helpful tools for data visualization. Colormap helps to colorize a plot of a dataset. For example, it is a common practice to present a pattern of meteorological data such as rainfall or temperature with colorized illustrations. This helps to display the severity and intensity of weather data. Here are MATLAB functions to set a colormap and add a colorbar to a plot:

Function	Description
`colormap`	Set or view colormap
`colorbar`	Add colorbar to plot
`caxis`	Set colormap limits

Here is a general syntax shows how to set a colormap:

Syntax

```
colormap(colormap_name(m))
```

The `colormap_name` defines a name of a standard colormap. The `colormap_name` is optional. If `colormap_name` is not defined, a default colormap is used. The `m` defines a number of colors in a colormap. The `m` is optional. If `m` is not defined, a colormap with 256 colors is used. To use a user-defined colormap, we can replace `colormap_name(m)` with a three-column array that contains RGB values of colors in a colormap. Note that, if we need to set a default colormap, we can simply use the `colormap` function without any colormap name.

Here is a list of common colormaps in MATLAB:

Colormap	Description
`parula`	Sequential (default) colormap
`Jet`	Sequential colormap
`cool`	Sequential colormap
`Hot`	Sequential colormap
`spring`	Sequential colormap
`summer`	Sequential colormap
`autumn`	Sequential colormap
`winter`	Sequential colormap
`gray`	Sequential colormap
`bone`	Sequential colormap
`hsv`	Cyclic colormap

`lines`	Qualitative colormap
`demcmap`	Colormaps for terrain elevation data

Figure 10.1
MATLAB colormaps

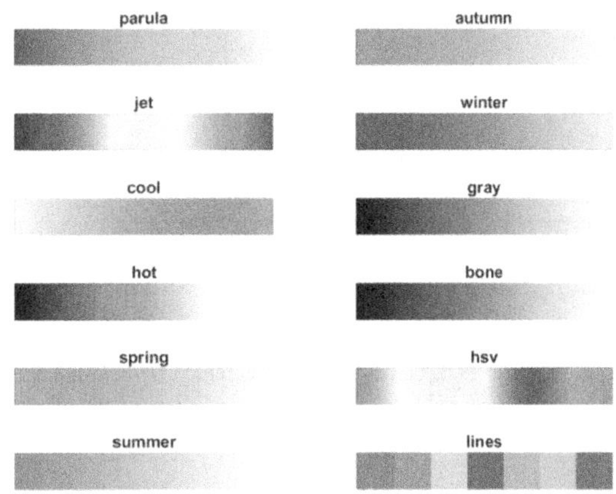

The lines colormap has 7 colors. If It is called to return more than 7 colors, it repeats those 7 colors in a cycle.

Note that, each of these built-in colormaps may be used in reverse order as well. To get a reversed colormap, we should use **`flipud`** function. For example, the original cool colormap is obtained by **`colormap(cool)`** while the reverse of cool colormap is obtained by **`colormap(flipud(cool))`**.

After we create a plot with a colormap, we may need to add a colorbar to a plot. It helps to display a value that each color represents. Here is a general syntax shows how to add a colorbar to a plot:

Syntax

```
colorbar
```

In the rest of this chapter we show how to use a colormap and colorbar in different types of plots.

10.2 Extract Colors from Colormap

Sometimes we may need to get an individual color or a subset of colors from a MATLAB colormap. Here is a general syntax shows how to extract colors from a MATLAB colormap:

Syntax

```
cmap = colormap_name(m)
```

The `colormap_name` defines a name of a standard colormap. The `m` defines a number of colors in a returned colormap. The `m` is optional. If `m` is not defined, then a colormap with 256 colors is returned. The `cmap` is a three-column array that contains returned colors from a colormap. Each row in the `cmap` represents one of these returned colors in a format of `[Red, Green, Blue]`.

Here is an example shows how to extract colors from a colormap

```
%Get 'cool' colormap with 9 colors
cmap = cool(9);

%Get the first color in colormap
%Output: 0     1     1
first_color=cmap(1,:);
disp(first_color)

%Get the seventh color in colormap
%Output: 0.7500    0.2500    1.0000
seventh_color=cmap(7,:);
disp(seventh_color)

%Get the first 3 colors in colormap
%Output:
%         0    1.0000    1.0000
%    0.1250    0.8750    1.0000
%    0.2500    0.7500    1.0000
colors=cmap(1:3,:);
disp(colors)
```

10.3 Create Colormap

We can create a user-defined colormap in MATLAB. We may use two methods to create a colormap. In the first method, a colormap is created from a complete list of colors. In other words, we already have all colors to be included in a colormap and we want to create a colormap from them. In the second method, a colormap is created from an interpolation of a limited number of colors. In other words, we only have a few colors and we want to generate more colors to create a colormap from them.

If we already have all colors to be included in a colormap, we can concatenate those colors and create a three-column array that each of its rows contains one of the colors. Then, this array can be used as a colormap. Here is a general syntax shows how to create a colormap in MATLAB:

Syntax

```
cmap = [ [R1, G1, B1]; [R2, G2, B2]; [R3, G3, B3]; ... ]
```

The `[R1, G1, B1]`; `[R2, G2, B2]`; `[R3, G3, B3]`; ... contain RGB values of colors to be used in a colormap.

Here is an example shows how to create a colormap from a list of colors. In this example, we create a colormap from a subset of 128 colors positioned from 64 to 191 in a cool colormap. To do that, first, we get a cool colormap with 256 colors. Then, we extract 128 colors positioned from 64 to 191 in this colormap by using (64:191,:) indexing and assign them to an array. Now, this new three-column array contains all 128 colors and can be used as a new colormap.

```
%Get 'cool' colormap with 256 colors
cmap = cool(256);

%Create colormap from 128 colors positioned from 64 to 191 in colormap
new_cmap = cmap(64:191,:);
```

Sometimes we need to create a colormap from a limited number of colors. For example, assume we have three colors indicating two ends and middle of a colormap and we need to create a diverging colormap with 256 colors from these 3 colors. In such cases, if we use a previous method to create a colormap, we get a colormap that only has 3 colors.

To get a proper colormap from a limited number of colors, first, we need to interpolate enough colors from initial colors, and then use these interpolated colors to create a colormap. To create a colormap from a limited number of colors, we can use the **interp1** function. To do that, first, we generate required colors from an interpolation of original colors, and then, we create a colormap from these new interpolated colors. For more detail on interpolation, refer to 1-dimensional interpolation section.

Here is a general syntax shows how to create a colormap from limited colors in MATLAB:

Syntax

```
cmap = interp1(linspace(1,N_cmap,N_col), col_arr, linspace(1,N_cmap,N_cmap))
```

The `N_col` defines a number of initial colors. The `N_cmap` defines the total number of colors in a colormap. The `col_arr` defines a three-column array containing initial colors that final colors are interpolated from them.

Here is an example shows how to create a colormap with 128 colors from 3 initial colors. In this example, we create a colormap that starts from blue, continues to yellow, and ends with red.

```
%Initial colors
blue_color=[0.14, 0.44, 0.63];
yellow_color=[0.94, 0.76, 0.05];
red_color=[0.66, 0.19, 0.14];

%Array that contains initial colors
colors_arr=[blue_color;yellow_color;red_color];

%Create colormap
N_colors=3; %Number of initial colors
N_colormap=128; %Number of colors in colormap
cmap = interp1(linspace(1,N_colormap,N_colors), colors_arr,
linspace(1,N_colormap,N_colormap));
```

10.4 Scatter Plot

Besides a line plot, a scatter plot is one of the most common plot types that is used to display data. In this type of plot, each pair of (x,y) is visualized by a single marker such a circle. In other words, y data are plotted versus x data using markers. Here is a MATLAB function to create a scatter plot:

Function	Description
`scatter`	Create scatter plot

Here is a general syntax shows how to create a scatter plot:

Syntax

```
scatter_object = scatter(x, y, sz, c, 'filled', mkr, 'Name1', Value1,
..., 'NameN', ValueN)
```

The `x` and `y` contain data to be plotted.

The `sz`, `c`, `'filled'`, and `mkr` represent optional arguments and `'Name1', Value1`, ..., `'NameN', ValueN` define optional comma-separated Name-Value pair arguments. As explained in an earlier chapter, in Name-Value pair arguments, the `'Name'` specifies a name of the optional argument, while the `Value` contains values to be assigned to this optional argument. We may use several optional arguments to customize a scatter plot. Here is a list of common optional arguments to customize a scatter plot. All arguments in this list are optional.

Arguments	Description	Example
`sz`	Set marker size in points squared	`36`
`c`	Set marker color	`[0.5,0.5,0.5]`
`'filled'`	fill interior of markers	`'filled'`
`mkr`	Set marker type	`'o'`
`'MarkerEdgeColor'`	Set marker edge color	`'MarkerEdgeColor',[0.5,0.5,0.5]`
`'MarkerFaceColor'`	Set marker face color	`'MarkerFaceColor',[0.5,0.5,0.5]`
`'LineWidth'`	Set marker edge width	`'LineWidth', 1`

If the `sz` is a single value, then it is used as a size for all markers. However, if we need to use varying marker sizes, then the `sz` should be a 1-d array that contains marker sizes for all data points. In such cases, the `sz` has one marker size value for each data point, and therefore, it has the same number of elements as `x` and `y`. If empty square brackets as `[]` is used in place of the `sz`, then a default value for the `sz` is used.

Similarly, if the `c` is a single color, then it is used as a color for all markers. To use a single RGB color, the `c` should be a 1-d row array such as [Red, Green, Blue]. If we need to colorize markers using a colormap, then the `c` should be a 1-d array that contains values that are used to map a colormap. In other words, markers are colorized based on values in the c array. In such cases, the `c` should have the same number of elements as x and y.

Note that, we can create axes and then add a scatter plot to that axes. For more details on how to create axes and add a plot to that axes refer axes section.

To explain how to visualize scattered data with MATLAB, let's consider an example. Assume we have seven pairs of data points in a form of (x,y) as (-6,36), (-4,16), (-2,4), (0,0), (2,4), (4,16), and (6,36). In other words, the x values are x=[-6,-4,-2,0,2,4,6] and y values are y=[36,16,4,0,4,16,36]. These data represent $y = x^2$. When we pass these data to MATLAB, it assigns each value from x to its corresponding value in y to create all (x,y) pairs. Here is an example shows how to plot these data using the `scatter` function.

```
%x and y data
x=[-6,-4,-2,0,2,4,6];
y=[36,16,4,0,4,16,36];

%Scatter plot of y versus x
scatter(x,y)
```

Figure 10.2
Scatter plot using the `scatter` function

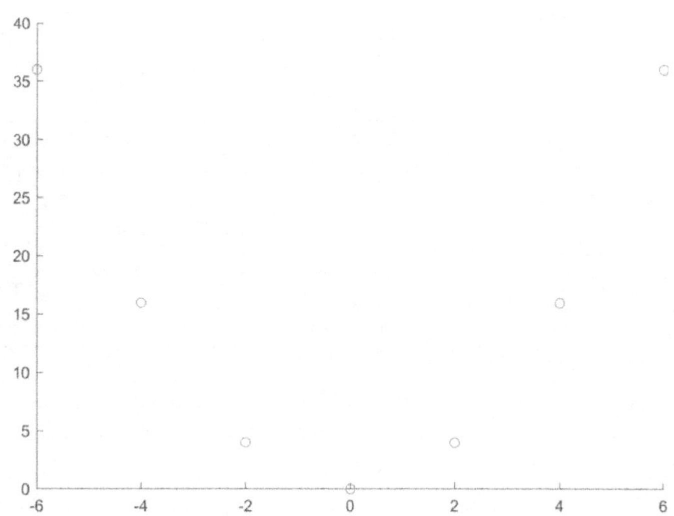

Similar to a line plot, we can customize a scatter plot. Here is an example shows how to customize a scatter plot. In this example, we create a scatter plot with a marker size of 100 points and colorize its markers. Assume we need to colorize each (x,y) point based on its $\sqrt{y}$ value. To do that, we create an array sq_y that contains values of $\sqrt{y}$. Now, we use an array sq_y in place of an argument `c` to colorize markers based on values in sq_y. Also, we use the `'filled'` argument to colorize an interior of markers. By default, MATLAB uses a default colormap to draw data. If we need to set any specific colormap, we need to use the `colormap` function and pass the desired colormap name to it. For example, here, we set a colormap to `'copper'` by using `colormap(copper)`. Note that, if we do not use the `colormap` function, then MATLAB uses a default colormap. After that, we add labels, set axis limits, and add grid lines, a colorbar, and axes outline to a plot. The values of a colorbar represent values in an array sq_y.

```
%x and y data
x=[-6,-4,-2,0,2,4,6];
y=[36,16,4,0,4,16,36];

%Calculate values to colorize markers based on them
sq_y=sqrt(y);

%Scatter plot of y versus x
scatter(x,y, 100, sq_y, 'filled')

%Set colormap
colormap(copper)

%Add labels
title('Scatter Plot')
xlabel('X Data')
ylabel('Y Data')

%Set axis limits
xlim([-8,8])
ylim([-10,40])

%Add grid lines
grid on

%Add colorbar
colorbar

%Add axes outline
box on
```

Figure 10.3
Customized scatter plot

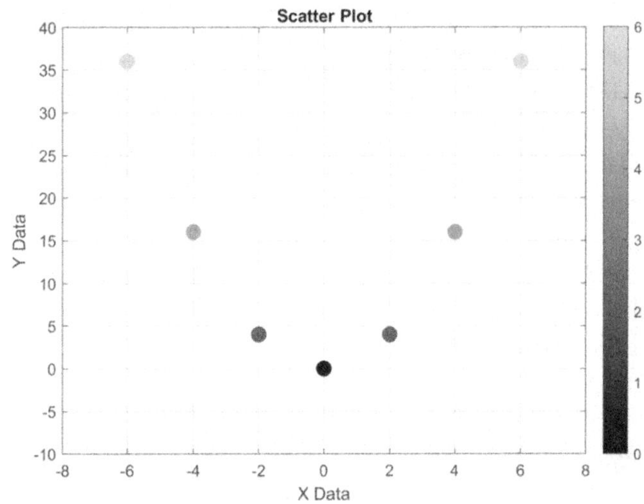

10.5 Contour and Image Plot

Sometimes we need to plot 3-dimensional data in a 2-dimensional space. In this type of plot, each data point is presented by (x,y,z). For example, data for a 2-d temperature map may be presented as (x,y,T), where x and y define a location of a point and T shows the temperature at that point. Here are MATLAB functions to create a 2-d plot from 3-d data:

Function	Description
`contourf`	Create filled contour plot
`contour`	Create contour plot
`imshow`	Plot image
`imagesc`	Plot image with scaled color
`pcolor`	Create pseudocolor plot
`clabel`	Label contour plot

Note that, we can create axes and then add any of these plots to that axes. For more details on how to create axes and add a plot to that axes refer axes section.

In this section, we explain how to work with the `contourf` function. Working with the other functions presented above is more or less similar to the `contourf` function.

Here is a general syntax shows how to create a filled contour plot:

Syntax

```
M = contourf(X, Y, Z, levels, 'Name1', Value1, ..., 'NameN', ValueN)
```

The `X` and `Y` contain coordinates of `Z`. The `Z` contains values to be plotted at `(X,Y)`. The `X`, `Y`, and `Z` are 2-d arrays with the same size. It means that, if `Z` is an array with a size of `(N,M)`, then `X` and `Y` should have a shape of `(N,M)` as well. Note that, we may use 1-d arrays for `X` and `Y` if `length(X)` is equal to the number of columns in `Z` and `length(Y)` is equal to the number of rows in `Z`. In other words, if `Z` has a size of `(N,M)`, then we may use 1-d arrays for `X` and `Y` if `length(X)` is equal to `M` and `length(Y)` is equal to `N`. The `X` and `Y` are optional and if they are not given, they are considered as `X=1:M` and `Y=1:N` .

The **`levels`** defines the numbers or positions of contour lines. If the **`levels`** is specified as a scalar `k`, then `k` contour lines are drawn. If the **`levels`** is an array, then contour lines are drawn at given levels. The **`levels`** is optional.

The **`'Name1', Value1`**, ..., **`'NameN', ValueN`** define optional comma-separated Name-Value pair arguments. We may use several Name-Value pair arguments to customize a filled contour plot. Here is a list of common Name-Value pair arguments to customize a filled contour plot. All arguments in this list are optional.

'Name'	Description	Example
`'LineColor'`	Set color of contour lines	`'LineColor', 'k'`
`'LineWidth'`	Set width of contour lines	`'LineWidth', 2`
`'LineStyle'`	Set style of contour lines	`'LineStyle', '--'`
`'ShowText'`	Add or hide contour labels	`'ShowText', 'on'`

To hide contour lines in a plot, we can use `'LineColor', 'none'` or `'LineStyle', 'none'` pair arguments. In this case, no contour lines are drawn.

Note that, by default, MATLAB uses a default colormap to draw data. If we need to set any specific colormap, we need to use the **`colormap`** function and pass the desired colormap name to it.

Here is an example shows how to visualize 3-d data in a 2-d space using MATLAB. In this example, first, we create 1-d xm and yn arrays containing 100 grid coordinates between -10 and 10. Then, we use the **`meshgrid`** function to map xm and yn values to 2-d grid arrays. We named these 2-d grid arrays as Xnm and Ynm. Next, we calculate Znm for each pair of (Xnm,Ynm) as $Z_{nm} = X_{nm}^2 + Y_{nm}^2$. Finally, we use the **`contourf`** function to plot these data and then we customize it.

```
%Generate 1-d grid coordinates
xm=linspace(-10,10,100); %Generate 100 points between -10 and 10
yn=linspace(-10,10,100); %Generate 100 points between -10 and 10

%Generate 2-d grid coordinates
[Xnm, Ynm] = meshgrid(xm,yn);

%Calculate 2-d Znm array
Znm=Xnm.^2+Ynm.^2;

%Filled contour plot of Xnm, Ynm, and Znm
contourf(Xnm, Ynm, Znm)

%Add labels
title('Filled Contour Plot')
xlabel('X Data')
ylabel('Y Data')

%Set axis limits
xlim([-10,10])
ylim([-10,10])

%Add colorbar
colorbar
```

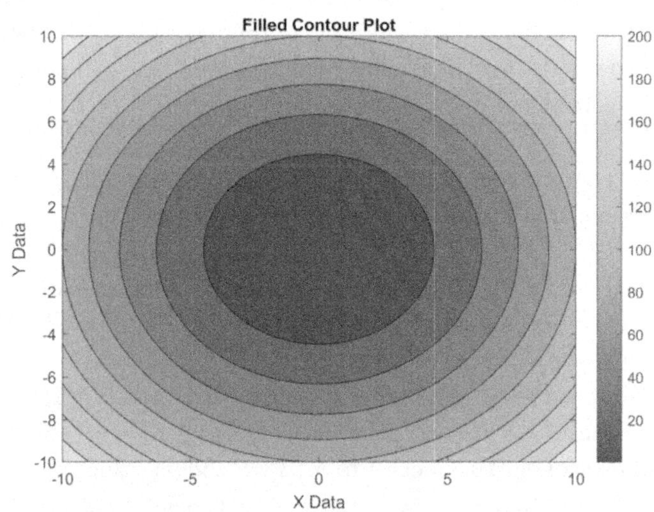

Figure 10.4
Filled contour plot using the `contourf` function

10.6 Bar Plot

We can use a bar plot to visualize data with bars. It is in particular helpful to visualize data that are categorized into several bins. In this type of plot, a series of (x,y) pairs are visualized by bars that each one is located at x and has a length of y. In other words, y data are plotted versus x data using bars. Here are MATLAB functions to create a bar plot:

Function	Description
`bar`	Create bar plot
`barh`	Create horizontal bar plot

Note that, we can create axes and then add any of these plots to that axes. For more details on how to create axes and add a plot to that axes refer axes section.

In this section, we explain how to work with the **bar** function. Working with the **barh** functions is similar to the **bar** function.

Here is a general syntax shows how to create a bar plot:

Syntax

```
bar_object = bar(x, y, width, 'Name1', Value1, ..., 'NameN', ValueN)
```

The **x** contains coordinates of bars. The **y** contains height values of bars at **x**. The **width** defines a relative width of bars as a ratio of width that a bar fills to available width for each bar. For example, the **width** equal to 0.6 means that 60 percent of space between bars is filled with bar width. If the **width** is equal to 1 then there would be no space between bars. The **width** is optional and by default is 0.8.

The **'Name1', Value1**, ..., **'NameN', ValueN** define optional comma-separated Name-Value pair arguments. We may use several Name-Value pair arguments to customize a bar plot. Here is a list of common Name-Value pair arguments to customize a bar plot. All arguments in this list are optional.

'Name'	Description	Example
`'EdgeColor'`	Set bar edge color	`'EdgeColor', 'k'`
`'FaceColor'`	Set bar face color	`'FaceColor', [0.5,0.5,0.5]`
`'LineStyle'`	Set bar edge line style	`'LineStyle', '--'`
`'LineWidth'`	Set bar edge line width	`'LineWidth', 2`

Here is an example shows how to visualize a bar plot with MATLAB. In this example, we plot x=[1,2,3,4,5,6] and y=[10,30,20,50,40,70] using the `bar` function.

```
%x and y data
x=[1,2,3,4,5,6];
y=[10,30,20,50,40,70];

%Bar plot of y versus x
bar(x,y)

%Add labels
title('Bar Plot')
xlabel('X Data')
ylabel('Y Data')

%Set axis limits
ylim([0,80])
```

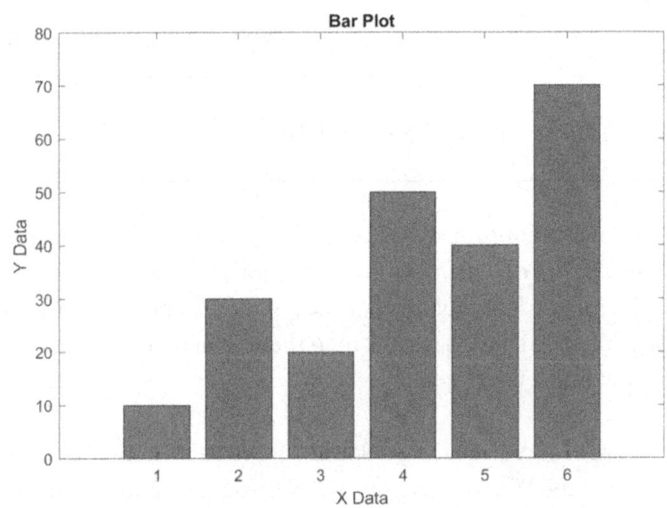

Figure 10.5
Bar plot using the `bar` function

10.7 Histogram Plot

One helpful method to visualize and inspect data is to plot a histogram of data. To find a histogram, first, a data range is split into several bins (intervals), and then, numbers of data points fall into each bin are counted. A histogram is a presentation of data counts in each bin. In other words, a histogram displays a distribution of data. Here are MATLAB functions to create a histogram plot:

Function	Description
`histogram`	Create histogram
`hist`	Create histogram (legacy version)
`histogram2`	Create bivariate histogram
`hist3`	Create bivariate histogram
`binscatter`	Create binned scatter plot

Note that, we can create axes and then add any of these plots to that axes. For more details on how to create axes and add a plot to that axes refer axes section.

In this section, we explain how to work with the **`histogram`** function. Working with the other functions presented above is more or less similar to the **`histogram`** function.

Here is a general syntax shows how to create a histogram plot:

Syntax

```
histogram_object = histogram(X, nbins, 'Name1', Value1, ..., 'NameN', ValueN)
```

The **`X`** contains data that their histogram is plotted. The **`nbins`** defines a number of bins. The **`nbins`** is optional.

The **`'Name1', Value1`**, ..., **`'NameN', ValueN`** define optional comma-separated Name-Value pair arguments. We may use several Name-Value pair arguments to customize a histogram plot. Here is a list of common Name-Value pair arguments to customize a histogram plot. All arguments in this list are optional.

'Name'	Description	Example
`'Normalization'`	Set histogram normalization	`'Normalization', 'pdf'`
`'BarWidth'`	Set relative width of bars	`'BarWidth', 0.8`
`'EdgeColor'`	Set bar edge color	`'EdgeColor', 'k'`
`'FaceColor'`	Set bar face color	`'FaceColor', [0.5,0.5,0.5]`
`'LineStyle'`	Set bar edge line style	`'LineStyle', '--'`
`'LineWidth'`	Set bar edge line width	`'LineWidth', 2`
`'BarWidth'`	Set relative width of bars	`'BarWidth', 0.8`
`'Orientation'`	Set histogram orientation	`'Orientation', 'horizontal'`

By default, the **histogram** function returns a histogram of data. If we need to get a probability density of data, we can use **'Normalization', 'pdf'** pair arguments.

Note that, MATLAB has a legacy **hist** function that returns a histogram of a dataset. Although the **hist** function is sufficient for most general purposes, it has limited capabilities compared with the **histogram** function. Here is a general syntax shows how to create a histogram plot using the **hist** function:

Syntax

```
hist(x, nbins)
```

The **x** defines an array that its histogram is calculated. The **nbins** defines the total number of bins in a histogram. The **nbins** is optional and by default is 10. Note that, if the **hist** function is called with an output argument, then it does not plot a histogram of data.

Here is an example shows how to visualize a histogram of data with MATLAB. In this example, first, we generate 1000 random data points that follow a standard normal distribution using the **randn** function. Then, we calculate and plot a histogram of these data within 20 bins using the **histogram** function. Note that, since data are generated randomly, we get slightly different results each time we run this code.

```
%x data
x=randn(1000,1); %Generate 1000 random points
                 %with normal distribution

%Histogram plot of x
h = histogram(x,20);

%Add labels
title('Histogram Plot')
xlabel('X Data')
ylabel('Counts')
```

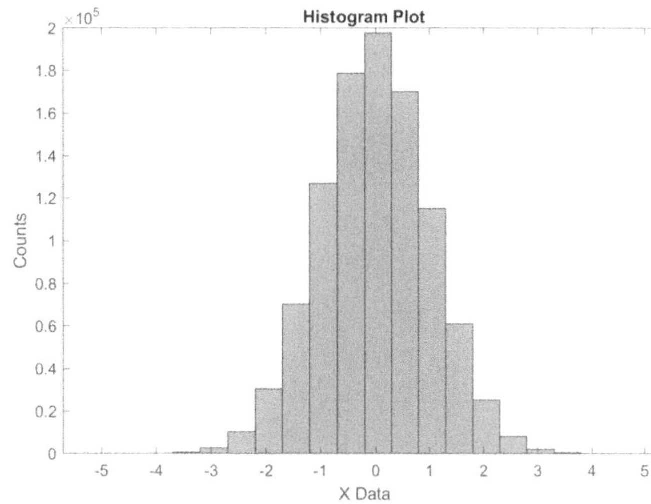

Figure 10.6
Histogram plot using the `histogram` function

10.8 Axes

In MATLAB, each figure contains one or more separate plots. Each of these plots in a figure is considered as one axes. In other words, each axes refer to one plot in a figure. For example, if we have 2 separate plots placed side by side in one figure, then we have two axes in that figure where each axes represents one of these two plots. Here are MATLAB functions to create a figure and add axes to that figure:

Function	Description
`figure`	Create new figure
`axes`	Create Cartesian axes

To explain axes in a figure, let's illustrate a figure that contains 3 plots with 3 axes. In this figure, two plots are placed side by side on the top of a figure with axes 1 and axes 2 and the third plot is placed underneath them with axes 3.

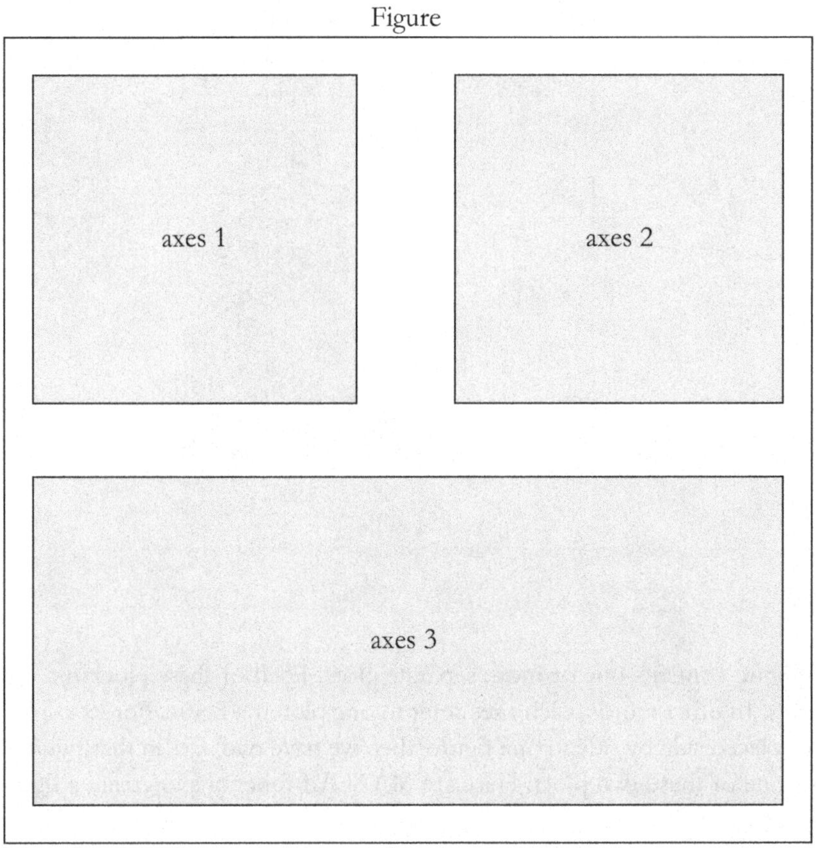

To add an axes to an existing figure, we can use the `axes` function. Here are general syntaxes show how to create a figure and add axes to that figure using the `axes` function:

Syntax

```
fig = figure(n)
axes_object = axes('Position', [left, bottom, width, height])
```

The `n` defines a figure number. The `n` is optional. If the `n` is not defined, the next incremented figure number is used. The `left`, `bottom`, `width`, `height` define a position and size of an axes inside a figure. The `left` and `bottom` define distances from a lower-left corner of a figure to a lower-left corner of axes. The `width` and `height` define the size of an axes.

Note that, if we need to add axes to an existing figure, we can use its figure number in the **figure** function to switch to that figure. By doing that, a specified existing figure becomes a current figure and all new axes are added to that figure.

After all axes are created in a figure, we can call axes one by one and plot data in each of them. Here are general syntaxes show how to call an axes axes_object1, axes_object2, ... and plot in each of them:

Syntax

```
axes(axes_object1)
plot(...)
...
axes(axes_object2)
plot(...)
...
```

In these syntaxes, we use the **plot** function. However, after we call an axes, we can use any plotting function to plot data in that axes.

Here is an example shows how to plot in axes. In this example, we create a figure that contains 2 axes. First, we generate a sequence of 1000 numbers between 0 and 2π. Then, we calculate y1 and y2 values as $y1 = \sin(x)$ and $y2 = \sin(2x)$. Then, we create a figure and add two axes to that figure. Next, we call the first axes and draw y1 versus x in that axes, and customize it. After that, we call second axes and draw y2 versus x in that axes, and customize it.

```
%x, y1 and y2 data
x=linspace(0,2*pi,1000); %Generate 1000 points between 0 and 2pi
y1=sin(x);               %y1=sin(x)
y2=sin(2*x);             %y2=sin(2x)

%Create axes
figure(1)
ax1 = axes('Position',[0.1, 0.1, 0.5, 0.5]);
ax2 = axes('Position',[0.65, 0.65, 0.25, 0.25]);

%Plot in ax1
axes(ax1)
plot(x, y1)
title('axes 1')
```

```
xlabel('x')
ylabel('y')
legend('sin(x)' , 'Location', 'northeast')

%Plot in ax2
axes(ax2)
plot(x, y2)
title('axes 2')
xlabel('x')
ylabel('y')
legend('sin(2x)' , 'Location', 'northeast')
```

Figure 10.7
Plot in axes

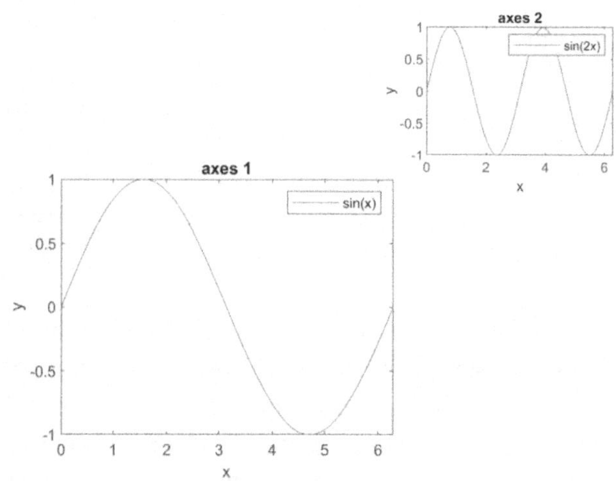

10.9 Create Subplots

It is probable that we need to display several plots together in one figure. It helps to compare and evaluate related data while they are drawn next to each other. As mentioned above, one method to have more than one plot in a figure is to create a couple of axes in chosen positions and then draw data in those axes. A simpler method to display several plots in one figure is to create a series of tiled axes and then draw data in those axes. These tiled axes are considered as subplots in a figure. Here are MATLAB functions to create subplots on tiled axes:

Function	Description
`subplot`	Add one subplot on tiled axes to current figure
`tiledlayout`	Create tiled layout
`nexttile`	Create axes in tiled layout
`stackedplot`	Create subplots with common x-axis

A simple method to create subplots on tiled axes is to use the **`subplot`** function. Unlike the **`axes`** function that creates an axes on any given position, the **`subplot`** function creates subplots on tiled axes. Each time we call the **`subplot`** function, it creates one subplot on tiled axes. Therefore, to create all subplots in a figure, we need to use the **`subplot`** function multiple times. Here is a general syntax shows how to add one subplot on tiled axes to a figure:

Syntax

```
axes_object = subplot(m, n, p)
```

The `m` and `n` define a number of rows and columns in a subplot grid, respectively. In other words, the `m` and `n` define the formation of subplots (tiled axes) to be an `m`-by-`n` grid. The `p` defines an index number of a subplot (axes) to be created. In other words, it creates a subplot with a given index and lets us drawing in that subplot. If a subplot with a given index already exists, it makes that subplot a current subplot and lets us customize it.

To explain how to use the **`subplot`** function to creates a grid of subplots, let's illustrate a figure with 6 subplots. Consider we want to create a figure that contains 6 subplots in a formation of 2 rows and 3 columns. Therefore, m=2, n=3, and p is between 1 to 6. For example, (m,n,p) for the first subplot is (2,3,1), for the second subplot is (2,3,2), and so on. Here, we illustrate (m,n,p) to be used in the **`subplot`** function for each of these subplots.

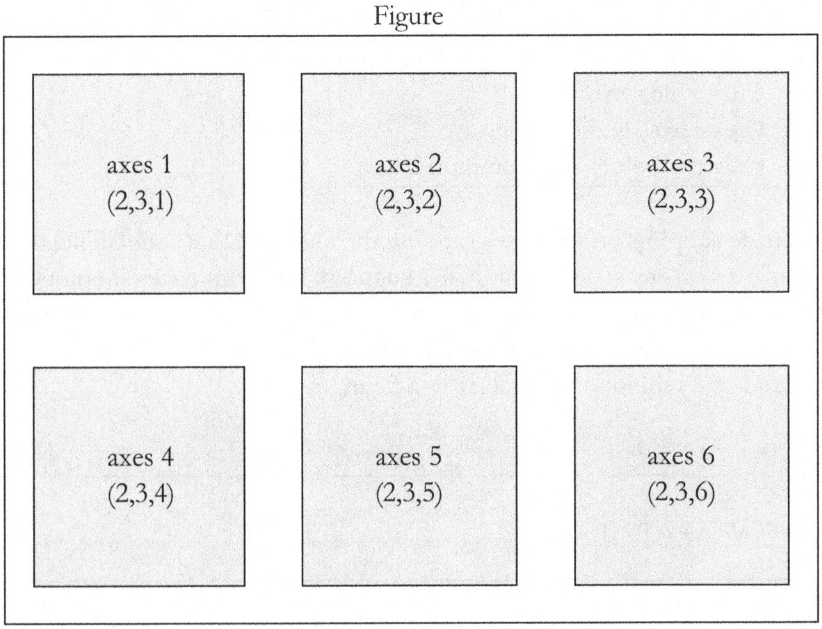

Here is an example shows how to create subplots. In this example, we want to create a figure that contains 6 subplots in a grid formation of 2 rows and 3 columns. First, we generate a sequence of 1000 numbers between 0 and 2π. Then, we calculate y1 to y6 values as $y1 = \sin(x)$, $y2 = \sin(2x)$, $y3 = \sin(3x)$, $y4 = \cos(x)$, $y5 = \cos(2x)$, and $y6 = \cos(3x)$. Then, we add the first subplot with axes index 1, draw y1 versus x in that subplot, and customize it. Next, we add the second subplot with axes index 2, draw y2 versus x in that subplot, and customize it. We continue until we plot all 6 subplots.

```
%x, y1, y2, y3, y4, y5 and y6 data
x=linspace(0,2*pi,1000); %Generate 1000 points between 0 and 2pi
y1=sin(x);               %y1=sin(x)
y2=sin(2*x);             %y2=sin(2x)
y3=sin(3*x);             %y3=sin(3x)
y4=cos(x);               %y4=cos(x)
y5=cos(2*x);             %y5=cos(2x)
y6=cos(3*x);             %y6=cos(3x)

%Plot in subplot with axis_index 1 (axes 1)
ax1 = subplot(2,3,1); %Add subplot with axis_index 1
plot(x, y1)
title('axes 1')
ylabel('y')
```

```
legend('sin(x)', 'Location', 'northeast')

%Plot in subplot with axis_index 2 (axes 2)
ax2 = subplot(2,3,2); %Add subplot with axis_index 2
plot(x, y2)
title('axes 2')
legend('sin(2x)', 'Location', 'northeast')

%Plot in subplot with axis_index 3 (axes 3)
ax3 = subplot(2,3,3); %Add subplot with axis_index 3
plot(x, y3)
title('axes 3')
legend('sin(3x)', 'Location', 'northeast')

%Plot in subplot with axis_index 4 (axes 4)
ax4 = subplot(2,3,4); %Add subplot with axis_index 4
plot(x, y4)
title('axes 4')
xlabel('x')
ylabel('y')
legend('cos(x)', 'Location', 'northeast')

%Plot in subplot with axis_index 5 (axes 5)
ax5 = subplot(2,3,5); %Add subplot with axis_index 5
plot(x, y5)
title('axes 5')
xlabel('x')
legend('cos(2x)', 'Location', 'northeast')

%Plot in subplot with axis_index 6 (axes 6)
ax6 = subplot(2,3,6); %Add subplot with axis_index 6
plot(x, y6)
title('axes 6')
xlabel('x')
legend('cos(3x)', 'Location', 'northeast')
```

Figure 10.8
Subplots with 2 rows and 3 columns

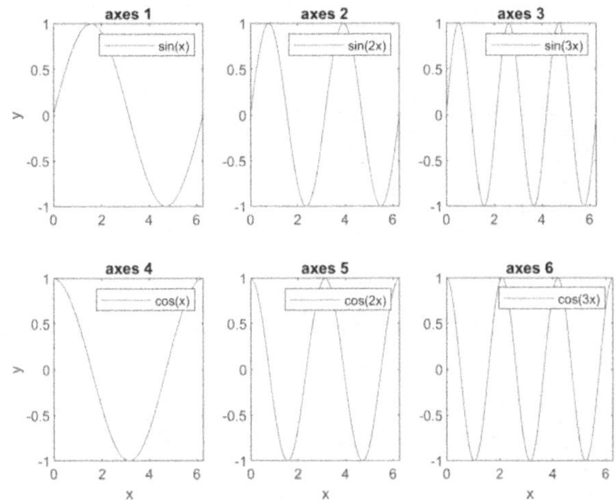

We also can create subplots on tiled axes using the `tiledlayout` and `nexttile` functions. Compared with the `subplot` function, the `tiledlayout` function provides better control over adjusting white spaces between plots or between edges of plots and edges of a figure.

10.10 Create Unequal Subplots

Sometimes we need to create a figure with unequal subplots. Creating unequal subplots is similar to create equal subplots, except that instead of plotting a subplot in one axes, we plot a subplot in place of multiple axes. Here is a general syntax shows how to add one subplot in place of multiple axes:

Syntax

```
axes_object = subplot(m, n, [p1, ..., pN])
```

The `m` and `n` define a number of rows and columns in a subplot grid, respectively. In other words, the `m` and `n` define the formation of subplots (tiled axes) to be an `m`-by-`n` grid. The `p1`, ..., `pN` define indexes of all axes that a subplot should be placed there. In other words, it creates a subplot in place of all axes defined by `p1`, ..., `pN`. For example, using `[p1,p2]` as [2,3] indicates to place a subplot in place of axes with indexes 2 and 3.

To explain how to create unequal subplots, let's illustrate a figure with 4 subplots. Consider we want to create a figure that contains 4 subplots in a formation of 2 rows and 3 columns. Therefore, m=2 and n=3. In each row we have two subplots in two sizes. Here, we illustrate (m,n,p) and (m,n,[p1, ..., pN]) to be used in the `subplot` function for each of these subplots.

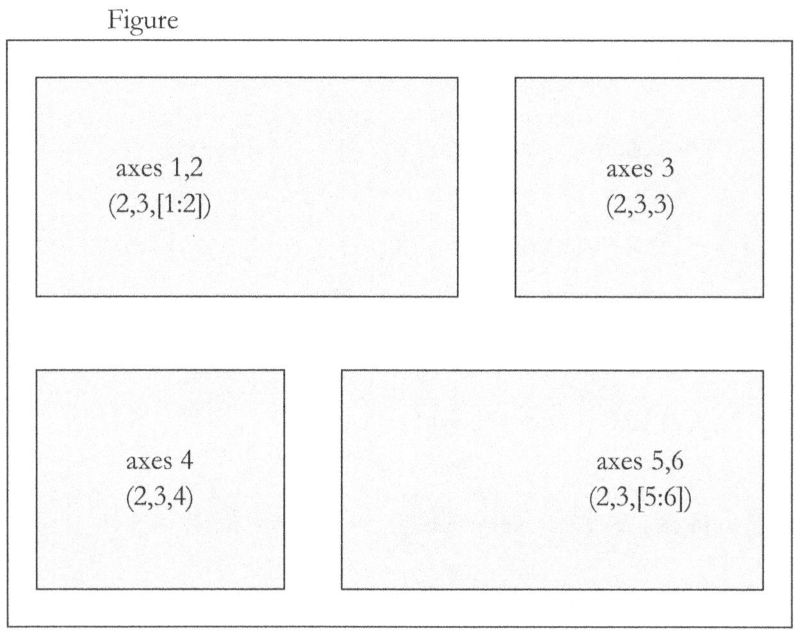

Here is an example shows how to create unequal subplots. In this example, we want to create a figure that contains 4 subplots in a grid formation of 2 rows and 3 columns. First, we generate a sequence of 1000 numbers between 0 and 2π. Then, we calculate y1 to y4 values as $y1 = \sin(x)$, $y2 = \sin(2x)$, $y3 = \cos(x)$, and $y4 = \cos(2x)$. Next, we add the first subplot at indexes of (2,3,[1:2]), draw y1 versus x in that subplot, and customize it. Next, we add the second subplot at indexes of (2,3,3), draw y2 versus x in that subplot, and customize it. We continue until we plot all 4 subplots.

```
%x, y1, y2, y3 and y4 data
x=linspace(0,2*pi,1000); %Generate 1000 points between 0 and 2pi
y1=sin(x);               %y1=sin(x)
y2=sin(2*x);             %y2=sin(2x)
y3=cos(x);               %y3=cos(x)
y4=cos(2*x);             %y4=cos(2x)

%Plot in subplot at indexes [1:2]
ax12 = subplot(2,3,[1,1:2]); %Add subplot at indexes [1:2]
plot(x, y1')
title('indexes [1:2]')
```

```
ylabel('y')
legend('sin(x)', 'Location', 'northeast')

%Plot in subplot at index 3
ax3 = subplot(2,3,3); %Add subplot at index 3
plot(x, y2)
title('index 3')
legend('sin(2x)', 'Location', 'northeast')

%Plot in subplot at index 4
ax4 = subplot(2,3,4); %Add subplot at index 4
plot(x, y3)
title('index 4')
xlabel('x')
ylabel('y')
legend('cos(x)', 'Location', 'northeast')

%Plot in subplot at indexes [5:6]
ax56 = subplot(2,3,[5:6]); %Add subplot at indexes [5:6]
plot(x, y4)
title('indexes [5:6]')
xlabel('x')
legend('cos(2x)', 'Location', 'northeast')
```

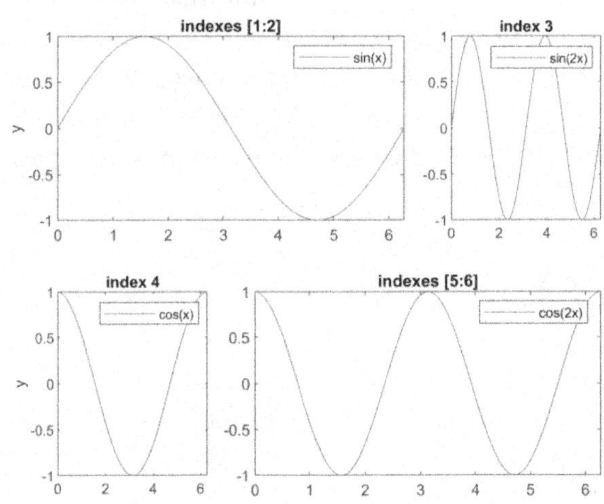

Figure 10.9
Unequal subplots

10.11 Procedural and Object-Oriented Plotting

Up to here, we mainly used a procedural method to plot data. In release 2014b, MATLAB provides an object-oriented plotting in addition to a procedural method. It this method, first, we create a figure axes (object), and then we work on this axes (object) to prepare the desired plot.

To explain how to use an object-oriented plotting, first, we use a procedural method to create a plot and then we show how to use an object-oriented plotting to draw the same plot.

Here is an example shows how to create a plot using a procedural plotting. This is how we plotted all previous plots. In this example, first, we plot y1, y2, and y3 versus x using the `plot` function. In this plot, we use a dashed line style as 'LineStyle', '--', dash-dotted line style as 'LineStyle', '-.', dotted line styles as 'LineStyle', ':', and circle marker points as 'Marker', 'o'. We set a plot title as 'Line Plot', x-axis label as 'X Data', and y-axis label as 'Y Data'. We set x-axis limits from 0 to 7 and y-axis limits from -20 to 100. We add major grid lines to both axes and a legend to a plot. Finally, we add a text 'The first peak' to a plot.

```
%x, y1, y2, and y3 data
x=[1,2,3,4,5,6];
y1=[0,30,20,50,40,70];
y2=[10,40,30,60,50,80];
y3=[20,50,40,70,60,90];

%Plot y1, y2, and y3 versus x
plot(x, y1, 'LineStyle', '--', 'Marker', 'o')
hold on
plot(x, y2, 'LineStyle', '-.', 'Marker', 'o')
plot(x, y3, 'LineStyle', ':', 'Marker', 'o')

%Add labels
title('Line Plot')
xlabel('X Data')
ylabel('Y Data')

%Set axis limits
xlim([0,7])
ylim([-20,100])

%Add grid lines
grid on
```

```
%Add legend
legend('y1','y2','y3', 'Location', 'northwest')

%Add text
text(1, 55, 'The first peak', 'FontSize', 12)
```

Figure 10.10
Plot with procedural method

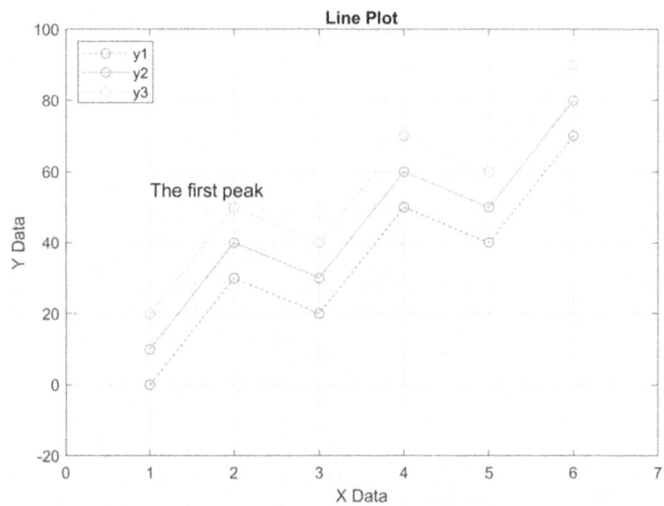

Now, we explain how to use an object-oriented plotting. To plot data using an object-oriented plotting, first, we need to create a graphics object. The outputs of functions that we use to create a plot are graphics objects. Therefore, to create a graphics object, we assign the output of a plotting function to an object. Similarly, we can assign the output of a function that we use to customize a plot to an object. After we create a graphics object, we start to customize that graphics object.

After a graphics object is created, we use dot notation to access or customize properties of that graphics object. Here is a general syntax shows how to use a dot notation to access properties of a graphics object:

Syntax

```
Property_Value = graphics_object.Property_Name
```

Here is a general syntax shows how to use a dot notation to customize properties of a graphics object:

Syntax

```
graphics_object.Property_Name = New_Property_Value
```

Most of the graphics object properties have the same names as the 'Name' in corresponding comma-separated Name-Value pair arguments. For example, the `plot` function has `'LineStyle', LineStyle_Value` pair arguments. In the same way, an object created by the `plot` function has a property named `LineStyle`. Here is a list of common Name-Value pair arguments and their equivalent graphics object properties for the `plot` function.

'Name', Value	Graphics Object Property	Description
`'Color', Color_Val`	`graphics_obj.Color=Color_Val`	Set plot color
`'LineStyle', Style_Val`	`graphics_obj.LineStyle=Style_Val`	Set line style
`'LineWidth', Width_Val`	`graphics_obj.LineWidth=Width_Val`	Set line width
`'Marker', Marker_Val`	`graphics_obj.Marker= Marker_Val`	Set marker type

Here is an example shows how to create a previous plot using an object-oriented plotting. The steps are similar to a procedural plotting except that we need to create a graphics object first. After we create a graphics object, we customize that graphics object. For example, consider a graphics object named h1. To set a line style of that graphics object, we use h1.LineStyle=Style_Val. We use the same method for the rest of the objects such as the ones created by the `legend` and `text` functions.

```
%x, y1, y2, and y3 data
x=[1,2,3,4,5,6];
y1=[0,30,20,50,40,70];
y2=[10,40,30,60,50,80];
y3=[20,50,40,70,60,90];

%Plot y1, y2, and y3 versus x
h1 = plot(x, y1);
hold on
h2 = plot(x, y2);
h3 = plot(x, y3);

%Set line styles
h1.LineStyle='--';
h2.LineStyle='-.';
h3.LineStyle=':';
```

```
%Set line type
h1.Marker='o';
h2.Marker='o';
h3.Marker='o';

%Add labels
title('Line Plot')
xlabel('X Data')
ylabel('Y Data')

%Set axis limits
xlim([0,7])
ylim([-20,100])

%Add grid lines
grid on

%Add legend
lgd = legend('y1','y2','y3');
lgd.Location='northwest';

%Add text
t = text(1, 55, 'The first peak');
t.FontSize=12;
```

The result from this example is the same as the one from a previous example.

10.12 Time-Series Plot

A time-series is a widely-used dataset with broad applications, particularly in scientific studies. A time-series refers to a dataset that contains data collected over time. These types of datasets are helpful to evaluate and study a trend of data during a given time period. Here are MATLAB functions to plot a time-series:

Function	Description
`plot`	Create line plot
`xticks`	Set tick locations for x-axis
`xticklabels`	Set tick labels for x-axis
`xtickformat`	Set tick labels format for x-axis
`datetick`	Set date-formatted tick labels

`xtickangle`	Set tick label angle for x-axis

MATLAB automatically sets tick locations when it plots data. We may use the **`xticks('auto')`** function to automatically reset tick locations to their defaults. Similarly, MATLAB automatically sets the tick labels format. We can use the **`xtickformat`** function to set tick labels format to set any specific date format.

In this section, we explain how to create a time-series with the **`datetime`** function and plot data associated with this time-series using the **`plot`** function. Note that, in addition to the **`datetime`** function, MATLAB also has the **`timetable`** and **`timeseries`** functions which provide a set of powerful and yet simple tools to work with date and time. For more detail on how to work with date, time, and time-series refer to date, time, and time-Series chapter. Here are MATLAB functions to create date and time:

Function	Description
`datetime`	Return date and time
`duration`	Represent time difference (duration)

Here is an example shows how to visualize time-series data with MATLAB. In this example, first, we create a time-series of 11 days from 2050-10-20 to 2050-10-30 using the **`datetime`** function. Then, we plot y data versus time. Next, we add labels, set x-axis limits, and add grid lines to x-axis. After that, we set ticks locators and ticks format. Finally, we use the **`xtickangle`** function to rotate and align ticks labels.

```
%Create datetime values for start and end dates
start_date=datetime(2050, 10, 20, 0, 0, 0);
end_date=datetime(2050, 10, 30, 0, 0, 0);

%Create duration equal to 1 day
dt=days(1); %Or dt=duration(24,0,0);

%Create daily time-series from 2050/10/20 to 2050/10/30
ts=start_date:dt:end_date;

%y data
y=[90,65,55,95,90,60,55,90,70,45,70];

%Plot y versus ts
plot(ts,y)

%Add labels
```

```
title('Time-Series Plot')
xlabel('Time')
ylabel('Y Data')

%Set axis limits
xlim([ts(1,1),ts(1,end)])

%Get current axes
ax = gca;

%Add grid lines
set(ax, 'XGrid', 'on')

%Set ticks locators
xticks('auto') %Not required
               %if xticks have not modified earlier

%Set ticks labels
date_labels=datestr(ts);
xticklabels(date_labels) %Not required
                         %if default xtick labels are acceptable

%Set ticks format
xtickformat('yyyy-MM-dd')
%Or datetick('x', 'yyyy-mm-dd', 'keeplimits', 'keepticks')

%Rotate ticks labels
xtickangle(0) %Not required
              %if default xticks orientation is acceptable
```

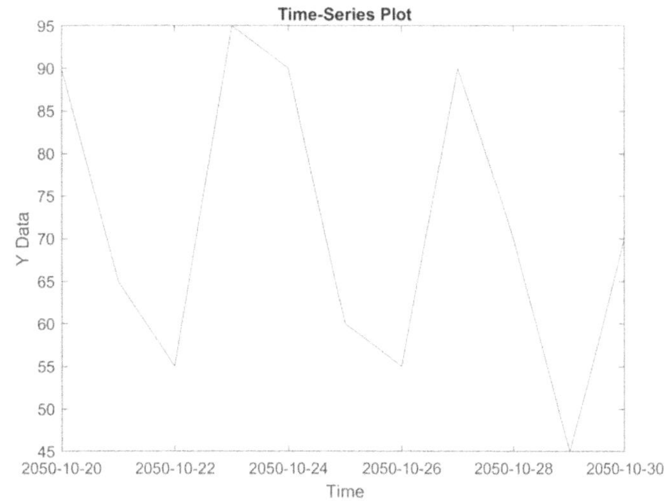

Figure 10.11
Time-series plot

10.13 The 3-Dimensional Plot

MATLAB provides several functions to display data in 3-d space. Here is a list of common MATLAB functions to create a 3-d plot:

Function	Description
`surf`	Create 3-d surface plot
`plot3`	Create 3-d line plot
`scatter3`	Create 3-d scatter plot
`bar3`	Create 3-d bar plot
`contour3`	Create 3-d contour plot

In this section, we explain how to work with the `surf` function. Working with the other functions presented above is more or less similar to the `surf` function.

Here is a general syntax shows how to create a 3-d surface plot:

Syntax

```
surface_object = surf(X, Y, Z, 'Name1', Value1, ..., 'NameN', ValueN)
```

The `X` and `Y` contain coordinates of `Z`. The `Z` contains values to be plotted at `(X,Y)`. The `X`, `Y`, and `Z` are 2-d arrays with the same size. It means that, if `Z` is an array with a size of `(N,M)`, then `X` and

`Y` should have a size of `(N,M)` as well. Note that, we may use 1-d array for `X` and `Y` if `length(X)` is equal to the number of columns in `Z` and `length(Y)` is equal to the number of rows in `Z`. In other words, if `Z` has a size of `(N,M)`, then we may use 1-d arrays for `X` and `Y` if `length(X)` is equal to `M` and `length(Y)` is equal to `N`. The `X` and `Y` are optional and if they are not given, they are considered as `X=1:M` and `Y=1:N` .

The `'Name1', Value1`, ..., `'NameN', ValueN` define optional comma-separated Name-Value pair arguments. We may use several Name-Value pair arguments to customize a surface plot. Here is a list of common Name-Value pair arguments to customize a surface plot. All arguments in this list are optional.

'Name'	Description	Example
`'EdgeColor'`	Set color of contour lines	`'LineColor', 'k'`
`'LineStyle'`	Set style of contour lines	`'LineStyle', '--'`
`'FaceColor'`	Set color of faces	`'FaceColor', 'interp'`
`'FaceAlpha'`	Set transparency of faces	`'FaceAlpha', 0.5`

To hide contour lines in a plot, we can use `'EdgeColor', 'none'` or `'LineStyle', 'none'` pair arguments. In this case, no contour lines are drawn.

Note that, by default, MATLAB uses a default colormap to draw data. If we need to set any specific colormap, we need to use the `colormap` function and pass the desired colormap name to it. Also, to set a shading of a plot, we can use the `shading` function.

Here is an example shows how to visualize a 3-d surface plot using MATLAB. Let's consider an example we used for a filled contour plot again. In this example, first, we create 1-d xm and yn arrays containing 100 grid coordinates between -10 and 10. Then, we use the `meshgrid` function to map xm and yn values to 2-d grid arrays. We named these 2-d grid arrays as Xnm and Ynm. Next, we calculate Znm for each pair of (Xnm,Ynm) as $Z_{nm} = X_{nm}^2 + Y_{nm}^2$. Finally, we use the `surf` function to plot these data and then we customize it.

```
%Generate 1-d grid coordinates
xm=linspace(-10,10,100); %Generate 100 points between -10 and 10
yn=linspace(-10,10,100); %Generate 100 points between -10 and 10

%Generate 2-d grid coordinates
[Xnm, Ynm] = meshgrid(xm,yn);

%Calculate 2-d Znm array
Znm=Xnm.^2+Ynm.^2;
```

```
%Surface plot of Xnm, Ynm, and Znm
s = surf(Xnm, Ynm, Znm);

%Add labels
title('Surface Plot')
xlabel('X Data')
ylabel('Y Data')
zlabel('Z Data')

%Set axis limits
xlim([-10,10])
ylim([-10,10])
zlim([0,200])

%Add colorbar
colorbar
```

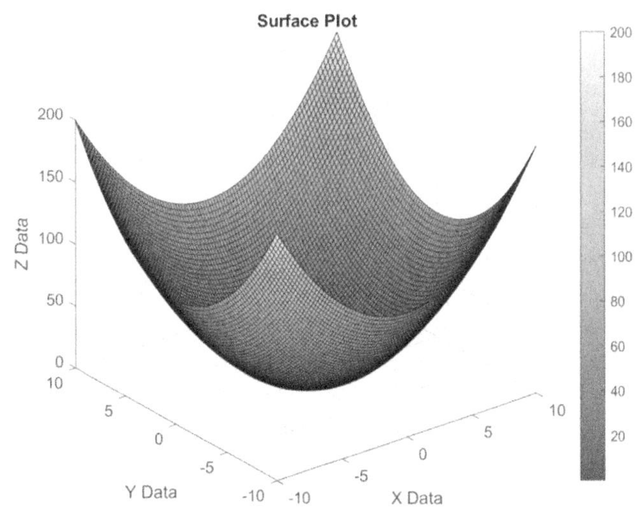

Figure 10.12
Surface plot using the `surf` function

10.14 Map Plot

A simple method in MATLAB to create a map and display data on that is to use the geographic axes. Here is a list of common MATLAB functions to create geographic axes:

Function	Description
geoaxes	Create geographic axes

`geoplot`	Display line on geographic map
`geoscatter`	Display scattered data on geographic map
`geobasemap`	Set basemap
`geolimits`	Set geographic map limits
`geotickformat`	Set tick label format of geographic map

The geographic axes provides several basemaps which may be used to create a map, and if needed, to visualize data on top of them. Some of the common basemaps are `'satellite'`, `'topographic'`, `'streets'`, `'landcover'`, `'colorterrain'`, `'bluegreen'`, and `'none'`.

Here is an example shows how to use the geographic axes. In this example, we show how to create a map of the Persian Gulf using the geographic axes. First, we create the geographic axes, and then we add a random sample point at (longitude=54, latitude=26) to a map. Next, we set a map extent. Finally, we add a label, text, and annotation to a map.

```
%Create geographic axes
gx = geoaxes; %Optional because we use geoscatter next

%Add point at (longitude=54,latitude=26) to map
geoscatter(26, 54, 100, [0.5, 0.2, 0.6], 'filled')

%Set basemap
geobasemap('landcover')

%Set map extent
latlim = [22,31]; %[y0,y1]
lonlim = [47,60]; %[x0,x1]
geolimits(latlim,lonlim)

%Add label
title('Map Plot')

%Add text
t = text(28.7, 49.5, 'Persian Gulf', 'FontSize', 16);
set(t, 'Rotation', -45)

%Add annotation
pos_x_norm = [0.6,0.55];
pos_y_norm = [0.6,0.48];
annotation('textarrow', pos_x_norm, pos_y_norm, ...
    'String', 'Sample Point', 'FontSize', 12, 'Color', [0,0,0])
```

MATLAB also has a Mapping Toolbox which provides several tools for working with geospatial data. Here is a list of common MATLAB functions to create a map plot:

Function	Description
worldmap	Create map axes of world or its regions
geoshow	Display map
mapshow	Display map without projection
demcmap	Set colormap for terrain elevation data
plotm	Display 2-d line on map
scatterm	Display scattered data on map
textm	Display text on map
setm	Set map properties
tightmap	Remove white space around map
geotiffread	Read GeoTIFF file
shaperead	Read shapefile
importdata	Read data from file

Here is an example shows how to use a Mapping Toolbox. In this example, we show how to create a map of the Persian Gulf using a Mapping Toolbox. First, we define a map extent and create a world map within these extend. Then, we set a map projection, and if required, we add coastlines to this map. Next, we load a land area and add that to a map. After that, we add a random sample point at (longitude=54, latitude=26) to a map. Finally, we add a label, text, and annotation to a map.

```
%Set map extent
latlim = [22,31]; %[y0,y1]
lonlim = [47,60]; %[x0,x1]

%Plot world map
ax = worldmap(latlim,lonlim);
%Or For world map use: ax = worldmap('World');

%Set map projection
setm(ax, 'MapProjection', 'mercator')

%Add coastlines to map (Optional)
%load coastlines
%plotm(coastlat,coastlon)

%Add land to map
```

```
land = shaperead('landareas', 'UseGeoCoords', true);
geoshow(ax, land, 'FaceColor', [0.15, 0.65, 0.6])

%Add point at (longitude=54,latitude=26) to map
scatterm(26, 54, 100, [0.5, 0.2, 0.6], 'filled')

%Add label
title('Map Plot')

%Add text
t = textm(28.7, 49.5, 'Persian Gulf', 'FontSize', 16);
set(t, 'Rotation', -45)

%Add annotation
pos_x_norm = [0.6,0.55];
pos_y_norm = [0.6,0.48];
annotation('textarrow', pos_x_norm, pos_y_norm, ...
    'String', 'Sample Point', 'FontSize', 12, 'Color', [0,0,0])
```

Note that, similar to how we use `scatterm` to add a random sample point to a map, we can use other MATLAB mapping functions to add elements to a map. For example, we can use the `contourfm` function to add a layer of a filled contour to a map.

There are cases that we prefer to plot a map that displays natural features. One method to create this type of map is to draw a topography relief map (terrain map) from a file that contains horizontal locations and vertical elevations of the earth surface. These data are commonly available as a GeoTiff file or as a .xyz file. The .xyz file is an ASCII file that contains three columns of data. In these files the first column has x (longitude), the second column has y (latitude), and the third column has z (elevation) data. One source to obtain these data is NOAA (National Oceanic and Atmospheric Administration) grid extract tool (https://maps.ngdc.noaa.gov/viewers/wcs-client).

Here is an example shows how to create a map from a .xyz file. In this example, we create a map of the Persian Gulf using a .xyz file. First, we download the Persian Gulf .xyz file from NOAA grid extract tool (https://maps.ngdc.noaa.gov/viewers/wcs-client) and save it as persiangulf.xyz in 'C:\Example' directory. To obtain this file, we extract a domain that its boundary is limited to 47.0 degrees in the West, 60.0 in the East, 22.0 in the South, and 31.0 in the North. After that, we read data in this file using the `importdata` function and store them in a variable named data. Then, we assign the first column in data to x, the second column to y, and the third column to z. Next, we generate 1-d arrays that contain grid coordinates in x and y directions. Using them, we generate 2-d arrays that contain grid coordinates and interpolate x, y, and z data to these 2-d grid arrays. After that, we define a map extent and create a world map within these extend. Then, we set a map projection. Next, we add terrain data to a map. After that, we add a random sample point at (longitude=54, latitude=26) to a map. Finally, we add a label, text, annotation, and colorbar to a map.

```
%Change folder
cd('C:\Example')

%Read xyz (terrain) file
%Source: https://maps.ngdc.noaa.gov/viewers/wcs-client/
%west=47.0, east=60.0, south=22.0, north=31.0 in signed decimal degrees
data=importdata('persiangulf.xyz');

%Assign data to x, y, and z
x=data(:,1); %First column contains x
y=data(:,2); %Second column contains y
z=data(:,3); %Third column contains z

%Generate 1-d grid coordinates
xm=linspace(min(x(:)),max(x(:)),100); %Generate 100 points
                                       %between min(x) and max(x)
yn=linspace(min(y(:)),max(y(:)),100); %Generate 100 points
                                       %between min(y) and max(y)

%Generate 2-d grid coordinates
[Xnm, Ynm] = meshgrid(xm,yn);

%Interpolate (x,y,z) data to 2-d Znm array
Znm = griddata(x, y, z, Xnm, Ynm, 'nearest');

%Set map extent
latlim = [22,31]; %[y0,y1]
lonlim = [47,60]; %[x0,x1]

%Plot world map
ax = worldmap(latlim,lonlim);
%Or For world map use: ax = worldmap('World');

%Set map projection
setm(ax, 'MapProjection', 'mercator')

%Add terrain to map
geoshow(ax, Ynm, Xnm, Znm, 'DisplayType', 'surface')
```

```
%Add point at (longitude=54,latitude=26) to map
scatterm(26, 54, 100, [0.5, 0.2, 0.6], 'filled')

%Add label
title('Map Plot')

%Add text
t = textm(28.7, 49.5, 'Persian Gulf', 'FontSize', 16);
set(t, 'Rotation', -45)

%Add annotation
pos_x_norm = [0.55,0.50];
pos_y_norm = [0.6,0.48];
annotation('textarrow', pos_x_norm, pos_y_norm, ...
    'String', 'Sample Point', 'FontSize', 12, 'Color', [0,0,0])

%Set colormap
%To set Znm limits use: demcmap([Low_Limit,High_Limit])
demcmap(Znm)

%Add colorbar
colorbar
```

Figure 10.13
The Persian Gulf map

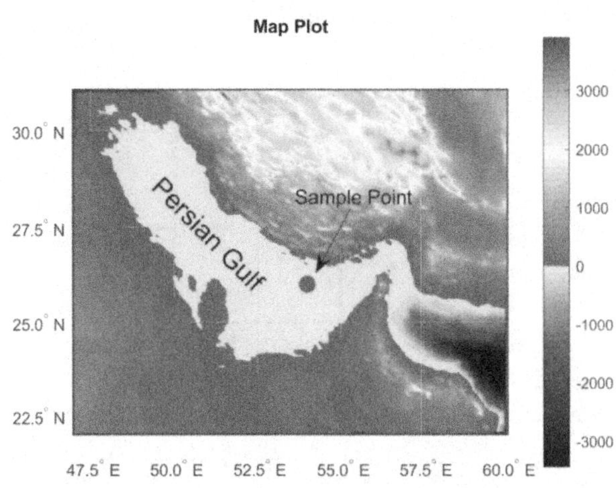

In addition to .xyz file, MATLAB provides tools to work with other geospatial data formats such as GeoTIFF and shapefile. We may obtain geospatial data from different sources. One public domain that contains map datasets is Natural Earth (www.naturalearthdata.com). It provides vector and raster data at 1:10 million, 1:50 million, and 1:110 million scales.

Also, there are several third-party packages for working with geospatial data in MATLAB. Among others, M_Map (Pawlowicz, R., 2020; www.eoas.ubc.ca/~rich/map.html) is helpful to create maps and analyze geospatial data. Some of the other mapping packages might be found on the MathWorks File Exchange (The MathWorks, Inc.; www.mathworks.com/matlabcentral/fileexchange). Note that, the third-party packages do not come with a standard version of MATLAB. Therefore, after MATLAB is installed, we need to download and set them up separately.

Chapter 11
Interpolation, Curve Fitting, Root Finding, and Numerical Integration with MATLAB

In this chapter, the basics of interpolation, curve fitting, root finding, and numerical integration with MATLAB are described. First, it is described how to generate 1-dimensional and 2-dimensional grid coordinates. After that, 1-dimensional and 2-dimensional methods for data interpolations are presented. Next, it is described how to fit a function to data. Then, it is explained how to find the roots of a function. It follows by descriptions of how to solve a system of linear equations. At the end, numerical integration is explained.

11.1 Generate 1-Dimensional Grid Coordinates

In earlier chapters, we explain how to generate a sequence of numbers in MATLAB. In practice, generating 1-d grid coordinates is similar to generating a sequence of numbers. In this section, we review again how to generate a sequence of numbers between two values with an evenly spaced step. Here are function and operator to create a sequence of numbers:

Function/Operator	Description
`:`	Generate evenly spaced sequence of numbers
`linspace`	Generate evenly spaced sequence of numbers

The `:` (colon) generates an evenly spaced sequence of numbers over an interval of `[start,stop]`. A resulted sequence includes a `start` value, but depending on a `step` value, it may or may not include a `stop` value. Here is a general syntax shows how to use the colon:

Syntax

```
xm = start : step : stop
```

The `start` defines a starting number in a sequence. The `stop` defines the end value in a sequence. Note that, depending on a `step` value, the `stop` itself may or may not be included in a sequence. The `step` defines an interval between every two consecutive numbers in a sequence. The `step` is optional and by default is 1.

Another method to generate a sequence of numbers is to use the `linspace` function. The `linspace` function generates an evenly spaced sequence of numbers over an interval of `[start,stop]`. A resulted sequence includes both `start` and `stop` values. Here is a general syntax shows how to use the `linspace` function:

Syntax

```
xm = linspace(start, stop, n)
```

The `start` defines a starting number in a sequence. The `stop` defines the end value in a sequence. Note that, a sequence includes both `start` and `stop` values. The `n` defines a number of samples to be generated. The `n` is optional and by default is 100.

To explain how 1-d grid coordinates are formed, let's illustrate a sequence of evenly spaced numbers with m members. The x1 to xm in this illustration represent numbers in this sequence.

Sequence xm:	x1	x2	x3	...	xm

Here are examples show how to generate a sequence of numbers.

```
%Generate numbers over [-10,10] interval with step=2
%Output: -10     -8     -6     -4     -2     0     2     4     6     8    10
seq=-10:2:10;
disp(seq)

%Generate 4 numbers over [-1,0.5] interval
%Output: -1.0000   -0.5000   0    0.5000
seq=linspace(-1,0.5,4);
disp(seq)
```

11.2 Generate 2-Dimensional Grid Coordinates

We can generate 2-d grid coordinates by using the following function:

Function	Description
`meshgrid`	Return 2 and 3-dimensional grid coordinates

The **meshgrid** function generates 2-d and 3-d grid coordinates. In this section, we explain how to use it to generate 2-d grid coordinates. Here is a general syntax shows how to generate 2-d grid coordinates:

Syntax

```
[Xnm,Ynm] = meshgrid(xm,yn)
```

The **xm** is a 1-d array contains **m** grid coordinates in the x-direction. Similarly, the **yn** is a 1-d array contains **n** grid coordinates in the y-direction. If a length of **xm** is equal to `M` and a length of **yn** is equal to `N`, then `Xnm` and `Ynm` have a size of `(N,M)`.

To explain how 2-d grid coordinates are formed, let's illustrate 2-d grid coordinates generated from 4 coordinates in the x-direction and 3 coordinates in the y-direction. Assume the xm contains 3 coordinates from x1 to x3 in the x-direction and yn contains 4 coordinates from y1 to y4 in the y-direction. Then, Xnm and Ynm have a size of (4,3) as:

xm	x1	x2	x3

yn
y1
y2
y3
y4

Xnm

x1	x2	x3
x1	x2	x3
x1	x2	x3
x1	x2	x3
x1	x2	x3

xm	x1	x2	x3

yn
y1
y2
y3
y4

Ynm

y1	y1	y1
y1	y1	y1
y2	y2	y2
y3	y3	y3
y4	y4	y4

Here is an example shows how to generate 2-d grid coordinates. In this example, we generate 2-d grid coordinates from 3 coordinates [1,2,3] in the x-direction and 4 coordinates [10,20,30,40] in the y-direction. The generated 2-d grid arrays Xnm and Ynm have a size of (4,3).

```
%Coordinates in x direction
xm=[1,2,3];

%Coordinates in y direction
yn=[10,20,30,40];

%Generate 2-d grid coordinates
[Xnm,Ynm] = meshgrid(xm,yn);

%Print Xnm
%Output:
%        1     2     3
%        1     2     3
%        1     2     3
%        1     2     3
disp(Xnm)

%Print Ynm
%Output:
%       10    10    10
%       20    20    20
%       30    30    30
%       40    40    40
disp(Ynm)
```

The 2-d grid coordinates have many 2-d and 3-d applications. For example, 2-d grid coordinates are used in 2-d data interpolation, 3-d data visualization, and two variables function z=f(x,y) calculation.

Here is an example shows how to use 2-d grid coordinates to calculate a function in a 2-d space. In this example, we want to calculate values of $Z_{nm} = X_{nm}^2 + Y_{nm}^2$ for x values of [1,2,3,4] and y values of [10,20,30,40]. Here, first, we create 1-d xm and yn arrays containing x and y grid coordinates. Then, we use the `meshgrid` function to map xm and yn values to 2-d grid arrays named Xnm and Ynm. Finally, we calculate Znm for each pair of (Xnm,Ynm). Note that, we use the dot in front of ^ operator as `.^` for an element-wise operation.

```
%Coordinates in x direction
xm=[1,2,3,4];

%Coordinates in y direction
yn=[10,20,30,40];

%Generate 2-d grid coordinates
[Xnm,Ynm] = meshgrid(xm,yn);

%Calculate 2-d Znm array
%Output:
%        101         104         109         116
%        401         404         409         416
%        901         904         909         916
%        1601        1604        1609        1616
Znm=Xnm.^2+Ynm.^2;
disp(Znm)
```

11.3 The 1-Dimensional Interpolation

MATLAB provides a function for 1-d univariate interpolations. This function helps to interpolate and find values at any given point from existing points. Here is a function to interpolate 1-d data:

Function	Description
`interp1`	Return 1-d interpolation values

For a 1-d interpolation, we can use the `interp1` function. Here is a general syntax shows how to find interpolated values for a 1-d dataset:

Syntax

```
vq = interp1(x, v, xq, method, extrapolation)
```

The `x` is a 1-d array that contains x-coordinates of known points. The `v` is an n-d array that contains values of known points as `v=f(x)`. In other words, `(x,v)` pairs represent known data points. Note that, a length of `v` along an interpolation dimension should be equal to a length of `x`. The `xq` is an array that contains x-coordinates for points where `vq` values are interpolated at those points. In other words, `(xq,vq)` pairs represent data points that we know their `x` values and we want to find their `v` values by interpolation.

The `method` defines the method of interpolation. The `method` is optional and by default is `'linear'`. Here is a list of common interpolation methods that can be used by the `interp1` function.

method	Description
`'linear'`	Use linear interpolation
`'nearest'`	Return value from nearest neighbor
`'pchip'`	Use cubic interpolation
`'cubic'`	Use cube interpolation
`'makima'`	Use modified Akima cubic Hermite interpolation
`'spline'`	Use Spline interpolation
`'previous'`	Return previous value
`'next'`	Return next value

The `extrapolation` defines an extrapolation strategy for points outside a data range. The `extrapolation` is optional. To specify an extrapolation method to be the same as an interpolation method, we can use `'extrap'` in place of the `extrapolation`. To fill out-ranged values with a single value, we can use a scalar in place of the `extrapolation`.

Here is an example shows how to interpolate 1-d data using the `interp1` function. In this example, we have known points as x=[0,2,4,6,8,10] and v=[0,4,16,36,64,100]. These data represent $v = x^2$. Now, assume we want to find vq values at xq=[1,3,5,7,9]. We use the `interp1` function to interpolate and find vq values at these x-coordinates from (x,v) points. We display original data and interpolated data. As we can see, although known values (x,v) follow $v = x^2$, the interpolated v values are not equal to x^2. It is because we use a linear interpolation. To get an accurate interpolation, we should use a higher-order interpolation method.

```
%x and v data
```

```
x=[0,2,4,6,8,10];
v=[0,4,16,36,64,100];

%xq data
xq=[1,3,5,7,9];

%Interpolate vq at xq
%Output: 2    10    26    50    82
vq=interp1(x, v, xq, 'linear');
disp(vq)

%Plot data
plot(x , v, 'LineStyle', '--', 'Marker', 'o')
hold on
scatter(xq, vq, 's', 'filled')
legend('Original Data', 'Iterpolated Data', 'Location', 'northwest')
```

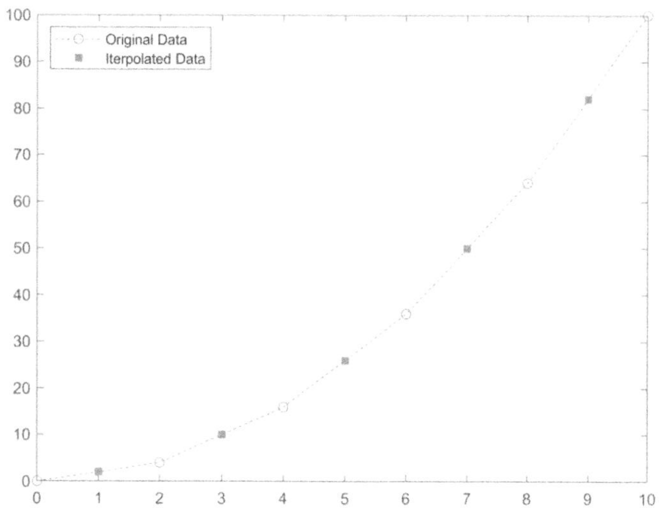

Figure 11.1
Linear interpolation using the `interp1` function

11.4 The 2-Dimensional Interpolation

MATLAB provides several functions for 2-d and multivariate interpolations. Here is a list of the most common functions to interpolate 2-d data:

Function	Description
`griddata`	Interpolate scattered data
`scatteredInterpolant`	Return interpolator function from 2-d or 3-d scattered data
`griddedInterpolant`	Return interpolator function from n-d gridded data
`interp2`	Return 2-d interpolation values from 2-d gridded data

The most helpful function for a 2-d interpolation is the **`griddata`** function. This function helps to interpolate values at given points from known scattered data. Here is a general syntax shows how to interpolate scattered data:

Syntax

```
vq = griddata(x ,y ,v ,xq ,yq , method)
```

The `x`, `y`, and `v` are 1-d arrays that contain coordinates of known points. In other words, `(x,y,v)` values represent known data points. The `xq` and `yq` are arrays that contain `x` and `y` coordinates for points where `vq` values are interpolated at those points. In other words, `(xq,yq,vq)` represent data points that we know their `x` and `y` values and we want to find their `v` values by interpolation.

The `method` defines the method of interpolation. The `method` is optional and by default is `'linear'`. Here is a list of common interpolation methods that can be used by the `griddata` function.

method	Description
`'linear'`	Use linear interpolation
`'nearest'`	Return value from nearest neighbor
`'cubic'`	Use cube interpolation

Here is an example shows how to interpolate scattered data using the `griddata` function. In this example, we show how to interpolate scattered (x,y,z) data that follow $z = x^2 + y^2$ equation to 2-d grid coordinates. First, we generate scattered (x,y,z) data. To do that, we generate 100 uniformly distributed random data points over an interval of (-5,5) for x and y data. Then, we calculate z values as $z = x^2 + y^2$. Next, we generate 1-d and 2-d coordinates over an interval of [-5,5] in x and y directions. Here, we use 50 coordinates in each direction. To get finer results, we can generate a finer grid with more coordinates, however, it may take a much longer time to interpolate. After that, we interpolate (x,y,z) scattered data to 2-d grid coordinates. Finally, we display interpolated data and scattered data. In the figure, interpolated data are displayed by filled contour and scattered data are displayed by black markers. Note that, since data are generated randomly, we get slightly different results each time we run this code.

```
%Define random range
low=-5.0;
high=5.0;

%Generate x data, 100 random points over (-5,5) interval
x=(high-low).*rand(100,1)+low;

%Generate y data, 100 random points over (-5,5) interval
y=(high-low).*rand(100,1)+low;

%Calculate z data
z=x.^2+y.^2;

%Generate 50 coordinates over [-5,5] interval in x direction
xm=linspace(-5,5,50);

%Generate 50 coordinates over [-5,5] interval in y direction
yn=linspace(-5,5,50);

%Generate 2-d grid coordinates
[Xnm,Ynm] = meshgrid(xm,yn);

%Interpolate data
Znm = griddata(x, y, z, Xnm, Ynm);

%Plot data
contourf(Xnm, Ynm , Znm)
hold on
scatter(x, y, 'k', 'filled')
```

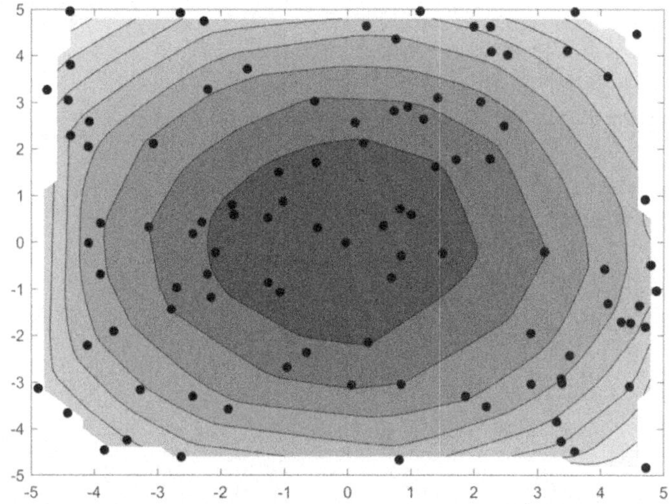

Figure 11.2
Scatter interpolation using the `griddata` function

When we are working with a large dataset, an interpolation can take a long time and lots of resources. One way to avoid that is to use the nearest-neighbor interpolation. In this method, when we want to find a value for a new point, instead of finding a value from an interpolation, a value from the nearest neighbor of this new point is returned. In general, this method is faster and less accurate compared to other interpolation methods.

The `griddata` function is helpful for cases that we need to interpolate unknown values from known scattered data once. However, if we need to repeat the interpolation of unknown values from the same set of known scattered data several times, then using the `griddata` function is not efficient anymore. For such cases that we have one set of known scattered data that is used repeatedly for interpolation, it is better to use the `scatteredInterpolant` function. The `scatteredInterpolant` function returns an interpolator function resulted from an interpolation. We can use this interpolator function to find values at new points. Here are general syntaxes show how to use the `scatteredInterpolant` function:

Syntax

```
F = scatteredInterpolant(x, y, v, Method)
vq = F(xq ,yq)
```

The `x`, `y`, and `v` are 1-d arrays that contain coordinates of known points. In other words, `(x,y,v)` values represent known data points. The `xq` and `yq` are arrays that contain `x` and `y` coordinates for points where `vq` values are interpolated at those points. In other words, `(xq,yq,vq)` represent data points that we know their `x` and `y` values and we want to find their `v` values by interpolation.

The `Method` defines the method of interpolation. The `method` is optional and by default is `'linear'`. To get value from the nearest neighbor, we can use `'nearest'` in place of the `Method`.

Note that, results from the `scatteredInterpolant` function are similar to results from the `griddata` function if we use the same interpolation method in both functions.

Here, we show how to use a previous example to interpolate scattered data using the `scatteredInterpolant` function. This time, we use a nearest-neighbor method for interpolation. Results from this example are similar to the ones from a previous example if we use a 'nearest' method in the `griddata` function. Note that, since data are generated randomly, we get slightly different results each time we run this code.

```
%Define random range
low=-5.0;
high=5.0;

%Generate x data, 100 random points over (-5,5) interval
x=(high-low).*rand(100,1)+low;

%Generate y data, 100 random points over (-5,5) interval
y=(high-low).*rand(100,1)+low;

%Calculate z data
z=x.^2+y.^2;

%Generate 50 coordinates over [-5,5] interval in x direction
xm=linspace(-5,5,50);

%Generate 50 coordinates over [-5,5] interval in y direction
yn=linspace(-5,5,50);

%Generate 2-d grid coordinates
[Xnm,Ynm] = meshgrid(xm,yn);

%Interpolate z=f(x,y)
F = scatteredInterpolant(x, y, z, 'nearest');

%Interpolate Znm at (Xnm,Ynm)
Znm = F(Xnm,Ynm);

%Plot data
```

```
contourf(Xnm, Ynm , Znm)
hold on
scatter(x, y, 'k', 'filled')
```

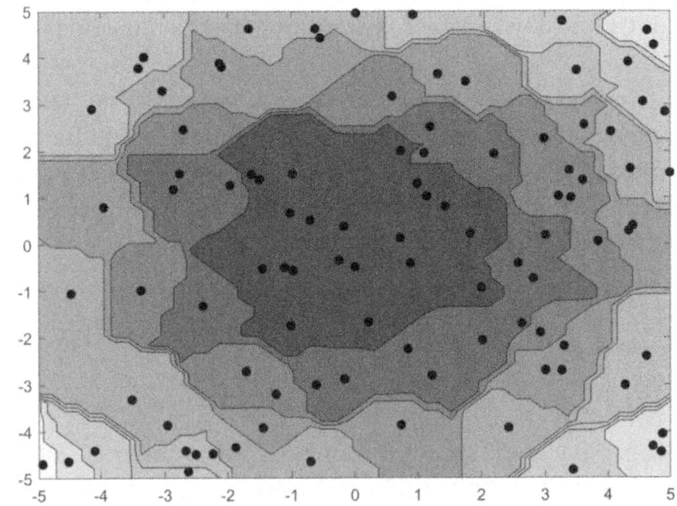

Figure 11.3
Scatter interpolation using the `scatteredInterpolant` function

11.5 Curve Fitting

Sometimes we have a dataset which we want to describe it by a mathematical function. The curve fitting refers to a process of finding a mathematical function that fits data points the best. MATLAB has the Curve Fitting Toolbox which is a powerful tool for curve fitting. In addition to curve fitting functions, it provides a Curve Fitting App with an interactive interface that allows users to fit a curve to data relatively easily. However, the Curve Fitting Toolbox is not part of standard MATLAB and its license should be obtained separately. To run a Curve Fitting App, we can either use the `cftool` command or we can go to the APPS tab and click on Curve Fitting.

Using the Curve Fitting App is useful if we need to fit a limited number of curves. However, if we need to repeat a curve fitting process many times, then it is more convenient to do it by using curve fitting functions inside a code. In cases that we do not have access to the Curve Fitting Toolbox, still we can use other MATLAB functions for curve fitting. In this section, we explain how to use MATLAB functions to fit a curve (a mathematical function) to data. Note that, these functions do not belong to the Curve Fitting Toolbox. Here are functions to fit a curve (a mathematical function) to data:

Function	Description
`lsqcurvefit`	Fit curve (function) to data using non-linear least squares

polyfit	Fit polynomial to data

Before using these functions, let's explain how a curve fitting works. Assume we have a dataset that can be presented by an equation as $y = p_1 x^{p_2} + p_3$, where p1, p2, and p3 are unknown parameters. To find these parameters, we use a curve fitting method. A curve fitting helps to fit this equation to data and find p1, p2, and p3 that represent data the best.

The simplest method to fit a function to data is to use the `lsqcurvefit` function. Note that, the `lsqcurvefit` function belongs to the Optimization Toolbox. This function employs nonlinear least squares to fit a given function to data. Here is a general syntax shows how to fit a function to data:

Syntax

```
p = lsqcurvefit(fun, p0, xdata, ydata)
```

The `fun` defines a function to be fitted to data. The `p0` contains initial guesses for unknown parameters (coefficients). The `p0` is an array which its length is equal to a number of unknown parameters (coefficients) in a function. The `xdata` contains x data (values of an independent variable). The `ydata` contains y data (values of a dependent variable) as `ydata=fun(xdata)`. The `p` is an array that contains parameter (coefficient) values obtained from a curve fitting. These are coefficients that result in the best-fitted function to data.

Before we start using the `lsqcurvefit` function, we need to define a function to be fitted to data. The simplest way for that is to define an anonymous function. We explained how to define and use an anonymous function in earlier chapters. Here is a general syntax shows how to define an anonymous function to be used for a curve fitting:

Syntax

```
fun = @ (p,x) expression
```

The `x` defines an independent variable. The `p` defines unknown parameters (coefficients) in a function to be found by a curve fitting. The `expression` represents a function to be fitted to data.

Here is an example shows how to fit a curve to data using the `lsqcurvefit` function. In this example, we have data that are originally generated from $y = 0.5x^3 + 20$ for x between -6 and 5 and then some random noises are added to them. Therefore, we choose the best fit function to be

$y = p_{(1)}x^3 + p_{(2)}$. To fit this function to these data, first, we define an anonymous function as `p(1).*x.^3+p(2)`, where p(1) and p(2) are unknown parameters (coefficients) we intend to find by a curve fitting. Note that, we use the dot in front of operators for an element-wise operation. We use the lsqcurvefit function with initial guesses of p0=[0.1,15] to fit this function to data and find p(1) and p(2). The results are p(1)=0.49 and p(2)=20.41, which are very close to actual values of p(1)=0.5 and p(2)=20. After that, we generate 100 points between -6 and 5 and calculate values for these points from a fitted curve. Finally, we display original data and fitted curve. In the figure, original data are displayed by circle markers and a fitted curve is displayed by a line.

```
%x and y data
xdata=[-6,-5,-4,-3,-2,-1,0,1,2,3,4,5];
ydata=[-86,-41.5,-14,10.5,17,19.5,17,24.5,22,32.5,55,81.5];

%Define anonymous function
fun = @ (p,x) p(1).*x.^3+p(2);

%Initial guesses
p0=[0.1,15];

%Fit function to data
p = lsqcurvefit(fun, p0, xdata, ydata);

%Print parameters
%Output: 0.4951   20.4121
disp(p)

%Calculate fitted values
x_fit = linspace(-6,5,100); %Generate 100 points between -6 and 5
y_fit = fun(p, x_fit);

%Plot data
scatter(xdata, ydata, 'filled')
hold on
plot(x_fit, y_fit)
box on
legend('Data', 'Fitted Curve', 'Location', 'northwest')
```

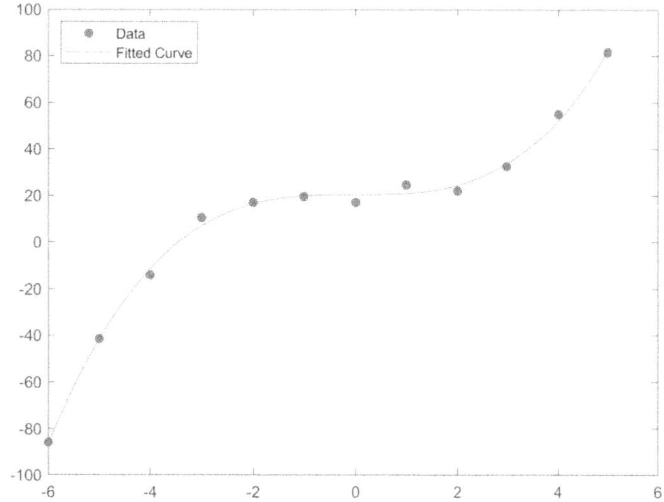

Figure 11.4
Curve fitting using the `lsqcurvefit` function

11.6 Curve Fitting by Optimization

Another method to fit a function to data is to use the **`fminsearch`** function from the Optimization toolbox. In this method, we minimize the sum of a squared error to find the best fit to data. Here is a function to find a minimum of a function:

Function	Description
`fminsearch`	Find minimum of function

Here is a general syntax shows how to minimize a function:

Syntax

```
p = fminsearch(fun, p0)
```

The **`fun`** defines a function to be minimized. The **`p0`** contains initial guesses for unknown parameters (coefficients). The **`p0`** is an array which its length is equal to a number of unknown parameters (coefficients) in a function. The **`p`** is an array that contains parameter (coefficient) values obtained from a curve fitting. These are coefficients that result in the best-fitted function to data.

As mentioned above, in this method, we find the best fit to data by minimizing the sum of a squared error. To do that, first, we define a function as **`sum((expression-ydata).^2)`** and then we find parameters (coefficients) that minimize this function. These parameters (coefficients) are the ones that provide the best fit to data. Here, the expression represents a function we want to fit to data.

Similar to a previous method, the simplest way to define a function is to use an anonymous function. Here is a general syntax shows how to define an anonymous function to be used for a function minimization:

Syntax

```
fun = @ (p) sum((expression-ydata).^2)
```

The `ydata` contain data for dependent variables. The `p` defines unknown parameters (coefficients) in a function to be found by a function minimization. The `expression` represents a function to be fitted to data.

Here, we show how to use a previous example to fit a curve to data using the fminsearch function. In this example, we want to fit $y = p_{(1)}x^3 + p_{(2)}$ to data. Therefore, we define an anonymous function as `sum(((p(1).*xdata.^3+p(2))-ydata).^2)`, where xdata and ydata contain data for independent and dependent variables, respectively, and p(1) and p(2) are unknown parameters we intend to find by minimization. Results from this example are similar to the ones from a previous example.

```
%x and y data
xdata=[-6,-5,-4,-3,-2,-1,0,1,2,3,4,5];
ydata=[-86,-41.5,-14,10.5,17,19.5,17,24.5,22,32.5,55,81.5];

%Define anonymous function
fun = @ (p) sum(((p(1).*xdata.^3+p(2))-ydata).^2);

%Initial guesses
p0=[0.1,15];

%Minimize function
p = fminsearch(fun, p0);

%Print parameters
%Output: 0.4951   20.4122
disp(p)
```

```
%Calculate fitted values
f = @ (p,x) p(1).*x.^3+p(2);
x_fit = linspace(-6,5,100); %Generate 100 points between -6 and 5
y_fit = f(p, x_fit);

%Plot data
scatter(xdata, ydata, 'filled')
hold on
plot(x_fit, y_fit)
box on
legend('Data', 'Fitted Curve', 'Location', 'northwest')
```

11.7 Root Finding

MATLAB provides functions to find roots of a function numerically. Here is a list of functions to find roots of a function:

Function	Description
`fzero`	Find root of non-linear function
`roots`	Find roots of polynomial

One method to find roots of a function is to use the **`fzero`** function. Here is a general syntax shows how to find roots of a function using the `fzero` function:

Syntax

```
x_root = fzero(fun, x0)
```

The **`fun`** defines a function to find its roots. The **`x0`** is a scalar that contains initial guess for a root. The **`x_root`** contains a root value for a function.

Note that, the `fzero` function returns one root at the time. It uses a given initial guess to look for a root of a function. If an input function has more than one root, then we need to repeat the process with one initial guess for each root.

As mentioned earlier, the simplest way to define a function is to use an anonymous function. Here is a general syntax shows how to define an anonymous function to find its roots:

Syntax

```
fun = @ (x) expression
```

The x defines an independent variable. The expression represents a function to find its roots.

Here is an example shows how to find roots of a function using the fzero function. In this example, we show how to find roots of $y = 2x^2 - 8$. This quadratic equation has two roots at x=-2 and x=2. To find roots, first, we define an anonymous function as 2*x^2-8. Then, we use an initial guess x0=-1 to find the first root and x0=1 to find the second root.

```
%Define anonymous function
fun = @ (x) 2*x^2-8;

%Find first root
%Output: -2
root_1 = fzero(fun, -1);
disp(root_1)

%Find second root
%Output: 2
root_2 = fzero(fun, 1);
disp(root_2)
```

Sometimes we need to find roots for a series of functions that have the same form but different parameters (coefficients). In such cases, it is easier to define function parameters as variables and pass parameter values to a function for each root finding. Here, we explain how to use variables as parameters and coefficients in a function to find its roots multiple times. The simplest method to do that is to define a function with only one argument representing an independent variable while all parameters in a function are replaced by variables. Another method is to define a function that has separate arguments for an independent variable and all parameters. In the next two examples, we explain how to implement these two methods.

Here is an example shows how to find roots of a function that takes its parameters from a code. In this example, we want to find roots of $y = ax^2 - b$, where a and b are variables. To find roots, first, we define a and b values in a code. Then, we define an anonymous function with only x argument. Finally, we use the fzero function to find its roots.

```
%Define a and b
a=2;
```

```
b=8;

%Define anonymous function
fun = @ (x) a*x^2-b;

%Find first root
%Output: -2
root_1 = fzero(fun, -1);
disp(root_1)

%Find second root
%Output: 2
root_2 = fzero(fun, 1);
disp(root_2)
```

Now, we show how to find roots for a previous example. This time, we define all `x`, `a`, and `b` as arguments in an anonymous function. Here, after specifying `a` and `b` values, first, we define an anonymous function with all `x`, `a`, and `b` as its arguments. Then, we use this function to define another anonymous function with only `x` argument. Finally, we use the `fzero` function to find the roots.

```
%Define a and b
a=2;
b=8;

%Define anonymous function with its variables
fun_with_variables = @ (x,a,b) a*x^2-b;

%Define anonymous function with x variable alone
fun = @(x) fun_with_variables(x,a,b);

%Find first root
%Output: -2
root_1 = fzero(fun, -1);
disp(root_1)

%Find second root
%Output: 2
root_2 = fzero(fun, 1);
disp(root_2)
```

11.8 Solve System of Linear Equations

MATLAB provides functions to solve equations. Here is a list of common functions to solve equations:

Function/Operator	Description
`\`	Solve for X in AX = B system of linear equations
`/`	Solve for X in XA = B system of linear equations
`linsolve`	Solve for X in AX = B system of linear equations
`solve`	Solve equations and systems
`dsolve`	Solve differential equations
`ode23`	Solve differential equations
`ode45`	Solve differential equations

One method to find a solution for a system of linear equations is to use the `\` (matrix left division or backslash) operator. Here is a general syntax shows how to solve for `X` in `AX = B` system of linear equations using \ :

Syntax

```
X = A\B
```

The `A` defines a coefficient matrix. The `B` contains values for the right side of equations. The `X` contains solutions.

To explain how to use \ to solve a system of linear equations, let's illustrate how to find A, X, and B in a system of linear equations AX = B. Assume we have a system that contains 3 linear equations as:

$$\begin{cases} 2x + 3y - 5z = -29 \\ -1x + 2y + 3z = 10 \\ 6x + 7y + 4z = 12 \end{cases}$$

We can write this system of equation in a matrix format as:

$$\begin{bmatrix} 2 & 3 & -5 \\ -1 & 2 & 3 \\ 6 & 7 & 4 \end{bmatrix} \times \begin{bmatrix} x \\ y \\ z \end{bmatrix} = \begin{bmatrix} -29 \\ 10 \\ 12 \end{bmatrix}$$

Then, by comparing these matrixes with the AX = B format, we can write A, X, and B as:

$$A = \begin{bmatrix} 2 & 3 & -5 \\ -1 & 2 & 3 \\ 6 & 7 & 4 \end{bmatrix} \qquad X = \begin{bmatrix} x \\ y \\ z \end{bmatrix} \qquad B = \begin{bmatrix} -29 \\ 10 \\ 12 \end{bmatrix}$$

Here is an example shows how to solve for X in AX = B system of linear equations using \ . In this example, we show how to find solutions for a system of linear equations demonstrated above. The solutions for this system of equations are x=1, y=-2, and z=5.

```
%Define coefficient matrix
%Output:
%        2     3    -5
%       -1     2     3
%        6     7     4
A=[[2,3,-5];[-1,2,3];[6,7,4]];
disp(A)

%Define right side matrix
%Output:
%      -29
%       10
%       12
B=[-29;10;12];
disp(B)

%Find solution for AX = B
%Output:
%       1.0000
%      -2.0000
%       5.0000
X = A\B;
disp(X)
```

11.9 Numerical Integration

MATLAB provides functions to find an integral of a function numerically. Here is a list of common functions to find an integral of a function:

Function	Description
`integral`	Return integral of function
`integral2`	Return double integral of function
`integral3`	Return triple integral of function
`trapz`	Return integral from function values
`quad`	Return integral of function (legacy version)

One method to find an integral of a function numerically is to use the `integral` function. Here is a general syntax shows how to find an integral of a function using the `integral` function:

Syntax

```
q = integral(fun, xmin, xmax)
```

The `fun` defines a function to find its integral. The `xmin` and `xmax` define the lower and upper limits of the integration, respectively. The `q` contains an integral value.

As mentioned earlier, the simplest way to define a function is to use an anonymous function. Here is a general syntax shows how to define an anonymous function to find its integral:

Syntax

```
fun = @ (x) expression
```

The `x` defines an independent variable. The `expression` represents a function to find its integral.

Here is an example shows how to find an integral of a function numerically using the `integral` function. In this example, we show how to find an integral of $y = 2x^3 - 5x$ from 0 to 10. An integral of this function from 0 to 10 is equal to 4750.

```
%Define anonymous function
fun = @ (x) 2.*x.^3-5.*x;

%Calculate integral from 0 to 10
%Output: 4750
q = integral(fun, 0, 10);
disp(q)
```

Chapter 12
Introduction to Signal Processing

In this chapter, the basics of signal processing with MATLAB are described. First, a wave function is explained. Then, a sampling frequency of data is described. After that, methods to control the quality of data and detrend data are presented. Next, it is described how time and frequency domains are related. Then, Fourier analysis and fast Fourier transform (FFT) are explained. It follows by descriptions of how frequencies are ordered in a fast Fourier transform. Next, double-sided and single-sided fast Fourier transforms are explained. Then, it is shown how to compute wave amplitudes from fast Fourier transform results. At the end, it is described how to estimate a power spectral density of a signal.

12.1 Wave Function

Before we start explaining a signal processing of waves, let's have a brief description of a simple wave. A mathematical function of a simple sinusoidal (harmonic) wave traveling in the positive x-direction is:

$$y(x,t) = A_w \sin(kx - \omega t + \varphi)$$

In this function, y is vertical position, x is horizontal position, t is time, A_w is wave amplitude, k is wavenumber in radian per unit distance, ω is angular frequency in radian per unit time (second), and φ is phase shift in radian.

A wavenumber and an angular frequency are:

$$k = \frac{2\pi}{\lambda}$$

$$\omega = 2\pi f_w = \frac{2\pi}{T_w}$$

$$f_w = \frac{1}{T_w}$$

Here, λ is wavelength, f_w is wave frequency in hertz (Hz), and T_w is wave period in second. Note that, the hertz (Hz) is defined as one cycle per second and presented as $(1/s)$.

We may consider a wave function for only one of a spatial or time domain. Characteristics of a wave in a spatial domain are represented by a wavenumber and wavelength. A wavenumber, k, shows the total number of full waves (oscillations) per unit distance. In other words, a wavenumber shows how many times a wave oscillates in a unit distance. A wavelength, λ, is a horizontal distance between two successive similar points. In other words, a wavelength is a distance that a wave travels in one full oscillation. A function of a wave that only travels in a spatial domain (for a fixed point of time such as t=0) is:

$$y(x, t = 0) = A_w \sin(kx + \varphi)$$

Similarly, characteristics of a wave in a time domain are represented by an angular frequency, wave period, and wave frequency. An angular frequency, ω, shows an angular displacement per unit time. A wave period, T_w, refers to the time that a wave requires to complete one full cycle of an oscillation. A wave frequency, f_w, which is an inverse of a wave period, shows the total number of full waves (oscillations) per unit time. A function of a wave that only oscillates in a time domain (for a fixed point of space such as x=0) is:

$$y(x = 0, t) = A_w \sin(-\omega t + \varphi)$$

Figure 12.1
A sinusoidal wave in spatial and time domains.

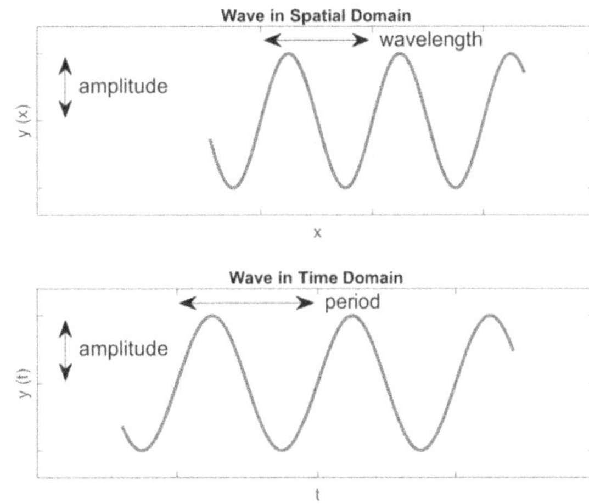

In the rest of this chapter, we only discuss a signal processing of waves in a time domain. A signal processing of waves in a spatial domain is similar to a time domain, except that a wave travels in space. Also, we use a frequency, f, with a unit of Hz, in all analyses. Note that, some texts or field of studies may prefer to use other formats of a frequency such as a normalized frequency or an angular frequency instead of a frequency.

12.2 Sampling Frequency

In signal processing, we usually work with measured or generated data which are stored as a sequence of discrete values. A sampling frequency, f_S, indicates a rate that these data are measured or generated. In other words, a sampling frequency shows how many data points are sampled per time unit. For example, if we measure a wave with 8 data points in every second, then a sampling frequency of this dataset is 8 samples per second or 8 Hz.

A sampling frequency is a key property of a time-series. The highest frequency that we can analyze in signal processing is equal to a half of a sampling frequency of a discrete signal. This is commonly known as the Nyquist frequency. For example, if we have a discrete signal with a sampling frequency of 8 Hz, then a frequency range we can work with is $0 < f \leq 4$ Hz.

A sampling duration, d, indicates a duration that data are measured or generated. A sampling duration shows for how long data points are sampled. For example, if we measure a wave for 128 seconds, then a sampling duration of this dataset is 128 seconds.

If we have a dataset that is sampled with a sampling frequency of f_s for a duration of d, then data points in this dataset have the following properties:

$$N = f_s \times d$$

$$\Delta t = \frac{1}{f_s}$$

Here, N is the total number of data points in a dataset, f_s is sampling frequency, d is sampling duration, and Δt is time interval between two successive data points.

Sometimes, a sampling frequency is confused with a wave frequency. A wave frequency describes how many full oscillations a wave completes per unit time, while a sampling frequency describes how many data points per unit time are sampled (obtained) from this wave. To clarify the difference between these two, let's have an example. Consider we have a wave that has a wave frequency equal to $f_w = 1$ Hz. It means that this wave has one full cycle per second. Now, assume we want to measure this wave with a sensor that is set to collect data every 0.125 seconds. In this setup, a sensor measures this wave 8 times per second. Therefore, while this wave has a wave frequency of $f_w = 1$ Hz, collected data from this wave has a sampling frequency of $f_s = 8$ Hz.

Figure 12.2
A sinusoidal wave with a wave amplitude of $A_w = 0.5$ m and wave frequency of $f_w = 1$ Hz. This wave is sampled with a sampling frequency of $f_s = 8$ Hz for a sampling duration of $d = 4$ seconds.

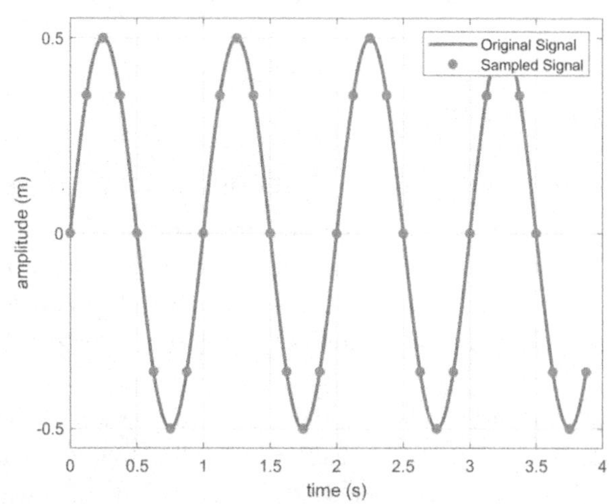

In signal processing, it is a common practice to sample data in a way that the total number of data points can be presented as 2^P such as one of the ..., 64, 128, 256, ... values. The reason is that some of the signal processing algorithms only work with a signal that its length is a power of 2. To obtain a signal with 2^P data points, we can choose a sampling frequency and a sampling duration that result in a signal with 2^P data points. For example, if $f_s = 8$ Hz and $d = 128$ seconds, then a signal length becomes $N = f_s \times d = 8 \times 128 = 1024$ which is equal to 2^{10}.

If a length of a signal is not a power of 2, we can change its length to become a power of 2. One method to change a signal length to a power of 2 is to pad (add) enough zeros to the end of a signal until its length becomes a power of 2. The other method to change a signal length to a power of 2 is to remove data points from the end of a signal until its length becomes a power of 2. For example, if we have a dataset that has 150 data points, we can either pad 106 zeros at the end of this signal to make its length equal to 256 or we can remove 22 data points from the end of this signal to make its length equal to 128.

Here is an example shows how to generate a simple signal. In this example, we generate a simple sinusoidal wave with a wave amplitude of 0.5 and a wave frequency of 1 Hz without a phase shift. To generate this wave, we use a sampling frequency of 8 Hz and a sampling duration of 128 seconds. A generated signal has 1024 data points with a time interval of 0.125 seconds.

```
%Wave amplitude
Aw=0.5;

%Wave frequency
fw=1;

%Sampling frequency
fs=8;

%Sampling duration
d=128;

%Total number of data points
N=fs*d;

%Time interval
dt=1/fs;

%Time data points
t=[0:1:N-1].*dt; %Or t=linspace(0,d-dt,N)
```

```
%Signal data points
y=Aw.*sin(2.*pi.*fw.*t);

%Plot signal
plot(t,y)
```

12.3 Control Data Quality

Before we use any dataset, we need to control the quality of that dataset and clean its data if it is necessary. It is particularly important if we are working with real-world data. In general, to clean data, we look for spikes, outliers, unacceptable values, and missing values in a dataset and remove or replace them with proper values.

A spike refers to a sudden rise or fall of a value in a signal. An outlier refers to a data point that does not follow the general trend of data. These spikes and outliers are usually caused by some kind of errors. These spikes and outliers in a dataset should be removed from a dataset and replaced by correct values.

An unacceptable value is a value that should not be presented in a dataset under circumstances that data are collected. For example, if we have a signal that all of its values should be positive, then any zero or negative value is unacceptable. These unacceptable data points should be removed from a dataset and replaced by acceptable values.

A missing value refers to a point in a dataset that there is no value for that point. For example, if a sensor that collects data stops reading for a period of time, then we do not have any values within that period. These missing data points should be replaced by available values.

In any of these cases, if there are few low-quality data points, they should be removed and replaced. However, if there are too many low-quality data points in a dataset, then the integrity of a dataset is affected and a dataset becomes unacceptable. In such cases, a dataset should not be used.

There are different methods to handle any of these low-quality data points. A preferable method is to replace them with data from another dataset if both datasets are almost identical. However, in practice, it is very rare to have two sets of identical datasets. A practical method to clean a dataset is to replace low-quality data points with values from their neighboring data points. In this method, each low-quality data point is either replaced with a value from its nearest neighbor or is replaced with a value that is obtained from an interpolation of neighboring data points.

One method to identify outliers is to use a z-score. To explain how it works, first, let's describe how data are distributed in a normal distribution. In a normal distribution, 99.73% of data in a dataset lie within 3 standard deviations of a mean value. It means that, if x is a data point that belongs to a dataset which has a mean value of $\bar{x}$ and a standard deviation of σ, then a probability that x falls in a range of $\bar{x} - 3\sigma \leq x \leq \bar{x} + 3\sigma$ is 0.9973, and a probability that x is in a range of $x < \bar{x} - 3\sigma$ or $x > \bar{x} + 3\sigma$ is 1-0.9973=0.0027. Similarly, in a normal distribution, a probability of $\bar{x} - 2\sigma \leq x \leq \bar{x} + 2\sigma$ is 0.9545 and a probability of $\bar{x} - \sigma \leq x \leq \bar{x} + \sigma$ is 0.6827. By knowing that, we can use a z-score, $z = (x - \bar{x})/\sigma$, as a threshold to find outliers. For example, if a z-score of a data point is equal or larger than 3, then a probability of that data point is not an outlier is equal or less than 1-0.9973=0.0027. In other words, a probability of that data point is an outlier is larger than 0.9973. Similarly, if a z-score of a data point is equal or larger than 2, then a probability of that data point is not an outlier is equal or less than 1-0.9545=0.0455. In other words, a probability of that data point is an outlier is larger than 0.9545. Although these thresholds are correct for a dataset that has a normal distribution, still they are used for datasets without a normal distribution.

In a z-score calculation, depends on a dataset, we may use a mean and standard deviation obtained from an entire dataset, or we may use a mean and standard deviation values calculated locally for each data point. If we use a mean and standard deviation of an entire dataset in a z-score calculation, then each data point is evaluated against all data points in a dataset. However, if we use a local mean and standard deviation values, then each data point is evaluated against its neighboring data points. For latter cases, it is usually easier to use moving average and moving standard deviation functions to slide a window over data and find mean and standard deviation for each data point from its neighbors.

Note that, MATLAB has the `fillmissing` and `filloutliers` functions that may be used to detect and replace missing and outlier data points.

Here is an example shows how to use a z-score to detect an outlier in a dataset. In this example, we have x and y data as y=f(x). All data points in y are between 0 and 10 except for one data point that is 37. Here, first, we show how to use a z-score to detect this outlier. Then, we label an outlier as `NaN`. Finally, we replace `NaN` with a value obtained from an interpolation of its neighbors.

```
%Data
x=[0,2,4,6,8,10,12,14,16,18];
y=[7,4,6,5,3,37,4,6,3,5];

%Mean value of data
y_mean=mean(y(:));
```

```
%Standard deviation of data
y_std=std(y(:));

%Calculate z-score
z_score=(y-y_mean)/y_std;

%Define z-score threshold
threshold=2;

%Replace outliers with NaN
%Output: 7     4     6     5     3   NaN     4     6     3     5
y(abs(z_score)>threshold)=NaN;
disp(y)

%Find NaN
nan_indx=find(isnan(y)==1);
not_nan_indx=find(isnan(y)==0);

%Interpolate missing values
%Output: 7.0000    4.0000    6.0000    5.0000    3.0000    3.5000
%        4.0000    6.0000    3.0000    5.0000
y(nan_indx) = interp1(x(not_nan_indx), y(not_nan_indx), x(nan_indx));
disp(y)
```

Here is another example shows how to use a z-score to detect an outlier in a dataset. In this example, we have x and y data as y=sin(x). All data points in y are between -1 and 1 except for one data point that is 10. Here, first, we show how to calculate a moving mean, moving standard deviation, and moving z-score. Then, we use these z-score values to label an outlier as NaN. Finally, we replace NaN with a value obtained from an interpolation of its neighbors.

```
%Data
x=linspace(0,4*pi,1000);
y=sin(x);
y(100)=10;

%Moving mean with window size of 9
rolled_mean=movmean(y,9,'Endpoints','shrink');

%Moving std with window size of 9
rolled_std=movstd(y,9,'Endpoints','shrink');

%Calculate moving z-score
```

```
rolled_z_score=(y-rolled_mean)./rolled_std;

%Define z-score threshold
threshold=2;

%Replace outliers with NaN
y(abs(rolled_z_score)>threshold)=NaN;

%Find NaN
nan_indx=find(isnan(y)==1);
not_nan_indx=find(isnan(y)==0);

%Interpolate missing values
y(nan_indx) = interp1(x(not_nan_indx), y(not_nan_indx), x(nan_indx));

%Plot data
plot(x, y)
```

12.4 Detrend Data

In most signal processing calculations, we need to use a dataset that does not have any trend in its signal. In other words, we need to use a signal that oscillates around a zero-line and has a mean value equal to zero. However, some datasets, in particular the ones that contain real-world data, might show some kind of a linear or non-linear trend. In such cases, we need to remove a trend from a dataset before using it for signal processing. For example, consider a dataset of air temperatures that are collected hourly for one year. In addition to hourly temperatures, these data points also contain footprints of a daily, weekly, and monthly air temperatures in their values. Now, if we want to study and analyze fluctuations of hourly air temperatures, we have to remove any mean or trend that is caused by daily, weekly, or monthly temperature variations. After removing means or trends from these data, only hourly air temperatures, which fluctuate around zero, remain. Here is a function to remove a trend from a dataset:

Function	Description
`detrend`	Remove polynomial trend from data

Here is a general syntax shows how to remove a trend from data:

Syntax

```
detrended_x = detrend(x, n, bp)
```

The `x` contains data to remove their trend. The `n` defines a degree of a polynomial trend to be removed from data. The `n` is optional. If the `n` is not defined, then the best fitted linear line is removed from data. To remove a mean value of data, we should use 0 or `'constant'` in place of `n`. To remove a linear trend from data, we should use 1 or `'linear'` in place of n. The `bp` defines sample values to be used as break-points. The `bp` is optional. If break-points are defined, then data between every two break-points are detrended separately.

Here is an example shows how to remove a trend from a dataset before using it for signal processing. In this example, first, we generate a simple sinusoidal wave with a wave amplitude of 0.5, a wave frequency of 1 Hz, a sampling frequency of 8 Hz, and a sampling duration of 128 seconds. Next, we add random noises and a linear trend to this signal. After that, we use the `detrend` function to remove a trend in this signal. Finally, we display both original and detrended signals. Note that, since noises are generated randomly, we get slightly different results each time we run this code.

```
%Wave properties
Aw=0.5;  %Wave amplitude
fw=1;    %Wave frequency

%Signal properties
fs=8;    %Sampling frequency
d=128;   %Sampling duration
N=fs*d;  %Total number of data points
dt=1/fs; %Time interval

%Time data points
t=[0:1:N-1].*dt;

%Signal data points
sinusoidal_signal=Aw.*sin(2.*pi.*fw.*t);
noise_signal=rand(1,N);
signal_trend=0.02.*t+5;
original_signal=sinusoidal_signal+noise_signal+signal_trend;

%Detrend signal
signal_detrended = detrend(original_signal);

%Plot signals
plot(t, original_signal)
hold on
```

```
plot(t, signal_detrended)
grid on
legend('Original Signal','Detrended Signal','Location','northwest')
```

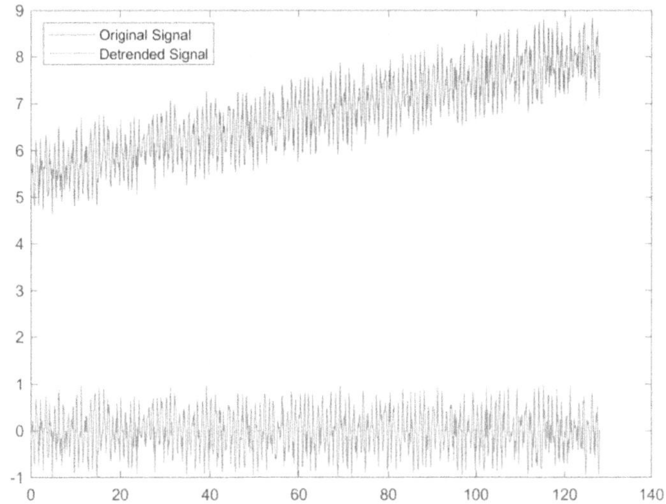

Figure 12.3
Remove a trend from a signal

12.5 Time and Frequency Domains

The main step in signal processing is to transform a signal from a time domain (or spatial domain) to a frequency domain. To transform a signal from a time domain to a frequency domain, first, we decompose an original signal in a time domain into several simple sinusoidal waves. In other words, we find a series of simple sinusoidal waves in a time domain which their superpositions generate an original signal. Now, by displaying amplitudes of these sinusoidal waves versus their wave frequencies, we present the signal in a frequency domain. In other words, amplitudes and frequencies of these sinusoidal waves are representations of the time domain signal in a frequency domain. In mathematics, the Fourier series is used to write a periodic function as a series of sine and cosine functions as:

$$y(t) = \frac{a_0}{2} + \sum_{n=1}^{N}(a_n \cos(n\omega t) + b_n \sin(n\omega t)) = \sum_{n=-N}^{N} c_n e^{in\omega t}$$

In this function, a_0, a_n, b_n, and c_n are Fourier series coefficients, and $i = \sqrt{-1}$ is an imaginary unit. The $a_0/2$, which is also known as a DC value (DC component), is a mean value of a time-series. This component can be considered as an amplitude of a cosine wave with a frequency of 0 Hz (e.g. Smith, 1997).

Here is an example shows the basic idea behind transforming a signal from a time domain to a frequency domain. In this example, a wave y(t) is decomposed into 3 sinusoidal waves y1(t), y2(t), and y3(t). Then, wave frequencies, fw, and wave amplitudes, Aw, of these three waves are displayed as pairs of (fw1,Aw1), (fw2,Aw2), and (fw3,Aw3). These pairs are transformations of y(t) from a time domain to a frequency domain.

Figure 12.4
Relationship between time and frequency domains (3-d presentation)

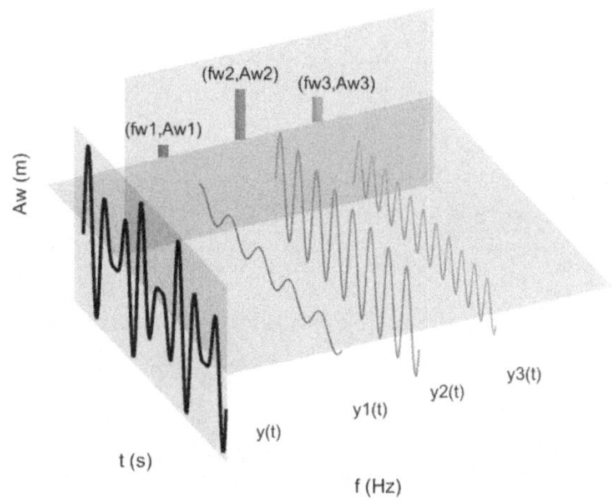

Here is a previous example, but this time in 2-dimension. It presents the basics of how to transform a signal from a time domain to a frequency domain.

Figure 12.5
Relationship between time and frequency domains (2-d presentation)

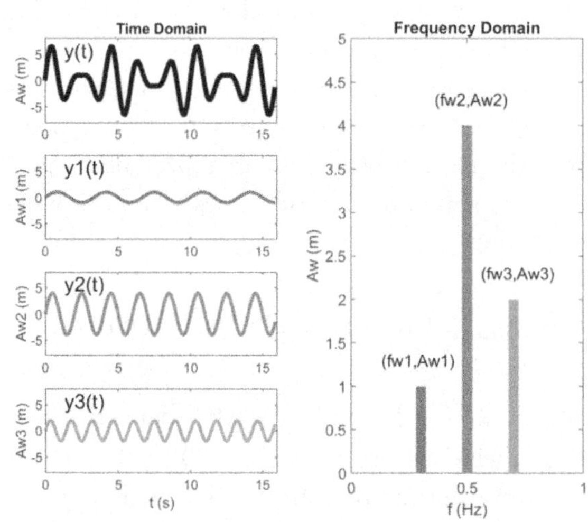

12.6 Fourier Analysis

A transformation of data from one domain to another domain has many applications in science and engineering. In mathematics, these transformations are known as Fourier analysis. In Fourier analysis, we may decompose a function into its oscillatory components or we may rebuild a function from its oscillatory components. Note that, sometimes Fourier analysis only uses to refer to a decomposition of a function into oscillatory components while rebuilding a function from oscillatory components is called Fourier synthesis.

In mathematics, a discrete Fourier transform (DFT) is used to transform a finite sequence of discrete data from one domain to another domain. A discrete Fourier transform (DFT) of a finite sequence of discrete data is written as:

$$X_k = \sum_{n=0}^{N-1} x_n e^{-i2\pi\frac{k}{N}n}$$

In this function, $x_0, x_1, ..., x_{N-1}$ are transformed to $X_0, X_1, ..., X_{N-1}$.

Similarly, an inverse discrete Fourier transform (IDFT) of a finite sequence of discrete data, which returns a Fourier series, is written as:

$$x_n = \frac{1}{N}\sum_{k=0}^{N-1} X_k e^{i2\pi\frac{n}{N}k}$$

In this function, $X_0, X_1, ..., X_{N-1}$ are inversely transformed back to $x_0, x_1, ..., x_{N-1}$. Here, k represents indexes in a frequency domain and n represents indexes in a time or spatial domain. If we are working with a time-series, then k/N represents the k-th frequency in a frequency domain and n/N represents the n-th point in a time domain.

Transformed values of $X_0, X_1, ..., X_{N-1}$ are complex numbers that each contains an amplitude and a phase of an associated sinusoidal wave. An amplitude and phase of sinusoidal waves associated with these transformed values can be obtained as:

Amplitude: $\frac{|X_k|}{N} = \sqrt{(\mathrm{Re}(X_k))^2 + (\mathrm{Im}(X_k))^2}/N$

Phase: $\mathrm{atan2}(\mathrm{Im}(X_k), \mathrm{Re}(X_k))$

Here, $\mathrm{Re}(X_k)$ is a real part, $\mathrm{Im}(X_k)$ is an imaginary part, and $|X_k|$ is a magnitude of X_k.

12.7 Fast Fourier Transform

In computer programming, a fast Fourier transform (FFT) algorithm is used to transform a signal from a time or spatial domain to a frequency domain. A fast Fourier transform is widely used in signal processing. Here are functions to transform signal between domains:

Function	Description
`fft`	Return 1-dimensional discrete Fourier transform (DFT)
`ifft`	Return 1-dimensional inverse discrete Fourier transform (IDFT)
`fftshift`	Shift zero-frequency component to center of spectrum
`abs`	Return absolute value (Return magnitude of complex number)

Here is a general syntax shows how to compute 1-d discrete Fourier transform (DFT) to transform a signal to a frequency domain:

Syntax

```
fft_results_2sided = fft(X, n, dim)
```

The `X` contains data in a time or spatial domain. The `n` defines a length of an output. The `n` is optional. If the `n` is not defined, then a length of an output array is equal to a length of an input array. If the `n` is smaller than a length of an input array, then an input array is truncated to make its length equal to `n`. If the `n` is larger than a length of an input array, then zeros are padded to the end of an input array to make its length equal to `n`. Note that, by increasing the `n` value, a frequency interval of returned FFT values decreases. The `dim` defines a dimension that transformations are computed along that dimension. The `dim` is optional. If the `dim` is not defined, transformations are computed along the first dimension that its length is not 1. Regarding FFT normalization in MATLAB, direct transforms are unscaled and inverse transforms are scaled by 1/n.

Note that, if a length of an input signal and a length of transformed values (FFT) are not equal, it is common to present a length of a signal by L and a length of the transformed values by NFFT.

As mentioned earlier, it is a common practice in signal processing to use a signal that its length is a power of 2 as 2^P. If we have a signal that its length is not a power of 2, we can either pad (add) enough zeros to the end of a signal until its length becomes a power of 2 or remove data points from the end of a signal until its length becomes a power of 2. To find out how many zeros should be padded to end of a signal to make its length a power of 2, we need to find an exponent of a next higher power of 2. For a signal with a length of L, an exponent of a next higher power of 2 that satisfies $2^P \geq L$ is obtained as:

Syntax

```
P = nextpow2(L)
```

Here, `P` is an exponent of a next higher power of 2 for a value of `L`. After we find a value of `P`, we need to pad $(2^P - L)$ zeros to the end of a signal to make its length a power of 2. Note that, instead of using the `nextpow2` function, we may find `P` from `P=ceil(log2(abs(L)))` as well.

For example, assume we have a signal that has 220 data points, which is not a power of 2. Using a previous equation, we find that an exponent of a next higher power of 2 for L=220 is P=8. Therefore, we pad $2^8 - 220 = 36$ zeros to the end of this signal to make its length equal to $2^8 = 256$.

As mentioned earlier, it is a common practice to remove any trend from data before using them for signal processing. However, if we do not remove a mean of a dataset from data, then we will have a value associated with f=0 Hz. This value is known as DC value (DC gain) and refers to the mean of a dataset.

12.8 Frequency Ordering of Fast Fourier Transform

Results from a fast Fourier transform (FFT) are evenly spaced in a frequency domain and have a frequency range from $-f_s/2$ to $f_s/2$. If an original signal only contains real values (not complex values), then outcomes of FFT are symmetrical around frequency 0.

Although FFT outcomes have a frequency range from $-f_s/2$ to $f_s/2$, the FFT results are not returned in this order. In fact, the `fft` function first returns results for positive frequencies, and then returns results for negative frequencies. For an even number of data points, results from a fast Fourier transform have frequency orders as:

```
[0, 1, 2, ..., (N/2-2), (N/2-1), (-N/2), (-N/2+1), ..., -2, -1] .* df
```

In this frequency sequence, which is for an even number of data points, the first element is always 0. This element represents a DC value, is unique, and is not repeated. Also, a frequency associated with $f_s/2$ is unique and is not repeated.

Similarly, for an odd number of data points, results from a fast Fourier transform have frequency orders as:

```
[0, 1, 2, ..., (N-1)/2-1, (N-1)/2, -(N-1)/2, -(N-1)/2+1, ..., -2, -1] .* df
```

Similarly, in a frequency sequence for an odd number of data points, the first element is always 0 (represents a DC value), is unique, and is not repeated. Also, there is no value associated with $f_s/2$.

In these frequency sequences, df or Δf is a frequency interval in a frequency domain which can be computed as:

$$\Delta f = \frac{f_s}{N} = \frac{1}{N\Delta t}$$

Here, Δf is a frequency interval between two successive frequencies, N is the total number of data points in a dataset, f_s is sampling frequency, and Δt is time interval between two successive data points.

Here are general syntaxes show how to obtain frequencies associated with FFT results if N is even and FFT results are symmetrical:

Syntax

```
frequencies = [0:1:N-1].*df %All frequencies
frequencies(N/2+1:end) = frequencies(N/2+1:end)-fs %Map negative frequencies
```

Similarly, we can obtain frequencies associated with FFT results for an odd number of data points. Here are general syntaxes show how to obtain frequencies associated with FFT results if N is odd and FFT results are symmetrical:

Syntax

```
frequencies = [0:1:N-1].*df %All frequencies
frequencies((N+1)/2+1:end) = frequencies((N+1)/2+1:end)-fs %Map negative
                                                            %frequencies
```

The `N` defines a length of a signal. The `df` defines a frequency interval. The `fs` defines a sampling frequency.

To better understand how FFT frequencies are ordered, we show how to assemble frequencies. Here is an example shows how to build a frequency sequence associated with FFT results for an even number of data points:

```
%Signal properties
fs=8;     %Sampling frequency
d=16;     %Sampling duration
N=fs*d;   %Total number of data points
dt=1/fs; %Time interval

%Frequency interval
df=fs/N;

%Frequencies
freq = [0:1:N-1].*df; %All frequencies
freq(N/2+1:end) = freq(N/2+1:end)-fs; %Map negative frequencies
```

Similarly, we can assemble FFT frequencies for an odd number of data points. Here is an example shows how to build a frequency sequence associated with FFT results for an odd number of data points:

```
%Signal properties
fs=5;     %Sampling frequency
d=15;     %Sampling duration
N=fs*d;   %Total number of data points
dt=1/fs; %Time interval

%Frequency interval
df=fs/N;

%Frequencies
freq = [0:1:N-1].*df; %All frequencies
freq((N+1)/2+1:end) = freq((N+1)/2+1:end)-fs; %Map negative frequencies
```

Note that, if we want to use frequency orders that starts at $-f_s/2$ and ends at $f_s/2$, we can use the **`fftshift`** function to shift a zero to the center of FFT results.

12.9 Double-Sided FFT and Single-Sided FFT

Results from a fast Fourier transform (FFT) have a frequency range from $-f_S/2$ to $f_S/2$. These outcomes are considered to be two-sided or double-sided. If an input signal only contains real values, then FFT outcomes are symmetrical around frequency 0. In such cases, it is common practice to only display FFT results for a frequency range from 0 to $f_S/2$. If FFT results are presented in a range from 0 to $f_S/2$, then they are considered to be one-sided or single-sided, as only half of the results are shown. Note that, regardless of a data type, if we need to reconstruct an original signal from FFT results, we should use two-sided FFT values in the `ifft` function.

To obtain one-sided FFT results, first, we keep FFT results that have a frequency range from 0 to $f_S/2$ and remove the rest. Then, we multiply all values that their frequencies are occurred on both sides by 2 to compensate for the other half that we removed. For an even number of data points, values for $f = 0$ (first element) and $f = f_S/2$ (center element) are unique and are not repeated on both sides. Therefore, we do not multiply them by 2. For an odd number of data points, a value for $f = 0$ (first element) is unique and is not repeated on both sides. Therefore, we do not multiply it by 2.

Here are general syntaxes show how to compute a one-sided FFT from a two-sided FFT if N is even and FFT results are symmetrical:

Syntax

```
fft_2sided = fft(signal)
fft_1sided = fft_2sided(1:N/2+1)
fft_1sided(2:end-1) = fft_1sided(2:end-1).*2
```

Similarly, we can compute a one-sided FFT for an odd number of data points. Here are general syntaxes show how to compute a one-sided FFT from a two-sided FFT if N is odd and FFT results are symmetrical:

Syntax

```
fft_2sided = fft(signal)
fft_1sided = fft_2sided(1:(N+1)/2)
fft_1sided(2:end) = fft_1sided(2:end).*2
```

After we obtain a one-sided FFT, we need to generate frequencies associated with these one-sided values. For an even number of data points, one-sided fast Fourier transform values have frequency orders as:

```
[0, 1, 2, ..., (N/2-2), (N/2-1), (N/2)] .* df
```

Similarly, for an odd number of data points, one-sided fast Fourier transform values have frequency orders as:

```
[0, 1, 2, ..., (N-1)/2-1, (N-1)/2] .* df
```

Here is a general syntax shows how to generate a sequence of one-sided frequencies associated with one-sided FFT results for both even and odd number of data points:

Syntax

```
freq_1sided = [0:1:floor(N/2)].*df
```

Here is an example shows how to compute a fast Fourier transform of a signal. In this example, first, we generate a signal from 3 simple sinusoidal waves with wave amplitudes of 0.1, 0.2, and 0.3, wave frequencies of 1, 2, and 3 Hz, a sampling frequency of 8 Hz, and a sampling duration of 16 seconds. Next, we remove a trend in this signal and compute FFT. After that, we show how to compute a one-sided FFT. Finally, we display magnitudes of a two-sided FFT and magnitudes of a one-sided FFT. In the figure, |FFT| represents a magnitude of FFT.

```
%Wave properties
Aw_1=0.1; %1st wave amplitude
Aw_2=0.2; %2nd wave amplitude
Aw_3=0.3; %3rd wave amplitude
fw_1=1.0; %1st wave frequency
fw_2=2.0; %2nd wave frequency
fw_3=3.0; %3rd wave frequency

%Signal properties
fs=8;     %Sampling frequency
d=16;     %Sampling duration
N=fs*d;   %Total number of data points
dt=1/fs;  %Time interval
df=fs/N;  %Frequency interval
```

```
%Time data points
t=[0:1:N-1].*dt;

%Signal data points
y_1=Aw_1.*sin(2.*pi.*fw_1.*t);
y_2=Aw_2.*sin(2.*pi.*fw_2.*t);
y_3=Aw_3.*sin(2.*pi.*fw_3.*t);
original_signal=y_1+y_2+y_3;

%Detrend signal
signal_detrended = detrend(original_signal);

%Compute fast Fourier transform (FFT)
fft_2sided = fft(signal_detrended);

%2-sided frequencies
freq_2sided = [0:1:N-1].*df; %All frequencies
freq_2sided(N/2+1:end) = freq_2sided(N/2+1:end)-fs; %Map negative
                                                    %frequencies

%Compute 1-sided FFT from 2-sided FFT if N is even
fft_1sided = fft_2sided(1:N/2+1);
fft_1sided(2:end-1) = fft_1sided(2:end-1).*2;

%1-sided frequencies
freq_1sided = [0:1:floor(N/2)].*df;

%Plot 2-sided FFT and 1-sided FFT
ax1 = subplot(2,1,1);
plot(freq_2sided,abs(fft_2sided))
title('Two-Sided FFT Results')
xlabel('f (Hz)')
ylabel('| FFT |')
xlim([-fs/2,fs/2])
ylim([0,40])

ax2 = subplot(2,1,2);
plot(freq_1sided,abs(fft_1sided))
title('One-Sided FFT Results')
xlabel('f (Hz)')
ylabel('| FFT |')
xlim([-fs/2,fs/2])
```

```
ylim([0,40])
```

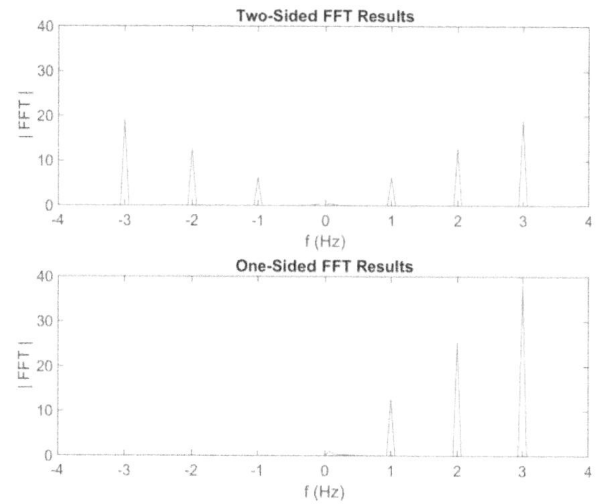

Figure 12.6
Fast Fourier Transform. Here, |FFT| represents a magnitude of FFT.

12.10 Wave Amplitudes from FFT

As mentioned earlier, a fast Fourier transform (FFT) algorithm transforms a signal from a time or spatial domain to a frequency domain by decomposing a signal to a series of sinusoidal waves. Now, if we have FFT results, we can obtain amplitudes of sinusoidal waves that an original signal is decomposed to them. In other words, we can use FFT results to compute amplitudes of sinusoidal waves that an original signal is made up of them.

To compute amplitudes of sinusoidal waves from FFT results, we divide magnitudes of FFT by a length of FFT. The outcomes are two-sided wave amplitudes. As mentioned earlier, outcomes of FFT for a signal with real values are symmetrical around frequency 0. In such cases, we can compute one-sided amplitudes from two-sided amplitudes. To obtain one-sided amplitudes, we keep amplitudes with a frequency range from 0 to $f_s/2$ and remove the rest. Then, we multiply values that their frequencies are repeated on both sides by 2 to compensate for the removed half.

Here are general syntaxes show how to compute one-sided amplitudes of sinusoidal waves if N is even and FFT results are symmetrical:

Syntax

```
fft_2sided = fft(signal)

Aw_2sided = abs(fft_2sided)./N
Aw_1sided = Aw_2sided(1:N/2+1)
Aw_1sided(2:end-1) = Aw_1sided(2:end-1).*2

freq_1sided = [0:1:floor(N/2)].*df
```

Similarly, we can compute amplitudes for an odd number of data points. Here are general syntaxes show how to compute one-sided amplitudes of sinusoidal waves if N is odd and FFT results are symmetrical:

Syntax

```
fft_2sided = fft(signal)

Aw_2sided = abs(fft_2sided)./N
Aw_1sided = Aw_2sided(1:(N+1)/2)
Aw_1sided(2:end) = Aw_1sided(2:end).*2

freq_1sided = [0:1:floor(N/2)].*df
```

Here is an example shows how to compute amplitudes of sinusoidal waves from FFT. Consider a previous example again. In this example, first, we generate a signal from 3 simple sinusoidal waves with wave amplitudes of 0.1, 0.2, and 0.3, wave frequencies of 1, 2, and 3 Hz, a sampling frequency of 8 Hz, and a sampling duration of 16 seconds. Next, we remove a trend in this signal and compute FFT. After that, we show how to compute one-sided amplitudes of sinusoidal waves. Finally, we display amplitudes of sinusoidal waves.

```
%Wave properties
Aw_1=0.1; %1st wave amplitude
Aw_2=0.2; %2nd wave amplitude
Aw_3=0.3; %3rd wave amplitude
fw_1=1.0; %1st wave frequency
fw_2=2.0; %2nd wave frequency
fw_3=3.0; %3rd wave frequency
```

```
%Signal properties
fs=8;    %Sampling frequency
d=16;    %Sampling duration
N=fs*d;  %Total number of data points
dt=1/fs; %Time interval
df=fs/N; %Frequency interval

%Time data points
t=[0:1:N-1].*dt;

%Signal data points
y_1=Aw_1.*sin(2.*pi.*fw_1.*t);
y_2=Aw_2.*sin(2.*pi.*fw_2.*t);
y_3=Aw_3.*sin(2.*pi.*fw_3.*t);
original_signal=y_1+y_2+y_3;

%Detrend signal
signal_detrended = detrend(original_signal);

%Compute fast Fourier transform (FFT)
fft_2sided = fft(signal_detrended);

%Compute 1-sided amplitudes from 2-sided FFT if N is even
Aw_2sided = abs(fft_2sided)./N;
Aw_1sided = Aw_2sided(1:N/2+1);
Aw_1sided(2:end-1) = Aw_1sided(2:end-1).*2;

%1-sided frequencies
freq_1sided = [0:1:floor(N/2)].*df;

%Plot wave amplitudes
plot(freq_1sided,Aw_1sided)
title('One-Sided Wave Amplitudes')
xlabel('f (Hz)')
ylabel('Aw')
xlim([-fs/2,fs/2])
ylim([0,0.4])
```

Figure 12.7
Amplitudes of sinusoidal waves

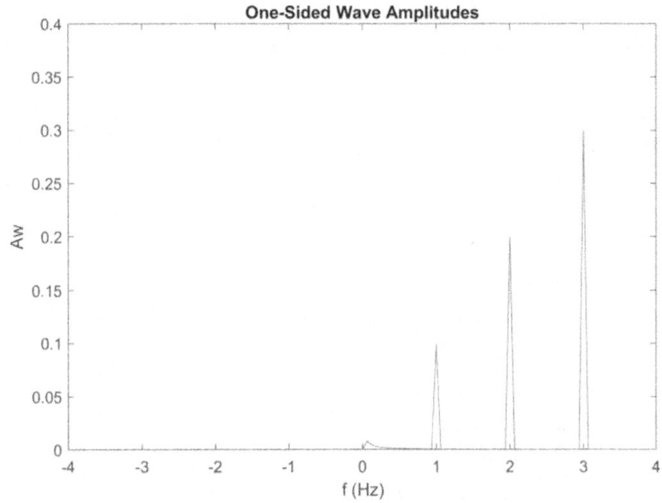

Note that, if FFT results are not symmetrical, then we need to compute two-sided amplitudes. Here are syntaxes show how to compute two-sided amplitudes if FFT results are not symmetrical:

Syntax

```
fft_2sided = fft(signal)
Aw_2sided = abs(fft_2sided)./N

freq_2sided = [0:1:N-1].*df %All frequencies

%If N is even
freq_2sided(N/2+1:end) = freq_2sided(N/2+1:end)-fs %Map negative
                                                    %frequencies
                                                    %if N is even

%If N is odd
freq_2sided((N+1)/2+1:end) = freq_2sided((N+1)/2+1:end)-fs %Map negative
                                                            %frequencies
                                                            %if N is odd
```

12.11 Estimate Power Spectral Density from FFT

If we consider that a Fourier transform shows how waves that form a time-domain signal are distributed in a frequency domain, then, a power spectral density (PSD) shows how powers of a time-domain signal are distributed in a frequency domain.

One simple method to estimate a power spectral density is to use results from a fast Fourier transform (FFT). The outcome of this method is commonly known as a periodogram and is a two-sided power spectral density. As mentioned earlier, outcomes of FFT for a signal with real values are symmetrical around frequency 0. In such cases, it is common to estimate a one-sided power spectral density (one-sided periodogram). To estimate a one-sided power spectral density, we keep values with a frequency range from 0 to $f_s/2$ and remove the rest. Then, we multiply values that their frequencies are repeated on both sides by 2 to conserve the power for the removed half.

Here are general syntaxes show how to estimate a one-sided power spectral density from FFT if N is even and FFT results are symmetrical:

Syntax

```
fft_2sided = fft(signal)

psd_2sided = 1/(fs*N).*abs(fft_2sided).^2
psd_1sided = psd_2sided(1:N/2+1)
psd_1sided(2:end-1) = psd_1sided(2:end-1).*2

freq_1sided = [0:1:floor(N/2)].*df
```

Similarly, we can estimate a power spectral density for an odd number of data points. Here are general syntaxes show how to estimate a one-sided power spectral density from FFT if N is odd and FFT results are symmetrical:

Syntax

```
fft_2sided = fft(signal)

psd_2sided = 1/(fs*N).*abs(fft_2sided).^2
psd_1sided = psd_2sided(1:(N+1)/2)
psd_1sided(2:end) = psd_1sided(2:end).*2

freq_1sided = [0:1:floor(N/2)].*df
```

Note that, MATLAB has a function named `periodogram` which may be used to estimate a power spectral density using a periodogram.

A unit of a power spectral density is presented as a time-series unit squared per unit of frequency. For example, if data in a time-series have a unit of meter (m), then a unit of power spectral density is m^2/Hz. Similarly, if data in a time-series have a unit of volt (V), then a unit of power spectral density is V^2/Hz.

Sometimes we need to present a power spectral density in decibel (dB) per unit of frequency. Here is a general syntax shows how we can obtain a power spectral density with a unit of dB/Hz:

Syntax

```
psd_dB_Hz = 10.*log10(psd)
```

Here, `psd` is a power spectral density in (unit squared)/Hz and `psd_dB_Hz` is a power spectral density in dB/Hz.

Here is an example shows how to estimate a power spectral density from fast Fourier transform (FFT) results. In this example, first, we generate a signal from 3 simple sinusoidal waves with wave amplitudes of 0.1, 0.2, and 0.3, wave frequencies of 1, 2, and 3 Hz, a sampling frequency of 8 Hz, and a sampling duration of 128 seconds. Next, we add random noises to this signal. Then, we remove a trend in this signal and compute FFT. After that, we show how to estimate a one-sided power spectral density. Finally, we display a power spectral density in a log-log scale. Note that, since noises are generated randomly, we get slightly different results each time we run this code.

```
%Wave properties
Aw_1=0.1; %1st wave amplitude
Aw_2=0.2; %2nd wave amplitude
Aw_3=0.3; %3rd wave amplitude
fw_1=1.0; %1st wave frequency
fw_2=2.0; %2nd wave frequency
fw_3=3.0; %3rd wave frequency

%Signal properties
fs=8;     %Sampling frequency
d=128;    %Sampling duration
N=fs*d;   %Total number of data points
dt=1/fs; %Time interval
df=fs/N; %Frequency interval

%Time data points
t=[0:1:N-1].*dt;
```

```
%Signal data points
y_1=Aw_1.*sin(2.*pi.*fw_1.*t);
y_2=Aw_2.*sin(2.*pi.*fw_2.*t);
y_3=Aw_3.*sin(2.*pi.*fw_3.*t);
noise_signal=0.05.*rand(1,N);
original_signal=y_1+y_2+y_3+noise_signal;

%Detrend signal
signal_detrended = detrend(original_signal);

%Compute fast Fourier transform (FFT)
fft_2sided = fft(signal_detrended);

%Estimate 1-sided power spectral density from 2-sided FFT if N is even
Pxx_2sided = 1/(fs*N).*abs(fft_2sided).^2;
Pxx_1sided = Pxx_2sided(1:N/2+1);
Pxx_1sided(2:end-1) = Pxx_1sided(2:end-1).*2;

%1-sided frequencies
freq_1sided = [0:1:floor(N/2)].*df;

%Plot power spectral density
loglog(freq_1sided,Pxx_1sided)
title('One-Sided Power Spectral Density')
xlabel('f (Hz)')
ylabel('PSD (m^2/Hz)')
xlim([5e-3,5])
ylim([1e-8,100])
```

Figure 12.8
Power spectral density from FFT

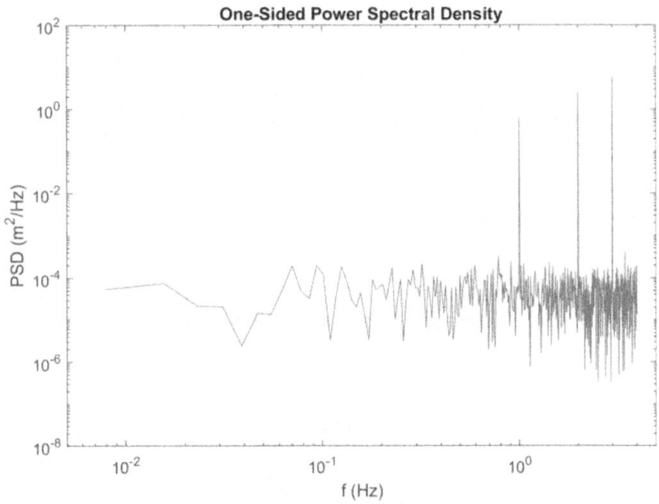

Note that, if FFT results are not symmetrical, then we need to compute a two-sided power spectral density. Here are general syntaxes show how to compute a two-sided power spectral density if FFT results are not symmetrical:

Syntax

```
fft_2sided = fft(signal)
psd_2sided = 1/(fs*N).*abs(fft_2sided).^2

freq_2sided = [0:1:N-1].*df %All frequencies

%If N is even
freq_2sided(N/2+1:end) = freq_2sided(N/2+1:end)-fs %Map
                                                    %negative frequencies
                                                    %if N is even

%If N is odd
freq_2sided((N+1)/2+1:end) = freq_2sided((N+1)/2+1:end)-fs %Map
                                                            %negative frequencies
                                                            %if N is odd
```

12.12 Estimate Power Spectral Density from Periodogram and Welch Method

MATLAB has the Signal Processing Toolbox which is a powerful tool for signal processing. It provides a series of functions to analyze signals. Note that, the Signal Processing Toolbox is not part of standard MATLAB and its license should be obtained separately. The Signal Processing Toolbox provides several functions to estimates a power spectral density of a signal. Here are functions to estimate a power spectral density of a signal:

Function	Description
`periodogram`	Estimate power spectral density using periodogram
`pwelch`	Estimate power spectral density using Welch method
`spectrogram`	Compute spectrogram

A simple method to estimate a power spectral density is to use the **`periodogram`** function. If we do not use any window function, then results from the periodogram function is identical to an estimation of a power spectral density using FFT.

Here is a general syntax shows how to estimate a power spectral density using a periodogram:

Syntax

```
[pxx, f] = periodogram(x, window, nfft, fs, freqrange)
```

The `x` contains time-series data. The **`window`** defines a window function to be used. The **`window`** is optional and by default a rectangular window is used. For more details on a window function, refer to basics of window function and digital filter chapter. The **`nfft`** defines a number of data points to be used in FFT algorithm. The **`nfft`** is optional. If the **`nfft`** is not defined then `max(256,2^nextpow2(length(x)))` is used. The **`fs`** defines a sampling frequency. The **`freqrange`** defines if to return a one-sided, two-sided, or centered two-sided spectrum. The **`freqrange`** is optional and by default is **`'onesided'`**. To get a two-sided or centered two-sided power spectral density, we should use `'twosided'` or `'centered'` in place of **`freqrange`**, respectively.

The **`pxx`** and **`f`** contain power spectral density values and associated frequencies, respectively. For one-sided spectrum, if **`nfft`** is even, a returned power spectral density has `(nfft/2 + 1)` data points with a frequency range of `[0,fs/2]`, and if **`nfft`** is odd, a returned power spectral density has `(nfft + 1)/2` data points with a frequency range of `[0,fs/2)`. Note that, if the **`periodogram`** function is called without any output argument, then it plots a power spectral density.

Another common method to estimates a power spectral density of a signal is the Welch method. In this method, first, a signal is divided into several segments that each has an overlap with its neighboring segments. Then, each of these segments is windowed with a window function before its power spectral density is estimated. Finally, a smooth power spectral density is obtained by averaging all power spectral densities obtained for all segments. Note that, a window function typically leaves values in the center of each segment untouched while it suppresses values at each end of the segment. This causes energy loss in each segment which should be (and is) compensated in the Welch method.

Here is a general syntax shows how to estimate a power spectral density using the Welch method:

Syntax

```
[pxx, f] = pwelch(x, window, noverlap, nfft, fs, freqrange)
```

The `x` contains time-series data. The `window` defines a window function to be used. The `window` is optional and by default a Hamming window is used. The `noverlap` defines a number of data points that overlap between two adjacent segments. The `noverlap` is optional. If the `noverlap` is not defined, then it chosen to have 50% overlap between segments. The `nfft` defines a number of data points to be used in FFT algorithm. The `nfft` is optional. If the `nfft` is not defined then `max(256,2^nextpow2(length(x)))` is used. The `fs` defines a sampling frequency. The `freqrange` defines if to return a one-sided, two-sided, or centered two-sided spectrum. The `freqrange` is optional and by default is `'onesided'`. To get a two-sided or centered two-sided power spectral density we should use `'twosided'` or `'centered'` in place of `freqrange`, respectively.

The `pxx` and `f` contain power spectral density values and associated frequencies, respectively. For one-sided spectrum, if `nfft` is even, a returned power spectral density has `(nfft/2 + 1)` data points with a frequency range of `[0,fs/2]`, and if `nfft` is odd, a returned power spectral density has `(nfft + 1)/2` data points with a frequency range of `[0,fs/2)`. Note that, if the `pwelch` function is called without any output argument, then it plots a power spectral density.

Commonly, an overlap in each segment is chosen to be equal to 50% of a segment length. In other words, the `noverlap` is chosen to be equal to half of the segment length. By defaults, the `pwelch` function divides a signal into 8 (or as close to 8) segments with 50% overlap. Also, typically one of the Hann or Hamming windows is chosen as a window function when the Welch method is used to estimate of a power spectral density. For more details on a window function, refer to basics of window function and digital filter chapter.

Resolutions of frequencies, `f`, and power spectral density values, `pxx`, depend on a number of data points that are used in FFT. In other words, a frequency interval of returned power spectral density values depends on `nfft`. To increase a resolution of `f` and `pxx`, we need to increase a value of nfft. Similarly, to decrease a resolution of f and pxx, we need to decrease a value of nfft. Note that, if nfft is larger than a length of a segment, then zeros are padded to end of each segment to make its length equal to nfft.

Here is an example shows how to estimate a power spectral density from periodogram and Welch methods. Consider a previous example again. In this example, first, we generate a signal from 3 simple sinusoidal waves with wave amplitudes of 0.1, 0.2, and 0.3, wave frequencies of 1, 2, and 3 Hz, a sampling frequency of 8 Hz, and a sampling duration of 128 seconds. Next, we add random noises to this signal. Then, we remove a trend in this signal and estimate a power spectral density from periodogram and Welch methods. Finally, we display power spectral densities in a log-log scale. Note that, since noises are generated randomly, we get slightly different results each time we run this code.

```
%Wave properties
Aw_1=0.1; %1st wave amplitude
Aw_2=0.2; %2nd wave amplitude
Aw_3=0.3; %3rd wave amplitude
fw_1=1.0; %1st wave frequency
fw_2=2.0; %2nd wave frequency
fw_3=3.0; %3rd wave frequency

%Signal properties
fs=8;     %Sampling frequency
d=128;    %Sampling duration
N=fs*d;   %Total number of data points
dt=1/fs; %Time interval

%Time data points
t=[0:1:N-1].*dt;

%Signal data points
y_1=Aw_1.*sin(2.*pi.*fw_1.*t);
y_2=Aw_2.*sin(2.*pi.*fw_2.*t);
y_3=Aw_3.*sin(2.*pi.*fw_3.*t);
noise_signal=0.05.*rand(1,N);
original_signal=y_1+y_2+y_3+noise_signal;

%Detrend signal
signal_detrended = detrend(original_signal);

%Estimate power spectral density using a periodogram
```

```
[pxx_periodogram, f_periodogram] = ...
    periodogram(signal_detrended, [], [], fs);

%Estimate power spectral density using the Welch method
[pxx_welch, f_welch] = pwelch(signal_detrended, [], [], [], fs);

%Plot power spectral densities
loglog(f_periodogram, pxx_periodogram)
hold on
loglog(f_welch, pxx_welch)
title('One-Sided Power Spectral Density')
xlabel('f (Hz)')
ylabel('PSD (m^2/Hz)')
xlim([5e-3,5])
ylim([1e-8,100])
legend('Periodogram', 'Welch', 'Location', 'northwest')
```

Figure 12.9
Power spectral density from a periodogram and Welch methods

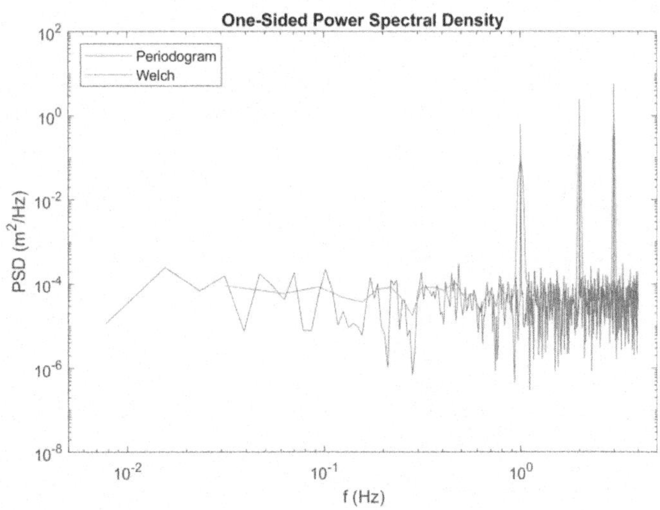

Chapter 13
Basics of Window Function and Digital Filter

In this chapter, the basics of window functions and digital filters are described. First, a convolution operation is explained. Then, a window function is described. After that, digital filters and their types are presented. Next, it is described how to compute basic low-pass, high-pass, band-pass, and band-stop filters. Then, it is explained how to design basic FIR filters with MATLAB. It follows by descriptions of how to smooth data. At the end, it is described how to filter out a particular frequency range from data.

13.1 Convolution

One mathematical operation that has several applications in digital filtering is convolution. In mathematics, convolution of two functions F and G is defined as an integral of the product of these two functions after one is mirrored and slid (shifted) across the other one. Convolution of two functions F and G is written as:

$$(F * G)(t) = \int_{-\infty}^{\infty} F(\tau)G(t-\tau)d\tau$$

In this function, t and τ are variables in function F and G. Both t and τ should represent the same variable and should be in the same domain. For example, both t and τ represent time in a time domain. Similarly, both t and τ represent a frequency in a frequency domain. Here, an asterisk sign, $*$, represents a convolution operation.

Convolution of two functions results in the third function that has a shape of one of the original functions modified by the second function. Consider a convolution operation of two functions as $(F * G)(t)$ where F is a function that its shape to be modified by a function G. In this case, a function F is an original function and a function G is a function that its values are used to reshape a function F. It means that, values in a function G are weights that a function F is reshaped based on them. In other words, a convolution operation returns weighted values of a function F at point t where weight values are obtained from a function G.

One application for a convolution operation is to calculate a weighted moving average of data. If a sum of all weights in a function G is equal to one, then a convolution operation, $(F * G)(t)$, returns a weighted average of a function F at point t where weights for an averaging calculation are obtained from a function G. It means that, convolution replaces each data point in a function F by a weighted average of a data point itself and its neighbors.

13.2 Window Function

A window function is a mathematical function that has a certain shape inside a given interval and typically is zero outside that interval. Commonly, window functions have a bell shape and are symmetrical around their center point. When a function or a data sequence is multiplied by a window function, all values that overlap with a window function are scaled proportional to values in window functions while all values that are outside an overlap interval become zero. In practice, first, a function or a data sequence is split into several segments, each with a length equal to a length of a window function, and then, each segment is manipulated (windowed) by a window function.

The most well-known window function is a rectangular window also known as a boxcar window. A rectangular window is a window function that all of its elements are one. It means that, when data are passed through a rectangular window, all values that overlap with a window function remain untouched while the rest of values become zero. A rectangular window function is presented as:

$$w(n_w) = 1$$

In this function, $w(n_w)$ is a window function, n_w is an element counter from 0 to $N_w - 1$, and N_w is a number of data points in a window function (length of a window function).

Another widely-used window function is a Hann window function which can be presented as:

$$w(n_w) = 0.5 - 0.5\cos\left(\frac{2\pi n_w}{N_w - 1}\right)$$

MATLAB provides several functions to create different window functions. Here is a list of common window functions:

Function	Description
`rectwin`	Return rectangular (boxcar) window
`triang`	Return triangular window
`blackman`	Return Blackman window
`hamming`	Return Hamming window
`hann`	Return Hann window
`bartlett`	Return Bartlett window
`blackmanharris`	Return Blackman-Harris window
`nuttallwin`	Return Blackman-Harris (Nuttall) window
`gausswin`	Return Gaussian window
`tukeywin`	Return Tukey window

Here, we describe how to create a Hann window function. Other types of window functions may be created similarly. Here is a general syntax shows how to create a Hann window function:

Syntax

```
window_function = hann(L, sflag)
```

The `L` defines a number of data points in a window function. The `sflag` defines if to create a symmetric or a periodic window function. The `sflag` is optional and by default is `'symmetric'`. To create a symmetric window function, we should use `'symmetric'` in place of `sflag`, and to create a periodic window function, we should use `'periodic'` in place of `sflag`. A symmetric window function is used for a filter design while a periodic window function is helpful for spectral analysis.

MATLAB also has one function that may be used to create different window functions. Here is a function to create a window function:

Function	Description
`window`	Return a window function

Here is a general syntax shows how to create a window function using the window function:

Syntax

```
window_function = window(@window_function_name, n, winopt)
```

The `@window_function_name` is a function handle that defines a window function to be created. For example, for the Hann window, a function handle is `@hann`. The `n` defines a number of data points in a window function. The `winopt` contains an additional value to be passed to a window function. For example, it may be `'periodic'` or `'symmetric'` for the `hann` function. Depends on a window function, the `winopt` might be optional or required.

Here is a list of common window types that can be created using the window function:

Window Function Handle	Description
`@rectwin`	Return rectangular (boxcar) window
`@triang`	Return triangular window
`@blackman`	Return Blackman window
`@hamming`	Return Hamming window
`@hann`	Return Hann window
`@bartlett`	Return Bartlett window

`@blackmanharris`	Return Blackman-Harris window
`@nuttallwin`	Return Blackman-Harris window based on Nuttall
`@gausswin`	Return Gaussian window
`@tukeywin`	Return Tukey window

MATLAB has the Window Visualization Tool that can be opened by using the **`wvtool`** command. It allows to visually inspect a window function in time and frequency domains. Also, MATLAB has Window Designer App that can be used to interactively design and analyze a window function. To run a Window Designer App, we can either use the **`windowDesigner`** command or we can go to the APPS tab and click on Window Designer.

Here is an example shows how to create a window function. In this example, we create rectangular, Blackman, Hann, and Hamming window functions. Here, first, we create symmetrical window functions with a length of 33, and then, we display these window functions.

```
%Length of window function
Nw=33;

%Create rectangular window function
win_rectangular = rectwin(Nw);

%Create Blackman window function
win_blackman = blackman(Nw);

%Create Hann window function
win_hann = hann(Nw);

%Create Hamming window function
win_hamming = hamming(Nw);

%Plot rectangular window function
ax1 = subplot(2,2,1);
plot(win_rectangular)
title('Rectangular window')
ylabel('W (n)')
xlim([0,34])
ylim([0,1.1])

%Plot Blackman window function
ax2 = subplot(2,2,2);
plot(win_blackman)
```

```
title('Blackman window')
xlim([0,34])
ylim([0,1.1])

%Plot Hann window function
ax3 = subplot(2,2,3);
plot(win_hann)
title('Hann window')
xlabel('Sample')
ylabel('W (n)')
xlim([0,34])
ylim([0,1.1])

%Plot Hamming window function
ax4 = subplot(2,2,4);
plot(win_hamming)
title('Hamming window')
xlabel('Sample')
xlim([0,34])
ylim([0,1.1])
```

Figure 13.1
Window function

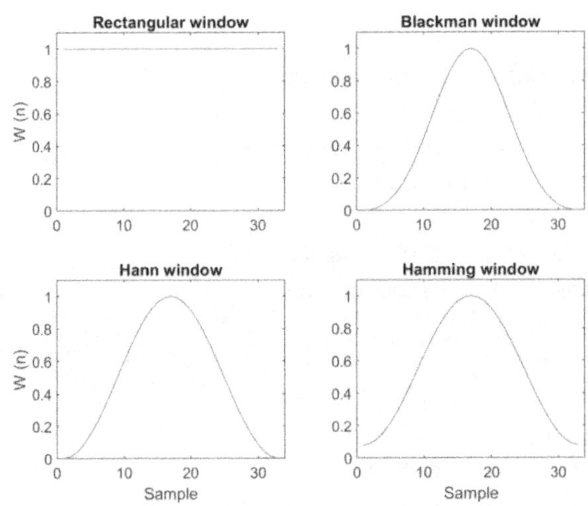

13.3 Digital Filter

A digital filter is a set of mathematical operations that are applied to data in order to modify and enhance (emphasize) or suppress (de-emphasize) certain properties of data. In signal processing, digital filters are widely used in order to pass (keep) part of a signal with specific frequencies and reject (remove or suppress) the rest (e.g. Smith, 1997). Here is a simple illustration of how a filter works:

```
Input Signal -----> Filter -----> Output Signal
```

For example, consider a measured signal with a sampling frequency of $f_s = 8$ Hz. As explained before, a frequency range in this signal that we can work with is between 0 and $f_s/2 = 4$ Hz. Now, assume we need to remove all values that have frequencies higher than 3 Hz. To do that, we use a filter that passes all values with frequencies equal or less than 3 Hz while rejects all values with frequencies larger than 3 Hz.

In a time domain, a digital filter is described by its impulse response and step response. An impulse response, also known as impulse response function (IRF), is a filter output (response) if a delta function (impulse) is used as a filter input. A delta function (impulse) is a function that is equal to 1 at a certain point (usually at x=0) and is 0 everywhere else.

Similarly, a step response is a filter output (response) if a step function is used as a filter input. A step function is a function that is equal to 0 for $x < 0$ and is equal to 1 for $x \geq 0$. Note that, a step response is equal to a cumulative sum of an impulse response.

In a frequency domain, a digital filter is described by its frequency response and phase response. A frequency response is a transformation of an impulse response to a frequency domain. In general, we mostly work with a magnitude of a frequency response, also known as a gain of a filter. A frequency response is usually presented in decibel (dB). Here is a general syntax shows how we can obtain a frequency response in dB:

Syntax

```
A_dB = 20.*log10(A)
```

Here, **A** is amplitude and **A_dB** is amplitude in decibel.

In general, there two types of digital filters, recursive filters and non-recursive filters. A recursive filter is a filter that uses values from both an input signal and previous step outputs at the same time as its inputs at each step. An impulse response for a recursive filter is referred to as an infinite impulse response (IIR). A non-recursive filter is a filter that only uses values from an input signal as its inputs and does not use any value from previous step outputs. An impulse response for a non-recursive filter is referred to as a finite impulse response (FIR).

Filters also can be causal or non-causal. A causal filter is a filter that its output is a function of past and present inputs. A non-causal filter is a filter that its output is a function of past, present, and future inputs. Similarly, filters might be linear or non-linear. A linear filter is a filter that its output is a linear function of its inputs. A non-linear filter is a filter that its output is not a linear function of its inputs.

An IIR filter with x as its input and y as its output is presented in a form of a difference equation as (here, * represents multiplication):

```
a0*y(n) = b0*x(n) + b1*x(n-1) + ... + bM*x(n-M)
                  - a1*y(n-1) - ... - aN*y(n-N)
```

Here, `x(n)` is input of a filter, `y(n)` is output of a filter, the `b0`, ..., `bM` are feed-forward coefficients of a filter, the `a0`, ..., `aN` are feed-backward coefficients of a filter, and max(M,N) shows a filter order.

Now, if all $a_k = 0$ except for $a_0 = 1$, then a filter becomes an FIR filter which is presented in a form of a difference equation as (here, * represents multiplication):

```
a0*y(n) = b0*x(n) + b1*x(n-1) + ... + bM*x(n-M)
```

Similarly, `x(n)` is input of a filter, `y(n)` is output of a filter, the `b0`, ..., `bM` are impulse responses of a filter, and `M` shows an FIR filter order. Note that, the `M`-th order FIR filter has `M+1` terms.

Digital filters are commonly presented by a rational transfer function. In this format, an IIR filter is presented as (e.g. Smith, 1997):

$$H(z) = \frac{\sum_{k=0}^{M-1} b_k z^{-k}}{\sum_{k=0}^{N-1} a_k z^{-k}}$$

Here, $H(z)$ is a z-transform of an impulse response. In other words, an inverse z-transform of $H(z)$ is an impulse response of a filter.

If all $a_k = 0$ except for $a_0 = 1$, then $H(z)$ becomes an FIR filter which is presented as:

$$H(z) = \sum_{k=0}^{M-1} b_k z^{-k}$$

In general, at each step, a filter uses a current data point along with several preceding data points from previous time steps to filter data. However, at the time that we have just started filtering a sequence of data, there might not be enough preceding data points. This causes a delay in filtering. For example, consider we have a filter that in each step it uses a current point along with two preceding points. Now, for the very first data point in a time-series there is no preceding data point. Similarly, for the second data point in a time-series there is only one preceding data point. Because of that, this filter cannot start working until it reaches the third data point in a time-series. This causes a 2 points delay in filtering. One method to remove delay from filtered data is zero-phase digital filtering, also known as forward-backward filtering. In this method, we apply a filter once in a forward direction and then once in a reverse direction to remove a delay from filtered data.

Generally, using a filter includes two steps, first, designing a filter, and second, applying a designed filter to data (filtering). We may apply digital filters to data in a time domain or in a frequency domain. To apply a filter in a time domain, we should convolve a signal in a time domain with an impulse response of a filter. To apply a filter in a frequency domain, we should multiply data in a frequency domain such as FFT results or a power spectral density by a magnitude of a filter frequency response. Note that, to apply a digital filter in a frequency domain, a frequency range and frequency interval of data should be the same as a frequency range and frequency interval of a frequency response.

13.4 Digital Filter Band-Forms

There are different digital filters each developed for a particular purpose. One common classification of filters is based on which frequencies are passed and which frequencies are rejected by a filter. There are four common types of filters based on a filter frequency response band-form, a low-pass filter, a high-pass filter, a band-pass filter, and a band-stop filter.

A low-pass filter is a filter that allows values with frequencies equal or smaller than a certain frequency to pass while it rejects values with frequencies larger than this certain frequency. This certain frequency that separates passing frequencies from rejecting frequencies is a cut-off frequency. Therefore, if we consider a cut-off frequency as f_c, then a low-pass filter keeps all values in a frequency range of $f \leq f_c$ while it removes all values in a frequency range of $f > f_c$.

Similarly, a high-pass filter is a filter that allows values with frequencies $f \geq f_c$ to pass while it rejects values with frequency $f < f_c$. Also, if we consider two cut-off frequencies as a lower cut-off frequency f_{cL} and a higher cut-off frequency f_{cH}, then a band-pass filter is a filter that allows values with frequencies $f_{cL} \leq f \leq f_{cH}$ to pass while it rejects values that are outside this frequency range. A band-stop (band-reject) filter is a filter that allows values with frequencies $f \leq f_{cL}$ or $f \geq f_{cH}$ to pass while it rejects values with frequencies $f_{cL} < f < f_{cH}$.

In filters, a frequency range that its values are passed is known as a passband of a filter and a frequency range that its values are rejected is known as a stopband of filter. In filter design, it is desirable to have a flat passband and stopband. However, typically by increasing the steepness of a transition band from a passband to a stopband, undesired ripples start to appear in a passband or stopband.

In an ideal filter, there is no transition from a passband to a stopband (vertical drop). However, in practice, a transition from a passband to a stopband or vice versa typically occurs through a frequency range. This frequency range that a transition between a passband and a stopband occurs is known as a transition band of a filter. It is preferable to make a transition band as sharp as possible to resemble an ideal filter. A steepness of a transition band is known as a filter roll-off. By increasing the number of terms in a filter (increasing a filter order), a filter transition between passband and stopband (roll-off) becomes sharper. Also, an IIR filter has a sharper roll-off compared to the same order FIR filter.

13.5 Basic Low-Pass FIR Filter

An ideal low-pass filter is a filter that allows values with frequencies $f \leq f_c$ to pass while it rejects values with frequency $f > f_c$. In other words, an ideal low-pass filter has a vertical drop from a passband to a stopband without any transition band between them. For example, consider we have a power spectral density with a frequency range of $0 \leq f \leq f_s/2$. Now, if we multiply (filter) this power spectral density by a frequency response of an ideal low-pass filter, all values in this spectrum with frequencies $f \leq f_c$ are left untouched while all values with frequency $f > f_c$ become zero.

A frequency response of an ideal low-pass filter with a cut-off frequency f_c can be presented in a frequency domain as:

$$H_{LowPass} = \begin{cases} 1 & |f| \leq f_c \\ 0 & |f| > f_c \end{cases}$$

Here, $H_{LowPass}$ is a frequency response of a low-pass filter.

If we transform back this ideal low-pass filter from a frequency domain to a time domain by using an inverse Fourier transform, the result would be a normalized sinc function as:

$$\text{sinc}(x) = \begin{cases} \frac{\sin(\pi x)}{\pi x} & x \neq 0 \\ 1 & x = 0 \end{cases}$$

Figure 13.2
Ideal low-pass filter

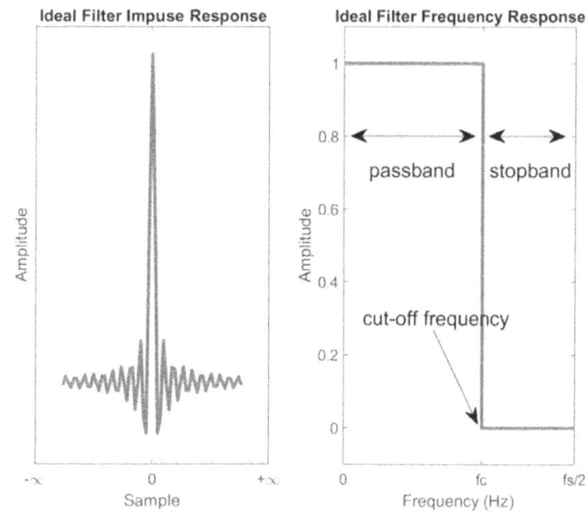

A normalized sinc function returns an infinite impulse response of a low-pass filter in a time domain. However, for practical purposes, we need to have a finite impulse response. To get an impulse response with a finite number of samples, we truncate an impulse response with a window function. This method is known as an FIR filter design by a window method.

The downside of truncating an impulse response is that it causes a filter to move away from an ideal filter. A simple method to truncate an impulse response is to use a rectangular window. However, using a tapered window such as a Bartlett window with an appropriate number of samples produces a better-behaved filter compared with using a simple rectangular window and could create a filter that is closer to an ideal filter.

An impulse response of a low-pass FIR filter designed by a window method, which is known as a low-pass windowed-sinc FIR filter, in a time domain is obtained as:

$$h(n_w) = \text{sinc}\left(2\frac{f_c}{f_s}\left(n_w - \frac{N_w-1}{2}\right)\right) \times w(n_w)$$

$$h_{LowPass} = \frac{h(n_w)}{\sum_{n_w=0}^{N_w-1} h(n_w)}$$

$$N_w = \frac{4}{(bw/f_s)}$$

In these functions, h is a windowed-sinc function, $h_{LowPass}$ is an impulse response of a low-pass windowed-sinc FIR filter, $w(n_w)$ is a window function, N_w is a number of data points in a window function (length of a window function), n_w is an element counter from 0 to $N_w - 1$, and bw is a width of a filter transition band (bandwidth). Note that, in this filter, a cut-off frequency should be $f_c \leq f_s/2$, a normalized width of a transition band, (bw/f_s), should follow $(bw/f_s) \leq 0.5$, and N_w should be an odd number.

To visualize how a low-pass filter works in a time domain, consider we have a signal that is made of many sinusoidal waves. Now, assume we want to remove waves that their frequencies are larger than a certain frequency from this signal. To do that, first, we decompose a signal into a series of time-series each contains one of the sinusoidal waves that an original signal is made up of them. Then, we remove all time-series that their waves have frequencies larger than this certain frequency. After we remove undesired time-series, we reconstruct a signal by adding remaining time-series together. The outcome of this process is the same as we apply a low-pass filter to an original signal.

Here is an example shows how to compute an impulse response and a frequency response of a low-pass windowed-sinc FIR filter. In this example, we generate a low-pass windowed-sinc FIR filter with a sampling frequency of 2 Hz, a cut-off frequency of 0.2 Hz, a filter length of 65, and an FFT length of 128.

```
%Low-pass windowed-sinc FIR filter properties
fs=2.0;   %Sampling frequency
fc=0.2;   %Cut-off frequency
n=64;     %Filter order (must be even)
NFFT=128; %Number of data points in FFT

%Window and filter length (must be odd)
Nw=n+1;

%Counter
nw=[0:1:Nw-1];

%Compute sinc function
h_sinc = sinc(2.*(fc./fs).*(nw-(Nw-1)./2));

%Create Hann window function
win = hann(Nw);
win = win.'; %Convert (transpose) row array to column array

%Window sinc function
h_windowed = h_sinc.*win;
```

```
%Compute impulse response of low-pass windowed-sinc FIR filter
impulse_response = h_windowed./sum(h_windowed(:));

%Compute frequency response of low-pass windowed-sinc FIR filter
N=NFFT*2;
frequency_response_2sided = fft(impulse_response, N);
frequency_response_1sided = frequency_response_2sided(1:N/2+1);

%1-sided frequencies
df=fs/N; %Frequency interval
frequency_1sided = [0:1:floor(N/2)].*df;

%Remove element associated with fs/2
frequency_response_1sided = frequency_response_1sided(1:end-1);
frequency_1sided = frequency_1sided(1:end-1);

%Plot impulse response
ax1 = subplot(1,2,1);
plot(nw, impulse_response)
title('Impuse Response (fc=0.2 Hz)')
xlabel('Sample')
ylabel('Amplitude')
xlim([-5,70])
ylim([-0.05,0.22])

%Plot frequency response
ax2 = subplot(1,2,2);
plot(frequency_1sided, abs(frequency_response_1sided))
title('Frequency Response (fc=0.2 Hz)')
xlabel('Frequency (Hz)')
ylabel('Amplitude (Gain)')
xlim([-0.1,1.1])
ylim([-0.1,1.1])
```

Figure 13.3
Low-pass windowed-sinc filter

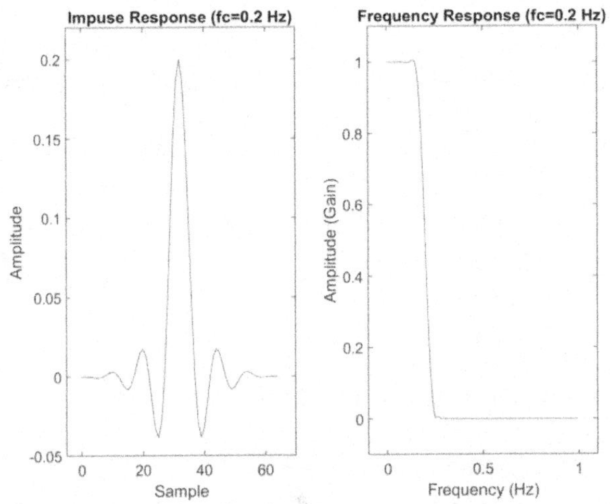

13.6 Basic High-Pass, Band-Pass and Band-Stop FIR Filters

If we have an impulse response of a low-pass windowed-sinc FIR filter, we can compute an impulse response of a high-pass windowed-sinc FIR filter as:

$$h_{HighPass}(n_w) = -h_{LowPass}(n_w)$$
$$h_{HighPass}(Center\ Point) = h_{HighPass}(Center\ Point) + 1$$

Here, $h_{HighPass}(n_w)$ is an impulse response of a high-pass windowed-sinc FIR filter and $h_{LowPass}(n_w)$ is an impulse response of a low-pass windowed-sinc FIR filter.

Similarly, we can compute impulse responses of band-pass and band-stop windowed-sinc FIR filters for a lower cut-off frequency f_{cL} and a higher cut-off frequency f_{cH} as (here, * represents a convolution operation):

$$h_{BandPass}(n_w) = h_{LowPass-Using\ f_{cH}}(n_w) * h_{HighPass-Using\ f_{cL}}(n_w)$$
$$h_{BandStop}(n_w) = h_{LowPass-Using\ f_{cL}}(n_w) + h_{HighPass-Using\ f_{cH}}(n_w)$$

Here, $h_{BandPass}(n_w)$ is an impulse response of a band-pass windowed-sinc FIR filter and $h_{BandStop}(n_w)$ is an impulse response of a band-stop windowed-sinc FIR filter.

A summation of all elements in impulse responses of windowed-sinc FIR filters are:

$$\sum_{n_w=0}^{N_w-1} h_{LowPass}(n_w) = 1$$

$$\sum_{n_w=0}^{N_w-1} h_{HighPass}(n_w) = 0$$

$$\sum_{n_w=0}^{N_w-1} h_{BandPass}(n_w) = 0$$

$$\sum_{n_w=0}^{N_w-1} h_{BandStop}(n_w) = 1$$

Figure 13.4
Basic FIR filters in time domain for fs=2 Hz and Nw=65

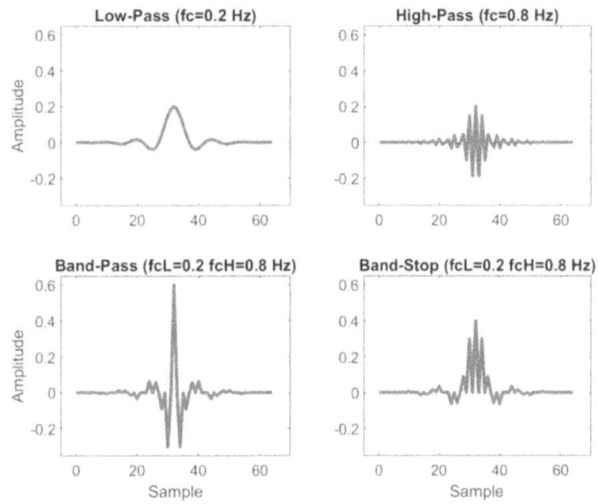

As mentioned earlier, a frequency response of a filter is a transformation of an impulse response of that filter to a frequency domain. Therefore, we can find frequency responses for previous filters by transforming their impulse responses to a frequency domain. Note that, if a length of an impulse response is smaller than a length of a frequency response we want to create, first, we have to pad enough zeros to the end of an impulse response to make its length equal to a length we need, and then transform it to a frequency domain.

Additionally, we can find a frequency response of a high-pass filter from a frequency response of a low-pass filter. If we have a frequency response of a low-pass windowed-sinc FIR filter, we can compute a frequency response of a high-pass windowed-sinc FIR filter as:

$$|H_{HighPass}(f)| = -|H_{LowPass}(f)| + 1$$

Here, $|H_{HighPass}(f)|$ is a magnitude (gain) of a frequency response of a high-pass windowed-sinc FIR filter and $|H_{LowPass}(f)|$ is a magnitude (gain) of a frequency response of a low-pass windowed-sinc FIR filter.

Figure 13.5
Basic FIR filters in frequency domain for fs=2 Hz and NFFT=128

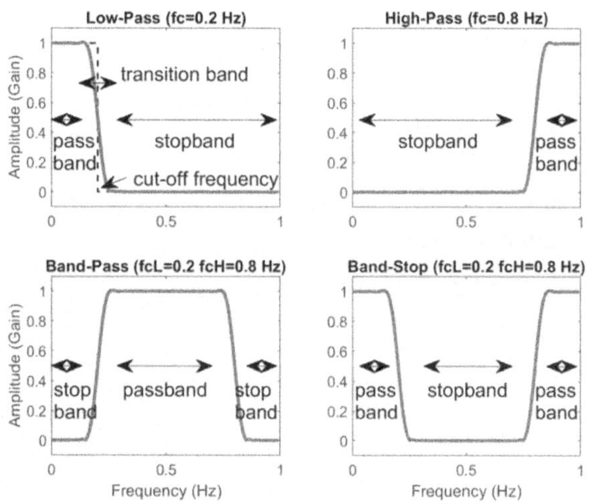

13.7 Design Basic FIR Filters with MATLAB

MATLAB provides functions that create basic FIR filters conveniently. Here are functions to design an FIR filter using a window method:

Function	Description
`fir1`	Design FIR filter using window method
`fir2`	Design FIR filter using window method
`firls`	Design FIR filter using Least-squares linear-phase
`freqz`	Return frequency response of digital filter

Here is a general syntax shows how to design an FIR filter using a window method and obtain an impulse response of a filter:

Syntax

```
b = fir1(n, Wn, ftype, window)
```

The `n` defines a filter order. Since a length of an FIR filter is equal to (filter_order+1), then a length of a filter is `(n+1)`, and therefore `(n+1)` filter coefficients are returned. The `Wn` defines a cut-off frequency of a filter as `Wn=fc/(fs/2)`, where `fc` is a cut-off frequency and `fs` is a sampling frequency. For band-pass and band-stop filters, the cutoff should be as `[WcL,WcH]`. The `ftype` defines a type of a filter. The `ftype` is optional. The `ftype` takes `'low'`, `'high'`, `'bandpass'`, `'stop'`, `'DC-0'`, and `'DC-1'`. The `window` defines a window function to be used in filter design. The `window` is optional and by default the Hamming window is used. Note that, length of a window function should be `(n+1)`.

The `b` contains `(n+1)` coefficients of an FIR filter. In other words, the `b` is an impulse response of an FIR filter.

Similarly, we can compute a frequency response of a filter. Here is a general syntax shows how to obtain a frequency response of a filter:

Syntax

```
[h,f] = freqz(b, a, n, 'whole', fs)
```

The `b` contains numerator coefficients of a filter transfer function. Similarly, the `a` contains denominator coefficients of a filter transfer function. By using `a=1`, a frequency response of an FIR filter is returned. The `n` defines a number of frequency data points to be calculated. The `n` is optional and by default is 512. The `'whole'` defines to return a two-sided frequency response. The `whole` is optional. If the `'whole'` is missing, then a one-sided frequency response is returned. The `fs` defines a sampling frequency. The `fs` is optional.

The `h` contains a frequency response of a filter. The `f` contains frequencies associated with values of a frequency response and has a range of `[0,fs/2)`.

Here is an example shows how to compute an impulse response and a frequency response of a low-pass filter. Consider a previous example again. This time we use the `fir1` and `freqz` functions to obtain an impulse response and a frequency response of a filter. In this example, we generate a low-pass filter with a sampling frequency of 2 Hz, a cut-off frequency of 0.2 Hz, a filter length of 65, and an FFT length of 128. The outputs from this example are the same as the ones from a previous example.

```
%Low-pass windowed-sinc FIR filter properties
fs=2.0;   %Sampling frequency
fc=0.2;   %Cut-off frequency
```

```
n=64;      %Filter order (must be even)
NFFT=128; %Number of data points in FFT

%Window and filter length (must be odd)
Nw=n+1;

%Counter
nw=[0:1:Nw-1];

%Impulse response of filter
impulse_response = fir1(n, fc/(fs/2), 'low', hann(Nw));

%Frequency response of filter
[frequency_response,frequency] = freqz(impulse_response, 1, NFFT, fs);

%Plot impulse response
ax1 = subplot(1,2,1);
plot(nw, impulse_response)
title('Impuse Response (fc=0.2 Hz)')
xlabel('Sample')
ylabel('Amplitude')
xlim([-5,70])
ylim([-0.05,0.22])

%Plot frequency response
ax2 = subplot(1,2,2);
plot(frequency, abs(frequency_response))
title('Frequency Response (fc=0.2 Hz)')
xlabel('Frequency (Hz)')
ylabel('Amplitude (Gain)')
xlim([-0.1,1.1])
ylim([-0.1,1.1])
```

MATLAB has the Filter Visualization Tool that can be opened by using the `fvtool` command. It allows to visually inspect a filter. Also, MATLAB has Filter Designer App that can be used to interactively design and analyze a filter. To run a Filter Designer App, we can either use the `filterDesigner` command or we can go to the APPS tab and click on Filter Designer. Similarly, MATLAB has Signal Analyzer App that can be used to interactively analyze signals. To run a Signal Analyzer App, we can either use the `signalAnalyzer` command or we can go to the APPS tab and click on Signal Analyzer.

13.8 Smooth Data by Moving Average

In data analysis and signal processing, it is common to encounter datasets that show rapid variations or contaminated with noises. This occurs in particular for data that are collected in the real world. In such cases, these rapid variations and noises make it difficult or impossible to follow the real trend in a dataset. Because of that, these variations and noises should be removed from a dataset before we start studying that dataset. One method to remove these variations and noises is to smooth data in a dataset. In general, a smoothing algorithm replaces all values that are away from the main trend of a dataset with values that resemble the general trend of data. This helps to capture important trends and patterns in a dataset. Here is a function to smooth data:

Function	Description
`conv`	Return convolution of two arrays
`smoothdata`	Smooth data
`smooth`	Smooth data

There are many methods and algorithms available to smooth data. One of the simplest methods to smooth data is to convolve data with a normalized window function which is a window function that a sum of its elements is equal to one. As mentioned earlier, if a sum of all weights in a function G is equal to one, then a convolution operation, $(F * G)(t)$, returns a weighted average of a function F at point t where weights for an averaging calculation are obtained from a function G. It means that, convolution replaces each data point in a function F by a weighted average of a data point itself and its neighbors. Now, if we use a normalized window function in place of G, a convolution operation slides a mirror of this normalized window function across a dataset and replaces each data point in a dataset by a weighted average of a data point itself and its neighbors.

For example, consider a dataset that contains L data points. We want to smooth this dataset by sliding a window with 3 equal members as [1/3,1/3,1/3] across a dataset using a convolution operation. Assume, we reach a data point x_n and its two neighbors x_{n-1} and x_{n+1}. Now, if we convolve these three data points with a sliding window, we replace x_n with $\frac{1}{3}x_{n-1} + \frac{1}{3}x_n + \frac{1}{3}x_{n+1}$. This method of smoothing data is known as a moving average or rolling average.

Similarly, instead of using a window that all of its members are equal, we can use a window with unequal members. It means that a contribution of each neighboring data point to an average value is weighted based on a neighboring point position. For example, if we have a window with unequal members as [1/4,1/2,1/4], we replace x_n with $\frac{1}{4}x_{n-1} + \frac{1}{2}x_n + \frac{1}{4}x_{n+1}$. This method of smoothing data is known as a weighted moving average.

In these examples, a window of [1/3,1/3,1/3] represents a normalized rectangular window with 3 data points, and a window of [1/4,1/2,1/4] represents a normalized triangular window with 3 data points. Note that, a sum of all elements in a normalized window function that is used for smoothing should be one.

To explain how a moving average with convolution works, let's consider a simple example. In this example, we illustrate how convolution rolls a window of [1/3,1/3,1/3] across a dataset with 10 data points. Each window contains a center data point and its two neighbors that are used to calculate an average in that window. Here, a rolling window 1 replaces a value of the first element with $\frac{1}{3}0 + \frac{1}{3}1 + \frac{1}{3}10$. It pads zeros to the left of an array to have 3 data points. Similarly, a rolling window 2 replaces a value of the second element with $\frac{1}{3}1 + \frac{1}{3}10 + \frac{1}{3}3$. It continues until a rolling window 10 replaces a value of the last element with $\frac{1}{3}9 + \frac{1}{3}2 + \frac{1}{3}0$. Again, it pads zero to the right of an array to have 3 data points.

Data	1	10	3	8	5	6	7	4	9	2
Rolling window 1	1	10								
Rolling window 2	1	10	3							
Rolling window 3		10	3	8						
Rolling window 4			3	8	5					
Rolling window 5				8	5	6				
Rolling window 6					5	6	7			
Rolling window 7						6	7	4		
Rolling window 8							7	4	9	
Rolling window 9								4	9	2
Rolling window 10									9	2
Moving average	3.66	4.66	7.00	5.33	6.33	6.00	5.66	6.66	5.00	3.66

Here is a general syntax shows how to convolve two arrays:

Syntax

```
convolution_results = conv(u, v, shape)
```

The `u` and `v` contain data of the first and the second arrays to be convolved, respectively. The `shape` defines a size of output results. The `shape` is optional and by default is `'full'`. To get a full convolution results, we should use `'full'` in place of the shape. To get convolution results with the same size as `u`, we should use `'same'` in place of the shape. To get convolution results without zero-padding, we should use `'valid'` in place of the shape.

Here are general syntaxes show how to smooth data by convolving data with a normalizes window function:

Syntax

```
win = rectwin(Nw)
win_norm = win./sum(win(:)) %Normalize window function
smoothed_data = conv(data, win_norm, 'same')
```

In this syntax, the `Nw` is a length of a window function. Commonly, `Nw` is chosen as an odd number to have the same number of data points on each side of the window center point. Here, we use a rectangular window function, however, we may use any other window function as well. We normalize a window function by its sum. In other words, a sum of all elements in a normalized window function should be one.

A similar method to smooth data is to use an impulse response of a low-pass filter instead of a normalized window function to smooth data. In this method, data are smoothed by convolving data with an impulse response of a low-pass filter. In general, this method is similar to a moving average method except that we use an impulse response of a low-pass filter instead of a normalized window function.

Here are general syntaxes show how to smooth data by convolving data with an impulse response of a low-pass filter:

Syntax

```
impulse_response = fir1(n, fc/(fs/2), 'low', rectwin(Nw))
smoothed_data = conv(data, impulse_response, 'same')
```

Here, the `n` is a filter order. A length of a filter is `(n+1)`. In this syntax, we use a rectangular window function, however, we can use any other window function as well.

Here is an example shows how to smooth data with a moving average. In this example, first, we generate a signal from 2 simple sinusoidal waves with wave amplitudes of 1.0 and 0.5, wave frequencies of 0.25 and 4.0 Hz, a sampling frequency of 32 Hz, and a sampling duration of 8 seconds. After that, we smooth this signal by using a normalized window function and impulse response of a low-pass filter. Finally, we display an original signal and smoothed signals. Note that, here we use the Hann window function in an impulse response calculation for comparison.

```
%Wave properties
Aw_low=1.0;  %Low-frequency wave amplitude
Aw_high=0.5; %High-frequency wave amplitude
fw_low=0.25; %Low-frequency wave frequency
fw_high=4.0; %High-frequency wave frequency

%Signal properties
fs=32;    %Sampling frequency
d=8;      %Sampling duration
N=fs*d;   %Total number of data points
dt=1/fs;  %Time interval

%Window and filter properties
fc=2.0;   %Cut-off frequency
n=32;     %Filter order (must be even)
Nw=n+1;   %Window and filter length (must be odd)

%Time data points
t=[0:1:N-1].*dt;

%Signal data points
y_low=Aw_low.*sin(2.*pi.*fw_low.*t);
y_high=Aw_high.*sin(2.*pi.*fw_high.*t);
original_signal=y_low+y_high;

%Smooth signal using normalized rectangular window function
win = rectwin(Nw); %Rectangular window function
win_norm = win./sum(win(:)); %Normalized rectangular window function
signal_windowed = conv(original_signal, win_norm, 'same');

%Smooth signal using impulse response of low-pass filter
impulse_response = fir1(n, fc/(fs/2), 'low', hann(Nw));
signal_lowpassed = conv(original_signal, impulse_response, 'same');

%Plot signals
plot(t, original_signal, 'LineWidth', 2)
hold on
plot(t, signal_windowed, 'LineWidth', 3)
```

```
plot(t, signal_lowpassed, 'LineWidth', 3)
xlabel('Time (s)')
ylabel('Amplitude')
legend('Original Signal', 'Smoothed (Normalized Window)', ...
    'Smoothed (Low-Pass Filter)', 'Location', 'southwest')
ylim([-2.6,1.6])
```

Figure 13.6
Smooth data by moving average

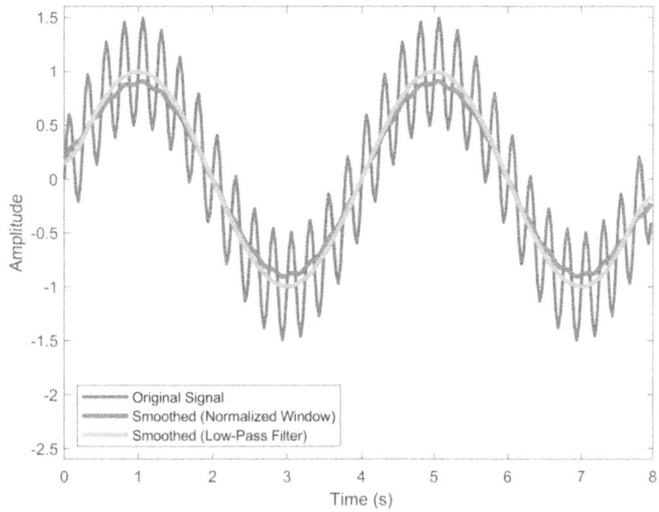

One application for smoothing data is to identify and replace outliers and spikes in a dataset. For a dataset that does not have rapid variations or noises, values of a smoothed dataset are very close to the values of an original dataset. Now, to identify outliers and spikes, we can subtract smoothed data from original data. Results from subtraction are small values except for data points that are outliers or spikes. After we identify these outliers and spikes, we can replace them with values from a smoothed dataset.

MATLAB provides the `movmean` function which returns moving mean values. It may be used to get similar values as the ones we get from convolution except for values close to edges of a dataset. The difference is that, convolution pads zeros to the edges of data to maintain a length of a window and averages data including these zeros, while the `movmean` function averages data at the edges without padding any zero. Also, MATLAB has the `smoothdata` and `smooth` functions which may be used to smooth data.

13.9 Smooth Data by Savitzky-Golay Filter

A more sophisticated method to smooth data is to use a Savitzky-Golay filter. A Savitzky-Golay filter is a digital filter that smooths data by convolving data inside a sliding window with coefficients obtained from a locally fitted polynomial to data inside that window. Here are functions to smooth data with a Savitzky-Golay filter:

Function	Description
`sgolayfilt`	Apply Savitzky-Golay filter to array
`sgolay`	Design Savitzky-Golay filter

Here is a general syntax shows how to use a Savitzky-Golay filter:

Syntax

```
fitered_results = sgolayfilt(x, order, framelen)
```

The `x` contains data to be filtered (here, to be smoothed). The `order` defines an order of a polynomial to be fitted to data. The `framelen` defines a number of data points in a filter window. The `framelen` must be an odd integer.

Here is an example shows how to smooth data with a Savitzky-Golay filter. Consider a previous example again. In this example, first, we generate a signal from 2 simple sinusoidal waves with wave amplitudes of 1.0 and 0.5, wave frequencies of 0.25 and 4.0 Hz, a sampling frequency of 32 Hz, and a sampling duration of 8 seconds. After that, we smooth this signal by using a Savitzky-Golay filter. Finally, we display original and smoothed signals.

```
%Wave properties
Aw_low=1.0;  %Low-frequency wave amplitude
Aw_high=0.5; %High-frequency wave amplitude
fw_low=0.25; %Low-frequency wave frequency
fw_high=4.0; %High-frequency wave frequency

%Signal properties
fs=32;    %Sampling frequency
d=8;      %Sampling duration
N=fs*d;   %Total number of data points
dt=1/fs;  %Time interval
```

```
%Window and filter properties
Nw=33;          %Window and filter length (must be odd)
poly_order=5; %Polynomial order

%Time data points
t=[0:1:N-1].*dt;

%Signal data points
y_low=Aw_low.*sin(2.*pi.*fw_low.*t);
y_high=Aw_high.*sin(2.*pi.*fw_high.*t);
original_signal=y_low+y_high;

%Smooth signal using Savitzky-Golay filter
signal_filtered = sgolayfilt(original_signal, poly_order, Nw);

%Plot signals
plot(t, original_signal, 'LineWidth', 2)
hold on
plot(t, signal_filtered, 'LineWidth', 3)
xlabel('Time (s)')
ylabel('Amplitude')
legend('Original Signal', 'Smoothed (Savitzky-Golay Filter)', ...
    'Location', 'southwest')
ylim([-2.6,1.6])
```

Figure 13.7
Smooth data by Savitzky-Golay filter

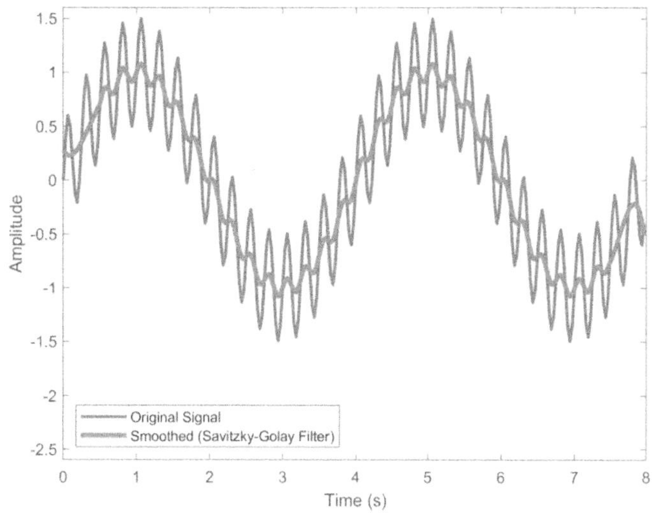

13.10 Smooth Data by Butterworth Filter

Another sophisticated method to smooth data is to use Butterworth or Chebyshev filters. A Butterworth filter is a filter that has a flat passband (without ripples) in its frequency response. A Chebyshev filter has a sharper roll-off compared with a Butterworth filter. However, unlike a Butterworth filter, a Chebyshev filter has ripples in its passband or stopband (they are not flat). Here are functions to smooth data with these filters:

Function	Description
`butter`	Design Butterworth filter
`cheby1`	Design Chebyshev (type I) filter
`filtfilt`	Apply digital filter in forward and reverse directions
`filter`	Apply digital filter in one direction

Here is a general syntax shows how to design a Butterworth filter:

Syntax

```
[b,a] = butter(n, Wn, ftype, 's')
```

The `n` defines an order of a filter. The `Wn` defines a cut-off frequency of a filter as `Wn=fc/(fs/2)`, where `fc` is a cut-off frequency and `fs` is a sampling frequency. For band-pass and band-stop filters, the cutoff should be as `[WcL,WcH]`. The `ftype` defines a type of a filter. The `ftype` is optional. The `ftype` takes `'low'`, `'high'`, `'bandpass'`, and `'stop'`. The `'s'` defines to return an analog filter. The `'s'` is optional. If the `'s'` is missing then a digital filter is returned.

The `b` contains numerator coefficients and the `a` contains denominator coefficients of a filter transfer function.

After we design a filter, we need to apply a filter to data. If we apply a filter in one direction, it can cause a delay in filtered results. For example, if we apply a symmetric filter with a length Nw in one direction, it causes a delay equal to (Nw-1)/2 data points in filtered outputs. In such cases, these delays in filtered data should be accounted for. To do that, we apply a filter in forward and reverse directions, which leads to zero-phase digital filtering, also known as forward-backward filtering, without any delay in outputs.

Here is a general syntax shows how to perform zero-phase digital filtering:

Syntax

```
fitered_results = filtfilt(b, a, x)
```

The `b` contains numerator coefficients of a filter transfer function. Similarly, the `a` contains denominator coefficients of a filter transfer function. The `x` contains data to be filtered.

Here is an example shows how to smooth data with a Butterworth filter. Consider a previous example again. In this example, first, we generate a signal from 2 simple sinusoidal waves with wave amplitudes of 1.0 and 0.5, wave frequencies of 0.25 and 4.0 Hz, a sampling frequency of 32 Hz, and a sampling duration of 8 seconds. After that, we smooth this signal by using a Butterworth filter. Finally, we display original and smoothed signals.

```
%Wave properties
Aw_low=1.0;  %Low-frequency wave amplitude
Aw_high=0.5; %High-frequency wave amplitude
fw_low=0.25; %Low-frequency wave frequency
fw_high=4.0; %High-frequency wave frequency

%Signal properties
fs=32;    %Sampling frequency
d=8;      %Sampling duration
N=fs*d;   %Total number of data points
dt=1/fs; %Time interval

%Filter properties
fc=2.0;          %Cut-off frequency
filter_order=4; %Filter order

%Time data points
t=[0:1:N-1].*dt;

%Signal data points
y_low=Aw_low.*sin(2.*pi.*fw_low.*t);
y_high=Aw_high.*sin(2.*pi.*fw_high.*t);
original_signal=y_low+y_high;

%Design Butterworth filter
[b,a] = butter(filter_order, fc/(fs/2), 'low');
```

```
%Apply filter to data
signal_filtered = filtfilt(b, a, original_signal);

%Plot signals
plot(t, original_signal, 'LineWidth', 2)
hold on
plot(t, signal_filtered, 'LineWidth', 3)
xlabel('Time (s)')
ylabel('Amplitude')
legend('Original Signal', 'Smoothed (Butterworth Filter)', ...
    'Location', 'southwest')
ylim([-2.6,1.6])
```

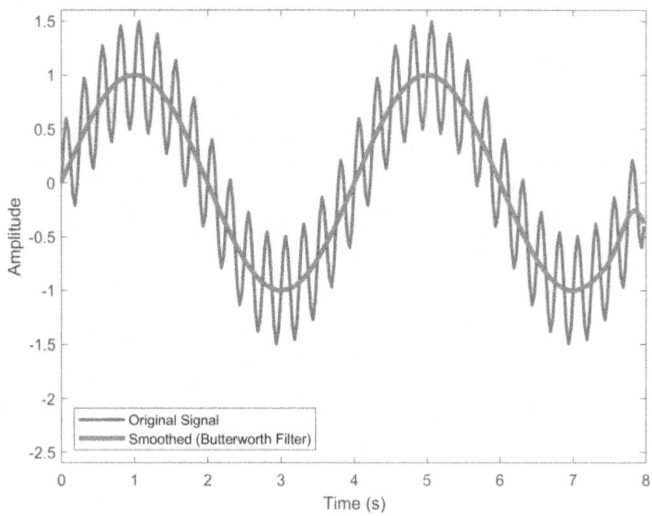

Figure 13.8
Smooth data by Butterworth filter

13.11 Filter Out Frequency Range from Data

In previous sections, we described how to smooth data. In general, to smooth data, we attempt to remove rapid variations and noises that have high frequencies from a dataset. In other words, to smooth data, we suppress values with high frequencies while we leave the rest of values untouched. In practice, we may need to perform similar filtering to keep any desired frequencies in a signal and filter out unwanted frequencies. For example, consider a signal that is sampled with a sampling frequency of $f_s = 8$ Hz. As explained before, a frequency range in this signal that we can work with is between 0 and $f_s/2 = 4$ Hz. Now, assume we only want to keep a part of a signal that has a frequency range between 1 Hz and 3 Hz and remove all other values from a signal. For this purpose, we have to use a band-pass filter to only keep values with a frequency range between 1 Hz and 3 Hz and remove the rest.

We can filter out frequencies from a signal either in a time domain or in a frequency domain. A process of filtering out frequencies in a time domain is similar to how we smooth data except that in data smoothing we only filter out high frequencies while here we filter out any desired frequency range. To filter out frequencies in a time domain, first, we choose a proper filter. For example, we may choose a proper windowed-sinc FIR filter. Then, we compute an impulse response of that filter. To filter data in a time domain, we convolve data by an impulse response of a filter.

Here is a general syntax shows how to apply a filter to data in a time domain:

```
filtered_data = (data_in_time_domain) * (h_IR)
```

Here, data are in a time domain, `h_IR` is an impulse response of a filter, and an asterisk sign, `*` , represents a convolution operation.

Similarly, to filter out frequencies in a frequency domain, first, we choose a proper filter. For example, we may choose a proper windowed-sinc FIR filter. Then, we compute an impulse response of that filter. Next, we compute a frequency response of a filter from its impulse response. Now, to filter data in a frequency domain, we multiply data, such as FFT results or a power spectral density, by a magnitude of a filter frequency response.

Here is a syntax shows how to apply a filter to data in a frequency domain:

```
filtered_data = (data_in_frequency_domain) x (|H_FR|)
```

Here, data are in a frequency domain, `|H_FR|` is a magnitude (gain) of a frequency response of a filter, and x represents multiplication. Note that, to apply a digital filter in a frequency domain, we have to make sure that a frequency range and frequency interval of data in a frequency domain is the same as a frequency range and frequency interval of a frequency response. For example, if we have a one-sided power spectral density with a frequency range of $0 \leq f \leq f_s/2$ and a frequency interval of df, then a frequency response of a filter should have a frequency range of $0 \leq f \leq f_s/2$ and a frequency interval of df.

Note that, we can also use any sophisticated FIR or IIR filters such as a Butterworth filter to design a proper filter and apply that filter to data in a time or frequency domain.

Here is an example shows how to filter out a particular frequency range from data in a time domain. In this example, first, we generate a signal from 3 simple sinusoidal waves with wave amplitudes of 1.0, 0.75 and 0.5, wave frequencies of 0.25, 2.0 and 4.0 Hz, a sampling frequency of 32 Hz, and a sampling duration of 8 seconds. Now, assume we want to keep all values with a frequency range of 1 to 3 Hz and remove the rest. Here we use two methods to show how to filter data. In the first method, we use a band-pass windowed-sinc FIR filter. In the second method, we use a band-pass Butterworth filter. Finally, we display an original signal and filtered signals.

```
%Wave properties
Aw_low=1.0;  %Low-frequency wave amplitude
Aw_mid=0.75; %Middle-frequency wave amplitude
Aw_high=0.5; %High-frequency wave amplitude
fw_low=0.25; %Low-frequency wave frequency
fw_mid=2.0;  %Middle-frequency wave frequency
fw_high=4.0; %High-frequency wave frequency

%Signal properties
fs=32;    %Sampling frequency
d=8;      %Sampling duration
N=fs*d;   %Total number of data points
dt=1/fs;  %Time interval

%Window and filter properties
fcL=1.0;        %Lower cut-off frequency
fcH=3.0;        %Higher cut-off frequency
n=64;           %Filter order (must be even)
Nw=n+1;         %Window and filter length (must be odd)
filter_order=4; %Filter order

%Time data points
t=[0:1:N-1].*dt;

%Signal data points
y_low=Aw_low.*sin(2.*pi.*fw_low.*t);
y_mid=Aw_mid.*sin(2.*pi.*fw_mid.*t);
y_high=Aw_high.*sin(2.*pi.*fw_high.*t);
original_signal=y_low+y_mid+y_high;

%Apply band-pass windowed-sinc filter to data
impulse_response = fir1(n, [fcL/(fs/2),fcH/(fs/2)], ...
    'bandpass', hann(Nw));
signal_filtered_windowed_sinc = conv(original_signal, ...
    impulse_response, 'same');
```

```
%Apply band-pass Butterworth filter to data
[b,a] = butter(filter_order, [fcL/(fs/2),fcH/(fs/2)], 'bandpass');
signal_filtered_butterworth = filtfilt(b, a, original_signal);

%Plot signals
ax1 = subplot(3,1,1);
plot(t, original_signal)
title('Original Signal')
ylabel('Amplitude')
ylim([-2.5,2.5])

ax2 = subplot(3,1,2);
plot(t, signal_filtered_windowed_sinc)
title('Signal Filtered by Windowed-Sinc')
ylabel('Amplitude')
ylim([-2.5,2.5])

ax3 = subplot(3,1,3);
plot(t, signal_filtered_butterworth)
title('Signal Filtered by Butterworth')
xlabel('Time (s)')
ylabel('Amplitude')
ylim([-2.5,2.5])
```

Figure 13.9
Filter data in time domain

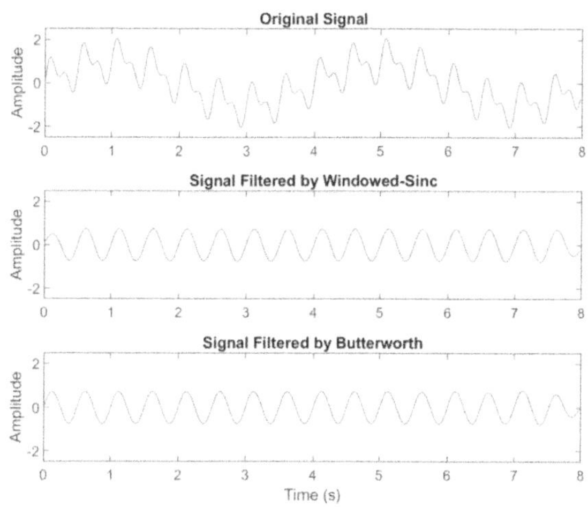

Here is an example shows how to filter out a particular frequency range from a power spectral density in a frequency domain. In this example, first, we generate a signal from 3 simple sinusoidal waves with wave amplitudes of 1.0, 0.75 and 0.5, wave frequencies of 0.25, 2.0 and 4.0 Hz, a sampling frequency of 32 Hz, and a sampling duration of 8 seconds. Then, we remove a trend in this signal and estimate its one-sided power spectral density using a periodogram. Now, assume we want to keep all values in this spectrum with a frequency range of 1 to 3 Hz and remove the rest. Here we use two methods to show how to filter frequencies in this spectrum. In the first method, we use a band-pass windowed-sinc FIR filter. In the second method, we use a band-pass Butterworth filter. Finally, we display an original signal and filtered signals. Note that, here, a frequency range of a power spectrum is `[0,fs/2]` while a frequency range of a frequency response is `[0,fs/2)`. Therefore, to have similar frequencies for both power spectral density and frequency response, we did not use the last data point in a spectrum.

```
%Wave properties
Aw_low=1.0;  %Low-frequency wave amplitude
Aw_mid=0.75; %Middle-frequency wave amplitude
Aw_high=0.5; %High-frequency wave amplitude
fw_low=0.25; %Low-frequency wave frequency
fw_mid=2.0;  %Middle-frequency wave frequency
fw_high=4.0; %High-frequency wave frequency

%Signal properties
fs=32;   %Sampling frequency
d=8;     %Sampling duration
N=fs*d;  %Total number of data points
dt=1/fs; %Time interval

%Window and filter properties
fcL=1.0;          %Lower cut-off frequency
fcH=3.0;          %Higher cut-off frequency
n=128;            %Windowed-sinc filter order (must be even)
Nw=n+1;           %Window and filter length (must be odd)
filter_order=4; %Butterworth filter order

%Time data points
t=[0:1:N-1].*dt;

%Signal data points
y_low=Aw_low.*sin(2.*pi.*fw_low.*t);
y_mid=Aw_mid.*sin(2.*pi.*fw_mid.*t);
y_high=Aw_high.*sin(2.*pi.*fw_high.*t);
original_signal=y_low+y_mid+y_high;
```

```
%Detrend signal
signal_detrended = detrend(original_signal);

%Estimate power spectral density using periodogram
[pxx,f] = periodogram(signal_detrended,[],[],fs);

%Apply band-pass windowed-sinc filter to data
impulse_response = fir1(n, [fcL/(fs/2),fcH/(fs/2)], ...
    'bandpass', hann(Nw));
[frequency_response_windowed_sinc,frequency_windowed_sinc] = ...
    freqz(impulse_response, 1, length(impulse_response)-1, fs);
signal_filtered_windowed_sinc = pxx(1:end-1,1) ...
    .*abs(frequency_response_windowed_sinc);

%Apply band-pass Butterworth filter to data
[b,a] = butter(filter_order, [fcL/(fs/2),fcH/(fs/2)], 'bandpass');
[frequency_response_butterworth,frequency_butterworth] = ...
    freqz(b, a, length(impulse_response)-1, fs);
signal_filtered_butterworth = pxx(1:end-1,1) ...
    .*abs(frequency_response_butterworth);

%Plot signals
ax1 = subplot(2,2,1);
plot(f(1:end-1,1), pxx(1:end-1,1))
hold on
plot(frequency_windowed_sinc, abs(frequency_response_windowed_sinc))
title('Filtered by Windowed-Sinc')
xlim([-1,16])
ylim([-0.5,3.5])
grid on
legend('PSD','Frequency Response')

ax2 = subplot(2,2,2);
plot(f(1:end-1,1), pxx(1:end-1,1))
hold on
plot(frequency_butterworth, abs(frequency_response_butterworth))
title('Filtered by Butterworth')
xlim([-1,16])
ylim([-0.5,3.5])
grid on
legend('PSD','Frequency Response')
```

```
ax3 = subplot(2,2,3);
plot(frequency_windowed_sinc, signal_filtered_windowed_sinc)
xlabel('Frequency (Hz)')
xlim([-1,16])
ylim([-0.5,3.5])
grid on
legend('Filtered PSD')

ax4 = subplot(2,2,4);
plot(frequency_windowed_sinc, signal_filtered_butterworth)
xlabel('Frequency (Hz)')
xlim([-1,16])
ylim([-0.5,3.5])
grid on
legend('Filtered PSD')
```

Figure 13.10
Filter data in frequency domain

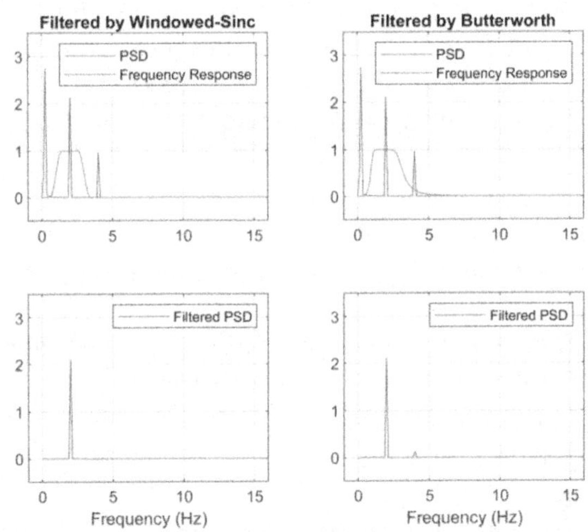

Chapter 14
Read and Write Data Files

In this chapter, it is described how to read data from files or write data to files. First, it is explained how to open and read text and ASCII files using the `fopen` function. Then, it is described how to open and read comma-separated values, CSV, files. After that, it is presented how to read text, ASCII, and CSV files as numerical arrays or tables. At the end, it is described how to save data to a file and how to load data from a file.

14.1 Read Text and ASCII Files with fopen

It is very likely that we may need to read (load) data from a file or write (save) data to a file when we develop a code. MATLAB provides several functions to work with data files. Here are common MATLAB functions to work (at low-level) with data files:

Function	Description
`fopen`	Open file and return a file identifier
`fread`	Read contents of binary file
`fgetl`	Read single line from file
`fwrite`	Write data to binary file
`ftell`	Return file current position
`fseek`	Move to given position in file
`fclose`	Close file
`split`	Split string
`strsplit`	Split string

To start working with a file in MATLAB, first, we need to open that file. To open a file in MATLAB, we use the `fopen` function. Here is a general syntax shows how to open a file in MATLAB:

Syntax

```
file_id = fopen(filename, permission)
```

The `filename` defines a file (name or path plus name) to be opened. If a file is in a current working directory, then a file name is enough, otherwise, a file path should be also included. The `permission` defines an access type to a file. The `permission` is optional and by default is `'r'`.

We may use different permissions for reading or writing in the `fopen` function. By default, the `fopen` function opens a file for reading in a binary mode. Here is a list of common permissions in the `fopen` function to open a file in a binary mode:

permission	Description
`'r'`	Open file for reading (default)
`'w'`	Open/create file for writing (overwrite file if existed)
`'a'`	Open/create file for writing (appending data to its end)
`'r+'`	Open file for reading and writing
`'w+'`	Open/create file for reading and writing (overwrite file if existed)

'a+'	Open/create file for reading and writing (appending data to its end)

By using previous permissions, a file is open in a binary mode. To open a file in a text mode, we should add `'t'` to the permission. For example, to open a file for reading in a text mode, we should use `'rt'`. Similarly, to open or create a file for reading and writing (overwrite a file if existed) in a text mode, we should use `'wt+'`.

To explain how to read data from a file, let's consider a sample dataset with 12 rows and 6 columns. The first two rows in this dataset contain dataset description line and column labels. In other words, the first two rows are headers. The first column in this dataset shows dates and columns 2 to 6 contain numbers.

```
Data File Containing Numerical Values
Date          Value_1     Value_2     Value_3     Value_4     Value_5
2050-10-20    1           10          0.1         100         0.01
2050-10-21    2           20          0.2         200         0.02
2050-10-22    3           30          0.3         300         0.03
2050-10-23    4           40          0.4         400         0.04
2050-10-24    5           50          0.5         500         0.05
2050-10-25    6           60          0.6         600         0.06
2050-10-26    7           70          0.7         700         0.07
2050-10-27    8           80          0.8         800         0.08
2050-10-28    9           90          0.9         900         0.09
2050-10-29    10          100         1           1000        0.1
```

Here is an example shows how to read data from a text file. In this example, first, we create a text file containing an above dataset and save it as datafile.txt in 'C:\Example' directory. After that, we open this file, read its data, and close a file. Then, we remove the first two lines, i.e. a file description line and column labels, from data. Next, we extract dates from the first column. Finally, we extract numerical values in columns 2 to 6 and convert them to an array. Here, we use the **strsplit** function to split a string in each line into its words. If values in each line are separated by a special character, we can use the second argument in the **strsplit** function to define a delimiter (separator).

```
%Change folder
cd('C:\Example')

%Open file
file_id = fopen('datafile.txt', 'r');

%Create empty cell
```

```
file_lines={}; %All text lines

%Read data in file
txt_line=fgetl(file_id); %Text line
while ischar(txt_line)
    line_words=strsplit(txt_line); %Split each line to its words
    file_lines{end+1,1}=line_words;
    txt_line=fgetl(file_id);
end

%Close file
fclose(file_id);

%Remove header lines
file_lines=file_lines(3:end);

%Extract dates of time-series
datetime_format='yyyy-MM-dd'; %Date format as YYYY-MM-DD
for i=1:length(file_lines)
    line_cell=file_lines{i};
    ts(i,1)=datetime(line_cell{1,1},'InputFormat',datetime_format);
    %Or line_cell=file_lines(i);
    %Or ts(i,1)=datetime(line_cell{1}{1,1}, ...
    %       'InputFormat',datetime_format);
end

%Extract data
for i=1:length(file_lines)
    line_cell=file_lines{i};
    data_cell{i}=line_cell(1,2:end);
    %Or line_cell=file_lines(i);
    %Or data_cell{i}=line_cell{1}(1,2:end);
end

%Convert cell to array
for i=1:length(data_cell)
    num_str=data_cell{i};
    for j=1:length(num_str)
        data(i,j)=str2num(num_str{j});
    end
end
```

Note that, reading ASCII files (or any files that can be edited by a text editor) are similar to text files, except that, we need to use that file extension instead of .txt extension when we use the `fopen` function to open that file.

Besides functions to work with binary files, MATLAB also has several functions that specifically work with text files. Here are common MATLAB functions to work with text files:

Function	Description
`textscan`	Read formatted data from text file
`fscanf`	Read data of text file
`sscanf`	Read formatted data from string
`fprintf`	Write data to text file

MATLAB has Import Tool that can be used to import data from a file. To run an Import Tool, we can either use the `uiimport(filename)` command or we can go to the HOME tab, VARIABLE section, and click on Import Data.

14.2 Read CSV Files

A common file format that is widely used to store tabular data is a comma-separated values, CSV, format. MATLAB provides functions to work with CSV files. Here are functions to read CSV files:

Function	Description
`csvread`	Read data from CSV file
`xlsread`	Read data from spreadsheet file

To read numerical data from a CSV file in MATLAB, we can use the `csvread` function. Here is a general syntax shows how to read a CSV file:

Syntax

```
M = csvread(filename, R1, C1)
```

The `filename` defines a CSV file name (name or path plus name) to be read. If a file is in a current working directory, then a file name is enough, otherwise, a file path should be also included. The `R1` and `C1` define a number of rows and columns to be skipped from the beginning of a file, respectively.

Here is an example shows how to read numerical data from a CSV file. Consider a previous dataset again. This time, we create a CSV file containing an above dataset and save it as datafile.csv in 'C:\Example' directory. After that, we read numerical data in this file using the `csvread` function. Here, we skipped the first two rows and the first column by using R1=2 and C1=1.

```
%Change folder
cd('C:\Example')

%Read data from CSV file
data=csvread('datafile.csv', 2, 1);
```

14.3 Read Text, ASCII, and CSV Files as Array

MATLAB provides functions to work with data files including text, ASCII, and CSV files. Here are functions to read text, ASCII, and CSV files (or any files that can be edited by a text editor):

Function	Description
`readmatrix`	Read matrix from file
`importdata`	Read data from data files
`dlmread`	Read data from ASCII-delimited file

Here is a general syntax shows how to load and read a data file:

Syntax

```
A = readmatrix(filename, 'NumHeaderLines', NumHeaderLines_Value, 'Range',
Range_Value, 'Delimiter', Delimiter_Value)
```

The `filename` defines a file (name or path plus name) to be read. If a file is in a current working directory, then a file name is enough, otherwise, a file path should be also included. The `'NumHeaderLines', NumHeaderLines_Value` pair arguments define a number of header lines in a file. The `'NumHeaderLines', NumHeaderLines_Value` are optional. If the `'NumHeaderLines', NumHeaderLines_Value` are not defined, then a number of header lines are detected automatically. The `'Range', Range_Value` pair arguments define a range of data to be read. The `Range_Value` is specified as `[start-row, start-column, end-row, and end-column]` or as `[start-row, start-column]`. If the `Range_Value` is given as `[start-row, start-column]` then data are read from defined start-row and start-column to the end of a file.

The 'Range', Range_Value are optional. The 'Delimiter', Delimiter_Value pair arguments define a string that separates values in a file. The 'Delimiter', Delimiter_Value are optional.

Here is an example shows how to read data from text and CSV files. Consider previous examples again. This time, we read data from text and CSV files using the **readmatrix** function. Here, we skip headers (the first two lines) and a date column (the first column) and only keep numerical values by using start-row=3 and start-column=2.

```
%Change folder
cd('C:\Example')

%Read data from text file
data_txt = readmatrix('datafile.txt', 'Range', [3,2]);

%Read data from CSV file
data_csv = readmatrix('datafile.csv', 'Range', [3,2]);
```

14.4 Read Text, ASCII, and CSV Files as Table

MATLAB provides several functions to work conveniently with different data files as tables. Here are functions to read text, ASCII, and CSV files (or any files that can be edited by a text editor) as a table:

Function	Description
readtable	Read table from file
readvars	Read variables from file
spreadsheetDatastore	Return spreadsheet datastore

Here is a general syntax shows how to load and read a data file as a table:

Syntax

```
T = readtable(filename, 'Delimiter', Delimiter_Value, 'HeaderLines',
HeaderLines_Value, 'Range', Range_Value)
```

The **filename** defines a file (name or path plus name) to be read. If a file is in a current working directory, then a file name is enough, otherwise, a file path should be also included. The

`'Delimiter', Delimiter_Value` pair arguments define a string that separates values in a file. The `'Delimiter', Delimiter_Value` are optional. The `'HeaderLines', HeaderLines_Value` pair arguments define a number of header lines to be skipped from the beginning of a file. The `'HeaderLines', HeaderLines_Value` are optional. If the `'HeaderLines', HeaderLines_Value` are not defined, then a number of header lines are detected automatically. The `'Range', Range_Value` pair arguments define a range of data to be read. The `Range_Value` is specified as one of the `'start-corner : end-corner'`, `'start-row : end-row'`, `'start-column : end-column'`, or `[start-row, start-column]`. If the `Range_Value` is given as `[start-row, start-column]` then data are read from defined start-row and start-column to the end of a file. The `'Range', Range_Value` pair arguments are optional.

Here is an example shows how to read data from text and CSV files into a table. Consider previous examples again. This time, we read data from text and CSV files using the `readtable` function.

```
%Change folder
cd('C:\Example')

%Read data from text file
data_txt = readtable('datafile.txt', 'HeaderLines', 1);
datetime_format='yyyy-MM-dd'; %Date format as YYYY-MM-DD
data_txt.Date=datetime(data_txt.Date, 'InputFormat', datetime_format);

%Read data from CSV file
data_csv = readtable('datafile.txt', 'HeaderLines', 1);
datetime_format='yyyy-MM-dd'; %Date format as YYYY-MM-DD
data_csv.Date=datetime(data_csv.Date, 'InputFormat', datetime_format);
```

14.5 Save and Load Data Files

In code developments, particularly in data analysis, we often need to save data for later use or load previously saved data. Here are common functions to save and load data in MATLAB:

Function	Description
`save`	Save variable (array) in workspace to file
`load`	Load variable (array) from file
`fwrite`	Write data to binary file
`fread`	Read data to binary file
`fprintf`	Write data to text file

`fscanf`	Read data of text file
`csvwrite`	Write data to CSV file
`csvread`	Read data from CSV file
`writematrix`	Write matrix to file
`readmatrix`	Read matrix from file
`writetable`	Write table to file
`readtable`	Read table from file
`importdata`	Read data from data files

Here are examples show how to save data to file. In these examples, we show how to save an array L=[[1,2,3,4,5];[6,7,8,9,10]] as a CSV file, binary file, text file, MATLAB .mat file, and labeled CSV file in 'C:\Example' directory. Note that, the **fprintf** function writes data in column order, therefore, we need to use a transpose of an array in the **fprintf** function to write data in correct order.

```
%Change folder
cd('C:\Example')

%Data
L = [[1,2,3,4,5];[6,7,8,9,10]];

%Save data as CSV file
csvwrite('csv_file.csv', L)

%Save data as binary file
file_id = fopen('binary_file.dat','w');
fwrite(file_id, L);
fclose(file_id);

%Save data as text file
writematrix(L, 'txt_file.txt')
%Or:
%file_id = fopen('txt_file.txt','w');
%fprintf(file_id, '%.4f %.4f %.4f %.4f %.4f \n', L.');
%fclose(file_id);

%Save data as .mat file
save('mat_file.mat', 'L') %Save variable L to file mat_file.mat

%Save data (with labels) as CSV file
T=table(L);
```

```
writetable(T, 'csv_file_with_labels.csv', ...
    'WriteVariableNames', true, 'WriteRowNames',true)
```

Now, we show how to read data from files that we saved in a previous example.

```
%Change folder
cd('C:\Example')

%Load CSV data file
data_csv = importdata('csv_file.csv');
%Or data_csv = readmatrix('csv_file.csv')
%Or data_csv = csvread('csv_file.csv')

%Load binary data file
file_ID = fopen('binary_file.dat');
data_binary = fread(file_ID, [2,5]);
fclose(file_ID);

%Load text data file
data_txt = importdata('txt_file.txt');

%Load .mat data file
data_mat = importdata('mat_file.mat');
%Or load('mat_file.mat'); %Load variable L from file mat_file.mat

%Load table data file
data_table = readtable('csv_file_with_labels.csv');
```

References

Pawlowicz, R., (2020). "M_Map: A mapping package for MATLAB", version 1.4m, [Computer software], available online at www.eoas.ubc.ca/~rich/map.html.

Smith, S. W. (1997). The scientist and engineer's guide to digital signal processing.

Index

Made in United States
Orlando, FL
18 August 2023

36219279R00233